The Political Economy of Financial Transformation in Turkey

T0298867

This volume provides a comprehensive study of Turkey's financial transformation into one of the most dynamic, if not trouble-free, emerging capitalist societies. While this financial evolution has underwritten Turkey's dramatic economic growth, it has done so without ameliorating the often persistently exploitative and unequal social structures that characterize neoliberalism today. Eschewing the interpretations of mainstream economics, *The Political Economy of Financial Transformation in Turkey* underscores both the quantitative significance of exponential growth in financial flows and investments, and the qualitative importance of the state's institutional restructuring around financial imperatives. This book presents today's reality as historically rooted; it is written by an interdisciplinary range of political economists, and critically examines Turkey's financial transformation, contributing to debates on the nature of peripheral financialization.

Galip L. Yalman is an Associate Professor (retired) of Political Science in the Department of Political Science and Public Administration at the Middle East Technical University, Ankara, Turkey. His research interests extend from state theory, to international and comparative political economy. He is the President of the Turkish Social Sciences Association.

Thomas Marois is a Senior Lecturer of Development Studies at SOAS University of London, United Kingdom, who specializes in finance and development in emerging capitalist societies. His current research focuses on the resurgence of public banks and their potential to support alternative green and equitable development strategies.

Ali Rıza Güngen is a political scientist and independent researcher, who received his PhD from the Middle East Technical University, Ankara, Turkey and was granted the Young Social Scientist award by the Turkish Social Sciences Association in 2013. His research currently focuses on sovereign debt management across the global South, and state restructuring and financial inclusion in Turkey.

Europa Perspectives: Emerging Economies

The Europa Emerging Economies series from Routledge, edited by Robert E. Looney, examines a wide range of contemporary economic, political, developmental and social issues as they affect emerging economies throughout the world. Complementing the *Europa Regional Surveys of the World series and the Handbook of Emerging Economies,* which was also edited by Professor Looney, the volumes in the *Europa Emerging Economies series* will be a valuable resource for academics, students, researchers, policy-makers, professionals, and anyone with an interest in issues regarding emerging economies in the wider context of current world affairs.

There will be individual volumes in the series which provide in-depth country studies, and others which examine issues and concepts; all are written or edited by specialists in their field. Volumes in the series are not constrained by any particular template, but may explore economic, political, governance, international relations, defence, or other issues in order to increase the understanding of emerging economies and their importance to the world economy.

Robert E. Looney is a Distinguished Professor at the Naval Postgraduate School, Monterey, California, who specializes in issues relating to economic development in the Middle East, East Asia, South Asia and Latin America. He has published over 20 books and 250 journal articles, and has worked widely as a consultant to national governments and international agencies.

The Islamic Republic of Iran: Reflections on an emerging economy
Jahangir Amuzegar

Argentina's Economic Reforms of the 1990s in Contemporary and Historical Perspective
Domingo Felipe Cavallo and Sonia Cavallo Runde

Handbook of Small States: Economic, Social and Environmental Issues
Edited by Lino Briguglio

Mexico under Misplaced Monopolies: Concentrated Wealth and Growing Violence from the 1980s to the Present
Francisco E. González

The Political Economy of Financial Transformation in Turkey
Edited by Galip L. Yalman, Thomas Marois and Ali Rıza Güngen

The Political Economy of Financial Transformation in Turkey

Edited by
Galip L. Yalman, Thomas Marois and
Ali Rıza Güngen

Routledge
Taylor & Francis Group
LONDON AND NEW YORK

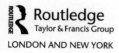

First published 2019
by Routledge
2 Park Square, Milton Park, Abingdon, Oxon OX14 4RN

and by Routledge
52 Vanderbilt Avenue, New York, NY 10017

First issued in paperback 2020

Routledge is an imprint of the Taylor & Francis Group, an informa business

© 2019 selection and editorial matter, Galip Yalman, Thomas Marois and Ali Rıza Güngen; individual chapters, the contributors

The right of Galip Yalman, Thomas Marois and Ali Rıza Güngen to be identified as the authors of the editorial material, and of the authors for their individual chapters, has been asserted by them in accordance with sections 77 and 78 of the Copyright, Designs and Patents Act 1988.

All rights reserved. No part of this book may be reprinted or reproduced or utilised in any form or by any electronic, mechanical, or other means, now known or hereafter invented, including photocopying and recording, or in any information storage or retrieval system, without permission in writing from the publishers.

Trademark notice: Product or corporate names may be trademarks or registered trademarks, and are used only for identification and explanation without intent to infringe.

by Taylor & Francis Books

Europa Commissioning Editor: Cathy Hartley

Editorial Assistant: Eleanor Catchpole Simmons

British Library Cataloguing in Publication Data
A catalogue record for this book is available from the British Library

Library of Congress Cataloging in Publication Data
Names: Güngen, Ali Rıza, editor. | Yalman, Galip L., editor. | Marois, Thomas, editor.
Title: The political economy of financial transformation in Turkey / edited by Galip L. Yalman, Thomas Marois and Ali Rıza Güngen.
Other titles: Europa emerging economies.
Description: Milton Park, Abingdon, Oxon ; New York, NY : Routledge, 2018. | Series: Europa emerging economies
Identifiers: LCCN 2018015598 | ISBN 9781857438116 (hardback)
Subjects: LCSH: Finance–Turkey. | Banks and banking–Turkey. | Global Financial Crisis, 2008-2009. | Turkey–Economic policy. | Turkey–Economic conditions–1960-
Classification: LCC HG187.T9 P65 2018 | DDC 332.09561–dc23
LC record available at https://lccn.loc.gov/2018015598

ISBN 13: 978-0-367-58496-2 (pbk)
ISBN 13: 978-1-85743-811-6 (hbk)

Typeset in Times New Roman
by Taylor & Francis Books

Contents

Figures

Tables

Boxes

Foreword

Turkey's neoliberal financial transformation, as part of a wider policy reorientation since the early 1980s, has been fairly extensively studied, if mostly from particularistic standpoints. This book differs from other volumes, due to its adherence to a critical political economy perspective (succinctly put forward in Chapter 1). Although the book includes (a) a historical narrative covering the period 1923–80, when monetary and financial policies were effectively geared towards the attainment of certain social and economic objectives, most notably import-substituting industrialization (Chapter 2); and (b) a review of Turkey's financial liberalization experience in the 1980s and the 1990s (Chapter 3), its main field of inquiry is Turkey's 'finance-led' capitalism since the early 2000s.

This sort of capitalism, which has been observed in many emerging economies in the modern era, exhibits not only an increasing dependence on ever-growing external financial transactions, but also necessitates a restructuring of state–capital relations and financial institutions in the (particular) national economy. These restructuring processes have strong affinities with (but do not fully correspond to) the financialization experience of the advanced capitalist economies, and hence deserve country-specific analyses.

This book on Turkey is a valuable excursion into this necessary field of research—a contribution building on its contributors' preparation of a comprehensive report on Turkey presented to the European Union (EU) under the Financialisation, Economy, Society and Sustainable Development (FESSUD) Project (2011–2016) (see http://fessud.eu/).

During Turkey's earlier phase of financial transformation, policymakers emphasized liberalizing financial transactions in stages, first in the domestic and later in the international sphere. The policy shift away from earlier practices of 'financial repression' was expected positively to contribute to economic growth and efficiency. Whether these gains were realized or not at the macro level is still subject to debate. But the recurrent financial crises suffered throughout the 1980s and 1990s provided ample evidence that a strategy of financial liberalization based primarily on deregulation was insufficient, and it must have been complemented with a competent institutional set-up and prudential regulations conducive to financial stability. Some contributors to this book would also point to the unequal and class-based social effects of this financial transformation.

To be fair, governments in Turkey prior to the financial crisis of 2001 were not against certain neoliberal reforms in the financial sector, and actually started to internalize best international practices, mainly in banking (efforts to comply with the Basel I accords during the 1990s are a case in point). In this context, it has to be noted that after the capital account liberalization of 1989, Turkey started to align itself towards finance-led growth, moving away from its earlier export-led growth pattern, and gradually becoming embedded into the global financial network.

The financial crisis of 2001, which was perhaps more severe than those in the previous two decades (see Chapter 4), made it clear that financial transformation within a liberal environment cannot be administered under a 'minimal' state (the brain-child of the neoliberal ideology). Obviously, neoliberal policies were mostly detrimental to the capability of the state to offer non-market co-ordination, but such a weakness in the case of managing finance-led capitalism was not tolerable. The severity of that crisis convinced the existing coalition government of the time to embark upon a radical (and 'qualitative', according to the contributors to the book) departure from the past mode of liberalization, by strengthening and 'internationalizing' public regulatory institutions.

In the wake of the 2001 financial crisis, the Turkish Government (under the aegis of the International Monetary Fund and the World Bank) restructured state financial agencies including the Ministry of the Economy, the Treasury, the Central Bank and other banking regulators, granting formal autonomy to the last two. Furthermore, autonomous regulatory bodies in other sectors (for example, in energy and telecommunications) were also established. The concentration of political and economic power in state financial agencies enabled these bodies to present their decisions to society as 'technical' matters—thus insulating themselves from class-based popular opposition—and in ways that projected the interests of financial capital as in the interests of all (Chapters 5–7).

Since coming to power in November 2002, the Adalet ve Kalkınma Partisi (AKP—Justice and Development Party) has generally adhered to this pattern of financial reform. Subsequent AKP governments have committed themselves to international capital mobility and hence to greater integration of Turkish financial markets into the global financial system. They have continued to adopt so-called best international financial practices and, until recently, preserved fiscal discipline. These attitudes have helped boost the confidence of international financial circles which have tolerated Turkey's rapidly rising current account deficits. Successive AKP governments have repeatedly amended the Banking Law and its by-laws (effectively in order to comply with EU norms) in order to make the banking sector (as the dominant component of the financial sector in Turkey) more competitive, better regulated and more stable. Apparently, this restructuring of the banking sector—by alleviating earlier financial distortions, capital inadequacies and improper risk-taking behaviour—helped Turkey to avoid the more serious repercussions of the 2008–09 global financial crisis that were felt elsewhere.

Notwithstanding the absence of an organized reaction of unions, workers and other popular movements to the neoliberal financial restructuring in capital's favour during the 2000s, Turkey's restructuring process has not been smooth because of difficulties in reconciling the diverse interests of capital, which are geographically, functionally and sociologically fractured. In attempts to settle these conflicts across various fractions of capital, successive AKP governments have been careful: (a) not to antagonize international capital; (b) to avoid an open confrontation with domestic financial capital; and (c) to encourage the rising 'Anatolian' entrepreneurial class and business community that is broadly supportive of the AKP. The abusive discourse of the AKP leadership towards the 'plotting' and 'exploiting' financiers in recent years should not be taken as an indication of a weakening in the AKP's resolve further to financialize the Turkish economy, but rather as growing difficulties in monitoring conflicts of interest within the capitalist class.

In recent years, there has been a tendency in Turkey to bring the autonomous regulatory agencies under the direct control of the government and to suppress the autonomy of the Central Bank. However, the concentration of economic and political power exercised through state financial agencies has not been eroded, but has actually risen. The rise in this concentration has coincided with the growing authoritarian tendency within the ruling cadre of the AKP (and President Recep Tayyip Erdoğan himself) in recent years.

The last part (Chapters 8 to 11) of this book provides detailed expositions and analyses of the ways through which the processes of financial transformation have affected and even reshaped other important constituents of the Turkish economy, including the corporate sector, SMEs, housing finance, and households. These chapters provide further support to the claim that AKP governments over their 16 years in power have deliberately promoted greater financial deepening as part of a finance-led strategy of capitalist development.

Turning back to the introductory chapter, by way of conclusion, it may be noted that three alternatives as a sequel to current neoliberal financial transformation in emerging economies can be identified. The first is the 'mainstream' alternative: that is, to intensify reform efforts in the same direction by improving the defective elements of the domestic financial system, by promoting fiscal stability, and by creating additional incentives for the private sector better to perform its economic tasks. The second is named as the 'heterodox' alternative, which envisages mitigating the excesses of financialization by allowing greater room for manoeuvre to policymakers in emerging economies in order to avoid cycles of boom and bust and other instabilities, together with a renewed emphasis on sustainable and equitable development. The third is seen as a 'critical' alternative, with the objective of transcending the financial oppression of capital over labouring and other popular classes. Undoubtedly, these are vital issues which cannot be fully dealt with within the limitations of the existing volume, but further research is welcomed.

As a final word, I would like to thank the contributors for the valuable task they have accomplished. I am sure that the readers of this book will learn a great deal from it, and enjoy it in equal measure.

Oktar Türel
Professor of Economics (retired)
Formerly at Middle East Technical University
Ankara, Turkey

Contributors

Hasan Cömert received his PhD from the University of Massachusetts at Amherst, USA, in 2011. Currently, Cömert is an Assistant Professor of Economics in the Department of Economics at Middle East Technical University (METU), Turkey. His research interests include central banking, financial markets, financial flows, developing countries and the Turkish economy. Dr Cömert has published several articles in Turkish and in English in domestic and international journals, including the *Cambridge Journal of Economics* and the *Canadian Journal of Development Studies.* He is the author of *Central Banks and Financial Markets: The Declining Power of US Monetary Policy* (Edward Elgar Publishing, 2013). In 2016, Rex McKenzie from Kingston University and Comert also edited a book on developing countries (also published by Edward Elgar) titled *Global South after the Crisis.* Comert also edited a book in Turkish titled *Looking at Turkey from the Lenses of Development Economics* (in Turkish; Kalkınma İktisadı Penceresinden Türkiye'ye Bakmak (edited with Emre Özçelik and Ebru Voyvoda, İletişim Publishing, 2017).

Demir Demiröz is a PhD candidate at the Department of Political Science and Public Administration, Middle East Technical University (METU), Ankara, Turkey. He has held graduate assistantship positions at METU and also Sabancı University. His main field of research is political economy. He is currently researching the development of business groups in Turkey.

Nilgün Erdem is an Independent Researcher who received her PhD in economics from the University of Ankara. In 1999–2000 she studied as a visiting researcher at the Department of Economics at the University of Notre Dame, USA. Her main interests are financial crises, hot money movements between developed and developing countries, international political economy, international financial architecture, labour markets and development.

İpek Eren Vural is an Associate Professor of Political Science in the Department of Political Science and Public Administration, at the Middle East

Technical University (METU), Ankara, Turkey. Her research interests lie in the fields of comparative political economy of public policy, particularly social policy and health policy. She has published numerous articles, book chapters and edited volumes on the political economy of pharmaceuticals, intellectual property rights, social policy and health policy in both Europe and Turkey. Her current research interests focus on the modalities and outcomes of financialization in the sphere of social reproduction, with particular reference to health care provision and financing systems. Her most recent published article on this line of research is titled "Financialisation in Health Care" in Social Science and Medicine in 2017.

Işıl Erol received her BSc. in City and Regional Planning (1998), her MSc in Economics (2000) from the Middle East Technical University (METU), Ankara, Turkey, and her MPhil in Land Economy (2001) and PhD in Real Estate Finance (2004) from the University of Cambridge. After completing her PhD Erol joined METU in the Department of Economics and worked there until 2013. Since August 2018, she has been an Associate Professor of Property, at Queensland University of Technology (QUT), School of Civil Engineering and Built Environment, Property and Planning in Brisbane, Australia. Her areas of speciality are in housing finance and mortgage markets, mortgage valuation with option pricing models, and Real Estate Investment Trusts. Her publications have appeared in the Journal of Housing Economics, Journal of Real Estate Finance and Economics, Urban Geography, Journal of Housing and Built Environment and Review of Urban and Regional Development Studies.

Ali Rıza Güngen is a political scientist and independent researcher. Dr Güngen received his PhD from the Middle East Technical University (METU), Ankara, Turkey, and was granted the Young Social Scientist award by the Turkish Social Sciences Association in 2013. Güngen is the co-author of the 2014 book *Financialization, Debt Crisis and Collapse* (in Turkish). His articles have appeared in *The Journal of Peasant Studies, New Political Economy* and *Amme İdaresi Dergisi*. His research currently focuses on sovereign debt management across the global South, and state restructuring and financial inclusion in Turkey.

Thomas Marois is a Senior Lecturer of Development Studies at SOAS University of London, United Kingdom, who specializes in finance and development in emerging capitalist societies. His current research focuses on the resurgence of public banks and their potential to support alternative green and equitable development. He is a member of the Municipal Services Project (https://www.municipalservicesproject.org/) and works closely with non-governmental organizations on topics of alternative finance and the public provisioning of essential services.

Aylin Topal is a faculty member of the Department of Political Science and Public Administration at Middle East Technical University (METU),

Ankara, Turkey. She is also the chairperson of Latin and North American Studies Program at the same university. Her main fields of research are political economy of development and agrarian change. She is the author of *Boosting Competitiveness through Decentralization: A Subnational Comparison of Local Development in Mexico*, (Burlington: Ashgate Publishing, 2012). She has also published several articles and chapters in edited volumes on regional, urban and rural development in Mexico and relations between the state, capital and labour under neoliberalism in Turkey.

Galip L. Yalman is an Associate Professor (retired) of Political Science in the Department of Political Science and Public Administration at the Middle East Technical University (METU), Ankara, Turkey. His research interests extend from state theory to international and comparative political economy. He is the author of *Transition to Neoliberalism: The Case of Turkey in the 1980s*, (İstanbul Bilgi University Press, 2009); "Crises as Driving Forces of Neoliberal 'Trasformismo': The Contours of the Turkish Political Economy since the 2000s" in Alan Cafruny et al. (eds.) *The Palgrave Handbook of Critical International Political Economy*, Palgrave-Macmillan, 2016; and co-editor of *Economic Transitions to Neoliberalism in Middle Income Countries,* (London, Routledge, 2010). He was the local co-ordinator in Turkey of FESSUD, Financialisation, Economy, Society and Sustainable Development, EU-funded Framework Seven Project, 2011–2016. He is currently President of the Turkish Social Sciences Association.

A. Erinç Yeldan Professor and Dean of the Faculty of Economics, Administrative and Social Sciences, and acting chair of the Department of International Relations at Bilkent University. He is the funding director of the Energy Policies Research Center at Bilkent; and serves as one of the 30 members of the International Resource Panel of the UN Environment Programme. He is also one of the executive directors of the International Development Economics Associates (IDEAs), New Delhi, India. Dr Yeldan received his PhD from the University of Minnesota, USA, and joined the Department of Economics at Bilkent in 1988. During 1994–95 he was a visiting scholar at the University of Minnesota where he taught Applied General Equilibrium Analysis. During 2007–08 he was a Fulbright scholar at the University of Massachusetts, Amherst and at Amherst College, USA. Dr Yeldan's recent work focuses on development macroeconomics, vulnerability and fragmentation of labour markets, de-industrialization, and economics of climate change, and on empirical, dynamic general equilibrium models. On these subjects Professor Yeldan has contributed over 50 refereed articles, written eight books, and participated in numerous project reports and briefings. In over 30 years of his professional experience as an educator, he has directed more than 20 master's theses and supervised six doctoral dissertations.

Acknowledgements

This book originates from a country-study report prepared as part of the research project, Financialisation, Economy, Society and Sustainable Development (FESSUD) (2011–2016), which has received funding from the European Union Seventh Research Framework Programme (FP7/2007–2013), (theme SSH) under grant agreement No. 266800.

The contributors of *Comparative Perspective on Financial System in the EU: Country Report on Turkey*, FESSUD Studies in Financial Systems No. 11, October 2013 (ISSN: 2052-8027), were P. Bedirhanoğlu, H. Cömert, İ. Eren, I. Erol, D. Demiröz, N. Erdem, A.R. Güngen, T. Marois, A. Topal, O. Türel, E. Voyvoda, G. Yalman and E. Yeldan,

The original report is available online at: http://fessud.eu/wp content/uploads/2012/08/Turkey-Studies.pdf.

We are also grateful to *Routledge Emerging Economies* series editor Professor Robert Looney, to Cathy Hartley (Regional Editor, *Western Europe,* and Commissioning Editor, Europa Publications) and to Eleanor Simmons (Editorial Assistant, Europa Publications) for their support and understanding during the preparation of our book.

Galip L. Yalman
Thomas Marois
Ali Rıza Güngen

1 Introduction

Debating Financial Transformation in Turkey

Galip L. Yalman, Thomas Marois and Ali Rıza Güngen

Turkey's neoliberal economy has evolved into one of the most dynamic among the emerging capitalist societies of the global South since the dramatic 2001 Turkish financial crisis, and it has once again become the darling of international financial circles, as it was in the 1980s. However, in due course, it also turned out to be one of the most debt-laden economies in the emerging market universe, with its persistent current account deficit, reflecting its economy's continued dependence on hot money flows. Concomitantly, eyebrows have been raised about the nature of its neoliberal transformation, as formal and informal relations between certain business groups and the political authorities have come under scrutiny. A major thrust of such questioning has been, however, to contrast the particularities of the Turkish political economy against an idealized type of market-based order that is assumed to reflect the distinctive features of Western capitalism, particularly in the neoliberal era.

Moreover, there have been increasing concerns about the deterioration of the political context, as the mode of governing of the political party that has been in power in Turkey since 2002 kept baffling observers of the Turkish case. While the Adalet ve Kalkınma Partisi (AKP—Justice and Development Party) was initially portrayed as the carrier of the mantle of the democratizing force in Turkish politics in the early 2000s, the party has started to attract growing criticism for becoming increasingly authoritarian in its political behaviour, particularly since 2012. This entailed not only an acknowledgement of significant backsliding in the areas of freedom of expression and freedom of assembly, the erosion of judicial and regulatory independence, wreaking havoc with the rule of law and the principle of separation of powers considered essential for a functioning market economy, as well as for a democratic form of government. It was also accompanied by a sudden reawakening to the pitfalls of the finance-dominated model of capital accumulation in the wake of very serious corruption allegations involving the very highest echelons of the AKP government. However, as there has been mounting criticism of increasing political interference in the financial sector, the AKP leadership chose to blame a shadowy 'interest rate lobby' for instigating instability for the sake of their vested interests. But this did not necessarily imply a criticism of monetary orthodoxy—far from it. While financial stability has been considered as the lynchpin of the AKP government's monetary and fiscal policies, reflecting its adherence to the neoliberal policy agenda at least until the 2008 global financial crisis, it seemed to have lost its saliency since then, as the country's financial system tended to straddle currency and maturity mismatches.

These developments underline the importance of the changes in the banking and financial sector both to Turkey's overall economic growth trajectory and to the underlying exploitative social structures that characterize neoliberal development strategies. However, given the predominance of liberal-individualist and statist-institutionalist approaches and schools of political economy in general, and the hegemony of neoliberalism in discourse, as well as in policymaking in particular, Turkey's financial transformation has been under-theorized and empirically under-explored from a critical political economy perspective. Hence, Turkey's variety of finance-led capitalism is to be defined not only by its increasing dependence on financial flows and investments in the national economy, but also by the qualitative analysis of the neoliberal and finance-led restructuring of state-capital relations, including the institutional apparatuses.

From this book's critical perspective, these changes have not been part of a class-neutral process, as they have primarily elevated the interests of major capital groups—which entailed the characteristics of both finance capital and financial capital (this conceptual distinction will be elaborated below)—above the interests of the poor, and wage earners in Turkey. Nor have the changes occurring in Turkey been limited within its national borders. The intensification of financial imperatives in Turkey's political economy has also altered the way in which both the economy and the society are integrated into the global financial market. However, Turkey's experiences with financial transformation show some variations with respect to the interpretations of financialization built upon the experiences of advanced capitalism. A major contribution of this volume, then, is to offer an alternative account on the basis of the financial transformation in Turkey as a variant of emerging capitalism in the global South.

This also explains why the title of the book is 'Financial Transformation' of Turkey, rather than, say, 'Financialization'. To be sure, this does *not* imply dismissing the 'financialization' literature or its import. Rather, it is to foreground the necessity of historicizing and specifying theory, based on concrete experiences, rather than grafting theory onto the realities of different societies like Turkey. Succinctly put, "the necessary historicity of our basic theoretical concepts require … further empirical definition", so that they could be employed for "the actual task of explanation" (Bromley 1994: 31). This also gains saliency, to avoid any tendency for country-specific, methodologically particularistic accounts, which has been a characteristic of many contemporary studies on Turkey (cf. Yalman 2016). Instead, the purpose of this book is to contribute to the development of "a common theoretical framework, using an empirically open methodology, to different societies" (Bromley 1994: 31).

We thus aim to introduce the contents of this book by first engaging in contemporary debates on financialization, arguing for the need for a conceptual framework to come to terms with historically distinct processes of financial transformation in general, in the emerging capitalist societies of the global South in particular. While some contributors to this book, benefiting from critical political economy and heterodox perspectives, preferred to refer to the concept of financialization, others employed terms such as finance-led capitalism in elaborating distinctive aspects of the Turkish transformation. Despite the heterogeneity in the use of terms, all of the authors made an effort to avoid grafting the concept of financialization as a ready-made framework onto the Turkish experience.

Then, we chart out, very briefly, the historical trajectory of Turkey's bank-based but increasingly market-oriented financial transformations. We move on to the alternatives to neoliberal intensification of financial imperatives. Our point is not simply to illustrate alternative approaches, but to underline the way they address the issues arising within the context of financial transformation. Finally, we review the problem of access to the financial system for many people in Turkey and point out the possibility of a pro-public approach to dealing with the often hectic financial transformation in Turkey, as well as in other emerging capitalist societies.

Debating 'Financialization' Today

Although it is considered a catch-all term that refers to a multiplicity of phenomena (Lavoie 2008: 332), financialization has gained saliency as a much-debated key concept to describe new trends in contemporary capitalism, thereby creating substantial disagreements among critical political economists, as well as heterodox and post-Keynesian economists, while being largely ignored by the mainstream economists (cf. Engelen and Konings 2010: 606; Palley 2007). Among the former, however, there are also those who underline the need for a proper analysis of how modern finance and capitalism function, but tend to dispense with the term altogether. By branding it as "an increasingly nebulous and even, arguably, unhelpful signifier", they put in doubt the usefulness of "the concept in attempting to understand contemporary capitalism and its specificities" (cf. Christophers 2015; Michell and Toporowski 2013). On the other hand, there have also been counter-arguments to the effect that financialization signifies a 'form of domination' through which finance has extended its influence into all realms of social life, to highlight the ways in which an economic system distributes power and affects the character of production and the distribution of income in the era of financial liberalisation (cf. Palley 2007; Picciotto 2011: 261; van der Zwan 2014). There is thus a predominant tendency to relate globalization and neoliberalization with financialization to account for capitalist transformation at the level of both the national state, and the global economy. Consequently, financialization studies in the 21st century have enjoyed the same meteoric rise in the field of the social sciences as did globalization and neoliberalization in the late 20th century.

Ironically, as the popularity of financialization rises and its usage becomes ever more widespread, its specific applicability seems to drain, if not erode its explanatory potential. As has been conceded even by those who are keen to employ it, it is not explicitly theoretically innovative in addressing its object of inquiry (Fine 2013a). As such, some of these accounts would be defended as providing less an explanation for financialization than an *interpretation* of it (Krippner 2012). Indeed, it remains unclear how financialization can be conceptualized in order to be utilized productively for the analysis of historically specific cases (Christophers 2015; Toporowski 2012), because, as has been acknowledged, it is often defined imprecisely across a burgeoning literature (Fine and Saad-Filho 2016). Nonetheless, as an analytical concept derived largely from the experiences of the global North, it is plausible to identify two broad perspectives: the first relating it to the growth of the financial sector in its operations and power, while the second views it as an epoch of capitalism in which the relationship between the financial sector and the real sector has been undergoing major changes (Sawyer 2013).

The pioneering and frequently quoted example of the first perspective has been provided by Gerald Epstein, who defines financialization broadly as the "increasing role of financial motives, financial markets, financial actors and financial institutions in the operation of domestic and international economies" (Epstein 2005: 3). While the growth of stock markets relative to banks in a financial system is considered as evidence of a more market-based economy, such a rapid expansion of financial markets, however, is said to blur the distinction between the banks and new financial institutions such as money market funds, and private equity and hedge funds, as well as the much-hyped contrast between bank-based and market-based financial systems (cf. Engelen et al. 2011: 230; Sawyer 2014; Stockhammer 2015). Building on the foundations set by Epstein, further elaborations have been largely empirical observations about i) the quantitative increases in the turnover of financial assets and liabilities (cf. Krippner 2011); and ii) the increased financial operations of firms and households relative to income. Thus, financialization has come to refer to a broad set of changes in the relationships between the 'financial' and the 'real' sectors, wherein the actions of financial actors or motives are privileged (Stockhammer 2011). That is, the concern is how different firms interact with and react to domestic and global financial markets. As such, financialization is considered a complicated process, entailing a "dialectical and contradictory relationship between the financial and real sides of the economy" that may affect different corporations in different ways. (Orhangazi 2008: 865; 2016:259). However, it has also been held that a dichotomous view of the economy implying clear-cut distinctions between the real economy and the financial sector is being undermined as finance has transcended its traditional intermediary role, while at the same time the financial motivations have become decisive even within the real economy (cf. Engelen and Konings 2010: 621; Sawyer et al. 2017; Stockhammer 2015).

Concomitantly, an important focus of the debate on financialization is concerned with the relationship between banking and industrial capital. While there is concurrence of opinion that there has been a significant transformation about the ways in which the process of capital accumulation is carried out, there appear to be significant differences in regards to both causes and consequences of this transformation. No less saliently, there is no concurrence of opinion in regards to whether this transformation process should be considered as a signifier of a new epoch. The *Monthly Review* school, characterized by the works of Paul Sweezy and John Bellamy Foster, among others, disputed that financialization signified a "new stage of capitalism". They have looked to the structural characteristics of contemporary capitalism via the quantitative growth in finance and increasingly large and recurrent crises, largely defined by the experiences of the global North and the USA in particular, to point to the emergence of a "new hybrid phase", monopoly-finance capital or finance capitalism (cf. Foster 2007, 2010; Peet 2011). The work of Gérard Duménil and Dominique Lévy similarly draws attention to how the current phase of finance-led capital accumulation is tied to the emergence of neoliberalism, itself an expression of the reasserted power of finance capital in power blocs (Duménil and Lévy 2005; 2011). Another good example of the second perspective expressed with the vocabulary of the French Regulation School is to characterize the changing relationship between the financial sector and the real sector as the development of a *finance-dominated* regime of accumulation and mode of regulation (cf. Demirovic and Sablowski 2013; Jessop and Sum 2014). However, 'finance-dominated capitalism' turns out to be a characteristic notion of post-Keynesian analysis as well, used interchangeably with financialization, implying the dominance of finance as a hindrance to investment in the real sector, as well as increasing income inequality and the falling share of labour income in the total economy (cf. Hein and Detzer 2014; Stockhammer 2011).

On the other hand, there are other major perspectives on financialization that contend, from a Marxist perspective, that it does, indeed, signify a new epoch, even though there are significant differences between them in accounting for the reasons of its emergence. One of them claims that financialization entails a "systemic transformation of mature capitalism" during which "commercial banks have become more distant from industrial and commercial capital". Thus, Hilferding's original thesis on finance capital is considered to be inadequate to come to terms with contemporary reality (Lapavitsas 2009; 2011). It has been argued that qualitative transformations have been taking place regarding both banking and industrial sectors, altering the conduct of both. As the non-financial corporations are said to become less reliant on outside finance in general, and bank loans in particular, for their operational investments, they would become 'financialized'—that is, their profits are to be generated out of the processes of circulation rather than deriving from surplus value generated in production (cf. Dos Santos 2009; Lapavitsas 2013: 145, 168). For these Marxian accounts, this leads to a new theorization of financial expropriation, or how banks have turned to the extraction of financial profits directly out of workers' income through increases in fees and commissions via the offering of new financial services—which nonetheless occurs alongside greater magnitude of open market operations. As this perspective reaffirms financialization as a distinct trajectory, there are other Marxian accounts, which tend to concur, but put forward a rather different mode of explanation that highlights the modalities by which social and economic reproduction increasingly occurs through financial means. In their view, too, financialization has to be recognized as an epoch in the history of capitalist development starting in the mid-1980s, as the accumulation and extended reproduction of capital becomes increasingly dependent upon finance in the form of interest-bearing capital (cf. Fine 2010; Chesnais 2014). Put differently, it implies the dominance of finance over industry as corporations have been observed to be relying less rather than more upon the financial system to fund their operations (Brown et al. 2015). This would imply that the financial system should be treated as a structured whole which is connected organically to real accumulation (Papadatos 2012).

However, for others while the growing reliance of nonfinancial firms on financial activities for profit making rather than through productive activities has been an important factor for developing a definition of financialization (Krippner 2011: 4, 23), this would not necessarily imply an entirely novel phase of capitalist development (ibid. 51). Indeed, it was earlier contended that what came to be referred to as the era of financialization need not be characterized as a new stage of world capitalism as periods of financial expansion were a recurrent pattern of historical capitalism as a world system (Arrighi and Silver 1999: 272; Arrighi 1994: 6). This would, in turn, generate the counter-argument that this is not simply the expansion of finance in scope and quantity, but also the subordination of such finance to interest-bearing capital in the form of assets that straddle the roles of money as credit and as capital (Fine 2013).

More pertinently, the financial expansion, however interpreted, would not necessarily imply that the financial economy has become entirely uncoupled from production (Krippner 2011: 4). As has been already observed:

> The very distinction between financial and industrial capital is becoming increasingly anachronistic as accumulation on a world scale is dominated by multinational corporations which take the form of financial holding companies closely integrated with multinational banks and financial institutions.
>
> (Clarke 1988: 4)

Such a blurring of frontiers between financial and non-financial activities would be manifested in the activities of the transnational corporations, organized and structured as groups of enterprises, in the form of holding companies, thus making them a locus for a global valorization of capital, where productive and financial valorization are closely intertwined. In fact, this would be identified as the main characteristic of 21st-century capitalism to the extent that a major characteristic of finance capital will no longer be an alliance of industrial companies and banks under the dominance of the latter, thereby also blurring the line between productive and interest-bearing capital (Serfati 2011; Chesnais 2016: 112). While there is a basic agreement that the fusion of banks with industrial capital does not imply the subordination of industrial capital by the banks, the changing relationship between the two need not imply the detachment of financial capital from productive capital in the contemporary era either (cf. Marois 2012a; Wood 2007). Nor a strict functional separation between finance and industry (Park and Doucette 2016: 534). This also brings into the debate a reminder about the need to distinguish finance capital from financial capital. While the latter refers to 'concentrated money capital operating in financial markets', the former designates 'the simultaneous and intertwined concentration and centralisation of money capital, industrial capital and commercial capital' (Chesnais 2016: 5) so that the process of production of value is subordinated to the needs of finance capital itself (Ticktin 2011: 10).

Another important aspect of the debate is concerned with the role of the state and its strategic selectivities in creating and perpetuating conditions conducive to financialization (cf. Fine 2010: 19; Jessop 2013; Krippner 2011: 2). In particular, its promotion of financial markets and its role in the commodification of the life cycle would be underlined (Zwan 2014). While much of the financialization literature has been generated from advanced capitalist countries, notably the USA, the United Kingdom, and Japan, there has been much emphasis on the role of the US state in particular as a key agent of global capital to come to terms with the crises in the era of finance-led neoliberalism (cf. Panitch and Gindin 2008). Therefore, it is deemed necessary from a critical political economy perspective, to perceive financialization as a political process driven by concrete social actors and engendered by specific strategies (García-Aras et al. 2017). In this regard, while class emerges as a central dynamic of financial transformation, it becomes salient to come to terms with the ways in which financialization shifts the balance of power between classes and reconfigures relations within the capital-owning classes. In particular, the specific ways in which contradictions endemic to the components of finance capital (industrial versus financial capitalist fractions) are internalized within particular organizational structures, such as holding companies, gain saliency (cf. Bryan et al. 2009; Harvey 2006: 320; Peet 2011). By the same token, there has been an increasing emphasis on the variegated characteristics of the process: that is, the variation it manifests as it unfolds in historically specific contexts, mediated by different institutional arrangements (cf. Brown et al. 2015; Engelen and Konings 2010: 604).

These issues gain significance not only for a comparative analysis of advanced capitalist countries, but as chapters in this book attest, the processes of financial transformation in emerging capitalisms as well (cf. Güngen 2012: 186). In any attempt to historicize financialization with regards to emerging capitalist societies, the analysis of the relations between the state, financial sector and the real sector becomes imperative. While the financialization literature of emerging capitalist societies is rather thin comparatively speaking, there has been a number of studies revealing important dimensions and contradictions of financial transformation in several regions of the global South. As a recent contribution by Adam Hanieh on the Gulf Cooperation Council underlines, financialization should not simply be equated with the expansion of financial assets and motives, as it is intimately connected to the changing dynamics of class formation (Hanieh 2016). In fact, Hanieh argued for the need to account for the specificities of 'place' and to better understand financial processes through a critical scalar and regional analytical lens, which in turn reveals valuable insights into associated class and state formation processes. The same study also warns against treating national economies as spatially bounded and methodologically divorced from international flows of capital. In fact, the liberalization of capital flows with its accompanying currency-convertibility has been an important facet of the financial transformation in peripheral economies over the last few decades. This has left them prone to the build-up of systemic risk as their financial sectors become fragile in the face of capital flows, whether intermediated through the banking system or as portfolio investments to equity and bond markets (cf. Claessens and Ghosh 2016).

No less significantly, the nature of a state's insertion into the global economy and changing forms of that modality necessitated further attention (Powell 2013). The effect of capital account liberalization has been growing public debt which, in turn, made these states subject to the vagaries of international financial markets and paved the way for increasing the degree of foreign ownership of domestic firms through privatizations, as well as mergers and acquisitions (cf. Correa and Vidal 2012; Painceira 2012). Indeed, the emphasis put on financial stability on the part of the monetary authorities in these countries will thus be interpreted as the expression of the dominance of finance, as reflected in the strategic selectivities of the states concerned (cf. Durand and Keucheyan 2015). However, the role of the state is not to be conceived merely as a transmission belt from the global economy to the national economy. Nor should the relative autonomy of the capitalist state imply a conception of the state being the locus of a coherent and rational policy external to capital. Rather the struggles among social forces located within each social formation should also be taken into account (cf. Panitch 1993; Poulantzas 1975: 158). A benefit of the nascent peripheral financialization literature is that it internalizes the diverse, variegated forms capitalism takes in different societies, whether or not they are to be described as examples of subordinate financialization (cf. Brenner et al. 2010; Lapavitsas 2013: 247; Lapavitsas and Powell 2013).

There are, in fact, several comparative studies bringing together variegated cases of financial transformations. In a comparative study of Mexico and Turkey, Thomas Marois argues for an analytical framework on the basis of Marxian-informed premises for studying 'emerging finance capitalism', defined as "the fusion of the interests of domestic and foreign financial capital in the state apparatus as the institutionalized priorities and overarching social logic guiding the actions of state managers and government elites, often to the detriment of labour" (Marois 2012: 38). More broadly, the specific historical and institutional trajectories of national process of capital accumulation are considered essential for the analysis of the financialisation of emerging capitalist economies (Kaltenbrunner and Karaçimen 2016: 289). Put differently, it is imperative to pay due attention to the specific modalities of state-capital relations and institutional forms that these relations give rise to in these countries as they are all located within global financial markets which are, indeed, dominated by those controlling the movement of capital flows.

There are also studies approaching these issues from an historical-institutionalist perspective, including those that attempt to overcome 'institutionally deterministic' versions which fail 'to explain structural changes in national financial systems'. One such study comparing the transformation of the Malaysian and Taiwanese financial systems aimed to illustrate how the bank-centred systems have been transformed as a result of the initiation of the market agents "to break through institutional heritages" (Zhang 2009). In a sense, it has tended to reiterate the claim made in regards to advanced capitalist economies—that the old distinction between bank-based and market-based finance has not disappeared, but has assumed new characteristics (Lapavitsas2013: 244), and is also valid in the case of the so-called second generation of newly industrializing countries.

By contrast, there are also studies which draw attention to the specific modalities of state-capital relations and institutional forms these relations give rise to, by focusing on the predominant form of corporate structure, i.e. conglomerates as key agents of financial transformation in several countries of the global South, from Latin America to East Asia. As already indicated, major capital groups which entailed the characteristics of both finance capital and financial capital, have been emerging as class actors *par excellence* in their respective environments. However, there are differences in the ways in which their role and context would be specified. These groups with their diversified structures are generally portrayed as both the participants of economic policymaking and beneficiaries of the financialization process in the Latin American context (cf. Jilberto and Hogenboom 2004; Lefort and Walker 1999/2000; Teubal 2004). Whereas it has been contended that the experience of their counterparts in South Korea, *chaebol*s, would make financialization a contested concept to the extent that the latter was understood as ascendancy or dominance of finance over industry. For the financial transformation in South Korea has not purportedly given rise to a 'new finance-led accumulation regime', as it simply reinforced the position of *chaebol*s comprising both industrial and financial companies within the political economy of the country (cf. Hart-Landsberg et al. 2007: 13–14; Park and Doucette 2016: 541–543). It is admittedly a relatively neglected field of study which needs further historically specific empirical analyses from a critical political economy perspective.

The Historical Trajectory of Turkey's Financial Transformation: Bank-based, but Market-oriented

As this book aims to highlight, the genesis of the financial transformation in Turkey could be traced back to the early republican era, from the 1920s onwards. Such a historical perspective indicates the critical role played by the state in different periods, notwithstanding the pursuit of qualitatively different strategies of capitalist development. Like most peripheral countries of the global capitalist system in the late 19th and early 20th centuries, the governing authorities aimed to create a national financial system that would seek to provide the financial support deemed essential for enhancing the developmental ambitions of the new republic. Having inherited two important banks from its predecessor, the Ottoman Empire—one foreign-owned, and one public—the need was still felt to found two new banks—one private, one public—that would contribute to the fulfilment of these developmental objectives. While the public one would take over the responsibility to issue money from the foreign bank which had this prerogative since the last few decades of the Ottoman Empire, the state-initiated private bank would assume the task of mobilizing scarce capital resources, thereby setting the stage for the evolution of closely knit relations between the banking and industrial sectors for decades to come. A process that would be given further stimulus with the establishment of a series of new special purpose public banks in the aftermath of the Great Depression, whereas the post-Second World War era would witness the proliferation of privately owned commercial banks. Hence, the need for new institutional arrangements for the banking sector, which would, in turn, pave the way for the formation of holding groups with their affiliated group banks that would emerge as a distinctive feature of the Turkish financial system (see Chapter 2). Closely knit entanglements between different capitalist interests tended to blur the frontiers between financial and non-financial sectors, as exemplified by the dominance of Turkish capital groups, especially since the 1960s.

As Ali Rıza Güngen (2012) points out, it is necessary to highlight the distinctive trajectories in Turkey due to the role of the state and the specific form financial deepening took in the neoliberal period. This involves tracing Turkey's transition to neoliberalism, its evolution into a more finance-led form through recurrent crises, and crystallized as variegated emergent form of finance-led capitalism. Accordingly, the establishment and formation of specific institutional mechanisms that characterized the long and protracted process of Turkish neoliberal transformation from the early 1980s to the late 1990s are presented in Chapter 3. In the wake of the two decades-long development planning experience that entrenched the bank-based nature of the Turkish financial system, with the addition of a series of publicly owned development banks, the transition in the 1980s to idealized neoliberal market-oriented development did not bring about an immediate shift in either Turkey's bank-based financial system or in bank ownership patterns, as both public and private banks remained major players in Turkey, while foreign control stayed well in the background.

Nonetheless, the wider liberalization of Turkey's economy did loosen control on financial transactions, leading to a phase of recurrent crises through the 1980s and 1990s, with the 2001 crisis being among the most dramatic and costly to Turkish society (see Chapters 3 and 4). Reflecting the specificity of Turkey, as in other emerging capitalist societies, the state-led resolution to the 2001 crisis "preserved, renewed, and intensified the structurally unequal social relations of power and class characteristic of finance-led neoliberal capitalism" in ways that disproportionately privileged the needs of financial capital over those of the poor and working classes (Marois 2011, 169). Moreover, since 2001 and under the ruling AKP government, Turkish authorities have aggressively restructured state and society in Turkey towards an intensely market-oriented strategy of development, including in its continued bank-based, but market-oriented financial system (see Chapters 5 to 7).

The 2008–09 global financial crisis exemplifies the depth of Turkey's financial transformation under neoliberalism. As Chapter 4 illustrates empirically, the 2008–09 crisis was in many ways distinct from previous crises under neoliberalism, being neither as severe financially but also being expressed more through trade channels. Indeed, international commentators have generally agreed that Turkey's financial sector, including the banks and more market-based institutions, proved relatively resilient. Yet Turkish authorities' response to the crisis maintained a neoliberal pattern of privileging the needs of capital in Turkey, albeit in complex and sometimes contradictory ways, while doing the least possible to address the needs of the poor and working classes (Muñoz-Martínez and Marois 2014).

The impact of and resolution to financial crises have proven constitutive of the evolving financial system and structures, which in turn feeds back onto wider economic and political practices—a point explored comparatively in Chapter 4, but also made in terms of the changing structures of the state apparatus, the banking sector, and the financial markets in Turkey (see Chapters 4 to 7). At the same time, financial transformation under conditions of neoliberalism has entailed the building-up of a more muscular and internationalized state financial apparatus (see Chapter 5). Contrary to the idealism of neoliberal thought and neoclassical economics, finance capitalism is characterized *by anything but a minimal state.* Governing authorities have restructured the state, concentrating political and economic power around state financial agencies such as the treasury, the central bank, banking regulators, and the ministry of finance and the economy. These financial institutions have gained formal independence: that is, greater insulation from popular democratic influence and working class priorities. Although several of the so-called independent regulatory agencies have been brought under the direct control of the political authorities since 2012, their insulation from democratic monitoring remains a constant.

The final four chapters of this book provide detailed analyses of the ways in which the process of financial transformation has affected important constituents of the Turkish economy, namely the corporate sector, small and medium-sized firms (SMEs), housing finance and households. Based on an analysis of Turkey's top 500 industrial firms, Chapter 8 aims to show the extent to which the financial transformation created new opportunities for the Turkish corporate sector in terms of financial channels as a source of profits, as well as mergers and acquisitions. Given the difficulties in measuring the percentage of financial profits within the total profits from the available data, the non-operating incomes of the top 500 industrial firms as a proportion of their net balance sheet profit are taken as an indicator of the dominance of financial activities for the non-financial corporations. This analysis is complemented by a presentation of how the new round of de- and re-regulation of the corporate sector in the post-2001 financial crisis era laid the foundations for the increasing significance of mergers and acquisitions (M&A) in the Turkish corporate sector, both in the real and financial components, at a historical juncture. Given the predominance of SMEs in the Turkish economy, both in terms of their share in total number of firms and the total number of workers employed, it is argued in Chapter 9 that the transformation of the Turkish financial system necessitates an analysis of the SMEs as a lynchpin of the differentiation between the financial and non-financial sectors. Indeed, this is in line with the argument that if there is a demarcation line to be drawn between financial and productive capital, that needs to be considered in regard to the SMEs that develop their activities at some distance from financial markets (Durand and Keucheyan 2015).

Construction in general, and housing in particular, have always been very important sectors of the Turkish economy, for channelling private sector investment, as well as for employment creation. Chapter 10 presents an analysis of both the housing market and housing finance in the context of the financial transformation since the 2000s, and tries to account for how the Turkish real estate market has become a rising star, while failing to respond to the need for affordable housing. It also provides a detailed analysis of new financial instruments introduced for the provision of housing finance, along with the changing role of the state within the housing sector with its direct involvement in the production and financing of housing via newly established agencies, thereby accelerating the commodification of land and the built environment.

Last but not least, as another important dimension of the debate on financialization, Chapter 11 focuses on the evolving nature of the relationship between the commercial banks and individuals/households, and highlights its distinctive characteristics in the Turkish context. In particular, it emphasizes that rising household debt and the growing reliance on consumer credits have not been class-neutral phenomena, entailing the transfer of resources from non-capital-owning classes to those who are in a position to benefit. Thus, it reinforces the disciplinary power of capital on labour and diffuses market logic into the everyday lives of average earners.

Since the 2008–09 crisis, successive AKP governments have pursued a strategy of trying to build Istanbul into a global financial hub, and in particular a new hub of 'green' or Islamic finance. Perhaps ironically, this new phase of financial transformation is being championed not by the private sector *per se*, but by the government and through the three remaining large state-owned commercial banks: Ziraat Bank, Halkbank and VakıfBank. To be sure, authorities are promoting market-based financial development and stock market growth, as discussed in Chapter 7. Yet for deep historical, economic and political reasons, the form financial transformation takes in Turkey is distinct from patterns identified in the advanced capitalist societies. In many ways, it is to this contemporary debate that this book seeks to contribute an alternative account.

Alternatives to Neoliberal Financial Transformation

While literature on financialization so far has been relatively blind to the specificities of emerging capitalist societies, at the same time the literature (on both the global North and South) has encountered theoretical and concrete difficulties with the question of alternatives. This problem has been under-theorized and -specified, especially from critical political economic perspectives. Indeed, both the mainstream and certain heterodox approaches have been relatively more active in addressing the concrete problems that have arisen within the context of contemporary financial transformation. It has been recently acknowledged that while there is a need to explore the possibilities for de-financialisation and for a socially and environmentally responsible financial sector, the calls for de-financialization have to recognize that the politically powerful financial sectors would fiercely resist any moves to transcend neoliberal financial transformation and thus try to make the likelihood of any such change a distant prospect (Sawyer 2017). A useful means of characterizing these alternatives is to debate the degree to which they seek to intensify, mitigate or transcend neoliberal financial transformation in society.

Mainstream Alternatives: Intensifying Financial Transformation

In conventional neoliberal and neoclassical academic and policy circles, there remains little to no alternative to intensified financial transformation. Indeed, even the unprecedented impact of the global 2008–09 financial crisis gave little pause to such advocacy. Instead, the recommendations coming out of the crisis included the need to 1) repair and reform the financial sector; 2) pursue fiscal adjustments to aid stability; 3) encourage emerging markets to develop their own domestic growth; and 4) help governments to create better incentives for the private sector as the key drivers of growth, employment, productivity (see Acemoğlu 2009; Rogers 2010). As F.S. Mishkin argues, "for emerging countries to reach the next stage of development and get rich, financial globalization must go much further than it already has" (2009: 140). Poverty and inequality, therein, are the consequence of an inability or unwillingness to enter into the global economic system, that is, to financially transform (2009: 142). To turn one's back on financial globalization, the benefits of private ownership, and market competition, then, spells economic disaster. International financial institutions, notably the World Bank, have advanced this line of argument since 2008–09.

Take for example the *World Development Report 2014*, which promotes financial inclusion and the deepening of access to financial markets. The Report innovates by suggesting that state regulatory and supervisory institutions are now needed to support extended financial transformation (World Bank 2013). Such state institutions are required for financial risk management—as the benefits reach the whole of society by linking investors and workers together while helping to prevent developmental setbacks (World Bank 2013: 8; 62). To manage financial risk, though, "resources should be provisioned for residual liabilities that the state may have to bear" (that is, socialized) (World Bank 2013: 33). Notwithstanding the rediscovery of the state in financial transformation and development, the international financial institutions and conventional economists underpin the fundamental need for universal private property protections and institutional frameworks that protect and enhance the market. None the less, there is a necessity for universal private property rights and market-enhancing institutional frameworks that preserve market-based economics (Calomiris and Haber 2014: 12–13; 35). A notable implication is that any move toward public ownership of banks, as one alternative strategy, would increase risk, encourage corruption, and undermine the economic benefits of market-oriented financial deepening (World Bank 2012: 117).

Heterodox and New Developmental Alternatives: Mitigating Excesses of Financial Transformation

Heterodox and new developmental scholars, by contrast, have pointed to the need for greater extra-market coordination of global finance in order to mitigate the excesses of financial boom-and-bust cycles (Epstein 2010). The contention is not to break with financial globalization, but to mediate the speed of transformation and to allow for greater domestic 'policy space' for emerging and developing countries in particular, and to negotiate their sequenced integration into global markets (cf. Grabel 2011). The *UNCTAD 2014 Trade and Development Report* exemplifies this heterodox approach to financial transformation. On the one hand, the Report's developmentalist orientation recognizes that foreign capital inflows are necessary for the development process, particularly for the purchase of capital goods that are not available domestically. On the other hand, however, these same inflows, if unregulated in terms of size and composition, can undermine growth and development while economic policy "room for manoeuvre" is constrained (UNCTAD 2014: 121). If left unmanaged, countries can suffer from repeated boom-and-bust cycles of capital abundance and scarcity, undermining long-term developmental prospects. As the Report (2014: 122) argues:

> Therefore, there is a strong case for governments to manage capital flows by seeking to influence not only the amount of foreign capital movements, but also their composition and use. Such a pragmatic and selective approach to capital flows, rather than unrestricted openness or a complete ban, could help maximize policy space within a given development strategy and given existing international institutional arrangements.

The Report highlights that some developing countries have successfully applied alternative capital flow management practices which, in their processes of financial transformation, have reduced financial vulnerability and enhanced resilience to global shocks (UNCTAD 2014: 146). A second related heterodox approach to alternatives involves renewed advocacy for public banks, notably the new multilateral development banks (the New Development Bank and the Asian Infrastructure Investment Bank) (Mazzucato and Penna 2015; Barone and Spratt 2015; Griffith-Jones et al. 2016). By privileging sustainable developmental goals over maximizing returns, public banks could spearhead a new phase of infrastructure and development-oriented lending. Public banks are also promoted as supportive financiers of SMEs as key drivers of domestic growth (Smallridge et al. 2013) (see Chapter 9 on SME financing and public banks in Turkey). Yet in this approach, the public banks are understood as fetishized institutions which, by virtue of being public, are most likely to differ from private sector institutions and to work in the public good. There is, however, good reason to be cautious of interpretations of public institutions as essentially good or bad, for this misses their complex historical social and class-based determinations (Marois and Güngen 2016).

Critical and Marxian-inspired Alternatives: Transcending Financial Oppression

Critical and Marxian-inspired critiques of financial transformation are in no short supply, evidenced most forcefully in the financialization and crisis literature discussed earlier. Yet for the most part critique has not been followed by a search for alternatives within the field of finance (Chesnais 2016).

Critical scholars tend more to make appeals for broad, left-oriented transformation in finance as part of an overall attempt to break with neoliberal capitalism (Harvey 2010; Albo 2012). As such, calls for some form of bank nationalization have increased, especially since the global financial crisis (Lapavitsas 2010). Yet these often lack detailed examples about which concrete strategies for change beyond neoliberal capitalism can be built, and often rely on static, essentialized (and often Keynesian) theorizations of public banking ownership and control. More promising approaches attempt to re-theorize the public sphere, under conditions of neoliberalism and financial transformation, in order to better understand the contradictions of already existing public banks, in order to elaborate on the transformative potential for substantively democratized pro-public financial institutions (Marois 2015 and 2018; cf. Cumbers and McMaster 2012). In not dissimilar fashion, strong gendered critiques of financialization have emerged since the global financial crisis, laying to waste conventional assumptions about universal equality before the marketplace (Roberts 2013). Such contributions emphasize how feminist approaches can help provide less partial accounts of financialization, by gendering capital itself (Pollard 2012). Aside from calls for more research into the gendered impacts of financialization, there is still too little attention to the problem of actual financial alternatives (a field dominated by questions of micro-finance and women's emancipation—see Kabeer 2005; Tiwari 2013). There is thus a great need within critical and Marxian-inspired fields of research to investigate concrete cases of financial provisioning that facilitate a structural break in financial oppression.

Contemporary Alternatives and Financial Inclusion in the Case of Turkey

The reality of Turkey is that since the 2001 crisis, the ruling AKP government has been aggressively pursuing neoliberal market-oriented strategies of financial transformation, albeit in sometimes unconventional ways, modified and conditioned by the particularities of Turkey's political economy. Turkey's financial transformation, however, did not alter the milieu of the post-financial liberalization era, characterized by boom-and-bust cycles of the economy. The dependence of the economy on capital inflows and existent fragilities has led to numerous discussions among state managers, implying a potential challenge to the neoliberal policy package in the aftermath of the 2008–09 global financial crisis. Supported by the authoritarian form of neoliberalism and the disproportionate impact of narrow policy circles with close ties to President Recep Tayyip Erdoğan, there remains the possibility that reforms, against the background of economic slowdown, can boost a neo-developmentalist policy framework. None the less, it has been neoliberal and mainstream recommendations which have given direction to Turkey's financial transformation in recent years. In the months following the 2016 coup attempt, the AKP government attempted to convert stocks into liquid assets by founding the Turkey Wealth Fund, and resorted to credit campaigns to avoid an economic slump. The government not only breached the legal public borrowing limit in 2017, but also socialized parts of the financial risks of small and medium-sized enterprises, paving the way for debt restructuring for thousands of firms. The economic boom, achieved via credit expansion, had come to an end by 2018, and the course of Turkey's financial transformation, alongside possible heterodox policy measures, rose once again to the top of the policy agenda.

Part of the Turkish economic policy responses in the aftermath of 2008–09 crisis dwell on financial inclusion, the new motto of development community. The reforms for inclusion are shaped in line with the demands of the financial sector, dominated by commercial banks, both public and private. The strength of these banks has been accompanied by the project of turning Istanbul into a regional financial hub in the medium term, and new capital market reforms for strengthening market finance (see Chapters 6 and 7). While setting the scene for the securitization of income streams and the inclusion of low-income segments of society into the financial sector, the reforms are in line with the mainstream alternatives perspective. Improving the institutional framework for enhancing the market underlay the recent capital market reforms.

For this reason, financial transformation in Turkey sits comfortably within the framework endorsed by the international financial institutions. There has been a drastic credit expansion in the post-2001 period, and the private sector campaigns for financial education in the mid-2000s. Meanwhile, the financial inclusion idea, refurbished by the G-20 and World Bank, began increasingly to affect the policy framework of the state financial authorities, the housing market boom and increased access to the credit created conundrums in the aftermath of the 2008–09 crisis (see Chapters 10 and 11).

In the Turkish case, the attempt at financial inclusion found its final form in the financial inclusion strategy (FIS—The Strategy for Financial Access, Financial Education, the Protection of Financial Consumers and Action Plans) of 2014 (FİK 2014), which aimed to expand formal financial services and increase financial literacy in order to avoid pitfalls such as over-indebted households and individuals. The need for a comprehensive framework has also derived from the need to expand the provision of credit in Turkey since 2010. In line with macro-prudential measures taken according to the official discourse, there was the need to devise action plans for the advance of savings and construction of conscious 'financial consumers'.

There are numerous reasons to criticize the FIS policymaking process and its implementation. First, the policymaking process has been conducted largely as a technocratic process and within closed circles. Second, the policymaking process found its counterpart in the overconfidence in the robustness of the financial sector. State authorities' belief in the smooth supply of financial services avoided any official attempt to reform the financial services, with the exception of a minor emphasis on the revision of fees and commissions received by the banking sector. Third, as it tends to frame women within their extended families, it is dubious that FIS will help women access the financial system independently. Fourth, enhanced access to the formal financial sector in Turkey under AKP governments went hand in hand with the increasing indebtedness of households. The promotion of FIS as a contemporary alternative which would provide reliable financial services to society at large, while yielding a pool of savings that will fund future productive investments, remain dubious. Last but not least, the competitiveness of Turkish capitalists depends to a great extent on low-wage and precarious employment, which in turn consolidates the barriers against the use of formal financial services by large sections of society. Despite falling levels of informal employment in recent years, employers in crucial sectors such as construction still benefit heavily from informal employment practices and subcontracting. These structural factors present additional problems to average earners and the poor in obtaining coveted investor or entrepreneur positions (Güngen 2018).

Access to financial services in Turkey remains a problem for women, students, people employed in unsecure jobs, and rural workers (Global Findex 2014 data can be accessed via databank.worldbank.org; see also Demirgüç-Kunt et al. 2015). It is possible to develop radical policy alternatives to neoliberal policymaking which strive to make the individual responsible and weaken discontent by the provision of enhanced but market-based opportunities for access to finance. A radical perspective may use public credit institutions to providing reliable and non-profit financial services to the poor and low-income groups. Departing from the dominant neoliberal perspective that transformed state-owned banks into for-profit financial institutions (Marois and Güngen, 2014) may form the essential first step. Going beyond the official financial inclusion discourse and discussing how to make finance pro-public—i.e. to make financial institutions serve the basic needs of people rather than including large segments of society in the financial sector in a position subordinate to the profit motives of banks—will necessitate a wider search for alternatives.

REFERENCES

Acemoğlu, D. (2009) "The crisis of 2008: Lessons for and from economics" *Critical Review*, 21(2-3): 185–194.

Arrighi, G. (1994) *The Long Twentieth Century*, New York: Verso.

Arrighi, G. and B. Silver (1999) "Conclusion" in G. Arrighi and B. Silver (eds.) *Chaos and Governance in the Modern World System*, Minneapolis: University of Minnesota Press, 271–290.

Barone, B. and S. Spratt (2015) Development Banks from the BRICS, *Institute of Development Studies Evidence Report* No. 111.

Brenner, N., J. Peck, and N. Theodore (2010) "Variegated Neoliberalization: Geographies, Modalities, Pathways", *Global Networks* 10: 182–222.

Bromley, S. (1994) *Rethinking Middle East Politics*. Austin: University of Texas Press.

Brown, A., M.V. Passarella and D. Spencer (2015) "The Nature and Variegation of Financialisation: A Cross-country Comparison" *FESSUD Working Paper Series* No. 127, November.
Bryan D., R. Martin and M. Rafferty (2009) "Financialization and Marx: Giving Labor and Capital a Financial Makeover" *Review of Radical Political Economics*, 41(4): 458–472.
Calomiris, C.W. and S. Haber (2014) *Fragile by design: banking crises, scarce credit, and political bargains*, Princeton, NJ: Princeton University Press.
Chesnais, F. (2014) "The power of financial capital and its links with productive capital" *IIRE Working Paper* No. 38.
Chesnais, F. (2016) *Finance Capital Today*. Leiden: Brill.
Christophers, B. (2015) "The Limits to Financialization", *Dialogues in Human Geography*, 5(2): 183–200.
Claessens, S. and S.R. Ghosh (2016) "Business and financial cycles in emerging markets: lessons for macroprudential policies", in D. Kang and A. Mason (eds.) *Macroprudential Regulation of International Finance: Managing Capital Flows and Exchange Rates*, Cheltenham, UK and Northampton, MA: Edward Elgar Publishing, 39–80.
Clarke, S. (1988) *Keynesianism, Monetarism and the Crisis of the State*. Aldershot: Edward Elgar Publishing.
Correa, E. and G. Vidal (2012) "Financialization and Global Financial Crisis in Latin American Countries", *Journal of Economic Issues*, 46(2): 541–548.
Cumbers, A. and R. McMaster (2012) "Revisiting Public Ownership: Knowledge, Democracy and Participation in Economic Decision Making", *Review of Radical Political Economics*, 44(3): 358–373.
Demirgüç-Kunt, A., L. Klapper, D. Singer and P. Van Oudhesden (2015) "The Global Findex Database 2014: Measuring Financial Inclusion around the World," *Policy Research Working Paper* No. 7255, Washington, DC: World Bank Group.
Demirovic, A. and T. Sablowski (2013) "The Finance-dominated Regime of Accumulation and the Crisis in Europe", *ANALYSEN*, Berlin: Rosa-Luxemburg-Stiftung.
Dos Santos, P. (2009) "On the Content of Banking in Contemporary Capitalism", *Historical Materialism*, 17(2): 180–213.
Duménil, G. and D. Lévy (2005) "*Costs and Benefits of Neoliberalism: A Class Analysis*", *Financialization and the World Economy*, G.A. Epstein (ed.), Northampton, MA: Edward Elgar Publishing, 17–45.
Duménil, G. and D. Lévy (2011) *The Crisis of Neoliberalism*. Cambridge, MA: Harvard University Press.
Durand, C. and R. Keucheyan (2015) "Financial Hegemony and the Unachieved European State", *Competition & Change*, 19(2): 129–144.
Engelen, E. and M. Konings (2010) "Financial Capitalism Resurgent: Comparative Institutionalism and the Challenges of Financialisation", in G. Morgan et al. (eds.) *Oxford Handbook of Comparative Institutional Analysis*, Oxford: Oxford University Press, 601–624.
Engelen, E. et al. (2011) *After the Great Complacence: The Financial Crisis and the Politics of Reform*, Oxford: Oxford University Press.
Epstein, G. (2010) "The David Gordon Memorial Lecture: Finance without Financiers: Prospects for Radical Change In Financial Governance", *Review of Radical Political Economics*, 42(3): 293–306.

FİK–Finansal İstikrar Komitesi (2014) *Finansal Erişim, Finansal Eğitim, Finansal Tüketicinin Korunması Stratejisive Eylem Planları*, June 2014, Ankara, *CMB website*, Accessed 13 November 2014.

Fine, B. (2010) "Neoliberalism as Financialisation", in A. Saad-Filho and G. Yalman (eds.) *Economic Transitions to Neoliberalism in Middle Income Countries*, London, Routledge, 11–23.

Fine, B. (2013) "Financialisation from a Marxist Perspective", *International Journal of Political Economy*, 42(4): 47–66.

Fine, B. and A. Saad-Filho (2016) "Thirteen Things You Need to Know About Neoliberalism", *Critical Sociology*, 43(4–5): 685–706.

Foster, J.B. (2007) "The Financialization of Capitalism", *Monthly Review*, 58(11) (April).

Foster, J.B. (2010) "The Financialization of Accumulation", *Monthly Review*, 62 (5) (October).

García-Aras, J., L. Horn and J. Toporowski (2017) "Perspectives on Financialisation and Crises in Europe", *Revista De Economía Mundial*, 46: 17–26.

Grabel, I. (2011) "Not your grandfather's IMF: global crisis, 'productive incoherence' and developmental policy space", *Cambridge Journal of Economics*, 35: 805–830.

Griffith-Jones, S., L. Xiaoyun, and S. Spratt (2016) *The Asian Infrastructure Investment Bank: What Can It Learn From, and Perhaps Teach To, the Multilateral Development Banks?*, Institute of Development Studies Evidence Report, No. 179.

Güngen, A.R. (2012) "Debt Management and Financialisation as Facets of State Restructuring: The Case of Turkey in the Post-1980 Period", unpublished PhD thesis, Middle East Technical University, Ankara.

Güngen, A.R. (2018) "Financial Inclusion and Policy Making: Strategy, Campaigns and Microcredit a la Turca", *New Political Economy*, 23(3): 331–347.

Hanieh, A. (2016) "Absent Regions: Spaces of Financialisation in the Arab World" *Antipode,* 48(5): 1228–1248.

Hart-Landsberg, M., S. Jeong and R. Westra (2007) "Introduction", M. Hart-Landsberg et al. (eds.), *Marxist Perspectives on South Korea in the Global Economy*, Aldershot: Ashgate, 1–29.

Harvey, D. (2006) *Limits to Capital*, London: Verso.

Harvey, D. (2010) "The enigma of capital and the crisis this time", paper prepared for the American Sociological Association Meetings, Atlanta, 16 August 2010. Retrieved from http://davidharvey.org/2010/08/the-enigma-of-capital-and-the-crisis-this-time

Hein, E. and D. Detzer (2014) "Finance-dominated capitalism and income distribution: a Kaleckian perspective on the case of Germany", Berlin School of Economics and Law and Institute for International Political Economy (IPE) Berlin, Germany, Working Paper, No. 42/2014.

Jessop, B. (2013) "Finance-dominated accumulation and post-democratic capitalism", in S. Fadda and P. Tridico, (eds.), *Institutions and Economic Development after the Financial Crisis*, London: Routledge, 83–105.

Jessop, B. and N.L. Sum (2014) *Towards a Cultural Political Economy*, Cheltenham: Edward Elgar Publishing.

Jilberto, A.F. and B. Hogenboom (2004) "Conglomerates and Economic Groups in Neoliberal Latin America", *Journal of Developing Countries*, 20: 3–4.

Kabeer, N. (2005) "Is Microfinance a Magic Bullet' for Women's Empowerment? Analysis of Findings from South Asia", *Economic and Political Weekly*, 4709–4718.

Kaltenbrunner, A. and E. Karaçimen (2016) "The Contested Nature of Financialization in Emerging Capitalist Economies", in T. Subasat (ed.), *The Great Financial Meltdown*, Cheltenham: Edward Elgar Publishing, 287–304.

Krippner, G. (2011) *Capitalizing on Crisis: The Political Origins of the Rise of Finance*, Cambridge, Massachusetts: Harvard University Press.

Krippner, G. (2012) "Reply to Critics", *Trajectories*, 23(2): 11–15.

Lapavitsas, C. (2009) "Financialised capitalism: crisis and financial expropriation", *Historical Materialism*, 17(2): 114–148.

Lapavitsas, C. (2010) "Systemic Failure of Private Banking: A Case for Public Banks", (162–199) *21st Century Keynesian Economics*, ed. by Philip Arestis and Malcolm Sawyer, Basingstoke: Palgrave Macmillan Houndmills.

Lapavitsas, C. (2011) "Theorizing Financialization", *Work, Employment and Society*, 25(4) 611–626.

Lapavitsas, C. (2013) *Profiting Without Producing: How Finance Exploits Us All*. London: Verso.

Lapavitsas, C. and J. Powell (2013) "Financialisation varied: a comparative analysis of advanced economies", *Cambridge Journal of Regions, Economy and Society*, 6(3): 359–379.

Lavoie, M. (2008) "Financialisation Issues in a Post- Keynesian Stock-flow Consistent Model", *European Journal of Economics and Economic Policies: Intervention*, 5(2): 331–356.

Lefort, F. and E. Walker (1999/2000) "Ownership and Capital structure of Chilean Conglomerates: Facts and Hypotheses for Governance", *Revista ABANTE*, 3(1): 3–27.

Marois, T. (2011) "Emerging market bank rescues in an era of finance-led neoliberalism: A comparison of Mexico and Turkey", *Review of International Political Economy*, 18(2): 168–196.

Marois, T. (2012a) *States, banks, and crisis: Emerging finance capitalism in Mexico and Turkey*. Cheltenham: Edward Elgar Publishing.

Marois, T. (2012b) "Finance, finance capital, and financialisation", in B. Fine and A. Saad-Filho (eds.) *The Elgar Companion to Marxist Economics*, Cheltenham: Edward Elgar Publishing.

Marois, T. (2015) "Banking on Alternatives to Neoliberal Development", in L. Pradella and T. Marois (eds.) *Polarizing Development: Alternatives to Neoliberalism and the Crisis*, London: Pluto Press, 27–38.

Marois, T. (2018) "Towards a Green Public Bank in the Public Interest" *Working Paper 2018*, Geneva: UNRISD.

Marois, T. and A.R. Güngen (2014) "Türkiye'nin Devlet Bankalarını Geri Kazanmak", *İktisat Dergisi (Special Issue)*, 527: 54–70.

Marois, T. and A.R. Güngen (2016) "Credibility and class in the evolution of public banks: the case of Turkey", *The Journal of Peasant Studies*, 43(6): 1285–1309.

Mazzucato, M., and C. Penna. 2015. *The Rise of Mission-Oriented State Investment Banks: The Cases of Germany's KfW and Brazil's BNDES*. SWPS 2015–2026.

Michell, J. and J. Toporowski (2013) "Critical Observations on Financialization and the Financial Process", *International Journal of Political Economy*, 42(4): 67–82.

Mishkin, F.S. (2009) "Why We Shouldn't Turn Our Backs on Financial Globalization", *IMF Staff Papers*, 56(1): 139–170.

Muñoz-Martínez, H. and T. Marois (2014) "Capital Fixity and Mobility in Response to the 2008–2009 Crisis: Variegated Neoliberalism in Mexico and Turkey", *Environment and Planning D: Society and Space*, 32: 1102–1119.

Orhangazi, Ö. (2008) "Financialisation and capital accumulation in the non-financial corporate sector: A theoretical and empirical investigation on the US economy: 1973–2003", *Cambridge Journal of Economics*, 32(6): 863–886.

Orhangazi, Ö. (2016) "Contradictions of Capital Accumulation in the Age of Financialization", in T. Subasat (ed.), *The Great Financial Meltdown*, Cheltenham: Edward Elgar Publishing, 248–265.

Painceira, J.P. (2012) "Developing Countries in the Era of Financialisation", in C. Lapavitsas (ed.) *Financialisation in Crisis*, Leiden: Brill.

Palley, T. (2007) "Financialization: What it is and why it matters" *Levy Economics Institute of Bard College Working Papers* 525.

Panitch, L. (1993) "Globalisation and the State" *The Socialist Register*, 30: 60–93.

Panitch, L. and S. Gindin (2008) "The Current Crisis: A Socialist Perspective", *Socialist Project E-Bulletin* No. 142, 30 September 2008.

Papadatos, D. (2012) "Central Banking in Contemporary Capitalism", in C. Lapavitsas (ed.) *Financialisation in Crisis*, Leiden: Brill.

Park, H. and J. Doucette (2016) "Financialization or Capitalisation? Debating Capitalist Power in South Korea in the Context of Neoliberal Globalisation", *Capital & Class*, 40(3), 533–554.

Peet, R. (2011) "Contradictions of Finance Capitalism", *Monthly Review*, 63(7): 18–32.

Picciotto, S. (2011) *Regulating Global Corporate Capitalism*. Cambridge: Cambridge University Press.

Pollard, J. (2012) "Gendering capital: Financial crisis, financialization and (an agenda for) economic geography", *Progress in Human Geography*, (37)3: 403–423.

Poulantzas, N. (1975) *Classes in Contemporary Capitalism*. London: New Left Books.

Powell, J. (2013) "Subordinate financialisation: a study of Mexico and its nonfinancial Corporations", PhD thesis. SOAS, University of London.

Roberts, A. (2013) "Financing Social Reproduction: The Gendered Relations of Debt and Mortgage Finance in Twenty-first-century America", *New Political Economy*, 18(1): 21-42.

Rogers, H.F. (2010) "The global financial crisis and development thinking", *Policy-Research Working Paper*, No. 5353, Washington, DC: World Bank.

Sawyer, M. (2013) "What Is Financialization?", *International Journal of Political Economy*, 42(4): 5–18.

Sawyer, M. (2014) "Bank-based versus Market-based Financial Systems: A Critique of the Dichotomy", *FESSUD Working Paper Series* No. 19.

Sawyer, M. (2017) "The Processes of Financialisation and Economic Performance", *Economic and Political Studies*, 5(1): 5–20

Sawyer, M. et al. (2017) "Financialisation, Economy Society and Sustainable Development: An Overview", *FESSUD Working Paper Series* No.206.

Serfati, C. (2011) "Transnational Corporations as Financial Groups",*Work, Organisation, Labour & Globalisation*, 5(1): 10–38.

Smallridge, D., B. Buchner, C. Trabacchi, M. Netto, J.J. Gomes Lorenzo and L. Serra (2013) *The Role of National Development Banks in Catalyzing International Climate Finance*. New York: Inter-American Development Bank–IDB.

Stockhammer, E. (2011) "Neoliberalism, Income Distribution and the Causes of the Crisis" in P. Arestis et al. (eds.) *The Financial Crisis: Origins and Implications*, Hampshire: Palgrave, 233–258.

Stockhammer, E. (2015) "Financialization: From Financial Deregulation to Boom Bust Cycles", *Perspectives*, Autumn 2015(3): 15–18.

Teubal, M. (2004) “Rise and Collapse of Neoliberalism in Argentina: The Role of Economic Groups” *Journal of Developing Societies*, 20(3–4): 173–188.

Ticktin, H. (2011) “The Nature of the Downturn/Depression”, in E.A. Tonak (ed.), *Critical Perspectives on the World Bank and the IMF*, İstanbul: Istanbul Bilgi University Press, 7–21.

Tiwari, M. (2013). “The global financial crisis and self-help groups in rural India: are there lessons from their micro savings model?”, *Development in Practice*, 23(2): 278–291.

Toporowski, J. (2012) “Neologism as Theoretical Innovation in Economics: The Case of ‘Financialisation’”, *SOAS, Department of Economics Working Paper Series*, No. 171.

United Nations Conference on Trade and Development (2014) *The Trade and Development Report 2014: Global Governance and Policy Space for Development*, Geneva: UNCTAD.

Van der Zwan, N. (2014) “Making Sense of Financialization”, *Socio-Economic Review* 12(1): 99–129.

Wood, E.M. (2007) “A Reply to Critics”, *Historical Materialism*, 15: 143–170.

World Bank (2012) *Global financial development report 2013: Rethinking the role of state in finance*, Washington, DC: World Bank.

World Bank (2013) *World Development Report 2014 Risk and Opportunity: Managing Risk for Development*, Washington, DC: World Bank.

Yalman, G.L. (2016). “Crises as Driving Forces of Neoliberal ‘Trasformismo’: The Contours of the Turkish Political Economy since the 2000s”, in Alan Cafruny et. al. (eds.) *The Palgrave Handbook of Critical International Political Economy*, New York: Palgrave Macmillan, 239–266.

Zhang, X. (2009) “From banks to markets: Malaysian and Taiwanese finance in transition”, *Review of International Political Economy*, 16(3): 382–408.

2 Putting the Turkish Financial System into Historical Perspective 1923–80

Galip L. Yalman

Introduction

It is fair to state that Turkish policymakers in the early Republican era, under Mustafa Kemal Atatürk's presidency (1923–38), aimed to establish and strengthen the country's financial institutions in order to develop the economy in general, and the industrial sector in particular. The financial sector subsequently tended to develop in accordance with the needs of the productive sector, as Turkish policymakers developed the financial instruments in accordance with the needs of the productive sector in the pre-1980 period. Put differently, the Turkish financial sector fulfilled the role of a financial intermediary especially geared to meet the productive sectors' need for financing, in line with the then dominant paradigm of the capitalist world, rather than being mainly concerned with the efficiency and performance of financial institutions themselves, as reflected in the paradigm shift of the post-1980 era.

By the same token, it is fair to say that while the nature of the Turkish economy's integration into the global economy has been a bone of contention among policymakers, the integration into the global economy has rarely been either perceived or presented as an end in itself; that is, until there would be a significant shift of emphasis from 1980 onwards. In that respect, the dependence of the Turkish economy on foreign savings has been a constant feature of Republican history, as well as being a source of tension and contention both within the Turkish power bloc, and with its relations with foreign creditors at different intervals. Thereby, achieving a balance between the developmental objectives and the requirements of adjustment to the changing modes of integration with the global economy has always had a bearing on the evolution of the Turkish financial system.

This chapter aims to present the development of the Turkish financial system by highlighting its institutional characteristics as a bank-dominated model with a three-pronged structure, comprising the Central Bank, deposit banks and the so-called special purpose banks from the early Republican era until the 1980s. However, it is also imperative to highlight the evolution of the relations between financial and non-financial sectors and the critical role played by the Turkish conglomerates in this regard, with the emergence of the so-called holding banks from the 1960s onwards.

The Rise of Finance in a Peripheral Economy

The 1923 Congress of Economics convened in İzmir on the eve of the foundation of the new Turkish Republic adopted the creation of a national economy as the basic strategy of the new state (Kuruç 1988: xxxvi). This is hardly surprising, as the establishment of a 'national economy' had been on the policymakers' agenda since the first decade of the century, well before the establishment of the Republic, having directly experienced the repercussions of financial and economic dependence of the Ottoman Empire on European powers and/or finance capital for the last vestiges of its statehood.[1] It is also to be noted that the participants of İzmir Congress were highlighting what they considered to be the prerequisites for the development of the prospective new state as an economically viable entity. In particular, there was an emphasis for the establishment of a national banking sector, given the lack of financial institutions that could meet the financing requirements of the prospective entrepreneurs (Akgüç 1987: 16–17). There were, of course, several banks that had been inherited from the Ottoman Empire. Among them were Ziraat Bank, established as the first state bank to provide agricultural loans, and the Ottoman Bank, a foreign-owned bank established as a consortium of British and French capital. Moreover, there were several banks established by local merchants and landowners in order to reduce their economic dependence on foreigners and non-Muslim minorities prior to and during the First World War (1914–18). In fact, these developments had laid the ground for the proliferation of several single-branch provincial banks during the first decade of the new Republic (Ökçün 1975: 460–467). In short, the objective of creating a national economy had made the establishment of a national banking sector an imperative.

> At the Lausanne Peace Conference (1922–3),which defined, amongst other things, the international economic framework for the new state, they succeeded in abolishing the regime of capitulations [i.e. trade concessions and legal privileges] that had provided special privileges to foreign citizens. The parties also agreed that the new republic would be free to pursue its own commercial policies after 1929.
>
> (Pamuk 2007: 276)

Thereby, after a brief spell tinkering with a seemingly liberal trade policy, the adjustment strategy brought to the agenda in the wake of the 1929 Great Depression, would entail the characteristic features of a neo-mercantilist development strategy, even though the impact of the global economic crisis on Turkey's foreign trade was relatively less severe compared with other peripheral economies (Tekeli and İlkin 1977: 31). The determination to initiate the industrialization of the country in the context of worsening economic conditions, however, could not be attributed solely to the vagaries of the global capitalist system. The strategy adopted in the wake of the Great Depression, *étatisme*—a form of state-led or 'statist' development—was thus understood as the duty of the state to participate in the economic life of the nation in order to guide it to prosperity. In that regard, it was generally interpreted as a rupture with its predecessor's manner of interventionism in economic and monetary affairs, as the Ottoman administration was not renowned for the nurturing of a private sector (cf. Pamuk 1998; 2014: 213).

However, Turkish policymakers of the time categorically rejected 'competition' as the basis of economic life, on the grounds that it would have a deleterious impact on the formation of national wealth (Kuruç 1988: xl fn16) However, this by no means implied a particularly anti-capitalist stance, as it had the support of the nascent business community at the time (Buğra 1994: 105). As a matter of fact, the anti-competition attitude of the Turkish *étatistes*showed striking parallels with the views of British Conservatives like Harold Macmillan who were, from the mid-1920s onwards, increasingly critical of the doctrinaire *laissez-faire* attitude of their party (Yalman 2009: 164). While there seemed to be an entrenched opinion that the *étatiste* experience has caused "insecurity in the business world and led to a tendency to avoid investments, to keep capital liquid, and to show interest in only short term undertakings" (Sarç 1948; Buğra 1994), the preference for a strategy that would assign the state a 'leadership' role in the co-ordination of investments had clearly been conditioned by a determination to enhance the prospects for private accumulation.

Moreover, even the contemporary advocates of market-based reforms acknowledge that the *étatiste* regime's policy orientation was characterized by a commitment to macroeconomic stability, both internally and externally (Gültekin 2012). Indeed, a balanced budget and strong currency would be the main objectives of monetary and fiscal policies to be pursued, given "the bitter legacy of the Ottoman experience with budget deficits, large external debt and inflationary [consequences of issuing] paper currency" (Pamuk 2007: 278).[2] The brunt of taxation was, however, born by the ordinary wage earners, as the level of taxation on merchants and industrialists was relatively much lower (Kuruç 1988: xlv-xlvii). Indeed, according to one estimate, real wages did not exceed their levels of 1914 during the *étatiste* era (Pamuk 2000: 331) which, in turn, implied the appropriation of lucrative profits in the industrial sector, as wage levels lagged behind the prices of industrial goods during 1933–39 (Boratav 1977: 48).

To the extent that the possibilities that the global economic crisis had created for overcoming the vicious circles of underdevelopment by weakening the links between the peripheries and the metropolises were perceived, *étatisme* was interpreted as a means of preventing the nascent industrial bourgeoisie from collecting the 'rents' of protectionism on its own (Kuruç 1988: xxxviii-xxxix; xliii; 1993: 66; Tekeli and İlkin 1977: 76–77), although there were also attempts to lure foreign capital investment into the country. However, this did not necessarily imply that *étatisme* had a restrictive effect on private investments. On the contrary, there is a convergence of opinion that the relations between the public and private sectors were complementary rather than antagonistic during the implementation of *étatist* policies, as promised by the key policymakers of the time (Kuruç 1993: 225; Boratav 1988: 57; Buğra 1994). Indeed, many advocates of a liberal economy would acknowledge that "etatism has not been a policy restricting private investments, but on the contrary has been a policy facilitating capital accumulation within the private sector" (Yaşa 1963: 103).

Most of the single-branch provincial banks established in the 1920s and/or inherited from the Ottoman era would not, however, survive the Great Depression.[3] A handful of these banks such as Türk Ticaret Bankası would be transformed, however, into private sector banks which had operated as national banks until the financial liberalization phase of the post-1980 era. Perhaps the most important private sector bank established in 1924, less than a year after the establishment of the Republic with the impetus of the founders of the republic, was İşbank (Türkiye İş Bankası). As it would bring together 'the most trustworthy, rich and politically reliable individuals' from several regions of the country as the founding members of the bank, they would be dubbed as '*affairiste*', implying that political expediency was as important a motive as initiation of capital accumulation in private hands (cf. Kocabaşoğlu 2001: 53; Pamuk 2014: 182). However, it would emerge as a leading institution of the Turkish financial system for decades to come, as it has been instrumental in inspiring a particular model of capital accumulation by initiating a series of participations in several sectors of the economy since its establishment.

Institutional Change in the Wake of Great Depression

Etatisme was to be grounded in a financial system that would entail the establishment of a series of *national* banks starting with the Central Bank of Turkey, thus laying the ground for the emergence of a *bank-based* financial system (Kocabaşoğlu et al. 2001: 262; Kuruç 1988: xlii; Marois 2012: 47–48; 109). In fact, the establishment of the Central Bank was perceived as an integral part of the decision to achieve and maintain macroeconomic stability, to be anchored on the stability of the exchange rate and as a prerequisite for integration into the global market (as the *sine qua non* of institutions required to manage inter-state financial transactions). For without the institution to issue the currency, it was reckoned that it would be difficult, if not impossible, to accomplish the latter objective.

Two important institutional developments critical to the pursuit of the macroeconomic objectives were initiated in 1930: The Law for Protecting the Value of Turkish Currency (Law no. 1567) and the Law for Establishing the Central Bank of Turkey (Law no. 1715). The former, enacted in February

1930, was construed as a key mechanism authorizing government intervention into currency and capital markets in order to maintain the external value of Turkish lira and/or to prevent capital flight (Boratav 2011: 405; Tekeli and İlkin 1977: 116; Tekeli and İlkin 1982: 290–291, Kuruç 2011: 284).[4] In fact, Law no. 1567 was no more than a piece of legislation that authorized the government to take all the necessary measures in order to achieve the objectives in question. While it was originally intended to remain in effect for three years, this particular law became an effectively permanent feature of Turkish legislation, as it allowed the government to extend the mandate by issuing decrees. Thus it remained in effect for the next six decades, with its purported objectives paid lip service by successive governments which issued the relevant decrees.

However, it was still the prerogative of a foreign bank, namely the Ottoman Bank, to issue money on the basis of an agreement signed with the Ottoman government in 1863 (Eldem 1999; Pamuk 1984: 130). The new Republic had been obliged to concur for the extension of this agreement for another ten years in 1925. The state authorities would soon start looking for ways in which they could replace this Ottoman legacy of a foreign bank acting as a 'state bank' with a Central Bank. This gained urgency in the light of difficulties encountered in achieving the objectives as envisaged with the enactment of the Law for Protecting the Value of Turkish Currency. This would, in turn, lead to the establishment of a consortium as a private corporation between the state, national and foreign-owned banks with the aim of maintaining the stability of the currency. The board of the corporation had comprised representatives of both foreign and national private banks, including those of the Ottoman Bank. There had apparently been substantial arm-twisting to encourage the banks' participation in the consortium, which would function until the Central Bank become fully operational. Its main function had been delineated as the co-ordination of foreign exchange trading in order to prevent speculative movements. It took more than a year after its establishment for the Central Bank to take over from the consortium, which continued to operate during this transition period (Tekeli and İlkin 1977: 116–117).

According to Law no. 1715, which remained in effect until 1971 with many amendments, the Central Bank is assigned with issuing money, protecting the value of the currency, adjusting the general liquidity of the economy, and lending to banks. In due course, from the 1950s onwards, it started to extend more loans to the Treasury and state economic enterprises in order to narrow the financing deficits of the public sector (BAT 2009). The establishment of the Central Bank was followed by the founding of several 'special purpose banks'. These state-owned banks provided the necessary financing for the establishment and subsequent operational requirements of the enterprises identified in the Industrial Development Plans, which were prepared during the 1930s.

Table 2.1 Public Commercial Banks in the early Turkish Republic

Public bank	*Year established*	*Development mission or target funding*
Ziraat Bank	1863/1888	Agriculture
Emlak Bank[5]	1926	Home mortgages and real estate loans
Sümerbank[6]	1933	State-owned enterprises and industrialization
Belediyeler Bank[7]	1933	Municipal infrastructure projects such as water, electricity, drainage, and the preparation of building plans
Halkbank	1933	Cooperatives, artisans, tradespersons and small-scale producers
Etibank[8]	1935	Electrical power generation capacity and the financing of mining and mineral marketing
Denizbank[9]	1937	Maritime development

Source: Akgüç 1987; BAT 1999, 2009.

Among these banks, the evolution of Ziraat Bank is indicative of the changing conceptions of policymakers as the Turkish economy had been undergoing changes in line with the developments in the global economy. In 1924, what was inherited as a state bank from the Ottoman Empire would be restructured as a private corporation, and it had been authorized to function as a commercial bank, along with its historical task of providing credit to the agricultural sector. However, with Law no. 3202 enacted in 1937, there had been a further attempt to restructure this bank by redefining it as a state economic enterprise in order to meet the financing needs of the agricultural sector in general, and agricultural co-operatives in particular (Akgüç 1987: 26; 34–35).[10]

Halkbank, founded initially under Law no. 2284 in 1933 as a credit union[11] by small co-operatives for the purposes of supplying tradesmen and artisans on favourable terms in order to promote economic development, became operational as a bank in 1938 (Akgüç 1987: 33). During 1938–50 Halkbank provided its loans through public funds named as the 'People's Fund'. It was authorized to open branches and grant loans to customers in 1950. Following its increase of capital in 1964, Halkbank became a more active player by establishing a nationwide network of branches. with a significant increase in the bank's deposit and lending volumes.

Sümerbank and Etibank were to continue to function not only as publicly owned banks, but also as publicly owned holding companies containing several state economic enterprises within their domain, long after the state-led strategy of industrial development had been superseded. It was contended that the establishment of Sümerbank in 1932 signified the initiation of a "new statist model of capital accumulation", while at the same time being a compromise between the representatives of the private sector and the advocates of this new model among policymakers at the time (Boratav 1977: 47; Kuruç 2011: 400–411; and also Kocabaşoğlu 2001: 261). For it had been organized in such a way that it would function both as a publicly owned group of industrial enterprises, and as a commercial bank providing credits to private sector enterprises. Indeed, both banks would remain as important institutions of the Turkish financial system until their dismantling as publicly owned holding companies and the subsequent privatization of their banking arms from the late 1980s onwards.

However, the *étatiste* period had also witnessed the closure of several foreign banks operating in Turkey, while a few, including the Ottoman Bank, would continue their operations well into the post-1980 era.[12] Consequently, the relative weight of foreign banks in terms of their share of total deposits and total credits had been steadily declining from the early years of the Republic until the end of the Second World War. Whereas those of the Turkish commercial banks had been on the rise, notwithstanding the fact that, as already mentioned, most of the provincial banks had terminated their activities during that period. However, the market share of the public banks was significantly higher than the other two sets of banks. According to the calculations by one economic historian (Tezel 2015: 149), the share of foreign banks in total deposits had declined from 78 per centin 1924 to 17 per centin 1946, while those of the Turkish commercial banks and public banks rose from 12 per centto 39 per centand from 10 per centto 44 percent, respectively. By the same token, the share of foreign banks in total credits declined from 53 per centto 13 percent, while those of the Turkish commercial banks and public banks rose from 5 per centto 28 per centand from 42 per centto 59 percent, respectively, in the same interval. These trends have been interpreted as a result of a deliberate strategic move on the part of the policymakers to end the stranglehold of foreign finance capital on the Turkish financial system (Tezel 1977: 224; 2015: 149). Furthermore, more than 70 per centof the total credit provided had been allocated to the business community outside the agriculture sector during 1924–38. This has, in turn, been interpreted as a major source of primitive accumulation for the merchants as most of the credits that were considered 'cheap' had been allocated to trading activities (cf. Günlük 1983: 192; Tezel 2015: 150). At the same time, the public banks actively promoted the development of state institutional capacity and the disciplining of a nascent working class, thus assuming a "place in state and class formation processes" in Turkey (Marois and Güngen 2016).

The year 1936 saw the enactment of the first Banking Law of the Republican era (Law no. 2999) which prescribed the scope and the ways in which the banks could participate in the industrial enterprises as important shareholders. It is possible to say that this law provided a legal basis for the kind of activities that İşBank had already been engaged for some time. Its rationale was to encourage the participation of the private sector banks in the establishment of industrial enterprises, given the lack of a capital market as a source of funds necessary for new investments (Kocabaşoğlu et al. 2001: 274). In the wake of the Great Depression, İş Bank had been identified as a 'national institution' that would contribute to the realization of the objectives of the First Industrial Development Plan of the early 1930s. In particular, its participation would concentrate on the production of raw materials and intermediate goods, along with its increasing involvement in the insurance business (Kuruç 1993: 243; Kocabaşoğlu et al. 2001: 260; 286–287). It is noteworthy, of course, that the development of İş Bank in particular, as one of the leading Turkish banks with significant investments in several industrial sectors, appears to provide some evidence in the Turkish context for the emergence of what Rudolph Hilferding had conceptualized as 'finance capital', entailing "an ever more intimate relationship" between banking and industrial capital (Hilferding 1910: Preface). The evolution of finance capital in Turkey, however, would manifest itself in a variegated form distinctive of Turkey's peripheral political economy, as exemplified by Sümerbank and İş Bank in the context of the *étatiste* experience: that is, banks (public or private) functioning as conglomerates without being formally structured as holding groups. By contrast, as will be elaborated in the next section, there would emerge from the 1960s onwards another institutional form: holding banks, where commercial banks are considered to be subordinated to the needs of industrial production (Marois 2012: 111; Şahinkaya, 1999: 100). Put differently, the blurring of frontiers between financial and non-financial activities within the groups was already emerging as a characteristic feature of capitalist development in a peripheral economy, albeit during periods that used to be characterized as state-guided and/or planned, with an emphasis on industrialization.

The Post-War Adjustment and the Evolution of the Banking Sector in the Context of Development Planning

In the wake of the Second World War, as the basic outlines of the post-war international economic order were emerging, the question of Turkey's integration into the global economy was coming onto the agenda once again. For the Turkish policymakers who had experienced the repercussions of being highly dependent on a single partner in its foreign trade relations—Germany's share in Turkey's foreign trade was no less than 45 per cent on average in the second part of the 1930s (cf. Pamuk 2000: 330)—the idea of being incorporated into a global economy that would open the possibility of multilateral trade relations was naturally quite appealing. The policymakers seemed to be confronted with a basic dilemma,however: how to re-integrate the Turkish economy into the global economy in accordance with the liberalization of international trade relations, as advocated by the designers of the new global economic order, while maintaining the objective of industrialization which was deemed essential for national development (Yalman 2009: 177).

In short, adjustment and industrialization were both conceived as desirable aims, notwithstanding the difficulties in reconciling them. Policymakers were to find themselves confronted with the difficult choice of opting for one or the other, almost periodically over the next four decades, as the Turkish economy increasingly became dependent on external sources for the financing of its development projects. This, in turn, indicated one of the key policy dilemmas that have confronted them. For the official policy line seemed to aim, more often than not, to diminish the dependence of the economy on foreign sources of finance for developmental purposes. In fact, it is possible to differentiate periods of economic history of the Turkish republican state in terms of the relative weights assigned to alternative sources of finance, in order to achieve policy priorities. With the transition to a multi-party system in the immediate aftermath of the Second World War, the parties vying for political power had both campaigned for the liberalization of the economy. While the Cumhuriyet Halk Partisi (CHP—Republican People's Party) could take pride in initiating the *economic aperture,* having already watered down the *étatiste* policies it had earlier implemented, its principal opponent, the Demokrat Parti (DP) championed the virtues of a liberal market economy.

By adopting a series of economic policy measures starting with the September 1946 devaluation, Turkish policymakers were intending a strategic shift by giving priority to adjustment rather than to industrialization in the context of a rapidly deteriorating international environment. The 1947 Development Plan of Turkey, which was prepared with the aim of receiving financial assistance from the USA prior to the establishment of Marshall Plan, and never officially implemented, reordered the priorities of development, acknowledged the importance of the development of private sector, and underlined the need for steps to be taken in agriculture, transportation and energy (Tekeli and İlkin 1974).

This change in policy priorities was reflected in the growth of financial sector. While fortunes made during the Second World War provided the funds for financing of new investments on the part of the would-be entrepreneurs in the late 1940s, the growth and strengthening of national banks can be seen as one of the characteristics of the 1945–60 period (Akgüç 1987: 38). With the foundation of 30 new banks in Turkey, the total number of banks rose to 60 in 1959 from 43 in 1944. During the same period, the number of bank branches increased from 405 to 1,759. While a few new public sector banks such as Deniz Bank and Vakıfbank were also established with laws enacted specifically for them in 1952 and 1954, respectively, most of the new banks were private banks which would initiate a new competitive environment with an emphasis on branch banking and deposit accumulation (Akgüç 1987: 39–40, 48; BAT 1999; Şahinkaya 1999: 95).[13] It was observed that the latter was a result of the fact that the interest rates and commission rates of banking transactions were being determined by the government, while the Central Bank remained the sole authority in making foreign exchange transactions. As branch banking became widespread, however, the local banks with regional character which had been given an impetus as important loci of capital accumulation in the early years of the Republic, were said to be withdrawing rapidly from the financial system (BAT 2009).

More saliently, there was also the establishment of yet another 'special purpose bank'. In contrast to the 1930s, however, the Türkiye Sinai Kalkınma Bankası (TSKB—Industrial Development Bank of Turkey) was established in 1950 as "the first private investment and development bank" of the country with the financial backing of the World Bank and the Central Bank of Turkey and shareholding of private commercial banks.[14] Set up with the mission of supporting the development of the Turkish private sector, TSKB was not only the bank capable of supplying the foreign currency credit needed to finance imports, it was also the only organization handling cash sales of foreign currencies released under the Marshal Plan in the early 1950s.[15] It had assumed a critical role in the development of import-substituting industrialization by providing credit support for a wide range of manufacturing activities before and after the adoption of development planning from 1962 onwards. By the same token, TSKB, with the loans provided on a project basis, would contribute to the development of the closely knit structure of the relations between financial and non-financial sectors.

The DP government, which came to power in 1950, had been advocating a liberal economic policy agenda as part of their efforts to put a distance between themselves and the *étatiste* heritage (Kocabaşoğlu et al. 2001: 368). However, it would soon be confronted with a predicament that would be the fate of many peripheral countries in the post-war international economic order. As they tried to cope with the problems of adjustment in accordance with the liberalization of international trade relations as advocated by the designers of the new global economic order, peripheral countries would all experience severe balance of payments crises. In the Turkish case, trade liberalization as stipulated by the Organisation for European Economic Cooperation had ended with 60 per centof import items being subjected to this policy. While governments attempted to finance the ensuing balance of payments deficit with a combination of US aid, "high interest cost private bank credits for exports" and the reduction of foreign exchange reserves, trade liberalization was going to be "*de facto* abandoned" at the end of the Korean War (Hiç 1972a: 182). This would, in turn, lead to the adoption of import-substituting industrialization policies, albeit in an *ad hoc* fashion, rather than planned, as there would be an accumulation of arrears, i.e. unpaid import bills. In fact, the DP government's decision to implement a restrictive import regime from 1953 onwards had the support of the incipient industrial bourgeoisie, which in due course would be advocating an 'investment programme' that would establish the priorities in the distribution of scarce foreign exchange resources (Yalman 2009: 204). For the arrears since 1952 had prevented the DP government from importing the raw materials and capital goods for their existing industries, as well as the new ones that they intended to establish.

By using deficit financing as a means of forced savings, the DP government was, in fact, initiating a process of capital accumulation that had been accompanied by soaring short-term credit provided by the commercial banks to the non-financial sectors in order to finance both the new investments and capitalization requirements of the latter.[16] However, this also coincided with a reversal of its liberal economic policy stance, thereby re-emphasizing the central role played by the state in the conduct of economic policy, as public investment constituted "the major driving force" with more than 50 per centof total investments (Hiç 1972a: 182). Moreover, it was pointed out that "the state banks played a key role in channelling foreign aid and credit as well as domestic public credit to private industry"' (Öncü and Gökçe 1991: 106). However, there was a significant departure from the *étatiste* period. For DP rule would denote the abandonment of two macroeconomic principles that characterized the *étatiste* period: namely, a balanced budget and a strong currency. It was the peculiarity of that government to pay lip service to the need for macroeconomic stability while refusing to implement a stabilization programme that would entail a realignment of the national currency with those of Turkey's trading partners, on the grounds that it would curtail its implementation of growth-oriented economic policies.

Having been emboldened by its incorporation into the North Atlantic Treaty Organization in 1952, as a result of its decision to take part in the Korean War, the Turkish government tried to make use of the so-called geostrategic importance of the country for the security of the US-led Western bloc in order to obtain as much US economic aid as possible. This had, in turn, led to the deterioration of relations between the DP government and the Bretton Woods institutions. For both the International Monetary Fund (IMF) and the World Bank were in principle against the use of foreign funds, whatever their form might be, as a means of avoiding or delaying the necessary adjustment for the realization of internal and external stability of the economy in question. As the economy was plagued by a prolonged crisis of balance of payments which, in turn, was fuelling discontent as a result of the disappearance of imported goods from the market and rising inflationary pressures, there was nonetheless fierce resistance on the part of the DP government to a stabilization programme, on the grounds that it would curtail economic growth. In that context, it would even resort to the sort of practices that had been anathema for the advocates of economic liberalization, by reintroducing a policy instrument employed during the Second World War: namely, the National Protection Law at the peak of the crisis in 1956, in order to cap price rises (Hiç 1972a: 184). Furthermore, the same year had also witnessed the establishment of a new body, the Regulatory Committee of Bank Loans, by a decree on under the provisions of the Law for Protecting the Value of Turkish Currency, in order to co-ordinate the distribution of bank loans on a sectoral and/or demand basis. The committee's decisions were to be binding for the banking sector.[17]

However, having exhausted all possible means of maintaining the import requirements of the economy, the DP government would finally succumb to pressures and adopt an IMF stabilization programme in 1958, primarily in order to satisfy international creditors. Restructuring of the external debt and a new import regime were two key features of the programme that would outlast its short-term effects. Thus, despite the fact that it was accompanied by substantial devaluation, the 1958 stabilization was intended to pave the way to achieve the necessary adjustment by enhancing rather than constraining the import capacity of the economy. The objective of the new import regime was not trade liberalization *per se*, but to put an end to the restrictive practices of the crisis years. As such, it would be instrumental for the implementation of the import-substituting industrialization strategy for the next two decades by preventing the *de facto* compression of imports for nascent industries (Yalman 2009: 221–222).

The adoption of the stabilization programme in August 1958 was to be preceded by a new Banking Law (Law no. 7129) in June of that year, which would also establish the Banks Association of Turkey (BAT) as the official representative body of all banks operating in Turkey (Marois 2012: 54). Its board of directors included the representatives of both public and private sector banks. Its founding principles, as stated in its statute were:

> to defend the rights and interests of banks within the framework of market economy and full competition principles in line with the principles and rules of banking laws and regulations; and to work for the purpose of the growth and healthy functioning of the banking system, and development of the banking profession, and increasing the system's competition power [sic.] as a whole; and to take or ensure that banks take, implement or demand the implementation of, decisions as required for prevention of unfair competition in the market.
>
> (BAT 2009)

As already noted, while 30 new banks had been established during 1945–60, a total of 14 banks (four of them being foreign banks) had to terminate their activities during the same period. While 10 of the national banks that closed had been established during the 1945–60 period, the origins of the foreign banks that closed could be traced back to the early 20th century (Akgüç 1987: 47–48). What is to be noted is the rise in the number of bank closures in the aftermath of the adoption of the stabilization programme in 1958. The total number of banks would fall to 52 (five of which were foreign owned) at the end of 1962, after reaching a peak of 62 in 1958 (Kocabaşoğlu et al. 2001: 378; Şahinkaya 1999: 95). In order to create an institutionalised mechanism to deal with failed banks, the Banks Liquidation Fund had been established with an amendment made to 1958 Banking Law following the military coup of May 1960. The Fund, in practice, would also function as an 'ex-post deposit guarantees' scheme to pay off the deposit holders, as all the liabilities of the failed banks had been covered (Atiyas 1990: 154). It could thus be seen as a precursor to the Savings Deposit Insurance Fund that would be forthcoming in the aftermath of the re-orientation of economic policies in the early 1980s. This rather turbulent period of bank closures also witnessed the first examples of forced mergers among some of these banks with the aim of strengthening their financial structures (Coşkun et al. 2012:10). The product of one such merger, Anadolu Bankası, would turn out to be a casualty of yet another round of bank closures and mergers in the 1980s.[18]

The 1961 Constitution, which came into effect following the military coup, had, in fact, paved the way for the emergence of a democratic form of the state in which the different sections of society would be given the opportunity to defend their socio-economic interests. But it was also significant for stipulating the establishment of the State Planning Organisation (SPO) without executive powers,in order to initiate the economic development of the country on a planned basis. The idea of planning was perceived as providing an effective instrument to utilize scarce national resources in a rational manner for the common good (Kepenek 1984: 152). According to a senior member of the SPO who had served as head of its economic planning department during the late 1970s, Five-Year Development Plans had facilitated rapid industrialization by means of financial repression, while maintaining relative macroeconomic stability (Türel 2009: 158). Indeed, economists with liberal views had already acknowledged that the 1962–70 era stood out as "the longest period of sustained high rate of growth", mainly due to the rapid development of the industrial sector (Hiç 1972a: 186). While the architects of the first two five-year development plans were reluctant to encourage interference in the mechanisms of the market, there was an acknowledgement of the fact that the functioning of the price mechanism in the context of a mixed economy could be limited by a variety of public controls in order to accomplish the desired objectives. Thereby, it was reckoned that it had been plausible to undertake interventions that would not be circumscribed, with the proviso of responding to "market failures" (Türel 2009: 158). In other words, the policy commitment to rapid industrialization would be identified as a basic cause of the continuation of the rise in public investment in the 1970s as well (Celasun 1990: 42). Although there were significant discrepancies between the plans' targets and investments undertaken, especially by the private sector, the period 1962–76 can be characterized as the heyday of import-substituting industrialization (ISI) or "what Albert Hirschman has called the easy stage of ISI" (Pamuk 2007: 283). As it also turned out to be a period during which both the real wages in the industrial sector and real incomes of producers in the agricultural sector were steadily on the rise, it led to the characterization of the period as one of "populist economic policies" (Boratav 1983). Development planning could thus be contemplated to function as a hegemonic apparatus, as it was seen as the lynchpin of a new democratic political order that strived to realize both economic development and social justice (Yalman 2002: 36). However, the Development Plans failed to accomplish one major goal that they had aimed for: namely, gradually diminishing the dependency of the economy on foreign resources (Kepenek 1984: 203).[19] In their search to increase the resources necessary for financing the investments, the planners would be obliged to acknowledge the need to find new sources of foreign finance that would enhance rather than curtail the capacity of the economy to achieve the planned targets, while avoiding creditors' effective control over policy objectives (Yalman 2009: 223).[20]

Notwithstanding these efforts, it was asserted that "the workings of the financial system was an important impediment in allocating savings into investments according to the requirements of development plans" (Atiyas and Ersel 1996: 104). For it was held that "the most distinctive characteristic of the Turkish financial system is the domination of monetary institutions" (Akyüz 1984: 74). Therefore, it was considered necessary to allocate "a larger portion of the funds at the disposal of the financial institutions [for] investment finance", while aiming "to change the composition of the financial assets in favour of the long term" (Akyüz 1984: 5). Others had, however, tended to put the blame on the state as the major factor affecting the business environment in the country, thus inhibiting a long-term commitment to industrial activities on the part of the entrepreneurs that would necessitate strategic planning (Buğra 1994: 91).

Meanwhile, the inadequacy of the efforts to increase domestic savings would be accompanied by the establishment of yet another batch of 'special purpose banks' from the early 1960s onwards as a mechanism of enhancing the use of public resources and/or special investment mechanisms for the realisation of plans' objectives (Kocabaşoğlu et al. 2001: 502–503). There were two such banks established as public sector banks in the early 1960s and another one in the 1970s. These were the Tourism Bank (1962), the State Investment Bank (1964),[21]and the State Industry and Workers' Investment Bank (1975).[22] In addition, there was also a private bank, the Industrial Investment and Credit Bank (1963) established in order to facilitate the channelling of private sector investments into the manufacturing industry in which İş Bank held the majority of shares. It was observed that the Second Five-Year Plan (1967–71) initiated several financing facilities for the private sector so that it could realize its investments in line with the plan targets. However, Law no. 933 enacted in 1967, which authorized the government to set measures for the encouragement of private sector activities by means of governmental decrees, was to be repealed by the Constitutional Court on the grounds that this authority could be used only by the Turkish Parliament. This, in turn, put further emphasis on the importance of existing 'special purpose banks' as intended in the Second Five-Year Development Plan, while efforts to establish yet another bank, the mooted Export and Development Bank, did not come to fruition (cf. Akgüç 1987: 50; Hiç 1972a: 188–189; 1972b: 314).

On the other hand, the liquidation of several banks in the wake of the 1958 Banking Law had made the policymakers cautious about the new bank entries. In fact, the Second and Third Five-Year Development Plans had specifically cautioned against the establishment of new banks, unless adequate financial resources had been secured. There were also suggestions for the merging of existing banks in order to reduce their transaction costs (Akgüç 1987: 50–51). Only one commercial bank that was a foreign capital bank would be licensed during the period in question, 1962–76. This was the American-Turkish Foreign Trade Bank, founded in 1964 (Kocabaşoğlu et al. 2001: 509) which remained in operation well into the 1990s, before it changed hands and names on two occasions between national and foreign owners, before eventually ceasing operations in 2005.

> It is thereby aimed that limited resources of the sector are distributed via existing banks in … in accordance with the ways stipulated under the plans. Working in an environment where there were no risks stemming from the changes and fluctuations in interest rates and foreign exchange rates and no product and price competition existed, the banks headed for widespread branch-banking in order to increase the deposits they collected with negative real interest rates.
>
> (BAT 2009: vii)

While the BAT tended to account for this state of affairs by putting the blame on the state for pursuing import-substituting industrialization via development planning, for others, these developments would underline the bank-based character of the Turkish financial system (Kocabaşoğlu et al. 2001: 516). As for the relations between the banking sector and the non-financial corporate sector, neoclassical economic observers of the Turkish economy would thus conclude with the benefit of hindsight:

> With the limited scope for equity and bond financing, private firms relied on deposit banks and their own resources for capital formation. This situation led to the evolution of sellers' markets for bank credits, large spreads in interest rates, and strong preference for a restrictive trade regime to sustain high-cost industries established for home markets.
>
> (Celasun and Rodrik 1989: 626)

However, the 1958 Banking Law would also be instrumental in encouraging the participation of the private sector banks such as İş Bank in newly established industrial firms as a mechanism of realising the objectives of the plans. Indeed, another significant feature of the 1958 Banking Law—which remained in force with some significant amendments until 1985—was that it had paved the way for the emergence of capital groups—'holdings' as they are known in Turkey—i.e. conglomerates that would increasingly characterize the Turkish financial system. This has been a clear trend, in line with developments in a number of developing countries, particularly in Latin America, where they constituted "the dominant form of private, domestically-owned capitalism", because of their size and diversified activities, as well as enhanced market power (Leff 1978, 1979). Moreover, what has been highlighted as a significant incentive for the formation of conglomerates in the credit-constrained Latin American economies, could be considered as an equally salient issue for the Turkish corporate sector. For the group structure would bring along a capability to allocate funds to different business units within the group, which has been dubbed as the formation of 'internal capital markets' or related lending (Tarzijan 1999; Lefort and Walker 2000).

A raft of legislation regarding the taxation of the corporate sector facilitated the formation of holding groups in Turkey from 1961 onwards.[23] However, no amendments would be made to the Commercial Law which was enacted in 1956 and came into effect in 1957, even though it did not entail any reference to a notion of 'groups'.[24] Nor for that matter, has there been any formal definition of 'holding' as such (Akgüç 1987: 60). While 18 such groups were formed by 1970, their number had reached 115 by 1976, and 210 by 1980 (Tekeli 1983: 2390–2391; Kazgan 1983: 2397). In due course, the number of capital groups with bank ownership reached 11 by the end of 1970s, while the relative weight of the banking sector in the Turkish financial system was found to have increased from 63.7 per cent in 1971 to 87 per centby the end of 1981 (Artun 1985: 48, 36). Concomitantly, it had been observed that the conglomerates with bank ownership had tended to dominate the list of Turkey's largest 100 firms during the same period, while the groups without bank ownership tended to lose their positions among that list (Kazgan 1983: 2406). As holding-banking was encouraged by the state with the motive of increasing private sector investments, it was held that the financial repression functioned as a source of primitive accumulation for the banking sector, and *ipso facto*, for the holding groups (Günlük 1983: 193, Akyüz 1990: 126). On the grounds of stabilizing and boosting the lending capabilities of the banking sector, the so-called 'holding banks' were allowed to extend unlimited credit to the firms within the group, thus making bank ownership a powerful lever of capital accumulation (Kocabaşoğlu et al. 2001: 490; Marois 2012: 54; Öncü and Gökçe 1991: 106). This process would be accelerated in the aftermath of the change in economic policy priorities from 1980 onwards with the removal of constraints on bank ownership. Thereby, a great portion of the privately held Turkish commercial banks would become 'holding-banks', where the ownership of a significant majority of a bank belonged to an industry or trade group (BAT 2009: 14). As has been observed with the benefit of hindsight:

> The benefits of financial liberalisation were used mostly by the business groups organised in the form of holdings. Turkish business groups were organised as holdings as the legal regulations made it much more profitable to do so.
>
> (Güngen 2012: 194)

It is therefore plausible to identify 'holding banks' as a key and constant feature of Turkish political economy transcending the fundamental re-orientation of economic policies taking place at significant intervals over the last half century. Overall, it could thus be concluded that this would ensue with the centralization and concentration of capital within the banking sector as 'holding banking' became an important part of the mode of accumulation by the Turkish conglomerates. In this regard, it is also to be noted that the rather intimate relations between the banking sector and non-financial corporations have manifested a variegated nature, as some leading Turkish groups such as Koç Holding would refrain from bank ownership well into the 1970s, while İş Bank itself would reflect all the characteristics of a conglomerate, even though it was not formally a holding as such.[25]

Towards the End of an Era: Crisis of ISI-led Development in the 1970s

The characteristic features of the bank-dominated financial system in Turkey would thus have a three-pronged structure, comprising the Central Bank, deposit banks and the so-called special purpose banks, i.e. investment and development banks as highlighted above. The enactment of a new Central Bank Law (No.1211) in January 1970 would shape Turkey's macroeconomic policy environment for the rest of the decade. This was to gain saliency as it vested the Central Bank with a new structure and brought significant changes to the legal status, organizational structure, duties and powers of the Bank.[26] The need for a new law was deemed necessary as the functioning of Central Bank since the end of the Second World War had reflected a fundamental shift from its founding principles, which were the maintenance of the macroeconomic stability anchored on the stability of the exchange rate. For the main function of the Central Bank had been provision of credits for the public sector during the 1950s and financing of investment projects in accordance with the priorities of the Five-Year Development Plans during the 1960s. In fact, Law no. 1211 was designed so as to give "the Central Bank the authority to make medium term rediscount and advance payment operations"[27] thus enabling it to implement monetary policy in line with the plans. The new law was to be interpreted in retrospect as a belated reflection of "planned economy" approach in Turkish central banking (Marois 2012: 56; Türel 2011: 129).

The strategic objective to reduce the dependence on foreign resources by no means stemmed from a desire to weaken the links with the global economy. The first decade of development planning coincided with the beginning of a long haul, at the end of which Turkish policymakers hoped to finalize their bid to become integrated with the economies of Western Europe. The Association Agreement with the European Common Market in 1963 had, in fact, been contemplated as the first step towards that eventuality. This would be followed by the 1970 Annex Protocol that would set Turkey on the path of an eventual customs union with the European Union (EU) 25 years later.[28] The signing of the Annex Protocol had come in the wake of yet another stabilization programme in August 1970 which aimed to resolve the balance of payments crisis, as both the trade deficit and the debt burden had more than doubled during the second half of the 1960s, while the current account deficit as a percentage of gross national product (GNP) decreased, mainly thanks to workers' remittances from Western European countries (Hiç 1972a: 190, 192). In fact, this would signify the dilemma faced by Turkish policymakers,as the decision to devalue had always been seen as a necessary, although regrettable means of adjustment that would pave the ground for the realization of the objectives of the industrialization strategy.[29] In order to overcome this dilemma, the Third Five-Year Development Plan strategy had been revised in order to facilitate the prospective economic integration with the European Economic Community (EEC—the forerunner to the EU), without forsaking the objectives of the industrialization strategy. Thus, the Third Plan (1973–77) reiterated the determination to reduce the dependence on foreign resources not by weakening the ties of the economy with the outside world, but rather by enhancing the vertical integration and competitiveness of the industrial structure. Eventually, Turkish–EEC relations would be put on hold in 1978 with the supportof significant sections of Turkish industrialists who had been until then critical of the terms of the Annex Protocol, while the Turkish government was striving to negotiate a rescheduling agreement with Turkey's creditors in the wake of a severe debt crisis (Yalman 2009: 225–227; 246–247).

Initially, the 1970 devaluation seemed to have accomplished the immediate objective of resolving the balance of payments crisis by encouraging the transfer of remittances by migrant workers abroad, as well as giving a jump-start to exports, mainly of textiles. After this brief interlude, which coincided with fundamental changes in the global economic order in the early 1970s, the Turkish economy would find itself heading towards a foreign exchange crisis of unprecedented magnitude. While there were obviously exogenous factors involved such as the quadrupling of international oil prices and the US arms embargo on Turkey in the aftermath of the 1974 Turkish intervention in Cyprus, the major cause of the deterioration in the foreign balance of payments was the phenomenal rise of the non-oil sector, particularly capital goods imports which would, in turn, lead to a desperate search for new sources of external finance. It was observed that the net use of foreign savings rose from −2.2 per cent of GNP in 1973 to 6.9 per cent in 1977 (Celasun and Rodrik 1989: 637). As a result, Turkish policymakers would be chided for attempting to avoid adjustment by borrowing in order to sustain the development strategy (cf. Derviş and Robinson 1978: 66; Derviş and Petri 1987: 243).

However, it was pointed out that, while foreign borrowing by the public sector remained well below 1 per cent of GNP during 1974–77, it did indeed finance the public sector; but it did so indirectly via the intermediation of the banking sector, and of the Central Bank in particular. Thus, the Central Bank appeared as the single largest source of financing, providing more than half of the funds needed (Celasun and Rodrik 1989: 638). In fact, Law no. 1211 gave the authority to the Central Bank, through rediscount transactions, to grant medium-term loans to industry. Thereby, there were a series of decisions by the Central Bank during 1973–75, to reduce the reserve requirements of banks to encourage them to award such loans for investment projects deemed a priority under the prevailing Five-Year Plan. By mid-1975 the reserve requirement for the loans that would be allocated for the medium-term requirements of the industry would come down from 20 per cent to zero percent. Moreover, the reserves previously deposited at the Central Bank would be reimbursed to the banks, provided that they utilize the funds for the completion of unfinished investment projects. The commercial banks were also encouraged to grant loans to borrowers who were investing in priority areas (Keyder and Ertunga 2012: 63; BAT 1999: 16).

Even if the public sector absorbed an increasing proportion of Central Bank resources, the representatives of Turkish industry noted that this should not lead observers to gloss over the fact that "the private sector had access to funds outside Central Bank resources" (TÜSİAD 1976: 68). It is also to be noted that Turkey's first brokerage house, Yatırım Finansman, was founded in October 1976 by 13 major banks led by İşbank and TSKB in an attempt to initiate the development of the capital markets.[30] Far from being 'crowded-out', as two prominent observers of the Turkish economy suggested, the private sector was the main beneficiary of the policies which were conventionally held responsible for the destabilization of the economy:

> To prevent private sector crowding-out and to ensure foreign exchange availability for its own needs, the government subsidised private sector foreign borrowing by providing blanket protection against foreign exchange risk. … [T]his type of external financing contained germs of its own destruction. The implicit subsidy on foreign borrowing was larger the greater the likelihood of a crisis; in turn, the crisis became more likely as borrowing skyrocketed. Hence, while the underlying cause of the deteriorating external balance has to be located in the public sector investment drive, what precipitated the debt crisis [of the late 1970s] per se was private sector borrowing behaviour, itself in turn conditioned by government policy.
>
> (Celasun and Rodrik1989: 634)

Blanket protection against foreign exchange risk that was alluded above had come in the form of Convertible Turkish Lira Deposits (CTLDs) during the mid-1970s. These were short-term foreign currency accounts held by foreign commercial banks with Turkish commercial banks, with a transfer guarantee from the Central Bank. They were originally designed to attract Turkish migrant workers' remittances, but, in practice, were widely used by the Turkish firms as a cheaper source of credit, thereby providing lucrative profits in the form of arbitrage, as well as providing an avenue for flight capital to return (Celasun and Rodrik 1989: 643; TÜSİAD 1976: 62). CTLDs were subsequently restructured in 1979 as foreign commercial bank deposits were given an exchange rate guarantee from the Central Bank on the basis of an agreement signed in London (Akgüç 1983: 68).

It is important to emphasize that the late 1970s witnessed not only a protracted balance of payments crisis in the form of a foreign debt crisis, but also an aggravated crisis of hegemony. Indeed, this particular crisis and its aftermath can be considered as an illustration of the validity of the Gramscian analysis that a crisis of hegemony is *ipso facto* a crisis of the state, the resolution of which necessitated not only a fundamental reorientation of economic policies, but also a change in the form of the state (Yalman 2009: 305). For the representative organizations of the Turkish bourgeoisie had started to see the rising class consciousness of the working class as a threat to the existing social order, while the trade unions became increasingly effective in defending their members' interests. Moreover, the large conglomerates would be irritated by the ways in which the coalition government that came to power at the beginning of 1978 had attempted to enhance public revenues by pushing forward a new tax law which never materialized, but perceived as a threat nonetheless (Kuruç 2010: 375, 392). Hence, the Turkish bourgeoisie would seek for new ways in which a restructuring of the political order could be carried out in order to guarantee the 'freedom of free enterprise'. This would subsequently be reflected in the strategic selectivities of the Turkish state that would shape the neoliberal transformation process in due course.

The late 1970s thus witnessed a critical shift of position on the part of the Turkish Industrialists and Businessmen's Association (TÜSİAD) as a prominent representative of the major conglomerates (Yalman 2009: 241–242; 247–248). For it was engaged in public campaigns to destabilize the government, which had been involved in a desperate effort to reschedule the existing foreign debt and obtain fresh loans. Such a turnaround in their policy orientation was also reflected in their opposition to the Fourth Five-Year Development Plan (1979–83) which sought to bring forward a new strategy that would combine the deepening of the industrial structure with a politics of redistribution (Kuruç 2010: 391–393).[31] It is also noteworthy that there was a last gasp effort on the part of the same government to initiate a series of changes to the 1958 Banking Law by issuing Decree 28 in July 1979, purportedly to facilitate the provision of credits so as to achieve production and investment targets of the Fourth Five-Year Development Plan. It also ostensibly aimed to prevent the concentration of capital in view of the closely knit relations between the bank ownership and the formation of holdings.[32] In fact, it included clauses that aimed to constrain the inter-locking directorships between the banks and industrial firms belonging to the same holding group, as well as clauses to limit the provision of credits to firms within the group by holding banks (that is, to constrain Turkey's particular form of finance capital). The timing of this decree could no doubt be seen as a response to TÜSİAD's publicity campaign. Although the government that initiated this decree fell from power only a few months later, the decree itself would remain in effect for another four years, until the military regime replaced it with another decree. During the period it remained formally in effect, but it did not make much of an impact on holding banking.

Meanwhile, the manifest opposition of conglomerates from 1978 onwards would, in turn, make them "one of the major forces advocating fundamental reform" (Krueger and Turan 1993: 345). It would thereby falsify the kind of arguments that purported to portray the Turkish business community as being denied the necessary means to function as an effective mechanism of special interest representation (cf. Buğra 1994: 237–238). With the adoption of a new IMF stand-by agreement in March 1980, following the 24 January 1980 stabilization measures, which initiated a process of market-oriented reforms, Turkey became a pioneer of a structural adjustment process that would go on to be widely experienced by the debtor economies of the South during the 1980s. Consequently, the Turkish experience of transition to neoliberalism and subsequently of financialization, as will be elaborated in the following chapters, would entail the restructuring of the state-market relations in a rather authoritarian political framework.

Notes

1 "Between 1854 and 1881, the Ottoman Empire went through one of the most critical phases of the history of its relations with European powers. Beginning with the first foreign loan contracted in 1854, this process was initially dominated by a modest level of indebtedness, coupled with sporadic and inconsequential attempts by western powers to impose some control over the viability of the operation. From 1863 on, a second and much more intense phase began, which eventually led to a snowballing effect of accumulated debts. The formal bankruptcy of the Empire in 1875 resulted in the collapse of the entire system in one of the most spectacular financial crashes of the period. It was only six years later, in 1881, that a solution was found in the establishment of the Ottoman Public Debt Administration that would control a large portion of state revenues." (Eldem 2005).

2 Put differently, "state finances remained the Achilles' heel of the Ottoman state" (Karaman and Pamuk 2010), accentuating its relative decline among European states until the World War I.

3 According to Akgüç (1987: 26), of the 29 local banks founded during 1924–1933 period, only six would continue to exist in the post-war era.

4 See Tekeli and İlkin (1977: 48–49) for the ways in which the value of the currency was determined until the 1930 Law; ibid. p.53 for the dependency of the monetary policy until 1930 on international financial circles; Kuruç (2011: 284–285) for the decision not to leave the determination the value of the currency to the financial markets.

5 Originally founded as Real Estate and Orphans Bank (REOB) in 1926, it was transformed as Real Estate and Credit Bank (RECB) in 1946 with enhanced financial resources. RECB had been merged with Anadolu Bankası in 1988 and given the name of Türkiye Emlak Bankası (Emlakbank). Its 96 branches were transferred to Halkbank in 2001, as it was put in the process of liquidation, to be eventually merged with Ziraat Bank and closed. Yet, the process of liquidation was brought to an end with Law no. 7020, dated 27 May 2017, and Türkiye Emlak

Bankası is said to start its operations in due course. http://www.emlakbank.com.tr/sayfalar.asp?LanguageID=1&cid=2&id=11&b=detay.

6 Sümerbank's assets and liabilities were transferred to Halkbank in 1993.

7 The Bank of Municipalities, founded in 1933 (Law no. 2301), was restructured in 1945 as Bank of Provinces (Law no. 4759) with a mandate to provide technical support as well as funds and loans to local governments (municipalities) for infrastructural investments. (http://www.ilbank.gov.tr/index.php?Sayfa=iceriksayfa&icId=3).

8 Etibank's assets and liabilities were transferred to Halkbank in 1998.

9 DenizBank was closed down in 1940 (Akgüç 1987: 32).

10 With Law no. 4603 passed on 25 November 2000; Ziraat Bank becomes a joint-stock company.

11 https://www.halkbank.com.tr/en/international-banking/97/history.

12 There were 11 foreign banks which had started their operations during 1909–23 (Artun 1985: 39), while nine foreign banks ceased their operations during 1929–36 (Akgüç 1987: 37). However, the lists of banks provided by these two references are not quite comparable with each other, since among the banks closed there were some which had started operating back in the 19th century. It was also noted that no new foreign banks were established during 1923–30 (Ökçün 1975: 475).

13 Of the three public sector banks established only one of them, Vakıflar Bankası, is still in operation today whereas four of the private sector banks (Yapı ve Kredi Bankası, Garanti Bankası, Akbank, Şekerbank) are, although some of them changed hands in due course (Şahinkaya 1999: 95).

14 Indeed, as stated in the website of TSKB, as of 2016, "Members of the Türkiye İş Bankası (Işbank) Group control a 50.33% stake in TSKB", http://www.tskb.com.tr/en/about-us/general-overview.

15 http://www.tskb.com.tr/en/history-of-tskb.

16 Whatever the source of their primary accumulation, according to one survey, 40% of the private sector firms which were in operation at the end of the 1960s had been established during the 1950s. Moreover, nearly 90% of these firms were in manufacturing industry (Soral, 1974: 30).

17 Addendum to Decree 14, dated 28 July 1955, for the establishment of "Banka Kredileri Tanzim Komitesi" published in *Official Gazette* on 14 February 1956. The committee would be comprised of relevant members of the government, Governor of CBRT, Secretary General of the Chambers of Commerce and Industry, and general managers of major commercial banks. In other words, it would coalesce together the representatives of the government, the business community and the banking industry. It had subsequently been incorporated into the Banking Law (No. 7129) and remained in effect until its abolition with the adoption of a new Central Bank Law (No.1211) in 1970 while its duties and powers had been assigned to the Central Bank.

18 See note 5 above.

19 It was calculated that more than half of the total foreign aid received during the First Five-Year Development Plan (1962–66) was used for foreign debt payments and interests (Alkin 1972: 248).

20 Boratav (1988: 102) calculated that the ratio of capital accumulation to GNP were near 17% for the 1962–76 period, and roughly one-fifth of which had been financed by foreign savings.

21 Devlet Yatırım Bankası (State Investment Bank), founded for the purpose of providing loans to state economic enterprises for their investments included in the plans, has been restructured in 1987 as its activity areas were redefined in line with the reorientation of economic policies from 1980 onwards and its name was changed as Türk Eximbank (BAT 2009, Şahinkaya 1999: 101).

22 Devlet Sanayi ve İşçi Yatırım Bankası (State Industry and Workers' Investment Bank), founded for the purpose of using the savings of Turkish workers working abroad, for investment in prioritized areas, was restructured by a Decree in 1983, changed its name as Development Bank of Turkey in 1988, and expanded its scope of activities when Tourism Bank was transferred to it with all its assets and liabilities in 1989. Eventually, with the enactment of Law no. 4456 in 1999, it had been redefined as a development and investment bank with the status of a private legal entity.

23 While it has been pointed out that the legal basis for the holding groups "was prepared upon the demands of certain big businessmen" (Buğra 1994: 136), this had been circumscribed with a series of tax benefits. Two main financial advantages for the holding groups as a result of the taxation legislation in the 1960s, however, were identified as follows: there was the requirement that taxes on revenues from participations are payable only in the following fiscal year. Moreover, there was the possibility of income shuffling to minimize the tax burden of the portfolio of companies under the holding company (TÜSİAD 2002: 128; Yurtoğlu 2000).

24 The introduction of 'groups' into the Turkish Commercial Law would have to wait for another fifty years until the adoption of a new Commercial Law which would be enacted in 2011 and came into effect in 2012.

25 See also Güven (2009: 106) who noted that there was "no single formula of industrial-financial relations in the [Turkish] private sector". Moreover, as Kazgan (1983: 2399) pointed out some private banks, such as Yapı Kredi Bank, functioning as conglomerates without formally structured as holding groups would be taken over and become holding banks in due course.

26 http://www.tcmb.gov.tr/yeni/eng/.

27 ibid.

28 See Yalman and Göksel 2017 for a brief historical review of Turkey-EU relations from a critical perspective.

29 It was pointed out that Turkish government had been obliged to have recourse devaluation on August 1970 due to pressures coming from the IMF and the Consortium for Aid (Hiç 1972b: 310), the latter being a legacy of the 1958 Stabilisation programme. Thereby, it was contended that the effectiveness of devaluation is debatable for the developing countries in solving their balance of payments problems (ibid: 312).

30 https://www.yf.com.tr/en/about-us/. Whereas Günlük (1983: 193–194) noted that while there had been two abortive efforts in the 1960s and 1970s to enact a law for the establishment of a capital market, the failure to legislate led to the emergence of an informal secondary market for the shares and bonds issued by the non-bank owning corporate sector. This was a process initiated largely by the latter which, in turn, created a set of dealers' as agents of this secondary market, referred to as "bankers".

31 Türel (2010: 412–415) provides a panoply of alternative strategic options which were apparently debated during the crisis period which ranged from an advocacy of export-oriented growth based on natural endowments to the promotion of further ISI, entailing variations of ISI in combination with export orientation. Kuruç (2010: 392) notes that Union of Industrialists, comprising many of the representatives of the groups, were initially more favourable to the deepening strategy of the Fourth Plan. However, they have declined in significance as the relations between the government and the conglomerates further deteriorated, while the Plan itself had been effectively shelved with the change of economic policy orientation from 1980 onwards.

32 The rationale of Decree 28 in changing some of the clauses of Banking Law no. 7129 (Taşçıoğlu 1998).

REFERENCES

Akgüç, Ö. (1983) "1982 Yılında Bankalar, Mevduat ve Krediler", *Banka ve Ekonomik Yorumlar*, 20(8): 59–79.

Akgüç, Ö. (1987) 100 *Soruda Türkiye'de Bankacılık*, Istanbul: Gerçek Yayınevi.

Akyüz, Y. (1984) *Financial Structure and Relations in the Turkish Economy*, Türkiye Sınai Kalkınma BankasıA.Ş., Istanbul.

Akyüz, Y. (1990) "Financial System and Policies in Turkey in the 1980s" in T. Arıcanlı, and D. Rodrik (eds.) *The Political Economy of Turkey Debt, Adjustment and Sustainability*, New York: Macmillan, 98–131.

Alkin, E. (1972) "Turkey's Foreign Trade", in *Problems of Turkey's Economic Development*,Vol.1, The Institute of Economic Development, Faculty of Economics, Istanbul University, 247–284.

Artun, T. (1985) "Türk Mali Sistemi 1980–1984" in B. Kuruç et al. (eds.) *Bırakınız Yapsınlar, Bırakınız Geçsinler: Türkiye Ekonomisi 1980–1985*, Ankara: Bilgi Yayınevi, 36–71.

Atiyas, İ. (1990) "The Private Sector's Response to Financial Liberalisation in Turkey: 1980-1982" in T. Arıcanlı and D. Rodrik (eds.) *The Political Economy of Turkey Debt, Adjustment and Sustainability*, New York: Macmillan, 132–155.

Atiyas, İ. and H. Ersel (1996) "The Impact of Financial Reform: The Turkish Experience", G. Caprio Jr. et al. (eds.) *Financial Reform: Theory and Experience*, Cambridge: Cambridge University Press, 103–139.

BAT–The Banks Association of Turkey (1999) *40th Anniversary of the Banks Association of Turkey and Turkish Banking System "1958–1997"*, Ankara: The Banks Association of Turkey.

BAT–The Banks Association of Turkey (2009)*50th Anniversary of the Banks Association of Turkey and Turkish Banking System "1958–2007"*, Ankara: The Banks Association of Turkey.

Boratav, K. (1977) "1923–1939 Yıllarının İktisat Politikası Açıından Dönemlendirilmesi" *Atatürk Döneminin Ekonomik ve Toplumsal Sorunları*, İktisadi ve Ticari İlimler Akademisi Mezunları Derneği, 14–16 January 1977 Symposium, Istanbul, 39–52.

Boratav, K. (1983) "Türkiye'de Popülizm: 1962–1976 Dönemi Üzerine Notlar", *Yapıt*, 1: 1–26.

Boratav, K. (1988) *Türkiye İktisat Tarihi 1908–1985*, Istanbul: Gerçek Yayınevi.

Boratav, K. (2011) "Serbest Sermaye Hareketleri ve Kriz-Küçülme Dönemeçleri 1990–2010" in S. Şahinkaya and İ. Ertuğrul (eds.) *Bilsay Kuruç'a Armağan*, Mülkiyeliler Birliği Yayın No. 2011/2, Ankara, 405–435.

Buğra, A. (1994) *State and Business in Modern Turkey: A Comparative Study*, New York: State University of New York Press.

Celasun, M. (1990) "Fiscal Aspects of Adjustment in the 1980s" in T. Arıcanlı, and D. Rodrik (eds.) *The Political Economy of Turkey Debt, Adjustment and Sustainability*, New York: Macmillan, 37–59.

Celasun, M. and D. Rodrik (1989) "Debt, Adjustment and Growth: Turkey" in J. Sachs (ed.) *Developing Country Debt and Economic Performance vol. III.*, Chicago: University of Chicago Press, 615–809.

Coşkun, M.N. et al. (2012) *Türkiye'de Bankacılık Sektörü, Piyasa Yapısı, Firma Davranışları ve Rekabet Analizi*, İstanbul: Türkiye Bankalar Birliği.

Derviş, K. and S. Robinson (1978) "The Foreign Exchange Gap, Growth and Industrial Strategy in Turkey: 1973–1983", *World Bank Staff Working Paper*, No.306.

Derviş, K. and P. Petri (1987) "The Macroeconomics of Successful Development: What are the Lessons?" *NBER Macroeconomics Annual*, Vol. 2: 211–262.

Eldem, E. (1999) "The Imperial Ottoman Bank: Actor or Instrument of Ottoman Modernization?" in K. Kostis (ed.), *Modern Banking in the Balkans and West-European Capital in the Nineteenth and Twentieth Centuries*, Aldershot: Ashgate, 50–60.

Eldem, E. (2005) "Ottoman Financial Integration with Europe: Foreign Loans, the Ottoman Bank and the Ottoman Public Debt", *European Review*, 13(3): 431–445.

Gültekin, B. (2012) "Liberalisation" in M. Heper and S. Sayarı (eds.) *The Routledge Handbook of Modern Turkey*, Routledge, 379–389.

Güngen, A.R. (2012) *Debt Management and Financialisation as Facets of State Restructuring: The Case of Turkey in the Post-1980 Period*, unpublished PhD thesis, Middle East Technical University, Ankara.

Günlük, A. (1983) "Türkiye'de Sermaye Piyasası", *Cumhuriyet Dönemi Türkiye Ansiklopedisi*, İletişim Yayınları, Istanbul, Vol. 1:191–197.

Güven, A.B. (2009) *Peasants, Bankers and the State: Forging Institutions in Neoliberal Turkey*, unpublished PhD thesis, University of Toronto, Toronto.

Hiç, M. (1972a) "Outline of Turkey's Monetary Policy and Economic Development 1950–1970" in *Problems of Turkey's Economic Development*, Vol. 1, the Institute of Economic Development, Faculty of Economics, Istanbul University, 179–192.

Hiç, M. (1972b) "The Question of the Balance of Payments Deficit and the August 10, 1970 Devaluation" in *Problems of Turkey's Economic Development*, Vol. 1, Institute of Economic Development, Faculty of Economics, Istanbul University, 285–314.

Hilferding, R. (1910) *Finance Capital. A Study of the Latest Phase of Capitalist Development*, T. Bottomore (ed.) London: Routledge & Kegan Paul.

Karaman, K. and Ş. Pamuk (2010) "Ottoman State Finances in European Perspective, 1500–1914", *The Journal of Economic History*, 70(3): 593–630.

Kazgan, G. (1983) "Büyük Sermaye Gruplarının Türkiye Ekonomisindeki Yeri", *Cumhuriyet Dönemi Türkiye Ansiklopedisi*, İletişimYayınları, Istanbul, Vol. 9: 2397–2410.

Kepenek, Y. (1984) *Türkiye Ekonomisi*, Ankara: Savaş Yayınları.

Keyder, N. and E. Ertunga (2012) *Para: Teori, Politika, Uygulama*, Ankara: Seçkin Yayıncılık.

Kocabaşoğlu, U. et al. (2001) *Türkiye İş Bankası Tarihi*, İstanbul: Türkiye İş Bankası Kültür Yayınları.

Krueger, A. and İ. Turan (1993) "The Politics and Economics of Turkish Policy Reforms in the 1980s", in R. Bates and A. Krueger (eds.) *Political and Economic Interactions in Economic Policy Reform*, Oxford: Basil Blackwell, 334–386.

Kuruç, B. (1988) "Sunuş" (Introduction) in Kuruç, B. (ed. 1988) *Belgelerle Türkiye İktisat Politikası, Vol.1 (1929–1932)*, Faculty of Political Science, Ankara, xxxi-lviii.

Kuruç, B. (1993) *Belgelerle Türkiye İktisat Politikası, Vol. 2 (1933–1935)*, Faculty of Political Science, Ankara.

Kuruç, B. (2010) "Bir Planın Anatomi Politiği: Dördüncü Planın Hazırlanışıve Sonu", in E. Türkcan (ed.) *Attila Sönmez'e Armağan: Türkiye'de Planlamanın Yükselişi ve Çöküşü 1960–1980*, İstanbul: İstanbul Bilgi University Press, 357–410.

Kuruç, B. (2011) *Mustafa Kemal Döneminde Ekonomi*, İstanbul: Bilgi Üniversitesi Yayınları.

Leff, N. (1978) "Industrial Organisation and Entrepreneurship in the Developing Countries: The Economic Groups", *Economic Development and Cultural Change*, 26(4): 661–675.

Leff, N. (1979) "'Monopoly Capitalism' and Public Policy in Developing Countries", *Kyklos* 32 (4): 718–738.

Lefort, F. and E. Walker (2000) "Ownership and Capital Structure of Chilean Conglomerates: Facts and Hypotheses for Governance", *Revista ABANTE*, 3(1): 3–27.

Marois, T. (2012) *States, Banks and Crisis: Emerging Finance Capitalism in Mexico and Turkey*, Cheltenham: Edward Elgar Publishing.

Marois, T. and A.R. Güngen (2016) "Credibility and Class in the Evolution of Public Banks: the Case of Turkey", *The Journal of Peasant Studies*, 43(6): 1285–1309.

Ökçün, G. (1975) "1919–1930 YıllarıArasında A.Ş. Olarak Kurulan Bankalar", in O. Okyar (ed.) *Türkiye İktisat Tarihi Semineri, 8–10 June 1973*, Ankara: Hacettepe Üniversitesi Yayınları, C13, 409–448.

Öncü, A. and D. Gökçe (1991) "Macro-Politics of De-Regulation and Micro-Politics of Banks"in M. Heper (ed.) *Strong State and Economic Interest Groups*, Berlin: de Gruyter, 99–117.

Pamuk, Ş. (1984) *Osmanlı Ekonomisive Dünya Kapitalizmi (1820–1913)*, Ankara: Yurt Yayınları.

Pamuk, Ş. (1998) "Ottoman Interventionism in Economic and Monetary Affairs", *Revue d'Histoire Maghrébine*, 25/91–92: 361–367

Pamuk, Ş. (2000) "Intervention during the Great Depression: Another Look at Turkish Experience" in Ş. Pamuk and J.G. Williamson (eds.), *The Mediterranean Response to Globalisation before 1950*, London and New York: Routledge, 321–339.

Pamuk, Ş. (2007) "Economic change in twentieth-century Turkey: is the glass more than half full?" in R. Kasaba (ed.) *The Cambridge History of Turkey, Vol. 4. Turkey in the Modern World*, Cambridge: Cambridge University Press, 266–300.

Pamuk, Ş. (2014) *Türkiye'nin 200 Yıllık İktisadi Tarihi*, Istanbul: Türkiye İş Bankası Kültür Yayınları.

Sarç, C. (1948) "Economic Policy of the New Turkey", *Middle East Journal*, 2(4): 430–446.

Soral, E. (1974) *Özel Kesimde Türk Müteşebbisleri*, Ankara: Ankara İktisadi ve Ticari İlimler Akademisi.

Şahinkaya, S. (1999) "1946–1979 Döneminde Bankalar, İhtisas Bankaları ve İktisat Politikaları", in Z. Rona (ed.) *Bilanço 1923–1998: Türkiye Cumhuriyeti'nin 75 Yılına Toplu Bakış*, Vol. 2, İstanbul: Tarih Vakfı Yayınları, 91–104.

Tarzijan, J. (1999) "Internal Capital Markets and Multimarket Contact as Explanations for Conglomerates in Emerging Markets", *Revista ABANTE*, 2(1): 3–22.

Taşçıoğlu, A. (1998) *Cumhuriyet Dönemi Bankalar Kanunları ve İlgili Yasal Düzenlemeler*, Türkiye Bankalar Birliği, Yayın No. 208, Istanbul: Türkiye Bankalar Birliği.

Tekeli, İ. (1983) "Türkiye'de Şirketlerin Gelişimi ve Kapitalin Yoğunlaşma Süreci", *Cumhuriyet Dönemi Türkiye Ansiklopedisi*, İstanbul: İletişim Yayınları, Vol. 9: 2386–2396.

Tekeli, İ. and S. İlkin (1974) *Savaş Sonrası Ortamında 1947 Türkiye Iktisadi Kalkınma Planı*, Ankara: METU.

Tekeli, İ. and S. İlkin (1977) *1929 Dünya Buhranında Türkiye'nin İktisadi Politika Arayışları*, Ankara: METU.

Tekeli, İ. and S. İlkin (1982) *Uygulamaya Geçerken Türkiye'de Devletçiliğin Oluşumu*, Ankara: METU.

Tezel, Y. S. (1977) "1923–1938 Döneminde Türkiye'nin Dış İktisadi İlişkileri", *Atatürk Döneminin Ekonomik ve Toplumsal Sorunları*, İktisadive Ticari İlimler Akademisi Mezunları Derneği, 14–16 January 1977 Symposium, Istanbul, 193–230.

Tezel, Y. S. (2015) *Cumhuriyet Döneminin İktisadi Tarihi (1923–1950)*, İstanbul: Türkiye İş Bankası Kültür Yayınları.

Türel, O. (2009) "Türkiye Ekonomisinin Neoliberal Yapılanma Sürecinde Bankacılığın Yeniden Düzenlenmesi, 1980–2007", in M. Özuğurlu et al. (eds.) *Alpaslan Işıklı'ya Armağan*, No: 31, Ankara: Mülkiyeliler Birliği Vakfı, 131–170.

Türel, O. (2010) "Türkiye'de 1978–1979 Bunalımı ve Merkezi İktisadi Planlama", in E. Türkcan (ed.) *Attila Sönmez'e Armağan: Türkiye'de Planlamanın Yükselişi ve Çöküşü 1960–1980*, İstanbul: İstanbul Bilgi University Press, 411–441.

Türel, O. (2011) "T.C. Merkez Bankasına Yeni Yasal Çerçeve: 4651 Sayılı Kanun Üzerine Gözlem ve Değerlendirmeler", *Geç Barbarlık Çağı 2*, İstanbul: Yordam Kitap, 127–139.

TÜSİAD (1976) *Turkey: An Economic Survey*, May, Istanbul: TÜSİAD.

TÜSİAD (2002) *Yeni Rekabet Stratejileri ve Türk Sanayisi* Yayın, No. TÜSİAD-T/ 2002-07/322, Istanbul: TÜSİAD.

Yalman, G.L. (2002) "State and Bourgeoisie in Historical Perspective: A Relativist Paradigm or A Panoply of Hegemonic Strategies?" in N. Balkan and S. Savran (eds.), *The Politics of Permanent Crisis: Class, State and Ideology in Turkey*, New York: Nova Science Publishers, 21–54.

Yalman, G.L. (2009) *Transition to Neoliberalism: The Case of Turkey in the 1980s*, İstanbul: İstanbul Bilgi University Press.

Yalman, G.L. and A. Göksel (2017) "Transforming Turkey? Putting the Turkey-European Union Relations into Historical Perspective", *Uluslararası İlişkiler*, 14(56).

Yaşa, M. (1963) "Domestic Sources of Capital" in *Capital Formation and Investment in Industry*, The Economic and Social Studies Conference Board publication, Istanbul.

Yurtoğlu, B. (2000) "Ownership, Control and Performance of Turkish Listed Firms", *Emprica. Journal of Applied Economics and Economic Policy*, 27: 193–222.

3 The Neoliberal Transformation of State and Market in Turkey

An Overview of Financial Developments from 1980 to 2000

Galip L. Yalman

Introduction

Turkey is a country where the need for adjustment has emerged periodically since the end of the Second World War. Indeed, as emphasized in the previous chapter, there were stabilization programmes every ten years or so for more than two decades in response to balance of payment difficulties encountered while pursuing a strategy of industrial development, whether planned or otherwise. But with the launch of the stabilization programme on 24 January 1980, there was an acknowledgement in the international financial community, as well as in political and business circles within Turkey, that it signified something qualitatively different this time. Indeed, this would initiate an ambitious programme of structural adjustment even before such a strategy was formally spelled out by the Bretton Woods institutions. Put differently, the programme is said to signify a radical change *both* in the mode of articulation of the Turkish economy within the global economy, and in the role that the state used to assume in the conduct of economic policy for most of the time since the establishment of the Turkish Republic in the early 1920s.

There would be an official denunciation of import-substitution industrialization as the source of balance of payment difficulties and macroeconomic instabilities, paving the way for the adoption of an export-oriented trade and development strategy based on a more market-directed system of resource allocation. More pertinently, this would set the stage for a process of financial liberalization with a series of ramifications for the Turkish financial system. No less saliently, it would entrench international finance capital as a key determinant of the developmental trajectory of the Turkish political economy, while Bretton Woods institutions would become integral constituents of the policymaking process.[1] In this regard, one of the striking changes of the 1980s was the perception of the integration into the global economy as an end in itself, at least at the level of discourse. The attempted adjustment was thus portrayed as entailing the integration of the Turkish economy into the global economy. What was actually in question was but a change in the mode of integration.

The modalities of the relations between states and markets that could be observed over the last few decades in many of the so-called emerging markets, as they have experienced economic and political crises while going through different phases of financial liberalization, could be contemplated as alternative strategies of adjustment to the vagaries of international financial markets. However, at the same time, it is also crucial to come to terms with these strategies as hegemonic projects to the extent that they fulfil certain functions in the reproduction of particular forms of social relations in historically specific contexts. Structural adjustment understood as such, did not signify simply a change in the mode of integration that would put an end to intermittent crises of foreign exchange. More fundamentally, it signified a new 'mode of living' more than anything else, marked by the availability of imported consumption goods that were instrumental in gaining the consent of the people, while the real wages of average earners declined throughout the 1980s (Yalman 2009: 250). Perhaps the most peculiar feature of the 'structural adjustment' episode in Turkey is the fact that it was attempted during a period in which a complete reorganization of the country's political structure was pursued. The military coup of 12 September 1980 signified not only a change in the political regime, but also a change in the form of the state which was institutionalized within the confines of the authoritarian 1982 Constitution, which remained in effect after the return to civilian rule in November 1983, and still is today (Yalman 2009: 298).

The role played by the capital groups as a key adjustment mechanism and class actor within the context of financial crises deserves special attention. This is essential to overcome the inadequacies of the dominant discourses which tend to analyze state–market relations severed from power relations. As pointed out in the previous chapter, the conglomerates referred to as holding companies in the Turkish context have turned out to be among the key actors in the political economy of Turkey from the 1960s onwards. Indeed, their diversified structures (banking, manufacturing, foreign trade, tourism, construction, energy, etc.) provided the necessary flexibility to alter the relative weight assigned to different domains of activity *within* the group, in accordance with the changing priorities of macroeconomic policies from 1980 onwards. In that sense, the behaviour of the groups in the context of the neoliberal transformation process was a confirmation of their capacity as a specific institutional form of capital for flexibility and adaptation. Moreover, an evaluation of the extent to which the bank-dominated financial system of the country has undergone changes could not be contemplated without taking into account the contours of the holding bank ownership structure during the process of financial liberalization. This, in turn, entails a focus on the specificity of the relations between the financial sector and the real sector in the Turkish context, with implications for the variegated nature of financialization in general.

First Phase of Financial Liberalization 1980–83

The '24 January 1980' Stabilization Package and Its Aftermath

The process initiated by the launch of the stabilization programme on 24 January 1980 was characterized by the following dual objectives: 'to remove the dominance of the state in key industries and in banking, and to minimize the state's intervention with the pricing and resource allocation processes of the market economy' (Taymaz and Yılmaz 2008). In line with the 'getting prices right' dictum of the era, which reasoned that the problems confronting the developing economies stem from policy-induced distortions (Lal 1983: 77), there was an attempt to initiate a rapid liberalization of money and foreign exchange markets, following the launch of the stabilization programme. Turkish policymakers seemed to heed the advice that this would do the trick by creating a competitive financial structure functioning efficiently (Artun 1983: 28; Ersel 1996). The basic argument used by the International Monetary Fund (IMF) and the World Bank to justify policies of financial deregulation was that the financial system in Turkey had been under severe 'financial repression' that led to inefficiency in the utilization of resources, lower economic growth in relation to low national saving and investment levels (Türel 2009: 135). However, the verdict of this advice, with the benefit of hindsight, would not be too inspiring, as reflected in a series of reports upon the developments in the Turkish economy:

> Despite impressive achievements over the past two decades, Turkey's economy has operated under a cloud of vulnerability-plagued by persistent fiscal imbalances, chronically high inflation, and sharp swings in the business cycle.
>
> (World Bank 2003b)

Not only macroeconomic stability was found to be elusive, but it "has worsened the climate for new capital formation in manufacturing, which is central to sustained industrialisation in the long run" (Celasun 1991). Thereby, the protagonists of the structural adjustment process pondered about the causes of "Turkey's record of failed reforms" so as to achieve "the primary objective of helping Turkey move to a path of sustained growth" (World Bank 2000a; 2003b).

These observations, thus, underline the need to refocus on the impact of the policies of financial liberalization on the relationship between the financial sector and the real sector. For the 'reform strategy' that was pursued, at least rhetorically, signified a rupture with the past experience as it put emphasis on competition and financial opening. This was to be achieved not only via trade liberalization for the domestic industry, but equally by easing entry into the bank-dominated financial sector. Yet, 'the Turkish reform strategy' was subsequently to be criticized for being 'overconfident in its reliance on competition among banks in developing financial markets', thereby reinforcing rather than weakening the oligopolistic structure of the banking industry (cf. Atiyas and Ersel 1996: 104; Sönmez 2001: 271; Ulagay 1987: 173). Put differently, 'Turkish financial liberalization did not correspond to a move toward a more competitive environment' (Boratav, Türel and Yeldan 1996). The oligopolistic characteristic would be sustained despite a slight decrease in the degree of concentration from the second half of the 1980s onwards (cf. Akgüç 1988: 5; Atiyas and Ersel 1996: 114, 138; Kocabaşoğlu et al. 2001: 599; Marois 2012: 109).

Box 3.1 Major Developments in the 1980s

- 1980 January 24, Stabilisation Programme
- 1980 June Three-year Stand-by Agreement with the IMF and the start of Structural Adjustment Loans by the World Bank
- 1980 June 4 Decree and 'July Banking'
- 1980 September 12, military coup
- 1981 Capital Markets Law no. 2499
- 1982 Bankers' Crisis
- 1983 Decree of Law on Banks no.70 effectively replacing Banking Law 7129 dated 1958
- 1983 Establishment of Saving Deposit Insurance Fund (SDIF) by Decree 70
- 1983 Decree 90 setting the rules for Lending Operations
- 1983 Decree 91 for Stock Exchange Market, replacing Law for Stock Market enacted in 1929
- 1983 November 6, return to civilian rule with parliamentary elections
- 1983 December–July 1984: Decrees 28 and 30 important steps for financial liberalization via 1930 Law Protecting the Value of Turkish Currency
- 1984 Establishment of the Housing and Public Partnership Directorate
- 1985 Shift of the financing of public sector deficit from the Central Bank to Government Debt Instruments by the Treasury, including foreign currency-denominated bonds, thus giving rise to substantial increases of interest burden on public finance
- 1985 Banking Law no. 3182. Mainly converting Decree 70 into a Law, with some modifications to bring Turkey in line with Bank of International Settlements requirements, capital adequacy, non-performing loan provisions, accounting/reporting standards, deposit insurance
- 1986 World Bank Financial Sector Adjustment Credit Agreement
- 1986 Istanbul Stock Exchange started trading
- 1986 Establishment of Interbank Money Market
- 1988 World Bank Second Financial Sector Adjustment Credit Agreement

- 1989 Decree 32 Convertibility of Turkish Lira, capital account liberalization
- 1989 World Bank ceases new adjustment loans

In the wake of the 24 January 1980 stabilization programme, there had been an attempt to liberalize the money market with the removal of interest rate ceilings on loans and deposits. This was intended to be put into effect as it would become customary to do so in due course, i.e. by way of a decree, dated 4 June 1980, based on Law no. 2279, dated June 1933, issued by the minority government which ruled the country for less than a year until the military coup in September 1980. This decision, in fact, stemmed from a commitment on the part of that government under the first Structural Adjustment Loan (SAL I) to be obtained from the World Bank. Even its timing was in line with that commitment, as SAL I indicated that it was to be implemented by the end of July 1980. The broad framework for the structural adjustment programme, however, had been delineated by the three-year stand-by agreement that the IMF entered into with the Turkish government in June 1980. As the World Bank proudly proclaimed, from the inception of the programme it was involved in a close working relationship with the IMF, providing five SALs in support of the liberalization process (World Bank 1984; Celasun and Rodrik 1989: 671). In fact, Turkey was known to have access to more than 70 per cent of all SALs given to the developing countries during this period (Yeldan 2001).

However, the banking community would not hesitate to contemplate its own way of determining the price of money, as the leading private banks reached a so-called gentlemen's agreement even before the decree was put into practice on 1 July 1980, notwithstanding the specific clauses of the decree which prohibited the Banking Association acting on behalf of the banks from setting limits on interest rates (Artun 1983: 36; TÜSİAD 1981: 80).[2] Hence it was to be dubbed 'July Banking'. And what is more striking is that this agreement was reached with the connivance of the Ministry of Finance and the public sector banks, and made public with a declaration in the press the day before the decree was due to come into effect (Aysan 1980: 7; Durakbaşa 1982: 8). It has subsequently led to a series of vociferous criticisms to the effect that it had produced an 'interest rate cartel'.[3] However, while the same decree also paved the way for the introduction of certificates of deposits (CDs) to be issued by the banks, as part of the initiative to kick-start the deregulation process, it would turn out to be a mechanism for the smaller banks to circumvent the gentlemen's agreement (Akyüz 1990: 99; Atiyas 1990: 135).

Contrary to what has been characterized as the new orthodoxy at the time, this initial step for financial liberalization did not lead to the unification of the credit market under the formal banking system, nor instigate an increase in the level of savings (cf. Fitzgerald and Vos 1989:7). Bringing 'financial repression' to an end did not necessarily lead to a rise in the level of savings in the Turkish context either. On the contrary, total savings in relation to gross national product (GNP) came down from around 20 percent in 1981 to just over 16 percent in 1984 in current prices (cf. Oyan and Aydın 1987: 103; Türel 1993: 164; see also Oyan 1987: 169–170; BEY January 1990: 34). Moreover, the segmented nature of capital markets which were yet to be regulated had been considered as providing a lifeline for the productive sectors which were desperate to get access to external sources of finance in the wake of the austerity policies that had been pursued since January 1980 (BEY July 1982:16). For the dealers functioning in the unorganized secondary market, known as 'bankers' in the Turkish context, would be instrumental in marketing the bonds issued by the corporate sector, thus alleviating, at least partly, its financial difficulties. Indeed, the amount of such bonds issued in 1980 was considered as breaking 'a remarkable record' in value terms over the previous decade, as well as in terms of its share doubling in all bond issues, although still less than a quarter of that of the public sector (TÜSİAD 1981: 77).

As mentioned in Chapter 2, there had already been attempts by the leading banks to establish brokerage houses for facilitating the issuance of bonds by the corporate sector at the peak of the crisis during the late 1970s. By the same token, some major capital groups which did not own a bank, had also established their own brokerage houses, partly because they were not allowed entry into the banking sector (Artun 1983: 77; Sönmez 1982: 188; BEY July 1981: 19; April 1986: 10). With the introduction of CDs, however, there would emerge a new category of dealers trading the CDs issued to them by the banks at a discount. Described as a version of Ponzi-type financing,[4] this caused an intense pressure on interest rates, which in turn provided a fieldday for a variety of formal and informal, large and small players involved who were able to exploit the lack of a proper regulatory framework for the financial sector. Concurrently, the rise of interest rates did not induce borrowers to decrease their leverage, described as distress borrowing, the consequence of which had been a significant rise in the non-performing loans of the banks (Atiyas 1990: 147; Atiyas and Ersel 1996: 105; Ekinci 1996).

Nor for that matter did the rise of interest rates constrain the phenomenal rise in the rate of inflation in the first year of the stabilization programme. As the Turkish government complied with its commitment to the IMF to stop capping the prices of the goods and services produced by the state economic enterprises (SEEs) this in turn propelled the private sector firms to raise their prices, as they were highly dependent on the former as suppliers of intermediate goods and energy. This had been accompanied by a significant reduction in direct central bank credit to SEEs, enabling a rise in the private sector's share in total domestic credit in due course (Celasun and Rodrik 1989: 695). Meanwhile, the corporate sector, having been confronted with the prospect of a squeeze on its profits as a result of austerity policies, justified by the World Bank in order "to restrain the growth of incomes and domestic demand" (World Bank 1983) on the one hand, and the soaring cost of loans it had to borrow on the other, had already started to complain about the impact of the new policy framework on its business activity. There were demands for special treatment from the authorities in charge of economic policy by the representatives of the conglomerates and the Chambers of Commerce and Industry. In particular, they had been looking for 'selective credits' by which they meant preferential rates to be applied to the loans they would be borrowing.[5] To a certain extent, such demands had been met in due course, as the rise in export credits was much faster than total credit expansion (Celasun and Rodrik 1989: 695; Ulagay 1987: 183).

The particular ways in which the tight money policy was implemented meant that it wreaked havoc with the monetarist creed to the extent that the Central Bank was allegedly sidelined as a key agent of monetary policy to manage aggregate demand (BEY January 1981: 23–24; Çölaşan 1983: 243). In fact, a new body, the Money and Credit Board (MCB), established as part of the reorganization of the management of the economy which concentrated authority in the Prime Minister's office, would effectively be in charge of money and credit (Ekzen 1984: 166; Sönmez 1980: 70). For instance, it was MCB that would determine the interest rates to be applied on 'selective credits' as an incentive mechanism, say, for exporters (Başbuğ1980: 32). It also set the minimum requirements to be met for establishing new banks and conditions of entry for the foreign banks (BEY January 1982: 34). These measures would be justified by the archetypal representative of the conglomerates 'that the introduction of market economy does not mean that the authorities need remain out of the picture altogether' (TÜSİAD 1982: vi). It seems that an alibi has also been provided by the propagators of the 'getting prices right' approach by resorting to second-best reasoning as they argued that it is "the form and extent of government intervention, not its complete absence" which is critical in an environment of risks and uncertainties (Lal 1983: 6, 105). Similarly, their Turkish counterparts contended that:

> [t]he dynamics of change in Turkish financial markets in the 1980s has to be sought in the logic and mode of state intervention rather than in its 'degree.'
>
> (Öncü and Gökçe 1991: 100)

The centralization of the decision-making process did not seem to bother the Bretton Woods institutions either, as long as ceilings on Central Bank credits to the public sector, identified as one of the principal conditions of the stand-by agreement, were complied with (World Bank 1983). On the other hand, there were concerns that it would curtail the legislative functions of the Turkish parliament. More pertinently, it would set in train criticisms to the effect that 'getting prices right' was no more than rhetoric which was not matched by the deeds of the policymakers. Indeed, a former chairperson of the Turkish Industrialists and Businessmen's Association (TÜSİAD) and head of a major conglomerate had acknowledged, with the benefit of hindsight, that the implementation of policy measures had caused too much uncertainty, as there were frequent changes in interest rates without consultation with the representatives of business community. However, there were also other prominent representatives of major groups who tended to view these vacillations in policy measures as 'course corrections' along the way.[6] These comments are, no doubt, in line with the general observation that the process of financial liberalization in Turkey coincided with a period of macroeconomic uncertainty and arbitrariness in policymaking (Kocabaşoğlu et al. 2001: 559; Boratav et al. 1995: 10).

As the cut-throat competition accelerated between the large and small banks to attract funds from the public, there was a further attempt by the leading banks to re-establish order, so to speak, in the aftermath of the changing political circumstances following the military coup. It was widely reported retrospectively that the large banks led by İşBank (private sector) and Ziraat Bank (public sector) would bring 12 banks to the table to sign a kind of a pact in order to abide by the terms of a new gentlemen's agreement (Aysan 1981; Çölaşan 1983: 127). It turned out to be an abortive attempt as İşBank announced only a month later that it considered both the June and December 1980 agreements null and void on the grounds that there were free riders within the banking community (Çölaşan 1983: 148). Consequently, İşBank would take the lead in raising interest rate on time deposits which would be an impulse for both the other banks and the 'bankers' to join the race. The upshot was effectively a variegated structure of the money market, with comparatively very low interest rates on sight/demand deposits, and no interest paid on commercial deposits.

Curiously, the Capital Markets Law (Law no. 2499) passed by the military regime in July 1981, as prescribed by World Bank's SAL II, in order to promote the development of financial markets along market-oriented principles, had effectively empowered the banks, as it entitled them to the monopoly of establishing mutual funds and investment trusts (Keyder 1992: 76; World Bank 1984).[7] However, this law was strongly criticized by the representatives of the corporate sector for failing to respond to the major problem of the corporate sector, namely, undercapitalization. Eradication of this inadequacy was, in turn, considered essential, if the corporate sector was to take the lead in undertaking the investments deemed vital for the industrialization of the country in a market-based financial system. There was also further criticism that the Capital Market Board, (CMB) established in February 1982, to implement the new Capital Market Law and to supervise all institutions operating in the securities market, was not envisaged by the law to function as an autonomous body, as it was to be regulated by the Ministry of Finance (BEY October 1981: 28, 14).

However, the new law did not affect the rush to acquire banks by many capital groups in the context of a highly speculative environment, as bank ownership "became the *sine qua non* of comparative advantage in financial markets" (Öncü and Gökçe 1991: 106). While there was still no entry into the banking system, the number of holding banks rose from 11 to 18 during 1980–82 (Artun 1985: 48).[8] A decision by the MCB (Decision no.55) in late 1981 had been identified as one important factor that contributed to the maintenance of the oligopolistic structure of the banking sector, by toughening the conditions of entry into the sector (ITO 1990: 11). It is to be noted, however, that there would be a steady increase in the number of foreign banks from four in 1979 to nine at the end of 1982 (Akgüç 1983: 59), as Law no. 2499 enabled foreign capital to buy securities in Turkish lira and repatriate profits freely.

By early 1982, the fieldday was over as the vast majority of the 'bankers' had been crushed by the devastating social and economic effects exerted on savers who had been lured into this 'bonanza' by channelling their savings to them.[9] Among the casualties, there were also quite a few newly acquired holding banks, thus bringing down the number of such banks to 14. Decree no. 28 of July 1979 had been instrumental for the military regime government in taking over these banks during the summer of 1982. The volatility of the situation, dubbed as the bankers' crisis, in the context of a military regime, also had a political fallout as Turgut Özal, known as the architect of the structural adjustment process from January 1980 onwards, had to resign from the government in July 1982 in which he was serving as deputy prime minister in charge of the economy. In fact, it would take more than a year to develop institutional mechanisms for a new regulatory framework by the military regime, with the appointment of a new economic team in charge of monetary and fiscal policies. Blatantly, the new economic team had portrayed 1982 as "another positive period in the structural adjustment process despite the chain of bankruptcies among the money brokers" (World Bank 1983). The new team would issue a series of decrees to reorganize the money markets and the banking sector. The decree issued in December 1982, to be effective from 1 January 1983, had put the banking sector once more in a central position in the determination of the interest rates.[10] Accordingly, interest rates on deposits would be determined by nine leading banks (ranked in terms of their share of total deposits). But the banks would be circumscribed by the variegated structure of the interest rates of which they would notify the Central Bank to be announced in the official gazette (Akgüç 1987: 204; ITO 1990: 14).

This decision, on the one hand, revived the criticisms about the formation of a cartel to determine the price of money, thereby a violation of market-based system, i.e., against the principle of getting prices right.[11] On the other hand, it was considered an inevitable decision to prevent a debacle for the corporate sector, including its integral component: that is, the banking sector (Cansen 1983: 36). In particular, it was held that it would be beneficial for the holding groups by reducing their costs of borrowing (BEY July 1983: 24). For the crisis was explained as the rise of deposit interest rates at abnormally high levels by the banks in competition with the 'bankers', causing high intermediation costs for the banking system which put their profitability at risk.

Moreover, the bank liquidity requirements, the rules of which showed substantial variation in time, were considered another important factor in increasing the intermediation costs of the banks. For that purpose, a unified reserve requirement system had been put in place in early 1983 (Keyder 1992: 72).[12] According to the World Bank, it was imperative to introduce measures designed to lower the cost of credit, along with those that would enable firms to revalue assets without initial tax liability, in order to respond to the undercapitalization problem of the corporate sector (World Bank 1983). So, overall, the decision to reduce and/or put a cap on interest rates was considered essentially as a bailing-out mechanism for the banks and *ipso facto* for the manufacturing industry, which was highly dependent on the banking sector for its survival, given its lack of equity capital in an inflationary environment. In fact, there had been a further reduction of interest rates from July 1983 onwards by the Ministry of Finance on both credits and deposits, while maintaining the already increased rate on sight/demand deposits intact (BEY July 1983: 60; December 1983: 44). Moreover, the Central Bank was instrumental in these bailing-out operations as there had been significant amounts transferred to the private sector through the reductions in reserve requirements and liquidity ratios, in order to alleviate the difficulties of some banks and enterprises (World Bank 1984; BEY December 1983: 44; March 1984: 20, 27). No less saliently, Law no. 2791 enacted by the military regime in January 1983 entailed critical amendments to the relevant taxation legislation in order to pave the way for the corporate sector to revalue its assets annually. (BEY December 1983: 44; Oyan 1987: 113).

Among the critical legislation put in place by the military regime, specific mention should be made of Decree on Banks no.70 in July 1983, coming in the wake of a new one-year stand-by agreement with the IMF upon the completion of the three-year arrangement made in June 1980. This decree would effectively function as a new legal framework for the banking sector in line with the recommendations of the World Bank (World Bank 1984), but without formally replacing the 1958 Banking Law. In a sense, the new economic team of the military regime was pursuing the same method of making significant amendments to the latter law by way of decree, as had been attempted prior to the January 1980 stabilization programme (see Chapter 2). Among the problems confronting the banking sector that Decree no.70 aimed to overcome, was the deterioration of financial structures of the banks, their undercapitalization in particular, and the loss of public confidence in banks and financial institutions (World Bank 1983). Hence a deposit insurance scheme in the institutional form of the Savings Deposit Insurance Fund (SDIF) was established to restore confidence in the banking system, while measures were introduced to strengthen the role of the Central Bank in the supervision of the banking sector. The SDIF replaced the Banks Liquidation Fund, a legacy of the banking crisis of the early 1960s, as mentioned in Chapter 2.[13] It is also noteworthy that the preamble of Decree no.70 identified increasing concentration and deterioration of the competitive environment in the banking industry as one of the reasons for the need to restructure the banking system. With that in mind, it set itself the task of making the necessary arrangements for foreign bank entry into the Turkish banking sector, a process in train since 1980, nonetheless duly celebrated by the World Bank as a stimulus for 'bank competition' (World Bank 1984).

Decree no. 70 aimed to redefine the relationship between the banks and the corporations by introducing new criteria such as limiting the provision of credit to the firms within the group by a holding bank with the total equity of the bank concerned (see Chapter 2). However, while Decree no. 28 of July 1979 had intended to constrain the so-called holding banking by bringing limits on the banks' participation in the corporations and the provision of credits to the firms within the group by holding banks, Decree no. 70 removed the former and widely extended the latter (cf. ITO 1990: 11; Kocabaşoğlu et al. 2001: 600; Taşçıoğlu 1998: 109). By explicitly stating that the limits introduced by Decree no. 28 for bank ownership would be lifted, it paved the way for new entries into the banking system. However, another piece of legislation, Decree no. 90 enacted by the military regime in October 1983 was also critical in this respect.[14] This was purportedly to outlaw usury by setting regulatory principles for lending activities. However, as it specified that the provisions of that decree would *not* apply to the banks in particular, it paved the way for the entrenchment of what came to be known as 'connected lending' between the banks and the groups which they belong to. Ironically, this 'connected lending' would later be seen as a problem to be dealt with: that is, as a cause of renewed crisis. Hence, if the ultimate aim was "to reduce the interlocking between banks and corporations" as prescribed by the World Bank, these set of decrees had rather the opposite effect (World Bank 1983; Kocabaşoğlu et al. 2001: 599–600; cf. Akgüç 1987: 206). The number of capital groups with bank ownership rose more than twofold, from 14 in 1984 to 34 in 1989.

Overall, it can be concluded that the first phase of financial liberalization in Turkey did not produce an outcome that has been highlighted as a defining feature of financialization (cf. Lapavitsas 2009, 2011). That is to say, commercial banks have *not* become more distant from industrial and commercial capital, notwithstanding the objectives reflected in the wording of World Bank's SALs and Decree no.70 to the contrary. The Turkish experience does not provide evidence for the detachment and/or the severance of financial from productive capital (cf. Wood 2007). Indeed, it emerges as a distinct modality of financialization that would not entail such a detachment, but rather the blurring of frontiers between financial and non-financial activities *within* the non-financial corporations too (cf. Serfati 2011; Türel 2009: 154), as the evolving process of financial liberalization revealed in its successive phases.

Second Phase of Financial Liberalization 1983–89: Market-oriented Institutionalization of a Bank-based Financial System

A cursory review of the relevant literature on the Turkish experience of financial liberalization would indicate the period from late 1982 onwards as one of the institutionalization of financial deepening, with an emphasis on the key role played by the banking sector fitfully being described as essentially comprising universal banks (cf. Kocabaşoğlu et al. 2001: 570–571; Türel 1993: 126; Marois 2012: 109). There was also an emphasis on the need for the development of an efficient capital market 'to act as a stimulus to increased bank efficiency' (World Bank 1984). Indeed, one of the final acts of the military regime before the transition to civilian rule was the enactment of Decree no. 91 for the establishment of İstanbul Stock Exchange (İSE) in October 1983, to further promote the development of financial markets along market-oriented principles. Decree no. 91 replaced the old law for the Securities and Stock Market (Law no. 1447) dating back to 1929. Thereby, securities markets that could hitherto be established with the decision of the government, could now be established by the Ministry of Finance on the proposal of CMB. But İSE, which had become inactive in the wake of the bankers' crisis, would not be able to start trading until 1986 (Pehlivan and Kirkpatrick 1992).

One of the priorities of the incoming Anavatan Partisi (Motherland Party) government led by Turgut Özal after the November 1983 general elections, was to renew its credentials as one that adhered to market-oriented reforms, while setting itself the task of fighting inflation. It also felt the need to distance itself from its predecessor team of economic management under the military regime. With that in mind, it would request the cancellation of the existing stand-by arrangement and its replacement with a new one-year arrangement by the IMF. The latter, in turn, would duly approve it in April 1984, as "the conditions of the new Standby" were "broadly similar to the previous one".[15] What had been prescribed, in fact, was yet another period of austerity, considered as "an essential prerequisite for a return to a sustainable growth path" (World Bank 1984). However, the implementation of IMF-guided stabilization programmes consecutively during 1980–85 was not accompanied by a contraction in the Turkish economy. In fact, there had been on average economic growth of nearly 5 per cent per annum which was maintained until 1988, even taking into account the economic contraction of 2.8 per cent in 1980. While this seemed to be an exception in the light of several other countries' experiences that pursued similar programmes, it was contended that the Turkish case should not be considered a 'success', or an exemplary case, as this growth was achieved at the expense of rising foreign debt. That is, it was mainly due to a steady inflow of foreign savings that indicated the policymakers' success in gaining the extraordinary support of international financial circles (Boratav 2004:159–161). Put differently, the Özal government's real achievement was to gain creditworthiness in the eyes of potential lenders to the Turkish economy (Şenses 1991; Yalman 2009: 280).

Ironically, the 1930 Law for Protecting the Value of Turkish Currency (Law no. 1567) (see Chapter 2) was still in effect during the first decade of financial liberalization in the 1980s when the real effective depreciation of the national currency was instrumental in gaining the competitive edge for the export orientation of the manufacturing industry. A series of decrees from late 1983 onwards under Law no. 1567 became important steps in the continuation of the process of financial liberalization, as well as introducing new institutional arrangements to prepare the transition to a market-based financial system. Decree no. 28 dated 28 December 1983 and Decree no. 30 enacted in July 1984, which replaced the former under the same law were, in particular, critical initiatives for setting the stage for external financial liberalization (Altınkemer and Ekinci 1992). The saliency of the latter had already been underlined by the World Bank, as it was anticipated that the capital account would begin to come under the pressure of repayments of rescheduled external debt from 1984 onwards (World Bank 1983). In fact, the World Bank was instrumental in initiating a 'medium term strategy' that would link the short-run objectives of a stabilization plan with a longer-run development plan. The second half of the decade would thus witness a return to five-year development plans with the adoption of the Fifth Five-Year Development Plan (1985–89). It was in line with the adjustment-with-growth maxim, as the World Bank itself was directly involved in the formulation of it (Yalman 2009: 252). Turkey would in fact become 'the darling of the Bank', as its total commitments exceeded a billion US dollars a year during the three-year period following the termination of the IMF stand-by agreement in 1985, making the Turkish portfolio the fifth-largest in the Bank by 1988 (World Bank 2006). In particular, the Financial Sector Adjustment Credit Agreement under SAL V in May 1986 made the related loan releases conditional on the radical restructurings proposed in financial institutions, instruments and policies (Ekzen 2004: 305; Türel 2009: 145).

Furthermore, the priority as envisaged in the SAL V was to reduce high real interest rates through a reduction in the operating costs of the banking system, conceived within the broader framework of the continuation of a stabilization programme,in order to reduce inflation 'to a level which will make interest rates attractive enough to encourage the growth of private investment' (World Bank 1984). However, having authorized the Central Bank to determine the interest rates on deposits, the Özal government had already pushed for an increase of interest rates on deposits on the grounds that they fell below the rate of inflation during 1983 (World Bank 1984). This paved the way for a partial liberalization, as the commercial banks became largely free to determine their own lending rates. These vacillations had, in turn, caused much consternation about the resulting uncertainty.[16] In particular, given the high rates of interest on bank credits, the financing requirements of the corporate sector became more and more acute, while the commercial banking system reduced its already low medium- and long-term credits to total credits ratio during 1982–88 (Ersel and Öztürk 1990). The spread between the average cost of deposits and the average cost of credits more than doubled during 1982–86 (Akyüz 1990: 111) which, in turn, meant the opposite of what had been anticipated by the World Bank.

The second phase of financial liberalization would thus witness frequent changes, at times on a monthly basis, in the ways in which interest rates were determined, as well as accompanying changes in reserve requirements and liquidity ratios, which were critical factors affecting the operating costs of the banking system (cf. Keyder 1992; Şenses 1991). In fact, there seemed to be an inverse relationship between the reserve requirements and liquidity ratios, reflecting a significant shift in the Özal government's policy of financing public deficit. If changes in the ways of determining interest rates was one key aspect of the financial liberalization process, another no less salient aspect concerned the determination of the exchange rate. In fact, a regime of managing real foreign exchange rates by frequent exchange rate adjustments had already been put into practice from May 1981 onwards. This policy of a daily adjusted crawling peg that was continued until 1989, had been instrumental in achieving real depreciation of the currency as a means of export promotion, which in turn resulted in currency substitution (Ekinci 1996). However, there were important shifts in the ways in which this policy of pursuing a 'realistic' exchange rate was put into effect, as it entailed a series of zigzags regarding the relationship between the authorities and the banking community. As the downside of this currency depreciation-based policy of export promotion was the increase in the relative size of the debt service, the Özal government would opt for domestic borrowing as the main mechanism to cope with the fiscal disequilibrium (Celasun and Rodrik 1989: 740). In line with this new policy of financing the deficit by domestic borrowing from 1985 onwards, the Central Bank tended to reduce reserve requirements, while liquidity ratios were raised to facilitate the government's borrowing from the financial markets by issuing treasury bonds with lucrative short-term returns (cf. Arın 2000: 277; Binay and Kunter 1998; Kepenek and Yentürk 2003: 260). Moreover, the new policy was grounded on a further entrenchment of the power of the executive at the expense of the legislature, as the budget law of 1985 authorized the Treasury with the power to borrow from the financial markets (Ekzen 1999: 411). Consequently, the principal of the debts incurred would not be reflected in the annual state budgets (Oyan 1997: 71). Furthermore, the Özal government would increasingly resort to the use of Extra Budgetary Funds (EBFs) as import surcharges or export subsidies, thereby setting in train a regime of multiple exchange rates in order to create and transfer funds to favoured sectors and/or firms and/or individuals (Rodrik 1990; Yalman 2009: 273–274). These were, in turn, criticized for giving discretionary power to the political authority in the allocation of a scarce resource, namely, foreign exchange earnings.

While it was observed that the pursuit of the interest rate policy prevented the development ofa capital market during the first half of the decade, thereby augmenting the dominance of the banking sector in the financial sector

(Akyüz 1985: 77), the issue of treasury bonds to be subscribed by the public at competitive interest rates was considered as a means of furthering the development of the capital market by the World Bank's SAL V programme (World Bank 1984). However, as the bulk of public debt carried a maturity of one year or less, new debt was issued primarily to roll over the old debt. In fact, the banking sector became the main interlocutor of the auction system established for government securities from 1985 onwards, as it could hold these as part of its liquidity requirement (cf. Arın 2000: 277; Binay and Kunter 1998; Rodrik 1990). However, the banks tended to increase interest rates on loans, as they increasingly faced a liquidity crisis as there was a movement away from deposit accounts towards treasury bonds, which was propelled by the reduction of interest rates on deposits (BEY October 1986).

Commercial banks were also allowed to accept foreign currency deposits from the residents of the country and to engage in foreign transactions. Through the communiqués that followed Decrees 28 and 30, the commercial banks authorized to conduct such transactions were identified.[17] Thereby, the banking system was able to expand by relying on foreign exchange denominated instruments, indicating a strong currency substitution effect (Ersel and Öztürk 1990). More pertinently, the capability to hold foreign currency deposits (FCDs) was considered as providing a lifeline for the banking community in general, as FCDs turned out to be the major mechanism for the deepening of the financial system (Kocabaşoğlu et al. 2001:574).[18] While these developments were generally perceived as signifiers of the liberalization of the foreign exchange regime, these decrees were also criticized for not being in line with the 'getting prices right' approach, as it had centralized the role of the Central Bank in the determination of exchange rate.[19]

This set in train a process of liberalization that was made possible as a result of the government's decision in 1985 to drop 'the general derogation' that was granted to Organisation for Economic Co-operation and Development (OECD) members in the OECD Code of Liberalisation of Capital Movements (Griffith-Jones et al. 2000).[20] In fact, the banks had been allowed by the Central Bank to determine the exchange rates in their purchase and sale of foreign currency from mid-1985 onwards. They had also been given the opportunity to provide export credits for their customers by borrowing short-term loans from international financial markets. In less than a year, however, the so-called 14 March 1986 decisions effectively brought to an end the determination of exchange rates by the banks, along with the decision to devalue the Turkish lira by about 5.25 per cent (BEY April 1986: 55). Once again this caused a wave of criticism that this measure was a retreat from a market-based system of determining prices, in this case, that of foreign exchange. They were also required to allocate reserve requirements for foreign exchange deposit accounts, starting from 31 December 1985, in a retroactive manner (Binay and Kunter 1998). The Central Bank decision that banks had to sell 20 per cent of their foreign exchange earnings to the Central Bank from 1 January 1986 had created cut-throat competition between the banks, forcing the small banks to obtain foreign exchange from the black market. This, in turn, had caused a widening difference between the rates announced by the Central Bank and those adopted by the banks, hence the decision to devalue. The reason for this abrupt change of policy stemmed from the government's concern to maintain a certain level of foreign exchange reserves. [21] For it had started to borrow short term in order to find the necessary foreign exchange to pay its long-term foreign debt, as there had been a steady rise in the share of short-term debt as a proportion of total debt (BEY May 1986: 18; Rodrik 1990).

While pre-occupied with the dual objectives of establishing its credentials as a pro-market administration and distancing itself from its predecessor, the Özal government would maintain for more than a year the legislative framework pertaining to the banking sector that it inherited from the military regime. And when it eventually enacted a new banking law (Law no. 3182) in April 1985, it would be more or less the transformation of Decree no. 70 into a law. Moreover, the new law also authorized the government to determine the lower and upper limits for interest rates on deposits, as well as to decide the partial or full liberalization of these rates. The government could, in turn, authorize the Central Bank to take such decisions, if it deemed it necessary to do so. While the new law was purportedly designed to bring the Turkish financial apparatus more in line with the Bank for International Settlements requirements, by instituting stronger capital adequacy and non-performing loan provisions (Ekinci 1996; Marois 2012: 106), it had effectively procured the bank-based nature of the Turkish financial system in which the profitability of the banks were maintained, notwithstanding the high costs of intermediation (Atiyas and Ersel 1996: 119; Sönmez 2001: 271).[22]

The new entry into the banking system which had been already facilitated by Decree no. 70 would be accelerated, along with the continued interest of the foreign banks in the Turkish market.[23] While the impact of foreign entry on the competitiveness of the banking sector in Turkey was found to be insignificant, contrary to McKinnon-Shaw's hypothesis (cf. Atiyas and Ersel 1996: 119; Pehlivan and Kirkpatrick 1992), the foreign banks were carving a lucrative niche for themselves in trade finance and funding operations at a time of intense export promotion. However, the Turkish case could be identified as an early, if not, a pioneering example in this regard, to the extent that the expansion of foreign banks into the domestic market through their involvement in activities unrelated to lending such as trade finance is considered an important aspect of financialization in developing countries (Bonizzi 2014). In fact, as trade finance was considered as a form of risk mitigation, the Turkish capital groups would also join in, thereby giving birth to a new generation of 'trade-finance banks', either in joint ventures with foreign banks or independently (Öncü and Gökçe 1991: 113).

While foreign bank entry did not significantly reduce the concentration ratio of the domestic banking sector (Pehlivan and Kirkpatrick 1992), it was observed that there had been a decline in the concentration ratios for private banks measured by the share of the three largest banks in total assets, (Atiyas and Ersel 1996: 115). However, the dominance of large state banks along with that of the holding banks, enabled by Law no. 3182 which either kept the related articles of Decree no. 70 intact or even further eased them, maintained the oligopolistic structure of the banking industry. Last but not the least, this second phase of financial liberalization had witnessed a new kind of financial institution, namely, 'Special Finance Houses' entering the arena by a decision of the Özal government immediately after taking office in December 1983.[24] Two of these Islamic, non-interest finance houses would start their operations from 1985 onwards and with a communiqué (dated 13 November 1985) on the basis of Decree no. 30, they were allowed along with the banks to engage in foreign transactions.

Although there was no doubt that a process of 'financial deepening' had been taking place, whether it resulted in the increased efficiency of the financial system became rather debatable (cf. Boratav et al. 1996; Türel 1993). Nor did it imply "a shift of portfolio selection from unproductive assets to those favouring fixed capital formation", once again contradicting the McKinnon-Shaw hypothesis (Köse and Yeldan 1996: 55). Indeed, the process of external financial liberalization seemed to have the dual effect of driving the funds away from productive investments and strengthening the position of the commercial banks, and *ipso facto* of the groups, by making them the key agents of the money markets in general and the foreign exchange market in particular (Yalman 2009: 284–285). This was said to make the banks 'the agents of the debtors', as it led to a concentration of loans to companies within the groups in the loan portfolios of the banks concerned (Akçaoğlu 1998: 86; World Bank 2000b). While this was a process to be augmented with a series of institutional changes, starting with the establishment of the Interbank Money Market, to be followed by Foreign Exchange Market within the Central Bank in 1986, it did not preclude the continuation of erratic policy changes in regards to the determination of both exchange and interest rates.

While the growth rate of credit extended to the private sector consistently exceeded the rate of output growth until 1987, high real interest rates have been considered an important factor by a World Bank study for the "lacklustre performance of private sector investment" (Chibber and van Wijnbergen 1988). Although there was a rise in private savings in the second half of the decade, this shift was accounted for as a result of the state functioning as an 'asymmetric risk holder' in the private sector's investment decisions in a variety of ways. On the one hand, incentives provided by the EBFs, especially for mass housing projects, tilted the composition of private investment in favour of non-tradables such as housing (Chibber and van Wijnbergen 1988). On the other hand, the shift in the Özal government's policy of financing public deficit that caused a decline in public savings while increasing the public sector debt were salient mechanisms in producing this outcome (cf. Arın 2000: 278; Celasun and Rodrik 1989: 747; Ersel and Öztürk 1990). Hence the World Bank was becoming "increasingly concerned" that the failure of the government "to get the macroeconomy under control ... was likely to lead to a crisis" (World Bank 2006).

If not a major crisis, the acceleration of inflation which, in turn, instigated a flight away from the Turkish lira forced the Özal government to resort to the adoption of stabilization measures, known as the 4 February 1988 decisions (Binay and Kunter 1998; Öniş 1991). Banks were thus authorized to set interest rates freely, but subject to maximum rates determined by the central bank (Şenses 1991). Indeed, the determination of interest rates on one-year deposits which had been left to the market by the Özal government on July 1987, would be capped at 65 percent following the 4 February 1988 decisions, while interest rates on credits were said to be soaring up to double that figure (BEY March 1988: 56). By the beginning of the following year, as the determination of interest rates on all kinds of deposits would be left to the initiative of the banks, there would be a differential on interest rates on one-year deposits ranging between 52 per cent and 85 per cent, as banks competed with each other to attract customers, while those on credit rose to 150 per cent (BEY April 1989).

It is also necessary to put this 'lacklustre' investment performance into context by recalling the series of laws enacted by the Özal government. In particular, the changes introduced in the taxation system and the efforts made to bolster the equity structure of the indebted corporations need to be underlined. On the one hand, 'the illiquidity problems' of the private sector were said to have 'required a relief in corporate taxes' (Celasun and Rodrik 1989: 749). On the other hand, the problem of non-performing loans would intensify the tensions between the creditor banks and the indebted corporations. Law no. 3332 (dated 31 March 1987) was an attempt to find a mutually satisfactory solution to this problem. Dubbed as 'the law for bailingout firms' (*şirket kurtarma kanunu*), it paved the way for the creditor banks to become majority shareholders in the indebted corporations (BEY May 1987: 59; Ulagay 1987: 197), thereby augmenting the closely knit relations between the banking sector and non-financial corporations.

Meanwhile, the changes introduced in the taxation system not only had a pro-capital, and anti-labour character, by undermining the progressive character of the income taxation and making the country a tax haven for the conglomerates and their shareholders (Boratav 2004: 154; Oyan 1987: 147–148).[25] But Law no. 3239 in particular was also criticized for bolstering the executive at the expense of the legislature, by giving all the powers to the government to initiate all the changes that it deemed necessary in the taxation system. Furthermore, it encouraged the issuing of bonds by the corporate sector, as it allowed the total amount of bonds issued to be deducted from the taxable revenues of the corporations concerned, asking those firms to pay 10 per cent withholding tax only. As a further incentive for the groups, a new financial instrument (*finansman bonosu*)—known in the Anglo-Saxon world as 'commercial paper'—was introduced in late 1986 to alleviate their financial difficulties, given the high rates of interest on bank credits (BEY December

1986). None the less, it was observed that the share of direct financing (i.e. bonds and finance bills) in total external funds was negligible during the second phase of financial liberalization, reflecting the underdeveloped nature of the private securities market. While the corporate sector relied more on its own resources, it tended to lean on short-term funds in its external financing (Ersel and Öztürk 1990).

In short, what the Turkish experience of financial liberalization highlighted, especially in its second phase, is that the increase in public debt and the use of incentive mechanisms ranging from several subsidy and bailing-out schemes, to a series of tax policy changes, were indicative of a transfer of resources to the corporate sector (Yalman 2009: 259). This is why it is important to underline the fact that the state continued to function as an 'asymmetric risk holder' for the corporate sector during the process of financial liberalization.

Third Phase 1989–2000: Capital Account Liberalisation and the Era of Financial Crises

There seems to be a convergence of opinion that the decision to liberalize the capital account in mid-1989 was the critical and final step to complete the process of financial liberalization (cf. Alper and Öniş 2003; Balkan and Yeldan 2002; Denizer 2000). It was put into effect by the outgoing Özal government with Decree no.32 issued on the basis of the extension of the mandate, prescribed by Law no. 1567. It thereby replaced Decree no. 30 which had set in train the second phase of financial liberalization. In fact, it put an end to the practice of implementing policy measures purportedly in compliance with the original objectives of Law no. 1567 as it paved the way for the convertibility of the Turkish lira.[26]

However, not only the timing of the decision was controversial, but also its consequences would be found wanting. According to those involved in the policymaking process at the time, it was a 'political decision' (Birand and Yalçın 2001: 334). While it was going to be criticized as a 'premature decision in the presence of pervasive macroeconomic instability and a severely under-regulated financial system' (Ersel 1996; Denizer et al. 2000), the political rationale behind this decision, it was argued, stemmed from the need to put an end to such instability. In the wake of February 1988 stabilization measures, it was reckoned that the ensuing convertibility of the Turkish lira would be essential to pave the way for a fully functioning market economy that would forestall the need for stabilization measures in the future (Birand and Yalçın 2001: 327).[27] In other words, the inability to cope with the fiscal adjustment was the underlying reason for this 'political decision' which was, apparently, taken against the advice of the Central Bank (Ersel 1996; Atiyas 2014). Paradoxically, it also meant a reversal in policy as the real effective appreciation of the national currency became an instrument to attract the so-called 'hot money flows'. This was said to be a process already initiated in the aftermath of the February 1988 stabilization measures, as the rate of depreciation of the Turkish lira was less than half of the rate of inflation for the 12 months preceding the decision to issue Decree no.32 (Rodrik 1990).

If an implicit objective was to facilitate the financing of public sector deficits without crowding-out private investment, as alleged at the time, the outcome turned out to be aggravating the fiscal problem (cf. Akyüz and Boratav 2003; Ersel 1996). For the dependence on the speculative short-term capital flows necessitated a higher return on domestic assets compared with the rate of nominal depreciation of the Turkish lira (Balkan and Yeldan 2002: 47). The shift of the financing of public sector deficit from the Central Bank to Government Debt Instruments (GDIs) by the Treasury,[28] including foreign currency-denominated bonds, from the mid-1980s onwards, was already giving rise to substantial increases of interest burden on public finance. With the completion of the final phase of financial liberalization, however, the short-term capital inflows turned out to be the basic mechanism for the financing of the public sector deficits. Thus, it signified the increasing dependence of the economy on private financial sources. In due course, what has been noted as a manifestation of financialization in the case of the USA would be equally pertinent for the Turkish case, as "high interest rates discouraged nonfinancial firms from borrowing to finance productive investment and instead directed corporate treasurers toward higher-yielding financial assets that could return invested capital more quickly" (Krippner 2011: 143).

Put differently, the following decade would witness a series of episodes that would disappoint the advocates of the policies of financial liberalization in general, and of capital account liberalization in particular, as the lynchpin of political and economic stability.[29] It is noteworthy that the World Bank seemed to be still preoccupied with "the primary objective of helping Turkey move to a path of sustained growth" (World Bank 2003b), as it would undertake a series of soul-searching studies after two decades of persistent implementation of the neoliberal policy agenda. The 1990s, perceived largely as 'a lost decade for Turkey'as in per capita terms Turkish gross domestic product (GDP) was only at around its 1990 level by the end of the decade (Yeldan 2002; Bedirhanoğlu and Yalman 2010: 115), would be characterized as an era during which Turkey could not realize its "potential to be a leader among emerging markets" (World Bank 2000a). In fact, the World Bank had decided back in 1989 "not to provide additional adjustment loans until Turkey could demonstrate progress on the structural problems destabilizing its economy" (World Bank 2005). Hence, previous attempts at stabilization would be found wanting as "they did not address the structural sources of the fiscal deficit". Among the structural reforms considered necessary was "financial sector reform" that would not only raise the efficiency of financial intermediation, but also contribute to increasing the productivity of the real sector. Thus, "a durable fiscal adjustment aimed at taming high inflation and breaking the grip of high real interest rates that constrain growth" was imperative (World Bank 2000a).

Paradoxically, these observations seem to provide supporting evidence for the contention—developed by those critical of neoliberal policy agenda—that 'financial liberalization resulted in a bifurcation of the financial system from the real economy' (Arın 2000: 275). This was a tendency that observers claimed was emerging throughout the 1990's, as "banking and financial institutions became disengaged from financing real production activities to the point where they became the dominant faction within capital and, therefore, able to manipulate the accumulation patterns" (Cizre and Yeldan 2005). In other words, the Turkish economy was said to be characterized by one of the defining features of financialization, to which I have alluded above: the detachment and/or the severance of financial from productive capital (cf. Lapavitsas 2009, 2011). However, by contrast, 'the breaking down of the earlier separation of activities between the financial and non-financial operations of the corporations' organized as 'holding companies' has been increasingly recognized as a significant feature of financialization (Chesnais 2016: 109, 112). Indeed, the characterization of the Turkish financial sector by the World Bank makes it quite clear that what is at issue is far from being a disengagement of financial capital from industrial capital. The following is the acknowledgement by the World Bank of the characteristics of Turkish capital groups which have already been delineated in Chapter 2:

> The Turkish financial sector consists in large part of financial-industrial conglomerates. Some of these have commercial banks at the center of their groups, surrounded by both financial and non-financial subsidiaries. Others are organized as holding companies owning banks and other financial and/or nonfinancial businesses, either directly or through parent-subsidiary structures. There are significant intra-group transactions and balances within these conglomerates, and many group companies can have loan and equity exposures to the same entities outside the group.
>
> (World Bank 2003a)

The post-1989 era had also witnessed a proliferation in the number of commercial banks, as bank ownership was perceived as a source of lucrative profits to be made either from trading GDIs or from the so-called 'connected lending' opportunities within the capital groups concerned (Güngen 2012: 257; Sönmez 2001: 271; Sönmez 2009: 53), while the banking sector was said to be receding from its basic function of intermediation (BRSA 2010).[30] Banks were said to refrain from lending in order to avoid increasing default risk in the corporate sector, as they found a secure alternative in the form of GDIs (Sak 1995: 118). While it had been the policy of some major Turkish conglomerates not to own a bank and/or a financing arm until the mid-1980s, there seems to have been a major shift in this regard, giving rise to the establishment of a series of new banks, many of which lacked 'critical size' in terms of capital adequacy and other related criteria in the following decade. In a sense, bank ownership came to signify a *quid pro quo* for the entry of newcomers into this rather privileged segment of the Turkish financial sector, as "banks became heavily dependent on interest earnings from government securities" (World Bank 2006). The 1990s would also witness a rising interest on the part of foreign capital that seemed to create a new niche for itself, as reflected in the increasing number of investment banks in Turkey (BRSA 2010; Ekzen 2004: 313).

However, this rush to establish new banks would be a rather hard experiment for many of the newcomers, which would reveal, in turn, the institutional weaknesses of the Turkish banking system. In fact, while the number of commercial banks would increase from 52 in 1988 to 62 in 1999, and that of investment banks from 10 to 19 (Ekzen 2004: 313; Yayla et al. 2008), out of the 22 new banks established during the 1990s, only 13 would survive by the end of the decade. Such culling of banks would not, however, be circumscribed by the new entries, as the total would reach 18, including both public and private commercial banks, some of which had been established in the pre-Second World War era, as well as some foreign-owned investment banks.[31] The deterioration of the banks' financial structures would be accounted for in terms of the tendency to move away from intermediation, coupled with group loans quite often exceeding the legal limits (cf. BRSA 2010; Kocabaşoğlu et al. 2001: 588; Sönmez 2009: 53). The tendency on the part of the commercial banks, both state and private, to borrow abroad in order to purchase government securities and to lend locally was considered as a process of building up problems for the banking sector (World Bank 2005). Interestingly, this phenomenon was characterized as one in which both banks and non-financial firms increasingly acted as 'institutional rentiers' (cf. Boratav et al. 1996; Cizre and Yeldan 2005), thereby diverting resources from productive forms of investment (Öniş 1996: 21).

The 1991 general elections that brought to an end eight years of single-party rule paved the way for successive coalition governments that would rule the country for the next 11 years. Hence, there has since been a predominant tendency to put the blame simply on the mismanagement of the economy by political agents (cf. Ulagay 1994:7; Öniş 1996: 11). Thus, the ensuing economic and financial crises that were experienced intermittently throughout the third phase of financial liberalization are interpreted as mainly resulting from 'policy mistakes' rather than identifying capital account liberalization as the culprit (cf. Ulagay 1994; Özatay 2009).[32] The World Bank tended to adopt such a perspective, summing up the policy making process as "a mix of borrowing and money creation, rather than making the structural changes needed to address the [fiscal] deficit" (World Bank 2000a).[33] In retrospect, there was a concurrence of opinion that the third phase of financial liberalization was prone to a 'crisis of public finance', as high real interest rates led to the debt/GNP ratiosescalating from 11.4 per cent in 1990 to 21.4 per cent in 1997 (cf. Oyan 1997: 65; Sönmez 2004: 269; Türel 2001).

The emphasis had been on monetary policy as market-based liquidity management under the guidance of the Central Bank had become the order of the day (cf. Sak 1995: 113). Indeed, the Central Bank had announced a monetary programme in 1990 as an integral part of a medium-term strategy (1990–94) which aimed to increase the net foreign assets and the share of Turkish lira liabilities, while decreasing the net foreign liability in its balance sheet (cf. Ekinci 1993: 199; Emir et al. 2000; Yülek 1998).[34] It has been acknowledged that both foreign assets and liabilities increased, but the programme failed to prevent the appreciation of the currency (cf. Binay and Kunter 1998; Ekinci 1993).[35] However, it would not be possible to maintain the announcement of a monetary programme in the subsequent years. The uncontrolled increase in foreign assets and currency substitution were considered the basic reason for this eventuality (Yentürk 1999: 100). More pertinently, the Central Bank failed to accumulate the necessary foreign exchange reserves to defend the domestic currency as it refrained from pursuing a policy of sterilized intervention during the 1989–93 period (Emir et al. 2000; Yentürk 1999:101). This may be seen at odds with the general tendency at the time on the part of many emerging economies, especially in Latin America, which sought to sterilize capital inflows through the pursuit of restrictive monetary policies (Eichengreen and Fishlow 1998: 26). However, this was said to be one of the reservations on the part of the Central Bank for the decision to issue Decree no.32, as it reckoned that it would be unrealistic to sterilize the ensuing capital inflows, given the shallowness of the domestic financial market (Ersel 1996: 48).[36] The inclination to bring down domestic interest rates on the part of the coalition government during 1992–93 seemed to be another factor for refraining from sterilization policies as the latter is said to prevent domestic short-term interest rates from converging towards international levels (cf. Reinhart and Reinhart 1998: 122; Yentürk 1999: 95).[37]

It is also noteworthy, however, that the institutional representatives of the capital groups were also critical of the economic policies pursued since the late 1980s. TÜSİAD would repeatedly call for a medium-term stabilization programme that should be prepared in concert with the representatives of private sector in order to establish economic and financial stability by bringing inflation under control (TÜSİAD 1992; 1994). Such calls would certainly undercut the political rationale for the convertibility of the Turkish lira, as it had become clear that achieving that objective was far from establishing the basis for economic stability. However, there were other representatives of the Turkish business community such as the then chairperson of Istanbul Chamber of Industry who would recommend a monetary policy that would put an end to the overvalued Turkish lira/high real interest rate spiral, characteristic of the post-1989 era in general. For in their view, this spiral had not only aggravated the fiscal crisis of the state, but also had detrimental consequences for those industrialists who were not part of the capital groups (cf. Ulagay 1994: 93–94, 126; Boratav 2004: 168). As large fiscal deficits led to high public sector borrowing requirements and high real interest rates, self-financing seemed to be order of the day for those who had the necessary means to do so. Hence, the relatively low ratio of credit to the private sector as a share of

GDP, in comparative terms (Türel 2004: 301; World Bank 2000b). More pertinently, the ensuing real appreciation of the Turkish lira, in order to attract capital inflows, was said to reduce the profitability of investment in tradable goods, thus further depressing private firms' willingness to invest in export-oriented industries (Rodrik 2009).

In this context, there were a series of institutional developments that would seek, on the one hand, to contribute to the deepening of financial markets, and on the other, to alleviate the dearth of funding for those segments of the corporate sector that did not have any organic relationship with financial capital. For the realization of the latter objective, two new institutions were established: KOSGEB (Small and Medium Industry Development Organization) in 1990; and the Credit Guarantee Fund in 1991 to develop policies specific to small and medium-sized enterprises, and provide the necessary funding for their implementation, respectively.[38] As for the former objective, banks and non-bank financial institutions would be provided a series of incentives with the amendments made to the Capital Market Law and relevant tax legislation. In 1991 offshore banking was encouraged by exempting such banks from being subjected to reserve requirements and liquidity ratios for the deposit accounts to be opened by the banks in Turkey and/or by non-residents (TÜSİAD 1992). By the same token, banks were allowed to issue asset-based securities that would not be subjected to reserve requirements and liquidity ratios in 1992, with the aim of bringing down their costs (TÜSİAD 1993). The earlier monopoly of the banks to establish mutual funds was also brought to an end by extending this right to the insurance firms and the dealers as well, with tax exemptions provided (cf. Sönmez 1998: 250; Sak 1995: 136; Türel 1993: 127–128). These, in turn, led to the formalization of a process, i.e. repurchase operations ('repos') which had already been set in train since 1987 with the opening of the repo and reverse repo market at the ISE in 1993 (cf. Kocabaşoğlu et al. 2001: 568; Keyder 1999: 357; TÜSİAD 2005). While lowering the costs of intermediation and enhancing the access to sources of finance were the rationale for providing these new incentives, their impact on the conduct of monetary policy by the Central Bank was debatable.

These incentives were basically seen as lubricating mechanisms to enhance the financing of public deficits, yet with serious implications for the Turkish economy in general, and Turkish banking in particular. They accentuated the tendency of the Turkish banking system to borrow from international financial markets to finance public deficits by holding Turkish lira-denominated government securities. In this way, an open foreign exchange position became a structural feature of the Turkish banking system (Alper and Öniş 2003; Ersel and Özatay 2008; Mercan and Yolalan 2000). This, in turn, meant a corresponding increase in risks for the banking sector with rising volatility in interest and foreign exchange rates throughout the 1990s (Özatay and Sak 2002a). As the exchange rate and the interest rate actually became exogenous variables, totally dependent on the decisions of international arbiters, it was argued that this process hindered the Central Bank's capacity to conduct monetary policy (Köse and Yeldan 1998: 62). The upshot seems to be that there were no trade-offs associated with the so-called 'Trilemma' as there was neither exchange rate stability nor any degree of monetary independence to accompany the dependence of the economy on capital inflows (cf. Aizenman and Glick 2008). Under these circumstances, the economy drifted towards the 1993–94 financial crisis, as chronic fiscal deficits coupled with high real interest rates led to unsustainable debt dynamics (Taymaz and Yılmaz 2008).

By contrast, there was a shift of policy on the part of the Central Bank with the adoption of a stabilization program on 5 April 1994 in the wake of a severe financial crisis,the basic trigger of which was the reversal of capital flows (cf. Boratav 2011: 419). In concurrence with an IMF stand-by agreement—the first since 1984—the Central Bank gave priority to "the stability of the financial markets" with its policy of sterilized intervention that would remain in effect until the next IMF stand-by agreement in December 1999. This policy shift was justified on the grounds that "non-sterilised intervention should not be a policy option in case of unsustainable fiscal stance" (Emir et al. 2000). As there would be a steady inflow of portfolio investments during 1995–97, there had been a significant increase in the foreign exchange reserves that was said to enhance the CBRT's resistance to speculative attacks in the midst of the Asian crisis and thereafter. The rise in the current account deficit during the same period was said to have been largely financed by the return of flight capital that had occurred in the wake of 1994 crisis (cf. Boratav 2011: 420; TÜSİAD 1996, 1997).

However, the destructive effects of the 1994 crisis would be reflected on the fiscal balances of the Turkish economy, as there was increased recourse to domestic borrowing in financing the increased budget deficit, with the consequence of high interest rates to make GDIs attractive. Ironically, the processes of financial liberalization which were supposed to reduce the costs of intermediation, instead functioned as mechanisms to finance the public deficit (cf. Binay and Kunter 1998; Emir et al. 2000). As open market operations and interbank markets were said to increase the ability of the Central Bank to control liquidity, the banking sector would be encouraged to purchase GDIs with reductions in the reserve requirements. It was believed that the higher the share of GDIs in the banks' balance sheets, the higher would be the reliance of the Treasury on bond financing for its deficit (cf. Akçaoğlu 1998: 94; Özatay and Sak 2002a).

Concurrently, the process of liberalization and market-driven economic policy had been identified as the basic philosophy of the five-year development plans during the 1990s. In particular, the Seventh Five-Year Development Plan (1995–99) was singled out as aiming to redefine the functions of the Turkish state as a regulatory state for the realization of the so-called "second generation structural reforms" (Yılmaz 2003: 254). However, the particular nature of domestic debt management did not necessarily provide supporting evidence for this aspiration. Rather it seemed that the Turkish state was functioning both as an actor in and an enabler of the Turkish capital markets: that is, assuming the role of a market-making authority, albeit with detrimental effects for the financial system.[39] Moreover, it was to be criticized as constituting an income transfer mechanism from wage earners to those who are in a position to lend to the state via the banking sector (Köse and Yeldan 1998: 63; Marois 2012: 114). In this regard, fiscal debt management appeared to be yet another manifestation of the functioning of the state as an asymmetric risk holder, thereby socializing the risk for the capital groups in particular (Marois 2012: 167; Yalman 2009: 298); while the Treasury as the banking supervisory authority during the 1990s created the so-called 'duty losses' for the state banks by treating their non-performing loans as far as the Treasury was concerned, as performing loans (cf. Marois 2012: 116; Özatay and Sak 2002b).

This state of affairs would pave the way for the re-emergence of the IMF as a key actor in economic policymaking from 1998 onwards for the next 10 years (BSB 2007). The initial step was to come in the form of a 'Staff Monitoring Program' which entailed 'quarterly monitoring' by IMF staff for an 18-month period starting in mid-1998, as described in the *Memorandum of Economic Policies* of 26 June 1998 by the Turkish government. The underlying rationale was "to preserve macroeconomic stability and reduce inflation" which would, in turn, require the implementation of "a comprehensive program of fiscal and structural reform". This would specifically entail "measures to strengthen the banking sector and supervision through more stringent enforcement of capital adequacy requirements and of the ceiling on banks' net open foreign exchange positions". In fact, such measures were in line with policy recommendations put forward in the report prepared by a group of economists for TÜSİAD in 1995, under the rubric of a new medium-term stabilization programme for Turkey (TÜSİAD 1995). Hence, these were subsequently to be criticized not only for being the programme of major capital groups, but also for paving the way for the domination of the Turkish economy by international finance capital in due course (cf. BSB 2008: 64; Boratav 2004: 199).

As the Turkish government would commit itself to increase the primary surplus of the budget, starting with the Staff Monitoring Program, it would set in train a very painful process for significant sections of Turkish society. Otherwise referred to as a finance-led transition (Marois 2012: 114), this signified a new phase of the neoliberal transformation, a process that would gain pace following the so-called 'twin crises' during November 2000–February 2001, in which a balance of payments crisis took place simultaneously with the crisis in the banking sector. But the striking feature of this crisis was that it had struck while the Turkish government had been diligently implementing a three-year IMF stand-by agreement that had been initiated in December 1999 (cf. Boratav 2001). The IMF had attempted to justify the need for such an agreement while monitoring the Turkish economy on the grounds that a new and more comprehensive programme of macroeconomic and fiscal adjustment was required to tackle excessive inflation (IMF 1999). In retrospect, the World Bank also considered that the crisis had been instrumental in getting policymakers to listen to the message on the need for structural reform as it had "little success" in this regard during 1994–98 (World Bank 2006). Meanwhile, the last year of the Staff Monitoring Programme had already witnessed a number of institutional changes that included a new Banking Law (Law no. 4389), the establishment of an independent bank regulatory and supervision agency (BRSA), and the lowering of the ceiling on banks' net foreign exchange positions, all intended to reform and strengthen the financial sector. The establishment of BRSA was to bring to an end the Treasury's role as the banking supervisory authority. There had been a series of significant amendments made to Law no. 4389 with a new law (Law no. 4491) enacted immediately after the stand-by agreement in December 1999, indicating the clout the IMF had gained (cf. IMF 1999; Türel 2004: 297; 2009: 137). The letter of intent by the Turkish government had also indicated that the sterilization of capital flows would be ceased in order to allow domestic interest rates to be 'fully market determined' (Demiralp 1999). This shift in monetary policy not only acknowledged the limitations that open-market operations, along with repos, brought for the conduct of monetary policy by the Central Bank and its limited capacity to sterilize international flows of money in particular. More saliently, it brought support to the contention that such shifts of policy underlined the state's diminished capacity to define nation-specific money (cf. Keyder 1999: 375–376; Bryan and Rafferty 2015).

Thus, the third phase of financial liberalization came to an end by underlining the increased dependence of the Turkish economy's growth prospects on capital flows. No less significant had been the role played by the financial crises as the main driving forces to ensure neoliberal transformation of state-market relations since the liberalization of the capital account in 1989, as they have been proved to provide a strong opportunity for overcoming reluctance to changes (OECD 2002). Indeed, post-2001 crisis developments have vindicated this, as will be discussed in the following chapters.

Notes

1 As it will be elaborated below, this could be seen as a perfect example of what has been problematized as 'the internationalisation of specific policy regimes' as the key players in policy regimes increasingly tended to include those outside the country as sources of policy ideas, policy design and implementation (cf. Jessop 2002).

2 This particular clause is said to have entailed a violation of the Banking Law no. 7129 (Başbuğ 1980: 33–34), and thus made The Association of Turkish Banks "meaningless as an organisational vehicle" (Öncü and Gökçe 1991: 109), since the BAT was given the task by this law "to ensure that banks take, implement or demand the implementation of, decisions as required for prevention of unfair competition in the market" (see Chapter 2).

3 This had been quite a popular dubbing used by several critiques of this agreement by the banks, including prominent representatives of the business community as well as economists most of whom were said to be supportive of financial liberalisation in principle.

4 The term Ponzi-type financing here refers to a Ponzi scheme where new investors are invited by offering relatively higher returns, in the form of short-term returns that are either abnormally high or unusually consistent. Perpetuation of the high returns requires an ever-increasing flow of money from new investors to keep the scheme going.

5 See, for instance, İ. Bodur, ISOD (Journal of Istanbul Chamber of Industry, 15 August 1980; Ş. Çavuşoğlu, Banka ve Ekonomik Yorumlar, August 1980.

6 Interviews conducted by the author with F. Berker and R. Koç in early 1989. See also Keyder (1992: 72) for a brief but more sympathetic account of these policy changes.

7 Yet no single bank had applied to establish such funds by the end of 1985, according to the chairperson of the Capital Market Board (BEY March 1986: 12). The first such fund would be established by İşbank in 1987 (Kocabaşoğlu et al. 2001: 571).

8 A few remaining local banks which originated in the early republican era were among those taken over by the capital groups which hitherto lacked a financial sector arm. An interesting example was Kocaeli Halk Bankası, founded in 1927, changed its name to Türk Ekonomi Bankası (TEB) when it was taken over by Çolakoğlu Holding in 1982, and subsequently became a foreign bank, when its majority shares were sold to BNP Paribas in 2005.

9 According to the chairperson of Capital Market Board, the number of dealers, with the status of banker, had come down to four at the end of 1982, from 279 in 1979 (BEY April 1986: 25). Among the casualties, there were better known ones such as Kastelli and Meban.

10 With this decree, the interest rates on sight/demand deposits had been increased from 5 per cent to 20 per cent, while those on 6- and 12-month deposits had been reduced from 50 per cent to 40 per cent and from 56 per cent to 45 per cent, respectively (Döşlüoğlu 1983). For the World Bank, these changes were meant to reduce the cost of credits for the banks (World Bank 1983).

11 See BEY February 1983 for the complaints of the Chairperson of Istanbul Chamber of Commerce; see also BEY July 1983:6 for the argument by an eminent liberal professor of economics that the decision to reduce interest rates was a violation of market-based economy principles enunciated by the 24 January 1980 programme.

12 Since 1980, a highly differentiated cash reserve requirements (with separate rates for sight and savings deposits and substantially lower rates for deposits used for specific purposes) were effective (World Bank 1983).

13 See Chapter 5 for a detailed analysis of SDIF which was under the supervision of the Central Bank until August 2000 when it was transferred to the then established Banking Regulation and Supervision Agency (BRSA).

14 This decree which replaced Law no. 2279 dated June 1933, while being amended with another decree in 1994, would remain in effect until 2012 when it was replaced by (Law no. 6361) Law on Leasing, Factoring and Financing Companies.

15 A year later, the discussions for the renewal of the stand-by agreement would be cut short in May 1985, thereby bringing the five year long relationship with the IMF on the basis of successive stand-by agreements to an end.

16 Even a key ally of the Özal government, the then chairman of TÜSİAD, would find the rise of interest rates unpalatable and even counterproductive as it would, in his view, further propel inflation rather than curtail it (BEY April 1984: 21).

17 By the same token, the foreign trade companies which would be allowed to seek credits from international financial markets were identified by the communiqués on the basis of Decree no. 30.

18 By the end of 1980s, FCDs was said to surpass the volume of the Turkish Lira denominated deposits in the balance sheets of the Turkish banking sector (Işık 2007).

19 Decree 92 (dated 6 October 1983) by the military regime had already amended some of the articles of the Law of CBRT, thereby giving it the capacity to govern foreign exchange and precious metal reserves. That meant, CBRT would be able to deal in those markets.

20 General derogation is a dispensation from all operations specified in the Code which came into existence in its current format with the formation of the OECD in 1961. In the case of Turkey, this remained in effect from 1962 to 1985 (Griffith-Jones et al. 2000).

21 Such shifts were to be interpreted as resulting from the ways in which financial liberalization policies had been put into effect, that is, in a trial and error manner (Kocabaşoğlu et al. 2001:566).

22 There are conflicting accounts about the profitability of commercial banks during the 1980s. While their profitability was said to be deteriorating due to widening margins between the interest rates on deposits and credits (Ulagay 1987: 196), there were also others who contended that real profits of the private commercial banks increased as much as five fold over the 1981–90 period, and being five times higher than the OECD average (cf. Akçaoğlu 1998: 92; Işık and Hassan 2002). The latter would be much more in line with the following: "countries with under-developed financial systems have significantly higher levels of bank profits and margins" (Demirgüç-Kunt and Huzinga 2000).

23 By the end 1988, the total number of banks had reached 60. There were 7 new commercial banks established during 1984–88 period, bringing the total number of such banks to 33. It is worth reminding that there were quite a few banks which were taken over by SDIF since 1984, while the number of state banks had come down from 12 to eight due to some enforced mergers. During the same period, the number of foreign banks entering the Turkish market were ten, thus bringing the total number of foreign banks from four in 1980 to 19 in 1988. It is to be noted, however, that most of the foreign banks simply entered by establishing a single branch (ITO 1990: 21). Moreover, the number of investment and development banks had risen from three to ten, some of them being foreign banks.

24 'Special Finance Houses' has been transformed into 'Participation Banks', gaining the 'bank' statute, two decades later, with the enactment of a new Banking Law No.5411 on November 2005.

25 Law no. 2970 (14 January 1984) allowed the corporations to be exempt from the Corporation tax, if and when they increase their equity by adding 80% of the income they would gain from the sale of their real estate and/or shares in other companies (BEY January 1986). Whereas Law no. 3239 of 4 December 1985 entailed an amendment to Law no. 5422 (Corporation Tax Law), while raising the corporation tax from 40 per cent to 46 per cent, it made the corporations effectively exempt from this tax as dividends were made not taxable, and allowed them to deduct the interest payments from their tax base (Önder 2003: 223).

26 When asked by the then Governor of CBRT, Rüştü Saraçoğlu, in the wake of Decree 32 about the reason for not repealing Law no.1567, Prime Minister Özal had responded that he needed such a piece of legislation that gave the government the authority to make any changes in the exchange rate regime that it deemed necessary (Birand& Yalçın 2001: 333).

27 In April 1990, the Turkish government notified the IMF that it was ready to fulfil the obligations in Article VIII of the IMF Articles of Agreement, that is, it is 'to obey the conditions of convertibility as defined' (Ersel 1996: 47).

28 The stock of GDIs soared from 6 per cent of GNP in 1989 to nearly 20 per cent in 1997 (Köse and Yeldan 1998: 62).

29 Ironically, Stanley Fischer, as the First Deputy Managing Director at the IMF, was defending the abortive attempt to put capital account liberalisation at the centre of IMF mandate by an amendment of the Articles of Agreement as 'promoting the orderly liberalisation of international capital markets' (Fischer 1997).

30 "Share of credits within total assets of banking sector which was 47% in 1990 has decreased to 33% in 2000. Similarly, the credit/deposit ratio which was 84 in 1990 has decreased to 51% in 2000. [Moreover,] the share of interest income from credits within total interest incomes has continuously decreased from 69% to 38%." (BRSA 2010). Thus, Turkey was considered as having "one of the lowest financial intermediation ratios among emerging markets, [as it] ranked second lowest among 14 emerging markets in 1997." (Van Rijckeghem 1999).

31 The fate of these 18 banks had been quite different, as some were to be merged with some public banks so as to be liquidated, while eight others would be taken over by SDIF during the last two years of the 1990s (cf. Kocabaşoğlu et al. 2001: 589; http://www.finansgundem.com/haber/hangi-banka-neden-kapandi/278020).

32 See Chapter 4 for a detailed analysis of the crises of 1994 and 2000/2001.

33 Interestingly, the World Bank was retrospectively chiding that it had 'little success in getting the policymakers to listen to the message on the need for structural reform' (World Bank 2005).

34 1990 was also the year when Turkey was first asked by the rating agencies to be included in their rating evaluations as the potential investors asked the rating agencies to provide their assessments of the Turkish economy. The rating process started in 1992 following the completion of the necessary procedures.

35 It had been observed that despite the growing importance of foreign exchange assets, they only accounted for 36 percent of the foreign exchange liabilities of the banking system during the 1990–99 period (Özatay and Sak 2002a).

36 "Financial markets remained shallow despite the liberalization efforts in 1990–2000. The ratio of asset size of financial sector (banks, insurance companies, financial leasing companies) to GDP was about 60% in 1990 and it was about 85% in 2000." (BRSA 2010). By contrast, this was considered a tremendous increase for the financial assets, magnifying their importance for the Turkish economy (Türel 2001b).

37 In fact, this entailed a policy controversy between the Treasury and the CBRT which eventually led to the resignation of the Governor of the Central Bank who was an advocate of tight monetary policy (cf. Ekinci 1993: 203; Ulagay 1994: 185, 259).

38 See Chapter 9 for more detailed information and analysis of these institutions.

39 cf. Clift 2012 for a similar characterisation of the role of the state in the neoliberal transformation in the French case.

REFERENCES

Aizenman, J. and Glick, R. (2008) "Sterilization, Monetary Policy, and Global Financial Integration", Working Papers, Santa Cruz Center for International Economics, No. 8–1.

Akçaoğlu, E. (1998) *Financial Innovation in Turkish Banking*, Capital Markets Board, Publication No. 127, Ankara.

Akgüç, Ö. (1984) "1983 Yılında Bankalar, Mevduat ve Krediler", *Banka ve Ekonomik Yorumlar*, 21(9).

Akgüç, Ö. (1987) *100 Soruda Türkiye'de Bankacılık*, İstanbul: Gerçek Yayınevi.

Akgüç, Ö. (1988) "1987 Yılında Bankalar, Mevduat ve Krediler", *Banka ve Ekonomik Yorumlar*, 25(8).

Akyüz, Y. (1985) "Türkiye'de Mali Sistem Aracılığıyla Kaynak Aktarımı: 1980 Öncesi ve Sonrası", in B. Kuruç et al. (contributors) *Bırakınız Yapsınlar, Bırakınız Geçsinler: Türkiye Ekonomisi 1980–1985*, Ankara: Bilgi Yayınevi, 72–93.

Akyüz, Y. (1990) "Financial System and Policies in Turkey in the 1980s" in T. Arıcanlı, and D. Rodrik (eds.) *The Political Economy of Turkey: Debt, Adjustment and Sustainability*, New York: Macmillan, 98–131.

Akyüz, Y. and K. Boratav (2003) "The Making of the Turkish Financial Crisis", *World Development*, 31(9): 1549–1566.

Alper, E. and Z. Öniş (2003) "The Turkish Banking System, Financial Crises and the IMF in the Age of Capital Account Liberalization: A Political Economy Perspective", Paper presented at the Fourth Mediterranean Social and Political Research Meeting, Florence &MontecatiniTerme19–23 March 2003, organised by the Mediterranean Programme of the Robert Schuman Centre for Advanced Studies at the European University Institute.

Altınkemer, M. and N. Ekinci (1992) "Capital Account Liberalisation: The Case of Turkey", *New Perspectives on Turkey*, 8(2): 89–108.

Arın, T. (2000) "Financial Markets and Globalisation in Turkey: Fiscal Crises of the State", in *Prof. Dr Yüksel Ülken'e Armağan*, İstanbul: İstanbul Üniversitesi İktisat Fakültesi, 254–287.

Artun, T. (1983) *Türkiye'de 'Serbest' Faiz Politikası*, İstanbul: TekinYayınevi.

Atiyas, İ. (1990) "The Private Sector's Response to Financial Liberalisation in Turkey: 1980-1982" in T. Arıcanlı, and D. Rodrik (eds.) *The Political Economy of Turkey Debt, Adjustment and Sustainability*, New York: Macmillan, 132–155.

Atiyas, İ. and H. Ersel (1996) "The Impact of Financial Reform: The Turkish Experience", in G. Caprio, Jr. et al. (eds.) *Financial Reform: Theory and Experience*, Cambridge: Cambridge University Press, 103–139.

Atiyas, I. (2014) "Enhancing Competition in a Post-Revolutionary Arab Context: Does the Turkish Experience Provide Any Lessons?" in I. Diwan (ed.) *Understanding the Political Economy of the Arab Uprisings*, London and Hackensack, NJ: World Scientific Publishing, 165–192.

Aysan, A.F. and P.C. Şanlı (2006) "Why Do Foreign Banks Invest In Turkey?", MPRA Paper No. 5491, posted 30 October 2007, http://mpra.ub.uni-muenchen.de/5491.

Aysan, M. (1980) "Banka Yöneticileri Sınavdan Geçiyor", *Banka ve Ekonomik Yorumlar*, 17(7).

Aysan, M. (1981) "Faiz Curcunası Özel Bankacılığın Geleceğini Tehdit Ediyor", *Banka ve Ekonomik Yorumlar*, 18(2).

Bakır, C. and Z. Öniş (2010) "The Regulatory State and Turkish Banking Reforms in the Age of Post-Washington Consensus", *Development and Change* 41(1): 77–106.

Balkan, E. and E. Yeldan (2002) 'Peripheral Development under Financial Liberalisation: The Turkish Experience', in N. Balkan and S. Savran (eds.), *The Ravages of Neoliberalism: Economy, Society and Gender in Turkey*, New York: Nova Science Publishers, 39–54.

Başbuğ, F. (1980) "Liberal Faiz Ekonomisi", *Banka ve Ekonomik Yorumlar*, 17(9).

BEY–Banka ve Ekonomik Yorumlar, *Monthly Journal*, various issues.
Binay, Ş. and K. Kunter (1998) "Mali Liberalleşmede Merkez Bankası'nın Rolü 1980–1997", TCMB Araştırma Müdürlüğü, Tartışma Tebliği No: 9803, Aralık.
Birand, M.A. and S. Yalçın (2001) *The Özal: Bir Davanın Öyküsü*, İstanbul: Doğan Kitap.
Bonizzi, B. (2014) 'Financialisation in Developing and Emerging Countries: A Survey', *International Journal of Political Economy*, 42(4): 83–107.
Boratav, K. (2001) "Finansal Kriz IMF'nin Eseridir", unpublished paper, Ankara: Ankara University Faculty of Political Science.
Boratav, K. (2004) *Türkiye İktisat Tarihi 1908–2002*, İstanbul: Gerçek Yayınevi.
Boratav, K. (2011) "Serbest Sermaye Hareketlerive Kriz-Küçülme Dönemeçleri: 1990–2010", in S. Şahinkaya and N.İ. Ertuğrul (eds.) *Bilsay Kuruç'a Armağan*, Ankara: Mülkiyeliler Birliği Vakfı, 405–436.
Boratav, K., O. Türel and E. Yeldan (1995) "The Turkish Economy in 1981-92: A Balance Sheet, Problems and Prospects",*METU Studies in Development*, 22(1): 1–36.
Boratav, K., O. Türel and E. Yeldan (1996) "Dilemmas of Structural Adjustment and Environmental Policies Under Instability: Post-1980 Turkey", *World Development*, 24(2): 373–393.
Bryan, D. and M. Rafferty (2015) "Decomposing Money: Ontological Options and Spreads", *Journal of Cultural Economy*, 9(1): 27–42.
BRSA (2010) "From Crisis to Financial Stability (Turkey Experience)", Working Paper, revised third edition, prepared with the contributions of BRSA, SDIF and CBRT.
BSB (2007) *IMF Gözetiminde On Uzun Yıl 1998–2008: Farklı Hükümetler, Tek Siyaset*, İstanbul: Yordam Kitap.
BSB (2008) *2008 Kavşağında Türkiye*, İstanbul: Yordam Kitap.
Cansen, E. (1983) "Faizlerve Enflasyon", *Banka ve Ekonomik Yorumlar*, 20(7).
Celasun, M. (1991) "Trade and Industrialisation in Turkey: Initial Conditions, Policy and Performance in the 1980s", paper presented at UNU/WIDER Conference, Paris, 31 August–3 September 1991.
Celasun, M. and D. Rodrik (1989) "Debt, Adjustment and Growth: Turkey" in J.D. Sachs and S.M. Collins (eds.) *Developing Country Debt and Economic Performance, Volume 3, Country Studies–Indonesia, Korea, Philippines, Turkey*, Chicago: University of Chicago Press, 615–808.
Chesnais, F. (2016) *Finance Capital Today*, Leiden: Brill.
Chibber, A. and S. van Wijnbergen (1988) "Public Policy and Private Investment in Turkey", Policy, Planning and Research Department working papers no. WPS 120, Washington, DC: World Bank.
Cizre, Ü. and E. Yeldan (2005) "The Turkish Encounter with Neo-liberalism: Economics and Politics in the 2000/2001Crises", *Review of International Political Economy*, 12(3): 387–408.
Clift, B. (2012) "Comparative Capitalisms, Ideational Political Economy and French Post-Dirigiste Responses to the Global Financial Crisis", *New Political Economy*, 17(5): 565–590.
Çölaşan, E. (1983) *24 Ocak Bir Dönemin Perde Arkası*, İstanbul: Milliyet Yayınları.
Demiralp, S. (1999) "Recent Developments in Turkish Economy, Economic Policies for the Year 2000 and Effects of These Policies on Financial Markets", *The ISE Review Special Issue: Turkish Economy and Capital Markets Towards a New Millennium*, 12(3): 29–34.

Demirgüç-Kunt, A. and H. Huzinga (2000) "Financial Structure and Bank Profitability", World Bank Policy Research Working Paper No. 2430.

Denizer, C. (2000) "Foreign Entry in Turkey's Banking Sector, 1980–1997", Policy, Research working paper no. WPS 2462. Washington, DC: World Bank.

Denizer, C.A., M.N. Gültekin, and N.B. Gültekin (2000) "Distorted Incentives and Financial Development in Turkey", paper prepared for "Financial Structure and Economic Development" conference organized by the World Bank, 10–11 February 2000, Washington, DC.

Durakbaşa, N. (1982) "Bankacılığımızda Faizve Kredi Uygulaması", *Banka ve Ekonomik Yorumlar*, 19(2).

Eichengreen, B. and A. Fishlow (1998) "Contending the Capital Flows: What is Different about the 1990s" in M. Kahler (ed.) *Capital Flows and Financial Crises*, Manchester: Manchester University Press, 23–68.

Ekinci, N. (1993) "Türkiye'de 1980 Sonrasında Para Politikaları" in İ. Önder et al. (eds.) *Türkiye'de Kamu Maliyesi, Finansal Yapıve Politikalar*, İstanbul: TarihVakfı Yurt Yayınları, 186–203.

Ekinci, N. (1996). "Financial Liberalisation under External Debt Constraints: The Case of Turkey", ERC Working Paper 96/05, METU Economic Research Center, Ankara.

Ekzen, N. (1984) "1980 Stabilizasyon Paketinin 1958, 1970 ve 1978–1979 Paketleri ile Karşılaştırmalı Analizi" in İ. Tekeli et al. (contributors) *Türkiye'de ve Dünyada Yaşanan Ekonomik Bunalım*, Ankara: Yurt Yayınları.

Ekzen, N. (1999) "İç Borçlanma", *Türk-İş Yıllığı '99, Yüzyıl/Binyıl Biterken Dünyada ve Türkiye'de Durum*, Ankara: Türk-İş Araştırma Merkezi, 405–416.

Ekzen, N. (2004) "Mali Yapı ve Liberal Politikalar", *'Liberal Reformlar' ve Devlet*, Ankara: KİGEM, 303–316.

Emir, O.E., A. Karasoy, K. Kunter (2000) "Monetary Policy Reaction Function in Turkey" paper presented in the conference titled "Banking, Financial Markets and The Economies of the Middle East and North Africa" Beirut, 25–27, May 2000, Research Department of the Central Bank of the Republic of Turkey.

Ersel, H. (1996) "The Timing of Capital Account Liberalisation: The Turkish Experience", *New Perspectives on Turkey*, 15(2): 45–64.

Ersel, H. and E. Öztürk (1990) "The Credit Delivery System in Turkey", The Central Bank of the Republic of Turkey, Research Department, Discussion Papers No. 9003, March.

Fischer, S. (1997) "Capital Account Liberalisation and the Role of the IMF", paper presented at the *Conference on Development of Securities Markets in Emerging Markets*, Inter-American Development Bank, Washington, DC, 28 October 1997.

Fitzgerald, E.V.K. and R. Vos (1989) "The Foundations of Development Finance: Economic Structure, Accumulation Balances and Income Distribution" in E.V.K. Fitzgerald and R. Vos (eds.) *Financing Economic Development: A Structural Approach to Monetary Policy*, Gower.

Griffith-Jones, S., R. Gottschalk and X. Cirera (2000) "The OECD Experience with Capital Account Liberalisation" Institute of Development Studies, University of Sussex, http://www.ids.ac.uk/ids.

IMF (1999) "IMF Turkey – IMF Mission for the 1999 Article IV Consultation Discussions and Third Review of the Staff Monitored Program, Concluding Statement, 2 July 1999", http://www.imf.org/external/np/ms/1999/070299.HTM

Işık, İ. (2007) "Bank Ownership and Productivity Developments: Evidence from Turkey", *Studies in Economics and Finance*, 24(2): 115–139.

Işık, İ. and K. Hassan (2002) "Cost and Profit Efficiency of the Turkish Banking Industry: An Empirical Investigation", *The Financial Review*, 37(2): 257–280.

İTO (1990) *Türk ve Yabancı Sermayeli Bankalar*, İstanbul Ticaret Odası, Yayın No. 1990/17.

Jessop, B. (2002) "The Political Economy of State Rescaling", *The Future of Capitalist State*, Cambridge: Polity Press, 172–215.

Kepenek, Y.and N.Yentürk (2003) *Türkiye Ekonomisi*, Remzi Kitabevi, İstanbul.

Keyder, N. (1992) "The Financial Transformation of the 1980s and the Behaviour of Velocity in Turkey", *New Perspectives on Turkey*, 8(2): 67–87.

Keyder, N. (1999) "Türkiye'de Para Bazı Seçimi ve Para Çoğaltanı (1980–1998)", *METU Studies in Development*, 26(3–4): 353–377.

Kocabaşoğlu, U. et al. (2001) *Türkiye İş Bankası Tarihi*, İstanbul: Türkiye İş Bankası Kültür Yayınları.

Köse, A.H. and E. Yeldan (1998) "Turkish Economy in the 1990s: An Assessment of Fiscal Policies, Labour Markets and Foreign Trade", *New Perspectives on Turkey*, Spring, 18.

Krippner, G. (2011) *Capitalizing on Crisis: The Political Origins of the Rise of Finance*, Cambridge: Harvard University Press.

Lal, D. (1983) *The Poverty of 'Development Economics'*, London: The Institute of Economic Affairs.

Lapavitsas, C. (2009) "Financialized Capitalism: Crisis and Financial Expropriation", *Historical Materialism*, 17(2): 114–148.

Lapavitsas, C. (2011) "Theorizing Financialization", *Work, Employment and Society*, 25(4): 611–626.

Marois, T. (2012) *States, Banks and Crisis: Emerging Finance Capitalism in Mexico and Turkey*, Cheltenham, UK: Edward Elgar Publishing.

Mercan, M. and R. Yolalan (2000) "The Effect of Scale and Mode of Ownership on the Turkish Banking Sector Financial Performance", *The ISE Review*, 15: 1–26.

Organisation for Economic Co-operation and Development (2002) *Regulatory Reform in Turkey: Enhancing Market Openness Through Regulatory Reform*, OECD.

Oyan, O. (1987) *24 Ocak Ekonomisinde Dışa Açılma ve Mali Politikalar*, Ankara: Verso.

Oyan, O. (1997) "Kamu Maliyesi", *Türk-İş '97 Yıllığı*, Vol.1, Ankara: Türk-İş Araştırma Merkezi.

Oyan, O. and A.R. Aydın (1987) *İstikrar Programından Fon Ekonomisine*, Ankara: Teori Yayınları.

Öncü, A. and D. Gökçe (1991) "Macro-Politics of De-Regulation and Micro-Politics of Banks" in M. Heper (ed.) *Strong State and Economic Interest Groups*, Berlin: de Gruyter, 99–117.

Öniş, Z. (1991) "The Evolution of Privatization in Turkey: The Institutional Contextof Public-Enterprise Reform" *International Journal of Middle East Studies*, 23, 163–176.

Öniş, Z. (1996) "Globalisation and Financial Blow-Ups in the Semi-Periphery: Perspectives on Turkey's Financial Crisis of 1994", *New Perspectives on Turkey*, 15(2): 1–23.

Özatay, F. (2009) *Finansal Krizler ve Türkiye*, İstanbul: Doğan Kitap.

Özatay, F. and G. Sak (2002a) "Financial Liberalization in Turkey Why Was the Impact on Growth Limited?" *Emerging Markets Finance and Trade*, 38(5): 6–22.

Özatay, F. and G. Sak (2002b) "Banking Sector Fragility and Turkey's 2000–2001 Financial Crisis", in S.M. Collins and D. Rodrik (eds.) *Brookings Trade Forum 2002*, Washington, DC: Brookings Institution Press, 121–160.

Pehlivan, H. and C. Kirkpatrick (1992) "The Impact of Transnational Banks on Developing Countries' Banking Sector: An Analysis of the Turkish Experience, 1980–1989", *British Journal of Middle Eastern Studies*, 19(2): 186–201.

Reinhart, C.M. and V.R. Reinhart (1998) "Some Lessons for Policy Makers Who Deal with the Mixed Blessing of Capital Inflows", in M. Kahler (ed.) *Capital Flows and Financial Crises*, Manchester: Manchester University Press, 93–127.

Rodrik, D. (1990) "Premature Liberalization, Incomplete Stabilization: the Özal Decade in Turkey". *NBER Working Papers*, No. 3300.

Rodrik, D. (2009) "The Turkish Economy After the Crisis", paper prepared for the 80th anniversary of the Turkish Economics Association, Ankara.

Sak, G. (1995) *Public Policies Towards Financial Liberalization: A General Framework and An Evaluation of the Turkish Experience in the 1980s*, Capital Markets Board, Publication No.22.

Serfati, C. (2011) "Transnational Corporations as Financial Groups" *Work, Organisation, Labour & Globalisation*, 5(1): 10–38.

Sönmez, A. (2001) *Doğu Asya 'Mucizesi' ve Bunalımı: Türkiyeiçin Dersler*, İstanbul: İstanbul Bilgi Üniversitesi Yayınları.

Sönmez, M. (1980) *Türkiye Ekonomisinde Bunalım: 24 Ocak Kararlarıve Sonrası*, İstanbul: BelgeYayınları.

Sönmez, M. (1982) *Türkiye Ekonomisinde Bunalım: 1980 Sonbaharından 1982'ye*, İstanbul: Belge Yayınları.

Sönmez, M. (1998) "1980 Sonrası Istanbul Menkul Kıymetler Borsası", in M. Sönmez (ed.) *75 Yılda Paranın Serüveni*, İstanbul: Türkiye İş Bankası Kültür Yayınları and Tarih Vakfı, 241–255.

Sönmez, S. (2004) "Neoliberal İktisat Politikaları: Kamu Maliyesinde Değişim ve Kriz", *'Liberal Reformlar've Devlet*, Ankara: KİGEM, 261–294.

Sönmez, S. (2009) "Türkiye Ekonomisinde Neoliberal Dönüşüm Politikaları ve Etkileri", in N. Mütevellioğlu and S. Sönmez (eds.) *Küreselleşme, Kriz ve Türkiye'de Neoliberal Dönüşüm*, İstanbul: İstanbul Bilgi Üniversitesi Yayınları, 25–76.

Şenses, F. (1991) "Turkey's Stabilisation and Structural Adjustment Programme in Retrospectand Prospect", *The Developing Economies*, 29(3): 210–234.

Taşçıoğlu, A. (1998) *Cumhuriyet Dönemi Bankalar Kanunları ve İlgili Yasal Düzenlemeler*, Türkiye Bankalar Birliği, Publication No. 208, İstanbul.

Taymaz, E. and K. Yılmaz (2008) "Integration with the Global Economy: The Case of Turkish Automobile and Consumer Electronics Industries", TÜSİAD-Koç University Economic Research Forum, Working Paper Series, Working Paper 0801, February.

Türel, O. (1985) "1980 Sonrasında Kamu Kesimive Finansman Üzerine Gözlemve Değerlendirmeler" in B. Kuruç et al. (contributors) *Bırakınız Yapsınlar, Bırakınız Geçsinler: Türkiye Ekonomisi 1980–1985*, Ankara: Bilgi Yayınevi, 94–130.

Türel, O. (1993) "1980–1992 Döneminde Türkiye'de Finansal Yapı ve Politikalar", İ. Önder et al. (contributors) *Türkiye'de Kamu Maliyesi, Finansal Yapı ve Politikalar*, İstanbul: Tarih Vakfı Yurt Yayınları, 119–185.

Türel, O. (2001) "Restructuring the Public Sector in Post-1980 Turkey: An Assessment", H. Hakimian and Z. Moshaver (eds.) *The State and Global Challenge*, Surrey: Curzon Press, 178–208.

Türel, O. (2004) "Mali Serbestleşme Sürecinde Bankacılık Kesimi", *'Liberal Reformlar' ve Devlet*, Ankara: KİGEM, 295–315.

Türel, O. (2009) "Türkiye Ekonomisinin Neoliberal Yapılanma Sürecinde Bankacılığın Yeniden Düzenlenmesi, 1980–2007", *Alpaslan Işıklı'ya Armağan*, Ankara: Mülkiyeliler Birliği Vakfı Yayınları, 131–168.

TÜSİAD (1981) *The Turkish Economy 1981*, İstanbul: TÜSİAD.

TÜSİAD (1982) *1982 Yılına Girerken Türk Ekonomisi*, İstanbul: TÜSİAD.

TÜSİAD (1992) *1992 Yılına Girerken Türk Ekonomisi*, İstanbul: TÜSİAD.

TÜSİAD (1993) *1993 Yılına Girerken Türk Ekonomisi*, İstanbul: TÜSİAD.

TÜSİAD (1994) *1994 Yılına Girerken Türk Ekonomisi*, İstanbul: TÜSİAD.

TÜSİAD (1995) *Türkiye için Yeni Bir Orta Vadeli İstikrar Programına Doğru*, İstanbul: TÜSİAD

TÜSİAD (1996) *1996 Yılına Girerken Türk Ekonomisi*, İstanbul: TÜSİAD.

TÜSİAD (1997) *1997 Yılına Girerken Türk Ekonomisi*, İstanbul: TÜSİAD.

TÜSİAD (2005) *Türkiye Sermaye Piyasalarının Gelişimine Yönelik Öneriler*, İstanbul: TÜSİAD.

Ulagay, O. (1987) *Özal Ekonomisinde Kim Kazandı Kim Kaybetti*, Ankara: Bilgi Yayınevi.

Ulagay, O. (1994) *Krize Adım Adım: Günah Sayılan Kehanet*, Istanbul: MilliyetYayınları.

Van Rijckeghem, C. (1999) "The Political Economy of Inflation: Are Turkish Banks Potential Losers From Stabilization?" *The ISE Review*, 10: 1–16.

Wood, E.M. (2007) "A Reply to Critics", *Historical Materialism*, 15(3): 143–170.

World Bank (1983) *Report and Recommendation of the President of the World Bank to the Executive Directors on a Fourth Structural Adjustment Loan in an Amount Equivalent to US $300.8 million to the Republic of Turkey*, 26 May 1983, Report No. P-3543-TU.

World Bank (1984) *Turkey – Fifth Structural Adjustment Loan Project*. Washington, DC: World Bank.

World Bank (2000a) *Turkey Country Economic Memorandum: Structural Reforms for Sustainable Growth*, Vol. 1: Main Report, 15 September 2000, Report No. 20657-TU.

World Bank (2000b) *Memorandum of the President of the International Bank for Reconstruction and Development and the International Finance Corporation to the Executive Directors on a Country Assistance Strategy of the World Bank Group for the Republic of Turkey*, 28 November 2000.

World Bank (2003a) *Non-Bank Financial Institutions and Capital Markets in Turkey*, A World Bank Country Study. Washington, DC: The World Bank.

World Bank (2003b) *Memorandum of the President to the Executive Directors on a Country Assistance Strategy of the World Bank Group for the Republic of Turkey*, 2 October 2003, Report No. 26756 TU.

World Bank (2005) *The World Bank in Turkey, 1993–2004 Country Assistance Evaluation*, Independent Evaluation Group, Report No. 34783, 20 December 2005.

World Bank (2006) *The World Bank in Turkey: 1993–2004: An IEG Country Assistance Evaluation*, http://www.worldbank.org/ieg

Yalman, G.L. (2009) *Transition to Neoliberalism: The Case of Turkey in the 1980s*, İstanbul: İstanbul Bilgi University Press.

Yayla, M., A. Hekimoğlu, M. Kutlukaya (2008) "Financial Stability of the Turkish Banking Sector" *BDDK Bankacılıkve Finansal Piyasalar*, 2(1): 9–26.

Yeldan, E. (2001) *Küreselleşme Sürecinde Türkiye Ekonomisi*, İstanbul: İletişimYayınları.

Yeldan, E. (2002) "On the IMF-Directed Disinflation Program in Turkey", in N. Balkan and S. Savran (eds) *The Ravages of Neoliberalism: Economy, Society and Gender in Turkey*, New York: Nova Science Publishers, 1–20.

Yentürk, N. (1999) "Short-term Capital Inflows and Their Impact on Macroeconomic Structure: Turkey in the 1990s", *The Developing Economies*, 37(1): 89–113.

Yılmaz, C. (2003) "Planning For Complex Modernity: The Turkish Case", *unpublished PhD. thesis*, Department of Political Science and Public Administration, Bilkent University, Ankara.

Yülek, M. (1998) *Financial Liberalization and the Real Economy*, Capital Markets Board, Publication no. 110.

4 A Tale of Three Crises Made in Turkey: 1994, 2001 and 2008–09[1]

Hasan Cömert and Erinç Yeldan

Introduction

Developing countries have encountered dozens of economic crises since the 1980s, due mainly to structural problems related to their integration into the global economy. The Turkish economy is by no means an exception, and suffered significantly from the crises of 1994, 2001 and 2008–09. This chapter investigates the tales of these three crises to shed light on the propagation mechanisms of crises and their implications for developing countries, given the Turkish experience.[2]

The main findings of the chapter are as follows: Although there are many specific characteristics of each crisis, it is possible to see significant similarities between the cases of the 1994 and 2001 crises. The crisis of 2008–09 can be considered unique in many aspects. In this sense, two tales can be told about the three crises in question. Some stylized observations verify this picture. First, unprecedented government deficits with a very high interest burden and relatively high inflation were the characteristics of the period before the crises of 1994 and 2001, while high private debt was the characterizing factor in the 2008–09. Second, in all three episodes, financial flows played a role to varying degrees. The sheer size of the financial shock relative to Turkey's reserves and gross domestic product (GDP) played a key role in the crises of 1994 and 2001, whereas it seemed to have played a secondary role in the most recent crisis. In the first two crises, a very sharp exchange rate, foreign currency reserves, and interest rate movements were observed. Third, the trade channel played a decisive role in the last crisis, whereas there was no decline in Turkish exports in the previous two crises. The 2008–09 crisis likely exposed the limitations of export-based strategies. Fourth, the Turkish government implemented very tight monetary and fiscal policies during the crises of 1994 and 2001 whereas fiscal and monetary policies were relatively expansionary during the most recent crisis. This was possible due to specific domestic and global factors, such as relatively low public debt levels and low borrowing costs, mostly related to low interest rates globally, itself a result of the enormous expansion of liquidity by developed economies. Fifth, unlike the other two cases, the crisis of 2008–09 took place in the midst of a severe global economic crisis, while the global economic environment was not exceptional in the previous crises. Sixth, the sensitivity of the labour market to crisis appears to have increased over time. In other words, the severity of the employment implications of crisis seems to have increased over time.

This chapter will address these issues in turn. The next part will give a brief account of the implications of the crises. With reference to a large set of variables, the third part will investigate the pre-crisis conditions in the three cases. In this vein, this part will benefit from the literature on early warning indicators. The aim of this section is to explore an overall picture of pre-crisis conditions in order to understand factors leading to the crises. Furthermore, the existing domestic and global conditions before the crises will be explored as well. The fourth part will discuss how the crises spread throughout the economy (and through which channels), with specific reference to financial flows and the trade channel. The fifth part will be about the general implications of the crises and the fiscal and monetary measures taken in response,and the last part will will conclude..

Immediate Implications of the Crises

An economic crisis can be defined in different ways. In textbook versions, two consecutive quarters of negative GDP growth are considered a recession. Relatively deep recessions are deemed as crises. In some cases, sharp movements in unemployment, inflation, interest rates and exchange rates can also be utilized to determine the periods of crises. Throughout this chapter, in order to make consistent comparisons, 'crisis' is defined as the period when quarterly real GDP recorded negative growth from the same quarter in the previous year. Accordingly, the Turkish economy has encountered four apparent economic downturns since the 1980s. Here, we will focus on the crises of 1994, 2001 and 2008–09, excluding the crisis of 1999 which can partially be explained by the devastating earthquake of August 1999 in northwestern Turkey.[3]

In general, the comparison between different crises in terms of GDP is based on annual real GDP growth rates.[4] Turkish GDP declined by 4.8 per cent, 5.7 per cent and 4.9 per cent annually in 1994, 2001 and 2008–09, respectively. If annual growth rates are considered solely, then the crisis of 2001 is apparently the harshest one the Turkish economy has experienced after 1945. However, quarterly data reveal more information about the duration and magnitude of the crises. For the three crises in question, quarter two (Q2) of 1994, Q2 2001 and Q4 2008 were the quarters where negative growth was first recorded in that year.[5] Similarly, the end periods of those recessions were Q2 1995, Q1 2002 and Q4 2009, respectively. The crises of 1994 and 2008–09 lasted four quarters, whereas the crisis of 2001 lasted three quarters, although the first positive growth in GDP recorded at the end of the crisis of 2001 was relatively very low, just over zero per cent. If seasonally adjusted real rates of GDP growth are taken into account, all three crises prevailed over four quarters. Figure 4.1 demonstrates that all three crises have a more or less classical V-shape, revealing that relatively monotonically decreasing growth rates are followed by monotonically increasing GDP growth rate (less negative rates) after the economy reaches its point of lowest negative growth.[6] Furthermore, we compared total output from the beginning and the end of the crises with that in the same previous period. Interestingly, irrespective of the duration of the crises, GDP declined by about 8 per cent (8.03 per cent in 1994, 8.18 per cent in 2001 and 8.53 per cent in 2008–09) in all three crises. As a result, although conventional understanding based on annual GDP growth comparisons implies that the most severe crisis in Turkey was in 2001, according to quarterly data the crisis of 2008–09 seems to have been at least as severe or even more severe than the 2001 crisis, irrespective of the fact that there was no financial collapse in 2008–09.

Indeed, Cömert and Uğurlu (2015) document that Turkish economic performance was one of the worst in the world in this period (see Table 4.1). Excluding very small countries from the sample, Turkish economic performance during the 2008–09 crisis was only marginally better than in a small number of former Eastern Bloc countries, including Latvia, Lithuania, Ukraine, Armenia and Russia, and raw material exporters, such as Botswana and Kuwait.

Although all three crises caused a severe decline in domestic production, the influence of each crisis on employment was significantly different. The severity of the employment implications of economic crises in Turkey appear to have gradually increased.[7] For example, as Figure 4.2 demonstrates, the unemployment consequences of the 1994 crisis are not very striking. However,

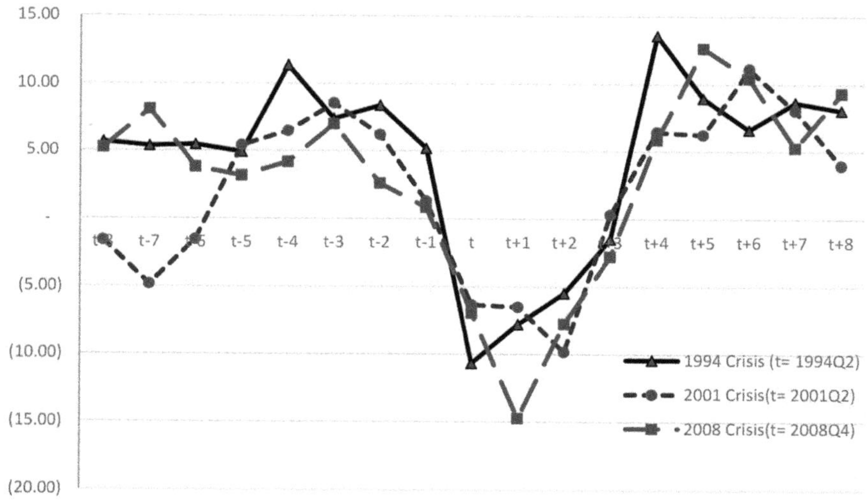

Figure 4.1 Turkish Growth Rate (compared with the same quarter of previous year), %
Source: Prepared by the authors based on TurkStat data.

Table 4.1 Growth Rates Across Selected Emerging Market Economies, %

	2002–06 average	*2007*	*2008*	*2009*
Latvia	8.99	9.6	-3.27	-17.72
Lithuania	8.01	9.79	2.91	-14.84
Ukraine	7.44	7.6	2.3	-14.8
Armenia	13.32	13.74	6.94	-14.15
Botswana	5.18	8.68	3.90	-7.84
Russia	7.03	8.53	5.24	-7.8
Kuwait	9.74	5.99	2.48	-7.07
Croatia	4.71	5.06	2.08	-6.94
Hungary	4.20	0.11	0.89	-6.76
Romania	6.16	6.31	7.34	-6.57
Moldova	6.80	2.99	7.8	-6.0
Bulgaria	5.95	6.44	6.19	-5.47
Turkey	7.21	4.66	0.65	-4.82
Mexico	2.76	3.13	1.21	-4.52
Paraguay	3.83	5.422	6.35	-3.96
Developing Countries	6.86	8.701	5.87	3.11
World	4.31	5.348	2.705	-0.381

Source: Cömert and Uğurlu (2015:10).

Turkey's unemployment rate reached very high levels after the initial periods of negative growth in production during the 2001 and 2008–09 crises (see Figure 4.2). This trend implies that some structural changes in the Turkish economy, such as a decreasing rural population, and increasing deregulation in labour markets, appear to have increased the sensitivity of the labour market to economic crises.[8] Furthermore, the recovery periods after the crises have not generated enough employment, and have been described as periods of 'jobless growth' by Telli et al (2006) and Yeldan (2011). In other words, on the one hand, the sensitivity of labour markets to declines in GDP growth seems to have increased between the 1994 and 2009 crises and, on the other hand, the time the economy needed to recover in terms of employment appears to have grown.

Pre-crisis Domestic and Global Conditions

The literature on early indicators discusses many different variables signalling a potential crisis in an economy. (see Kaminsky et al. 1998 and Frankel and Saravelos 2012). In this part, we explore the movements in variables such as the public debt to GDP ratio, the current account, interest rates, inflation, foreign currency reserves, and exchange rates in the periods leading to the crises, in order to understand the immediate factors contributing to the crises.

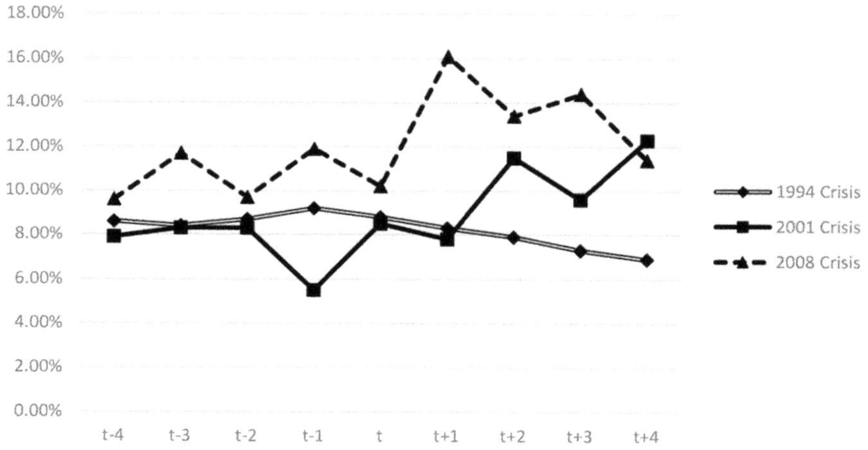

Figure 4.2 Unemployment Rate During Crises (6-monthly)
Source: Prepared by the authors based on Central Bank of the Republic of Turkey data.

The developments in the government budget balance, understood as government revenue minus government expenditure and related variables such as interest payments and government borrowings are crucial indicators to assess the fiscal sustainability of an economy affecting overall economic health.[9] A persistent deterioration in these variables is seen as a signal of a possible crisis (Sachs 1989). Indeed, in the case of many developing country crises, such as the Turkish crisis of 1994, a deterioration pattern in budget variables was very apparent. In the Turkish case, budget indicators reached alarming levels before the crises of 1994 and 2001. As can be seen from Figure 4.3, the reasons behind a high debt burden before the 1994 crisis were high primary budget deficits, together with high interest payments. The primary budget was in surplus in the period leading to the 2001 crisis due to tight fiscal policies. At the end of 1999, an International Monetary Fund (IMF)-sponsored stability programme was implemented with the aim of bringing the budget and inflation under control. Although the government initially reached its primary budget surplus targets, this did not prevent a deterioration in overall budget balance due to increasing interest payments (Akyüz and Boratav 2003).

The government budget demonstrated a very significant improvement before the period leading to the crisis of 2008–09. Decreasing interest payments and a primary budget surplus of around 5 per cent of GDP until 2006 brought about a very significant improvement in the overall balance. A slowdown in economic growth after 2006 and the output declines after the fourth quarter of 2008, together with a relatively expansionary fiscal policy, caused a gradual deterioration in the overall balance from 2006 onward. However, as Figure 4.3 demonstrates, interest payments were not unmanageable. Indeed, the improvement trend in interest payments was not reversed. Therefore, as opposed to the case of 1994 and 2001, overall budget variables did not cause alarm bells to ring prior to the crisis of 2008–09.

Interest payments are the product of the cost of borrowing (interest rates) and the stock of debt. As Figure 4.4 demonstrates, interest on government bonds remained at very high levels before the periods leading to the crises of 1994 (about 70 per cent) and 2001 (in the range of 60 to 70 per cent). However, since the stock of public debt was still at low levels, the burden of interest payments was not out of control in the case of the 1994 crisis, whereas in 2000 relatively high interest rates combined with high levels of accumulated public debt (about 60 per cent of GDP) caused only a short-lived mild improvement in the overall budget balance, despite high primary budget surpluses.

One of the most distinctive characteristics of the 2008–09 crisis was Turkey's moderate stock of public debt (about 40 percent) with low funding costs (low interest rates on government bonds) in comparison to earlier periods. Interest rates on government bonds were less than about 18 per cent before the 2008–09 crisis and surprisingly started to decline at the outbreak of the 2008–09 crisis (Figure 4.4). After a gradual and considerable decrease, interest rates declined to below 10 per cent. However, interest rates before the crises of both 1994 and 2001 followed a very similar pattern, remaining at around 70 and 80 per cent for more than two years, and jumped to even higher levels as the crises began.[10]

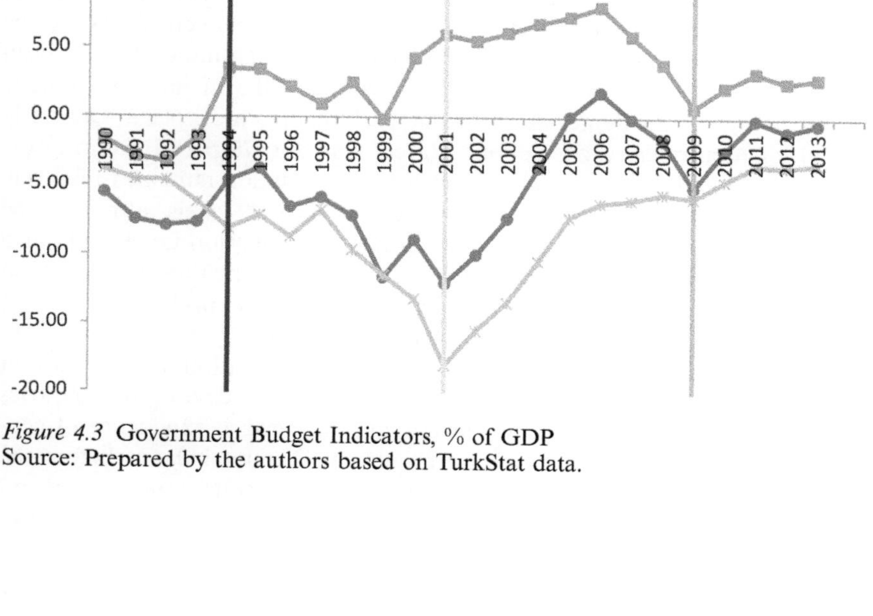

Figure 4.3 Government Budget Indicators, % of GDP
Source: Prepared by the authors based on TurkStat data.

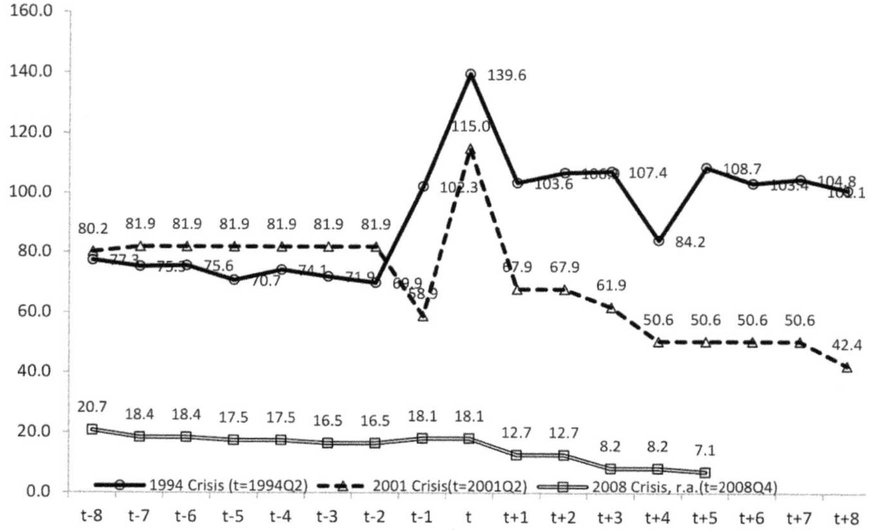

Figure 4.4 Government Bond Yields, Maturity of 6–24 Months
Source: Prepared by the authors based on TurkStat data.

The inflation rate can signal important information about the economic fragility of a country. High inflation and high nominal interest rates can feed each other in some cases. Furthermore, persistently high inflation may feed uncertainty and create significant distortions preventing investors from embarking new projects.[11]

Historically, the Turkish economy has had a severe inflation problem. From 1990 to the 1994 crisis, the average rate of inflation was above 60 per cent. From the end of the 1990s to the 2001 crisis, although inflation was still in double digits, it was on a declining trend and fell to 36 per cent thanks to the exchange rate peg policy of the 1999 disinflation programme. As can been seen from Figure 4.5, in both episodes a sudden hike in inflation, mostly related to significant depreciation in the Turkish lira, took place. Quarterly annual inflation rates reached about 125 per cent and 70 per cent during the crisis of 1994 and 2001, respectively. In contrast, inflation remained relatively under control (below 10 per cent) before the 2008–09 crisis, although the central bank had difficulty in reaching its intended inflation targets (about 5 per cent). In short, the economic outlook in terms of inflation was worst in 1994; inflation rate was high but exhibited a declining trend in the 2001 episode, and it was relatively moderate during the 2008–09 crisis.

Many researchers argue that a significant deterioration in the current account is an early signal for severe economic crises in developing countries (Kaminsky et al. 1998). When we investigate the Turkish experience of economic crises, a marked deterioration in current account balance before the crises of 1994 and 2001 is very apparent. In these episodes, current account

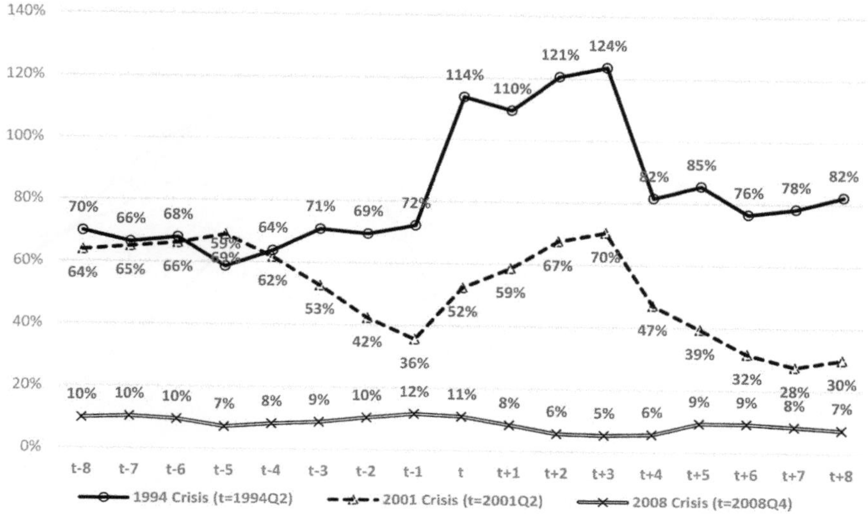

Figure 4.5 Annual Inflation Rate
Source: Prepared by the authors based on Central Bank of the Republic of Turkey Statistics.

balances were negative and worsening for about five to six quarters before national production started to decline. Furthermore, in both episodes, the current account deficits reached their maximum levels around the period when output growth started to turn negative. For the 2008–09 crisis, the current account exceeded 4 per cent of GDP after 2004 and remained at around 6 per cent for about eight quarters before the initial impact of the crisis was felt on production. In all cases, as expected, a sharp decline in production brought about an improvement in the current account. Furthermore, this positive effect was sustained for about a year. However, in the crisis of 2008–09, the current account deficit persisted in the midst of very large production declines. The current account deteriorated rapidly and reached more than 6 per cent of GDP in a very short time. As can be seen from Figure 4.6 below, although the movement in the current account balance in the episodes of the 1994 and 2001 were almost identical, they exhibited a very different structural pattern in 2008–09. This observation is in line with the findings of Comert et al. (2015). Using a range of statistical methods, they demonstrate that a structural break in the Turkish current account might have taken place around 2000. The enormous amount of global liquidity made the unprecedented levels of the current account deficit possible during this period.

Persistent current account deficits imply the accumulation of large foreign liabilities. Developing countries cannot pay back their external liabilities with their domestic currencies, which had been termed as the 'original sin' or the 'hierarchy of money'(Eichengreen et al. 2003; Eichengreen et al. 2013). In a

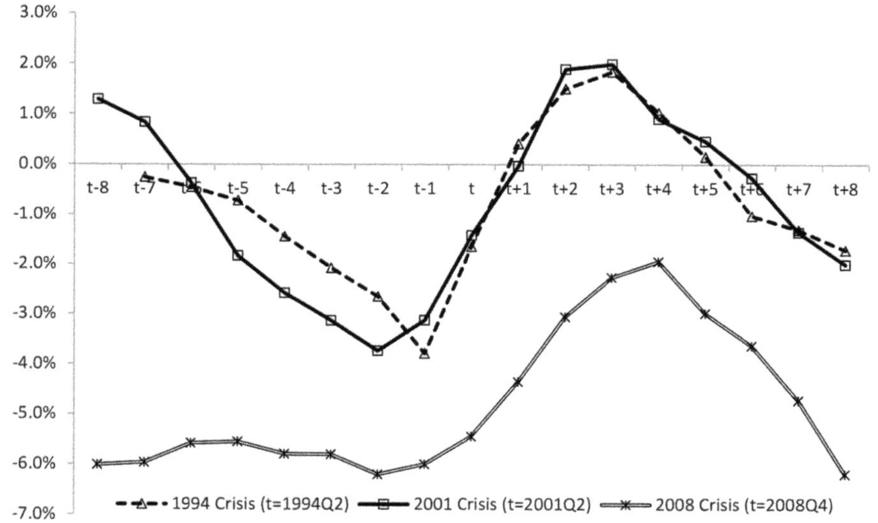

Figure 4.6 Current Account Balance, % of GDP
Source: Prepared by the authors based on Central Bank of the Republic of Turkey data.

world in which a strict hierarchy of money prevails, developing countries are forced to accumulate foreign exchange reserves even under flexible exchange rates regimes. Therefore, the amount of foreign reserves relative to liabilities (and relative to GDP) is another crucial indicator of possible vulnerabilities. Figure 4.7 demonstrates the general picture of reserves to short-term debt ratio during the crises. Complementing many other findings, the Turkish economy was caught in the crisis of 1994 with very low levels of reserves relative to its short-term debt. The reserves to short-term debt ratio critically declined to 30 per cent before the crisis. In the 2001 crisis, the reserves to external debt ratio was not as bad as the 1994 crisis, although the deterioration in the reserve position for two consecutive quarters before the output decline started was striking in the 2001 crisis. As Figure 4.7 depicts, compared with the previous two crises, the 2008–09 crisis is unique in terms of the reserves position. The Turkish economy entered the 2008–09 crisis with an ample amount of reserves in a global environment in which US interest rates were falling drastically.

Political and Geopolitical Configuration

Political structures and geopolitical factors significantly influence the trajectory of an economy. In certain political and geopolitical scenarios, potential risks materialize. Therefore, it is also important to understand the political and geopolitical configurations for the three crises investigated here.[12] The

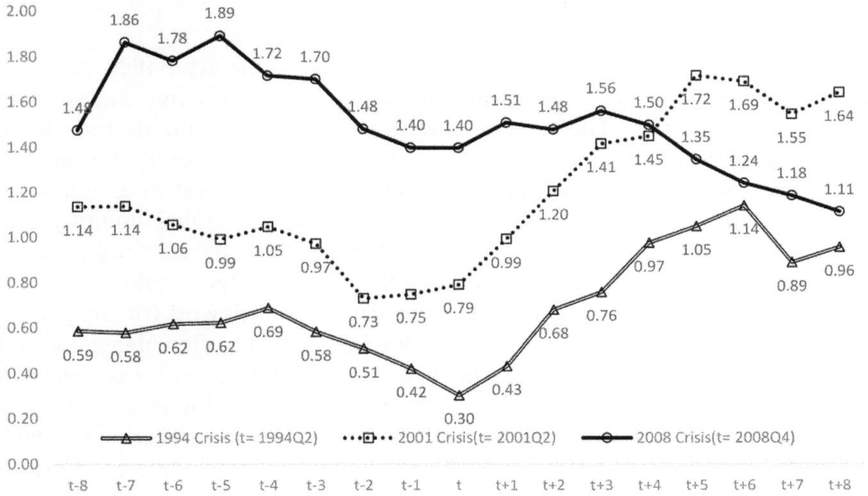

Figure 4.7 Reserves over Short-Term External Debt, ratio
Source: Prepared by the authors based on Central Bank of the Republic of Turkey, and TurkStat data.

Turkish economy was led in the 1994 and 2001 crises by relatively fragile coalition governments. In the case of the 1994 crisis, domestic conflicts, especially in the south eastern part of Turkey, increased existing uncertainties in the economy. Likewise, prevailing domestic problems within the coalition government and between the Prime Minister and the President increased economic fragility in 2001 (Marois 2012: 166). The Turkish economy faced the 2008–09 crisis with a relatively strong, single-party government, controlled by the Adalet ve Kalkınma Partisi (Justice and Development Party). In short, it is likely that domestic political configurations exacerbated existing fragilities before the 1994 and 2001 crises. Domestic and political conditions were relatively favourable in 2008-09, although this did not prevent the economy from experiencing one of the worst crises in its history.

The global economic outlook was slightly different before the crises of 1994 and 2001. The 1994 crisis took place in a period of global upswing although there was a mild slowdown in 1993. The crisis of 2001 took place at the end of a global upswing despite the fact that, the 1997 Asian Crisis and the 1998 Russian and Brazilian crises caused a slowdown in the global economy. Furthermore, global growth was also affected negatively by the 11 September attacks in the USA in 2001. However, the global economy recovered quickly and entered into a relatively long period of growth during 2001–07. As opposed to the other two cases, the crisis of 2008-09 took place in the midst of a severe global economic crisis triggered by the US sub-prime mortgage crisis. As Figure 4.8 shows, particularly advanced countries, which have been the main source of demand for goods and services of developing countries, encountered a massive reduction in GDP growth.

As experienced during the last global crisis, the monetary policy stance of developed countries has considerable influence on the economic trajectory of developing countries. The adverse effects of a deterioration of the global economic outlook can be mitigated via expansionary monetary policies. In this sense, the movements of the US Federal Reserve interest rate, indicating the Fed policy stance, can give some clues about the global liquidity and interest rates. High (or low) Fed interest rates may be an indication of increasing (or decreasing) attractiveness of US and other developed economies' financial assets, which sometimes causes slowdowns (or surges) in financial flows to developing countries, forcing them to offer higher interest rates to attract financial flows. The Fed's main interest rate was stable at around 3 per cent from mid-1992 to 1994 (Figure 4.9). In this sense, there was no exceptional monetary move by the Fed before the Turkish crisis of 1994. None the less, the Fed gradually increased its interest rate while the Turkish economy was passing through a very deep crisis in 1994 (and as Mexico entered the peso crisis of 1994). As it was a very gradual increase taking a long time, this may not be considered an exceptional development in global financial markets, even though this move may not be considered beneficial for the Turkish economy. The Fed monetary policy was relatively tight before the crisis of 2001. However, there was very sharp easing during the 2001 crisis. The Turkish economy and other developing countries benefited from this situation in the form of an abundance of financial inflows, especially after 2002.

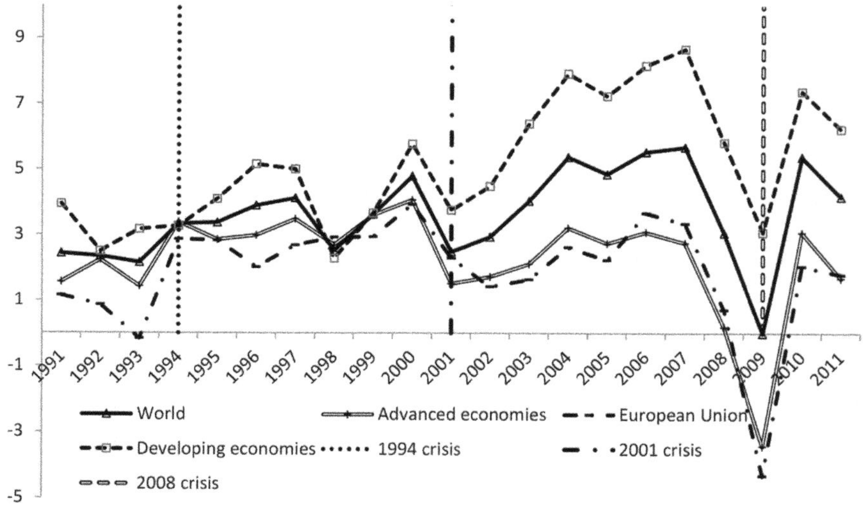

Figure 4.8 GDP Growth by Country Groups
Source: Prepared by the authors based on World Bank Development Indicators.

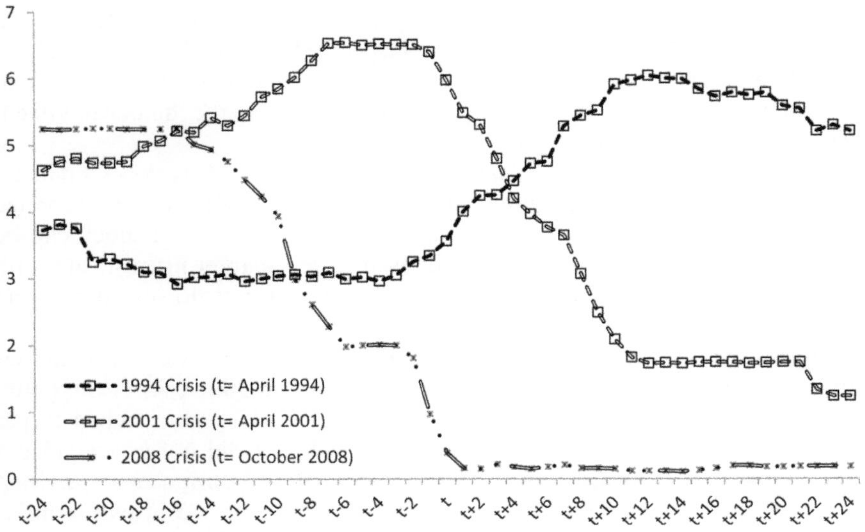

Figure 4.9 Effective Federal Reserve Funds Rate
Source: Prepared by the authors based on St Louis's Fed data.

The crisis of 2008–09 was exceptional in terms of global liquidity and interest rates. The Fed and the central banks of many other advanced countries embarked on significant expansionary monetary policies. This led to close-to-zero interest rates and liquidity bonanzas in advanced economies. Turkey and many other developing countries enjoyed these developments by welcoming this liquidity into their economies, as well as cutting their own policy rates. As discussed in the following sections, one of the reasons behind the absence of financial reversals from Turkey and many other developing countries and the very quick recovery of the flows, was the expansionary monetary policy stance of advanced countries.

How did the Crises Spread?

As documented above, global forces seem to have a very strong influence on the main economic trends in Turkey, as in other developing countries (Rey 2015; Benlialper and Cömert 2015). In this vein, the Turkish crises under investigation were either triggered or exacerbated by global factors in the form of financial flows or/and trade shocks. The Turkish economy experienced a significant financial reversal during the crises of 1994 and 2001. However, although the economy experienced a sharp decline in financial flows during the 2008–09 crisis, overall there was almost no reversal in financial flows. (see Figure 4.10). In this sense, the magnitude and duration of the financial shock that the Turkish economy encountered in the most recent crisis was low relative to that of the previous financial crises. Negative net financial flows lasted three quarters, six quarters and only one quarter during the crises of 1994, 2001 and 2008–09, respectively. Partially, as a result of these differences in financial shocks, while there were massive bankruptcies in Turkish financial markets in the previous two crises, the financial system weathered the crisis relatively well in 2008–09.

The difference between the magnitude and duration of Turkey's financial shocks has also had different implications for the country's reserves, exchange rates and interest rates. In this sense, the severity of a financial shock can be detected in the movements of central bank reserves, market interest rates and exchange rates, which may be transmitted to output losses and rising inflation.

Figure 4.11 shows that currency depreciation pressure was much milder during the 2008–09 global crisis than in the 1994 and 2001 crises. Maximum monthly appreciation of the US dollar against the Turkish lira reached 50 per cent and about 30 per cent in 1994 and 2001, while it did not exceed 15 per cent in 2008–09. Furthermore, monthly depreciation continued for at least four months in the previous two crises, but in 2009 it ended in two months. Here, it could be argued that due to foreign exchange interventions by the central bank (the selling of reserves to mitigate the overvaluation of dollar) exchange rate pressure might have been eased in the recent global crisis. However, the pressure on central bank reserves in the last crisis was of a shorter duration and the magnitude of the pressure was less. In the third

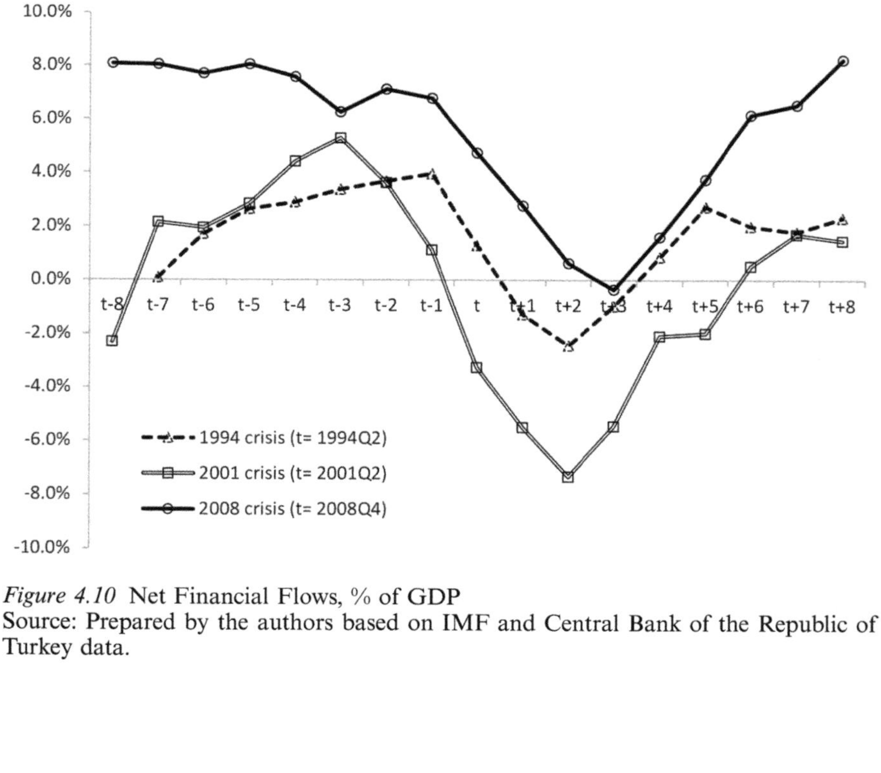

Figure 4.10 Net Financial Flows, % of GDP
Source: Prepared by the authors based on IMF and Central Bank of the Republic of Turkey data.

quarter of 2008, the reserves of the Central Bank amounted to US $76 billion, falling to a low of $63 billion in 2009. The foreign reserves lost accounted for 17.0 per cent of total reserves. By contrast, reserve depletion during the 2001 crisis was 36.0 per cent and in 1994 more than 50.0 per cent.

It can be argued that high interest rates might have substituted for reserve operations to mitigate the depreciation pressure on the Turkish lira during the global crisis. If this had been the case, higher interest rates might have been observed in times of low reserve losses. Indeed, this might even have been considered as a choice of the Central Bank, to intervene in the financial market via raising interest rates rather than depleting foreign exchange reserves and allowing exchange rates to depreciate. However, interest rate movements closely followed exchange rates and reserves. Overnight market interest rates and interest rates on public debt instruments reached unprecedented levels in the crises of 1994 and 2001, in which reserve losses and exchange rate hikes were observed. Interbank overnight rates reached 400 and 350 per cent in 1994 and 2001, respectively, while rates reached a maximum of just 16 per cent in 2009.[13 14]

Another channel through which the Turkish economy was hit by the 2008–09 global crisis was the trade channel. Even though the crises of 1994 and 2001 brought about an increase in Turkish exports, partially due to large depreciations in the Turkish Lira, during the 2008–09 global crisis, a substantial fall in export earnings was recorded. Annually, export earnings declined by more than 20 per cent in 2009. The first quarterly negative growth in exports was observed in the fourth quarter of 2008 and prevailed for four

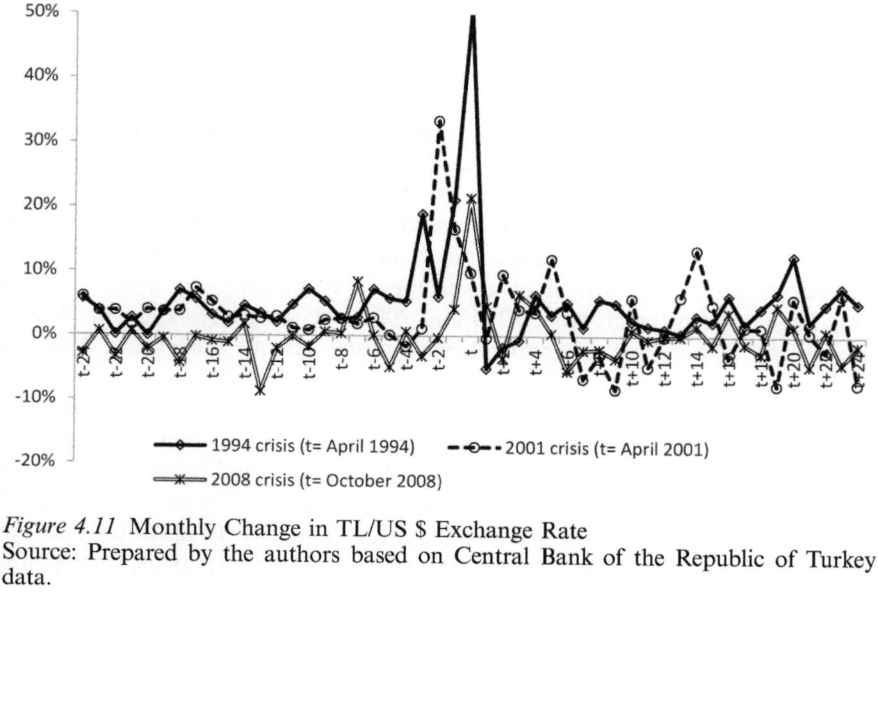

Figure 4.11 Monthly Change in TL/US $ Exchange Rate
Source: Prepared by the authors based on Central Bank of the Republic of Turkey data.

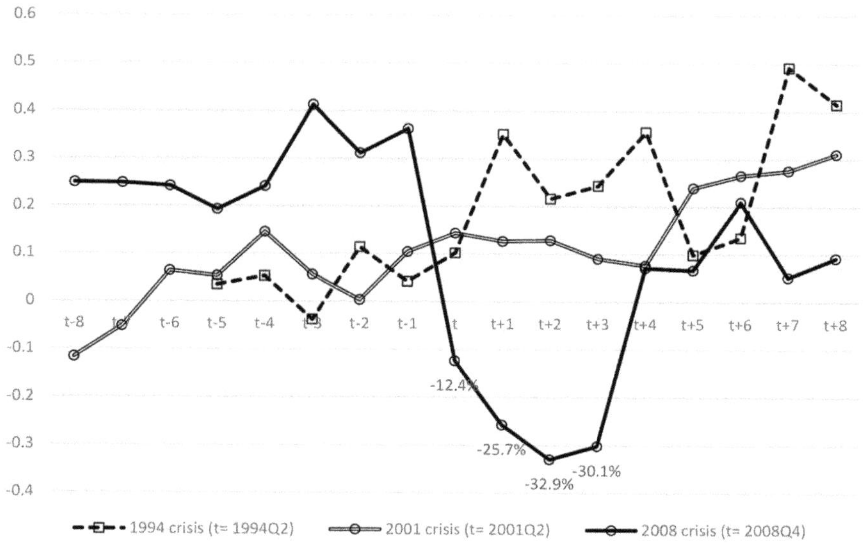

Figure 4.12 Quarterly Annual Growth Rate of Exports
Source: Prepared by the authors based on Central Bank of the Republic of Turkey data.

quarters. In other words, the duration of the crisis and duration of the negative export growths coincided. The main reason for this export shock was that the biggest export partner of Turkey, the European Union, was in a deep crisis and hence demand from most parts of Europe substantially declined.

Fiscal and Monetary Responses[15]

Differences in the government's fiscal and monetary responses to the three crises are striking and can help to explain the differences in performance of the Turkish economy in these episodes. As can be seen in Figure 4.13, government expenditure was reduced significantly during the crises of 1994 and 2001, whereas it did not decline much in the case of the 2008–09 crisis. Indeed, although the growth of government expenditure was negative for a long time in both the crises of 1994 and 2001, the economy experienced only one period of negative government expenditure growth during the 2008–09 crisis.

The striking difference in the fiscal stance of the government during the three crises can be followed by focusing on the primary balance and general government budget balance (see Figure 4.3). On an annual basis, there was an improvement in both the primary balance and general government budget balance just after the crises in 1994 and 2001. This clearly indicates that the government squeezed its spending in those episodes (that is, undertook

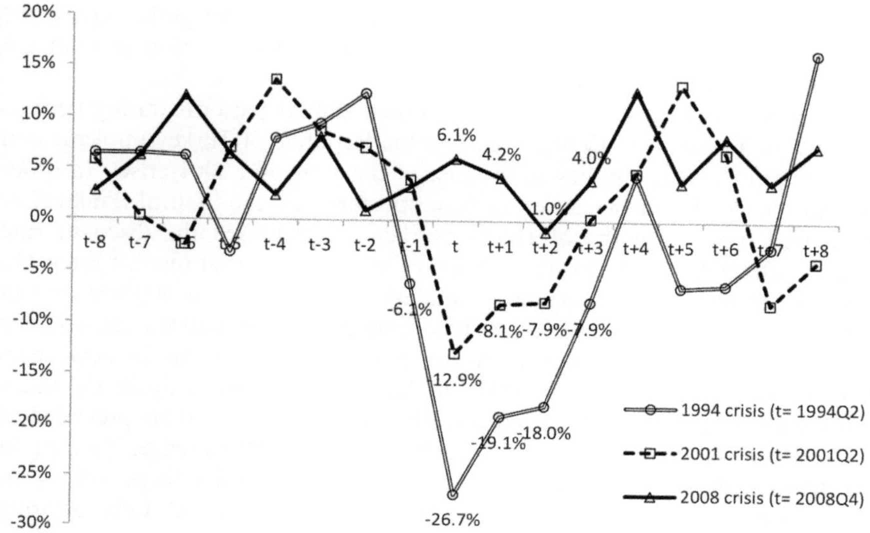

Figure 4.13 Growth of Quarterly Real Government Spending (compared with the same quarter of previous year)
Source: Prepared by the authors based on TurkStat data.

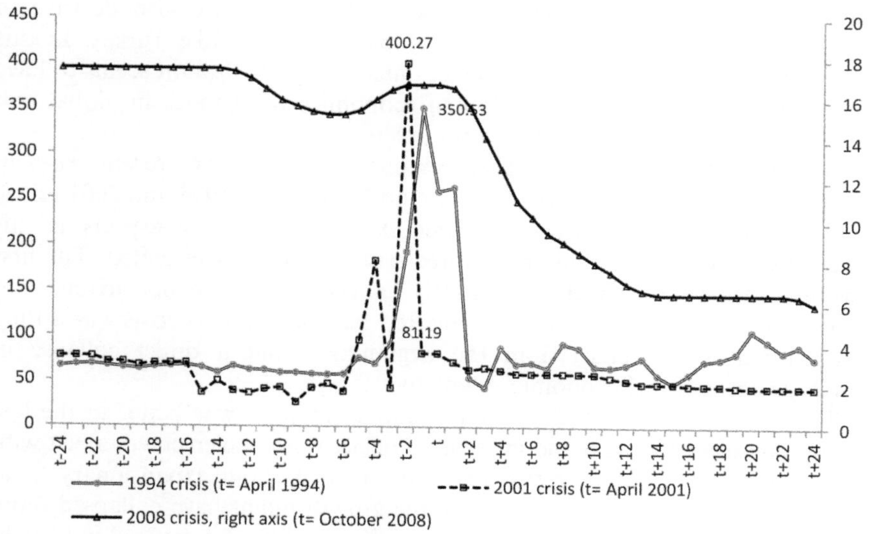

Figure 4.14 Interbank Over-Night, Call-money Interest Rates
Source: Prepared by the authors based on Central Bank of the Republic of Turkey data.

austerity measures). However, in response to the 2008–09 global crisis, the government loosened fiscal policy, which led to a deterioration in both the primary and general budget balance.

Monetary and fiscal policies have followed similar patterns during periods of crisis in Turkey. The Central Bank of the Republic of Turkey implemented a very tight monetary policy in the case of the 1994 and 2001 crises. In order to halt the trend of depreciation in domestic currency, the Central Bank either decreased funding in the overnight markets or increased the discount rate significantly, which led to very high spikes in money market interest rates. On average, as stated above, overnight interest rates were about 400 per cent in 1994 and 350 per cent in 2001 just before production growth turned negative (Figure 4.14). In other words, these two crises began after the financial markets largely froze up. Massive IMF funding seems to have calmed the interbank markets in 2001, whereas a disturbance in money markets prevailed in 1994. However, during the last crisis, the Central Bank increased funding in the money markets and took additional measures in order to provide sufficient liquidity to the market. As a result, market interest rates steadily decreased, falling below 10 per cent in a very short time period.

Conclusion

As the Turkish economy demonstrates, developing countries encounter and experience economic crises under different circumstances. Moreover, global factors, such as financial reversals and trade shocks, are also decisive in shaping the dynamics of crises in developing countries like Turkey. In this sense, the increasing degree of trade and financial globalization seems to have increased the sensitivity of developing economies to changes in global risk appetite and trade flows. Turkey is no exception.

Although there are many differences in the emergence of recent crises in Turkey, significant similarities can be found between the 1994 and 2001 crises. The crisis of 2008–09 can be considered exceptional in many aspects. In this sense, two tales can be told about three crises we have investigated. The first two episodes were deemed to be mostly finance-led and finance-driven, with repercussions on the real sectors thereafter; but the 2008–09 crisis was a fully fledged real sector crisis from the beginning, amid a direct collapse in employment and real economic productivity.

The pre-crisis macroeconomic and political outlook was better in the last crisis. Expansionary fiscal and monetary policies were implemented, albeit with some delays as opposed to the first two crises. Without expansionary fiscal and monetary policies, Turkish economic growth might have collapsed more dramatically in the last crisis. Global liquidity conditions recovered quickly in developing countries, including Turkey, thanks to unprecedented interest rate cuts and quantitative easing. However, in the most recent crisis, the Turkish economy experienced one of its worst economic downturns in its history in terms of output losses and unemployment, even though its financial markets remained resilient. In this sense, the 2008–09 crisis should be treated differently from the first two. A massive trade shock together with a certain degree of slowdown in financial flows can be devastating for a developing country such as Turkey. There is no doubt that in the deteriorating external environment, the necessary adjustments that lie ahead for attaining economic stability in Turkey and the emerging market economies will be more costly and difficult.

Notes

1 We are very grateful to Selman Çolak, Ali Riza Güngen, Thomas Marois, Oktar Türel and Galip Yalman for their very helpful comments and suggestions. All remaining errors and omissions are our own.

2 Özatay (2009), Rodrik (2009) and Türel (2010) investigate the crises Turkish economy has experienced since the 1980s.

3 Although the East Asian crisis of 1997 and, in relation to this the Russian crisis of 1998 had a role in the crisis of 1999, it is very difficult to disentangle the roles of these events in the 1999 Turkish crisis.

4 Recently, Turkish Statistical Institute has made very signficant updates in Turkish GDP series. These updates did not considerably change the growth rates around the crises years in question. Therefore, our analysis cannot be considered sensitive to these updates. However, there is a very huge discerapancy between new series and old ones after 2011. Up to now, Turkish Statical Institute has not satisfactorily explained the reason behind this.

5 However, it is important to note that Turkish quarterly annual growth was 1.3 and 0.9 in 2001Q1 and in 2008Q3. In this sense, the crisis of 1994 began with a very high GDP decline in 1994Q2 (about 10 percent). However, sharp output declines in the other two crises followed slowdowns in GDP growth. Based on this observation, Türel (2010) argues that even though the crisis of 2001 and 2008–09 took place in the downswing pahase of the national medium term cycle, the crisis of 1994 took place in upswing period of the national medium term cycle.

6 Although Figure 4.1 gives us important information about the trajectory of the crises, it would be misleading to consider overall severity of the crises by investigating only this figure due to the level effects. The crisis of 2008–09 started in 2008Q4 and became influential throughout 2009Q1, 2009Q2 and 2009Q3. In general output levels are considerably lower during the winter in Turkey and many other developing countries, which can exaggerate percentage output declines.

7 As Türel (2010) argues, one should be cautious about employment data in Turkey due to many changes made in the coverage and definitions of the employment variables.

8 A high share of rural employment in total employment would decrease pass through from output decline to the labor market due to the fact that agricultural goods demands would have less income elasticity. Turkish labor markets have been deregulated significantly through time; in many sectors, this might have enabled employers to decrease labor force in response to decline in demand for their production. Furthermore, working age household members planting their own land are considered self-employed in the agricultural sector. Therefore, as long as they plant their own land, they will not be considered unemployed. However, when they move to the city, they will be considered unemployed unless they will find a job or stop searching for a job. As a result, along with declining share of agriculture and migration to cities, labour market sensitivityto the crises can increase.

9 Especially, the first generation models of crises are based on deterioration of public balance (Krugman 1979).
10 Thanks to positive domestic and global outlook, interest rates entered into a declining trend after a short time in the 2001 crisis whereas they remained at very high levels after 1994.
11 There is no consensus in the literature about the optimum rate of inflation. However, by all standards, inflationary trends in Turkey in the 1990s and the beginning of 2001 can be considered very high and detrimental to the economy.
12 Here, we only consider indicators of very broad political and geopolitical factors without almost any elaboration. However, a through political economy analysis requires much more attention to the details regarding these factors and distributional and other conflicts in an economy.
13 The movements in exchange rates, reserves and interest rates can be summarized by a simple exchange rate index as well. We calculated an exchange rate index for three different crises periods. The implication of the index is very clear cut. Turkish economy encountered very high pressure on financial markets in the criss of 1994 and 2001 whereas the combined pressure on exchange rates reserves and interest rates was not very considerable in the recent crisis.
14 As will be discussed, this trend was also part of the expansionary monetary policy stance of Turkish central bank.
15 A detailed account of the fiscal and monetary responses to the recent crisis in Turkey can be found Cömert and Çolak (2014).

REFERENCES

Akyüz, Y. and K. Boratav (2003) "The making of the Turkish financial crisis", *World Development*, 31(9): 1549–1566.

Benlialper, A. and H. Cömert (2015) "Global constraints on central banking: The case of Turkey", *ERC-Economic Research Center Working Paper*, No 15/13, Middle East Technical University.

Cömert, H. and S. Çolak (2014), "The impacts of the global crisis on the Turkish economy and policy responses", *ERC-Economic Research Center Working Paper*, No 14/17, Middle East Technical University.

Cömert, H., U. Ünal and G. Yüksel (2015) "The investigation of recent trends in Turkish current account", in *EY International Congress on Economics II (EYC2015), November 5–6, 2015, Ankara, Turkey* (no. 258). Ekonomik Yaklasim Association.

Cömert, H., and E.N. Uğurlu (2015) "The impacts of the 2008 global financial crisis on developing countries: The case of the 15 most affected countries", *ERC-Economic Research Center Working Paper*, no. 15/09, Middle East Technical University.

Eichengreen, B., R. Hausmann and U. Panizza (2003) "The pain of original sin", in B. Eichengreen and R. Hausmann (eds.) *Other People's Money: Debt Denomination and Financial Instability in Emerging Market Economies*, University of Chicago Press, Chicago, 13–38.

Frankel, J., and G. Saravelos (2012) "Can leading indicators assess country vulnerability? Evidence from the 2008–2009 global financial crisis", *Journal of International Economics*, 87(2): 216–231.

Kaminsky, G., S. Lizondo and C.M. Reinhart (1998) "Leading indicators of currency crises", *International Monetary Fund Staff Papers*, 45(1): 1–48.

Krugman, P. (1979) "A model of balance of payments crises", *Journal of Money, Credit and Banking*, 11(3): 311–325.

Mehrling, P. (2013) "The inherent hierarchy of money", in Taylor, L., A. Rezai and T. Michl (eds.) *Social Fairness and Economics: economic essays in the spirit of Duncan Foley*, London and New York: Routledge, 394–405.

Özatay, F. (2009) *Finansalkrizlerve Türkiye*, İstanbul: Doğan Kitap.

Rey, H. (2015) "Dilemma not trilemma: the global financial cycle and monetary policy independence", *National Bureau of Economic Research Working Paper*, no. 21162.

Rodrik, D. (2009) "The Turkish economy after the crisis", *Turkish Economic Association Discussion Paper*, no. 2009/9.

Sachs, J.D. (1989) "Introduction", in J. Sachs (ed.) *Developing Country Debt and the World Economy*, Chicago, IL: University of Chicago Press, 1–34.

Telli, C., E. Voyvoda and E. Yeldan (2006) "Modeling general equilibrium for socially responsible macroeconomics: Seeking for the alternatives to fight jobless growth in Turkey", *METU Studies in Development*, 33(2): 255.

Türel, O. (2010) "Türkiye'de 1994, 2001 ve 2008–2009 ekonomik krizlerinin karşılaştırmalı analizi", *Ekonomik Yaklasim*, 21(75): 27–75.

Yeldan, E. (2011) "Macroeconomics of growth and employment: The Case Turkey", *ILO Employment Working Paper*, no. 108, International Labour Organisation: Geneva.

5 The Transformation of the State Financial Apparatus in Turkey since 2001

Thomas Marois

In Turkey, as in all emerging capitalist societies, the transition to and consolidation of neoliberalism has entailed the simultaneous financial transformation of the state apparatus. Neoliberalism, as a loose class-based ideology that suggests all developmental problems are best resolved via exposure to the market, involves complex matrixes of market-enhancing policies that have radically transformed state–society relationships. In some cases, neoliberal policies have, arguably, neutered state capacity to effect extra-market coordination and development, as in the cases of privatization and forms of liberalization. Yet at the same time neoliberalism has tended to increase the power and autonomy of specific, often finance-based, and increasingly centralized state authorities: treasuries, ministries of the economy, central banks, and the political executives. Such transformation is deeply political and entails inherently unequal social and class-based dimensions.

Such is the case in Turkey, whose society has witnessed and participated in the institutionalization of neoliberalism and state restructuring processes since the 1980s. From a Marxian-inspired political economic interpretative lens, these historic changes reflect a class-based strategy of development and form of capital accumulation premised on privileging the needs of foreign and domestic capital over those of Turkey's working classes and peasantry. Neoliberal transformation in Turkey, as elsewhere, has not been smooth, always meeting contestation and resistance. This contestation has not always or only manifested in the classic capital–labour form. In Turkey conflicts (and collaborations) have emerged between the so-called Istanbul and Anatolian, as well as domestic and foreign, fractions of capital; between different organizations of labour; and as well as between Turk and Kurd, to mention but a few. For this reason when we speak of neoliberalism in Turkey it must be qualified as *variegated* (Peck and Theodore 2007; Muñoz-Martínez and Marois 2014). That is, Turkish neoliberalism carries all the general characteristics of an attack on popular and working class aspirations by capital and by neoliberal advocates. Yet neoliberalism is also differentiated by the historical specificity of capitalism in Turkey, its class- and socially divided society, and its integration into the world market.

The transformation of the state's financial apparatus is a defining feature of contemporary neoliberal capital accumulation in Turkey. Politically authored economic openings since the 1980s—for example, capital account liberalization in 1989—have systematically increased the significance of foreign and domestic finance capital in Turkish society (see Chapter 3 in this volume). Yet the finance-led aspects of neoliberal transformation have been crisis-prone, giving rise to costly crises in 1982, 1994, 2001 and most recently in 2008–09 (see Chapter 4). Recurrent financial crisis and recovery processes have not led to an abandonment of market orthodoxy, but to the entrenchment of political, institutional and material commitments to protecting market-oriented development in Turkey, as elsewhere (Marois 2011; World Bank 2013). From the vantage point of finance and a Marxian-inspired institutional approach, I argue that neoliberal consolidation in Turkey has meant constructing a more muscular state financial apparatus. Turkish state authorities have developed new material and institutional capacity to overcome recurrent crises to the benefit of financial capital and without sacrificing underlying neoliberal strategies of development. While developing since the 1980s, it was not until after Turkey's massive 2001 crisis that this form of emerging finance capitalism consolidated such that the interests of domestic and foreign financial capital serve as "the institutionalized priorities and overarching social logic guiding the actions of state managers and government elites, often to the detriment of labor" (Marois 2012: 38). This has neither been a straightforward process unfolding at the behest of financial capital, nor has it occurred irrespective of the shifting accumulation strategies of productive and commercial capital in Turkey.

I argue this by first explaining the qualitative break that occurred in 2001. Second, I explore the wider context of Turkish authorities internalizing international best practices as 'emerging financial strategy' to help encourage finance-led capitalist consolidation. Third, I shift focus to the deliberate internal institutional restructuring and empowerment of Turkey's financial apparatus. Finally, I focus in on the build up of the state's material capacity to manage finance in contemporary capitalism. This is followed by a brief conclusion.

The 2001 Turkish Financial Crisis as Qualitative Break

It could not have been known at the time, and it surely was not on the minds of the governing coalition or the crisis management team led by Kemal Derviş. Yet the 2001 financial crisis and subsequent state-led, state-orchestrated recovery process has subsequently become the marker of qualitative change in the developmental trajectory of Turkey. In short, the 2001 crisis now demarcates a new phase in Turkish political economic history. My task here is not to elaborate on the economic dynamics of the crisis, as these are covered elsewhere in this collection (see Chapters 3 and 4) and widely in the literature on this subject. Rather, this section offers background on the generally agreed upon point that the 2001 crisis provided the opportunity for governing authorities to consolidate the state's neoliberal and financial transformation as a conjunctural, yet fundamentally qualitative, break.

The 2001 Crisis and 'Transition to a Strong Economy' Recovery Programme

The 2001 financial crisis in Turkey erupted out of two decades of neoliberal policymaking, which started to come to a head in the mid-1990s through rising public and private sector debts, exacerbated by the 1999 International Monetary Fund (IMF) Disinflation programme (Akyuz and Boratav 2003; see also Chapters 3 and 4). In February 2001, after months of instability, the crisis broke as US $5 billion in capital flight ate away at Turkey's modest foreign reserves and as the accumulation of bad banking debts, both public and private, was exposed. In response, the coalition government and the new, unelected Minister of the Economy, Kemal Derviş, introduced the neoliberal-inspired 'Transition to Strong Economy' (TSE) recovery programme in April. The goal of the TSE, in the words of Derviş, was to institutionally 'separate the economic from the political' (quoted by the Banks Association of Turkey—BAT—in 2001)—that is, to internalize market imperatives into policy formation, depoliticize the process, and ensure that the needs of capital trump popular concerns. Officials framed the TSE as necessary to eliminate Turkey's structural economic problems, increase resilience against external shocks, reduce inflation, gain control over public sector debts, and to strengthen the financial system and market discipline (BAT 2009b: 21).

The TSE programme gave rise to the 2001 Banking Sector Restructuring Programme (BSRP), a key moment in Turkey's modern financial transformation. In retrospect, state authorities have framed the 2001 BSRP as responsible for purging Turkey's earlier financial distortions and for creating an efficient, competitive, well-regulated and stable banking sector (BRSA 2002; 2009: viii). And, in neoliberal terms, these assessments are largely correct in the post-2001 era. The 2001 BSRP effectively restructured the sector so it conformed to market imperatives, while instituting regulations that reduced some of the more risky activities of the banks (see Chapter 5). As a first step, the BSRP began to re-regulate banks and enhance supervision, in a sense containing the pure neoliberal logic of market determination. That is, state authorities had to save financial capitalism from orthodox neoliberalism (Marois 2011). State authorities materially bolstered Turkey's failed economic strategy by socializing (that is, recapitalizing) some US $45 billion in accumulated banking losses between the public and private banks, and by actively dealing with the failed banks held within the Saving Deposit Insurance Fund (SDIF). Authorities also legally enabled the restructuring of private bank and productive sector debts so that non-performing loans (NPL) appeared as performing for the time, the so-called 'Istanbul Approach' (BRSA 2003: 47–52).

Institutionally, the government gave the Bank Regulation and Supervision Agency (BRSA; created just before the outbreak of crisis in 2000) new powers and charged the institution with resolving the current crisis and for building state capacity to manage future financial risks within Turkey's borders (according to European Union—EU—financial standards). The BRSA initiated a series of significant financial reforms that included higher capital adequacy requirements for the banks; higher capital requirements for bank mergers and acquisitions; adjustments to credit limits; reworked NPL provisions; clearer accounting rules for banks linked to other companies (holding groups); improved balance sheet reporting; and so on. Corporate and tax legislation also required that the Turkish financial-industrial groups separate out their financial and corporate operations, as these were intimately interlinked pre-crisis. In July 2001 the government allowed the Capital Markets Board of Turkey to establish a derivatives market under the İstanbul Stock Exchange (İSE) to expand and deepen domestic financial markets as an alternative form of finance (see Chapter 7). The initial BSRP changes and the rise of the BRSA also paved the way for the internalizing of so-called international best practices.

International Best Practices as Emerging Financial Strategy

Turkey's response to the 2001 crisis was hardly just a national affair. Turkey exists within an international hierarchy of states, dominated by the advanced capitalist societies of the USA and Western Europe, and a capitalist world market characterized by intense competitive imperatives and managed by powerful international financial institutions such as the IMF and World Bank. Since the mid-1990s, moreover, political and economic decisions have been heavily influenced by the instabilities in emerging capitalist societies, given the 1994 Mexican, 1997 East Asian, and the 1998 Brazilian and Russian crises. International and domestic policymakers and global capital were concerned with developing national capacities to avert and/or overcome financial crises in ways that do not threaten underlying neoliberal accumulation opportunities (for example, foreign reserve accumulation, as discussed below). These structural international dynamics inform and influence the decisions made by Turkish authorities, which in turn re-shape the nature of the world market. The EU, too, has been a key influence behind Turkey's emerging financial strategy.

In Turkey prior to the 2001 crisis, governing authorities were not averse to neoliberal reforms. Indeed, authorities responded to and aimed to internalize often foreign-crafted international best practices. This is not to say such practices unfolded without contestation or at the pace desired by neoliberal advocates. However, the neoliberal setting of international best practices in finance has a powerful influence on emerging capitalist policy formation in its seemingly commonsense, technical, depoliticized approach.[1] In this way, financial reforms can be narrated as if they were outside wider social relations of power, exploitation and domination. The economic and financial aspects of Turkey's EU accession exemplify this process.

A significant step towards Turkey's internalizing international best practices came in December 1999 with the Helsinki European Council's declaration of Turkey as a candidate for EU membership (Bedirhanoğlu et al. 2013: 178–80). The declaration required Turkey to prepare a National Programme for the Adoption of the *Acquis* (NPAA). The *acquis communautaire* comprises a common body of rights and obligations binding all EU members. The first Accession Partnership document signed with Turkey was on 8 March 2001 (at the peak of the 2001 crisis) and it included a wide range of objectives and short-term priorities. Those measures in the NPAA most related to the financial transformation of the state included official commitments to some of the most neoliberal of EU economic reforms. These included implementing an IMF- and World Bank-backed disinflation and structural reform programme; swift market-oriented financial reforms; fiscal reforms; state-owned enterprise privatization; and central bank independence (modelled on EU norms). These restructuring measures closely reflected those embodied in the 2001 TSE and BSRP. Early assessments of the programme believed EU accession would generate more virtuous and sustained cycles of development, given EU best practices as an anchor rooting Turkish development policy (cf. Öniş 2006: 254).

A second NPAA in June 2003 focused on enhancing the market-orientation and competitiveness of Turkey's economy in preparation for EU accession. The programme again highlighted the economic need for privatization, for transferring market regulation functions to independent agencies, and for reducing macroeconomic uncertainty—that is, the deepening of neoliberal rule. To this end, Turkish authorities established new independent regulatory agencies in sectors including energy and telecommunications, acting to depoliticize (or, in Derviş's words, to 'separate the economic from the political') economic processes. The 2003 NPAA also gave importance to approximating the EU system of taxing financial instruments. For capital markets, the NPAA called for the adoption of EU standards of financial reporting to enhance transparency, driving financial development. Special emphasis was also given to public disclosure, the protection of investors, and exchange systems. That is, to bolstering the state financial apparatus.

Throughout this period, the internationalization of Turkey's banking sector (the dominant form of financial institution in Turkey; see Chapter 6) was of major concern for international financial institutions and the EU. After coming to power in 2002, the Adalet ve Kalkınma Partisi (AKP—Justice and Development Party) amended the 1999 Banking Law repeatedly. The changes desired were prepared according to EU legislation and aimed at crafting a new banking law. In October 2005 the EU started accession negotiations with Turkey, and in November state authorities promulgated the new Banking Law No. 5411, written with the intention of ensuring that the needs of international financial investors are met so that the government could assure the recycling of capital inflows to service growing public and private debts. The law included provisions for consolidated regulation and supervision, corporate governance, consumer rights, among other things. That is, the law aimed to restructure and internationalize the state and financial apparatus. But the law also sought to place a sharper wedge between political and economic institutions in Turkey by transferring the regulation and supervision of some non-bank financial institutions from the Treasury to the BRSA. All related sub-regulations that would enhance compliance with EU regulations were completed by November 2006.

It is important to note that the 2005 Banking Law partially reversed certain earlier liberalization measures, insofar as it gave state financial authorities greater power to manage and intervene in the banking sector by, for example, limiting the number of banks, raising capital requirements, and limiting new bank licensing. Yet the Banking Law also deepened market rule by, for example, allowing for outsourcing of banking activities (formalized in the Outsourcing Regulation of 2006). As one indication of how domestic governance institutions internalize international neoliberal norms, however, the BRSA understands bank outsourcing as a natural consequence of competition and new technologies, both of which will help to increase productivity and efficiency insofar as it offers bankers more flexible and cost-effective solutions in the workplace (BRSA 2009: 26).

Turkey's emerging financial strategy and transformation processes have also evolved in line with the international best practices set by the Basel Accords (I–III). These Accords formalize non-binding, but highly influential regulatory best practices for the global banking industry and national regulators, with the latter held to account for their response to these measures. The Accords are issued by the Basel Committee of Banking Supervision, headquartered at the highly secretive Bank for International Settlements in Basel, Switzerland (Seabrooke 2006).

Turkey had worked toward Basel I compliance since 1989. The adequacy of Basel I for accounting for credit risks, however, was increasingly in question especially given the spate of emerging market crises, capped off by Turkey's in 2001. After the 2001 crisis, Turkish authorities began working towards internalizing elements of the emerging Basel II framework for risk management, corporate governance, accounting, information systems, and so on. Capital adequacy was targeted at 12 per cent. In March 2003 the Banks Association of Turkey (BAT) established the Basel II Working Committee which evolved into the Basel II Co-ordination Committee, comprising financial élites from the Treasury, BRSA, Central Bank, the Capital Markets Board of Turkey (CMB) and BAT. The Committee formed a discussion platform in preparation for BaselII implementation. This led to the writing of the 'Road Map for Transition to Basel II', which was published by the BRSA in May 2005 (BAT 2009b: 51). BRSA authorities had planned to implement Basel II by late 2008; however, the 2008–09 crisis delayed the process until June 2012 (and has since given rise to Basel III, of which implementation has been delayed until 31 March 2019). In practice, the banking sector regularly shows capital adequacy well in excess of Basel II requirements, reaching as high as 19 per cent (see Chapter 6).

As a further commitment to international best practices, Turkey joined the joint IMF and World Bank Financial Sector Assessment Programme (FSAP) in 2006. Subsequent Turkish FSAP updates call for deepening Turkey's supervision and regulatory capacity, especially relative to risk management (IMF 2012: 26). Then in 2009 Turkey became part of the Basel Committee on Banking Supervision. Membership within this élite financial club is expected to enhance the convergence of Turkish regulations with international best practices. According to a 2011 Progress Report, the Turkish banking sector was characterized by resilience to the global financial crisis, robust financial ratios, improved efficiency in financial intermediation, and moderate banking sector concentration. It was also indicated that the alignment with the EU *acquis* on banks and financial conglomerates and financial market infrastructure was at a high level. On 21 December 2016 the European Commission recognized Turkey's bank regulation and practice as equivalent to the EU's. None the less, recommendations such as full bank privatization have not been followed (as shall be discussed below). Until the AKP government declared an ongoing state of emergency following the 15 July 2016 coup attempt, the government had been largely committed to implementing international best practices intended to smooth and moderate free-flowing capital, rather than erect any barriers to capital mobility (cf. Muñoz-Martínez and Marois 2014). There are now regular incidents of President Recep Tayyip Erdoğan clashing with the principles of central bank independence and the setting of interest rates vis-à-vis the value of the Turkish lira and inflation rates.

International authorities like the IMF, while cautious, have generally welcomed financial restructuring since 2001. The regulation of financial markets is a field in which Turkey has already ensured a successful alignment with the acquis. As Basel II Accords have also been accepted by the EU as the main regulatory framework since 2006, Turkey's implementation of Basel II principles have helped to harmonize its financial regulations with those of the EU. As of mid-2015, the Central Bank reports that banking sector liquidity is strong and that banks in Turkey "are able to meet the legal liquidity coverage ratios put into effect by the BRSA in early 2015 in line with Basel III regulations" (CBRT 2015: 27).

Box 5.1 Major Financial Institutional Developments in Turkey since 2001

- April 2001 Transition to Strong Economy Programme
- April 2001 Amendment to the Central Bank Law on Independence of the Central Bank, maintaining price stability becomes the main objective via inflation targeting in due course
- May 2001 Banking Sector Restructuring Programme

- 2005 Banking Law No. 5411:
  - aimed at a national banking system fully integrated into the international financial system
  - the regulation and supervision of non-bank financial institutions was transferred from the Treasury to the BRSA
- 2005 "Road Map for Transition to Basel-II":
  - formal institutionalization has been postponed in the wake of US sub-prime crisis
- 2005 Establishment of Turkish Derivatives Exchange
- 2007 Housing Finance Law No.5582:
  - to enable banks to pool mortgages and securitize housing loans
- 2007 Insurance Law No. 5684
- 2011 Establishment of Financial Stability Committee:
  - to better detect, manage and mitigate aggregate and systemic financial risks
- 2012 Capital Market Law No.6362
  - İstanbul Stock Exchange renamed Borsa İstanbul in April 2013
- 2012 Basel II Implementation

Building the State's Institutional Financial Apparatus

The financial restructuring that occurred after the 2001 crisis is closely intertwined with the rise to power and permanence of the AKP majority government in 2002. The AKP supported and then deepened the processes of financial transformation triggered by the 2001 crisis. In its first years, the AKP government showed a strong commitment towards fiscal discipline and reform, which helped raise investor confidence, which has been the basis of Turkish recovery (Öniş 2006: 253). Thus, while this process occurs in an international context, financial transformation is also a deeply national affair and it involves the political transformation of public institutions such as the Central Bank and the BRSA.

In Turkey there is no single authority in charge of supervision of all the institutions in the financial sector. The authorities responsible for supervising and regulating the respective financial institutions are the CMB, the Undersecretary of the Treasury under the Prime Ministry of the Republic of Turkey, and the Banking Regulation and Supervision Agency.

The Central Bank of the Republic of Turkey

The standard functions of modern central banks include implementing monetary and exchange rate policies and managing the national currency. In the early 20th century, however, central bank functions often involved crafting domestic policy to pursue national developmental goals (see Chapter 2). When established in 1931, the Central Bank of the Republic of Turkey was

Table 5.1 Supervision and Regulation of the Turkish Financial System, 2016

Financial Institutions/Instrument	*Regulatory Institution and Responsibilities*
Banks and other Credit Institutions: – Banks (Public and Private) – Leasing – Factoring – Financial Companies	Banking Regulation and Supervision Agency (BRSA) Core responsibilities include the supervision of all banks, financial holding companies, leasing companies, factoring companies and consumer finance companies, and regulations regarding their activities.
Capital Market Institutions: – Mutual (investment) funds – Intermediary institutions – Real estate investment trusts – Pension funds	Capital Markets Board (CMB) Core responsibilities include the supervision and regulation of securities brokers.
Insurance Companies	Undersecretariat of the Treasury Core responsibilities include public finance, implementation of fiscal policy, and supervision and regulation of insurance companies.
Payment Systems	Central Bank of the Republic of Turkey (CBRT): Core responsibilities include the implementation of monetary policy and exchange rate regime to achieve price stability and financial stability, management and supervision of payment and settlement systems
Savings Insurance System	Savings Deposit Insurance Fund (SDIF) Core responsibilities include protecting the rights and interests of deposit holders, and resolution of banks.

Source: BAT 2015, I-14; http://www.tcmb.gov.tr/.

mandated to bolster national economic development and to act as the treasurer to the government. Later, the January 1970 Central Bank Act (Law No. 1211) mandated authorities to manage monetary policy in line with five-year development plans. Since the 1980s, however, neoliberal advocates have sought to de-politicize central banks by instituting market mechanisms in central bank operations and by erecting institutional barriers between national financial and monetary policy formation, on the one hand, and the political executive and wider democratic processes, on the other hand. This separation is pitched as necessary for reducing corruption and ensuring efficient market processes. Central bank independence and price stability mandates are now definitive features of modern, neoliberal central banking. Central banks can intervene in the market from time to time to smooth excessive fluctuations in inflation, or the value of the currency, and to accumulate foreign exchange reserves, but only so long as their actions remain subordinate to achieving price stability.

The severity of the 2001 crisis opened an opportunity for the government, in tandem with the international financial institutions, to push forward with market reforms. Changes to the Central Bank Law in April 2001, as part of the TSE programme, transformed the institution's mandate. Its new primary objective would be to achieve and maintain price stability. To this end, the Law granted the Central Bank enhanced institutional independence from the government and the Treasury. While the Central Bank was still allowed to pursue growth or employment initiatives, it could not do this if the activity contravened its price stability imperative. At the same time, the Central Bank could no longer extend loans or grant credit to public institutions or the Treasury, as these were now deemed as inflation-generating mechanisms. To bolster its institutional independence and help mitigate political interventions, the government extended the rights and tenures of senior Central Bank executives. The 2001 Law also allowed for the formation of the Monetary Policy Committee (MPC), which centralized and insulated decision-making processes. The MPC members include the Central Bank Governor (as Chair), Deputy Governors, a member to be elected by and from among the Board members and a member to be appointed by a joint decree on the recommendation of the Governor. A representative from the Treasury may participate in board discussions, but cannot vote. Aspects of these measures had been signalled in the early stages of the 2001 crisis. Turkey's December 2000 Letter of Intent to the IMF made clear Turkey's commitment to a new central bank law and inflation targeting to be enacted by the end of April 2001.

Turkey's inflation-targeting regime unfolded in two phases: an implicit inflation-targeting phase from 2002 to 2005 and an explicit inflation-targeting phase since 2006. The first phase enabled the build-up of capacity in the Central Bank and for a transitional period for markets. The second phase since 2006 has formally targeted inflation primarily through the use of short-term interest rates. The actual target level is not set in full independence by the CBRT, but in consultation with the government, and the levels have varied from year to year. For example, in 2002 the annual inflation target was set at 35 per cent, while actual inflation was recorded at 29.7 per cent (see http://www.tcmb.gov.tr/). In 2006, the inflation target was set at 5.0 per cent while actual inflation was recorded at 9.7 per cent. Since 2012, the inflation target has been 5 per cent, with recorded inflation overshooting this target each year: 6.2 per cent in 2012, 7.4 per cent in 2013, 8.2 per cent in 2014, and 8.8 per cent in 2015. While exceeding targets, Turkey has nonetheless witnessed a somewhat structural break in high inflation since 2002 (see Chapter 4). According to the Banks Association of Turkey, the transformation of the Central Bank and greater institutional independence has facilitated the effective struggle against inflation (BAT 2005: 25). A more critical account would link inflation-targeting to the privileging of financial imperatives within the state apparatus, insofar as it seeks to protect the value of capital assets in Turkey, on the one hand, and to suppress workers' wages below rates of inflation under neoliberalism that also help reduce inflationary pressures. The impact of the 2008–09 global crisis on Turkey, however, has influenced Central Bank authorities to take up the concern for financial stability alongside its price stability imperative (Aslaner et al. 2015).

The Central Bank Risk Centre

According to the repealed Article 44 of Central Bank Law No.1211, the fundamental objective of the Risk Centre (established in 1951) is to ensure that the customers or loan applicants of banks and financial institutions can access credits and assist them in their credit decisions (CBRT 2011: 63). While initially dealing with banks, in June 2000 the Risk Centre began dealing too with factoring and financial leasing companies and beginning in February 2005 with consumer financing companies, and then most recently in October 2007 with asset management companies (CBRT 2011: 63). As of 2017, there were 178 participants included within the Risk Centre, which include 52 banks, 14 financing companies, 13 asset management companies, 26 financial leasing companies, 61 factoring companies, eight insurance companies, a Credit Guarantee Fund, the Union of Agricultural Credit Co-operatives, and the Borsa Istanbul, in addition to the SDIF and CMB (which provide information resources). In line with the Basel Committee on Banking Supervision, Turkish authorities have decided that banks in Turkey should develop their own internal risk control mechanisms. To this end, authorities decided to transfer Risk Center activities to the BAT (as a substantial part of the Turkish financial system consists of banks) (CBRT 2011: 64). This was institutionalized in Law No. 6111 of February 2011 (which superseded earlier provisions under Article No. 1211 of the Central Bank Law).

The Bank Regulation and Supervision Agency (BRSA)

Since its establishment in 1999 (under the Bank Act No. 4389) and coming into operation in August 2000, the BRSA has become a key institution within Turkey's financial apparatus (BRSA 2015). The logic behind its foundation involved drawing together Turkey's otherwise fragmented bank regulatory apparatus under one roof. The 1990s had proven especially volatile financially and international financial institution pressure for a more independent bank regulator had grown. Like the Central Bank, governing élites endowed the BRSA with regulatory independence in order to pursue the goal of safeguarding the banking sector. Its capacity and expertise were immediately tested, given the role assigned to it in 2001 to help overcome the crisis and to restructure the banking sector (under the BSRP). Since 2001, the BRSA has been building up operational capacity in the areas of regulation, auditing, licensing and enforcement, information management, research, and international relations. In terms of its core roles, the BRSA is charged with regulating accounting, risk, and information systems, as well as dealing with leasing, factoring, asset management, and some financing companies (as these are often tied to the banks). To assess and rate the banks' financial structures, the BRSA uses the so-called 'CAMELS' system: C → Capital Adequacy; A → Asset Quality; M → Managerial Ability; E → Earnings; L → Liquidity; S → Sensitivity to Market Risk.

These institutional roles are guided by the BRSA's fundamental goal, which is "to ensure the confidence and stability in financial markets, to provide effective operating of loan system and to safeguard the rights and interests of depositors" (BRSA 2015: 14). As of 2018, the BRSA is bound by the 2005 Banking Law (No. 5411; last updated in 2015); the Law on Bank Cards and Credit Cards (No. 5464); the Financial Leasing, Factoring and Financing Companies Law (No. 6361); and the Law on Payment and Security Settlement Systems, Payment Services and Electronic Money Institutions (No. 6493).

The BRSA plays a key role in mediating the internationalization of the financial apparatus and finance capital in Turkey. In the authoring of financial regulations, the BRSA explicitly aims to approximate EU and international best practices and the Basel Accords (BRSA 2015: 16). The BRSA is responsible for signing official Memorandums of Understanding (MoU) with other national regulators, and has penned 34 MoUs since its inception, with 19 of these since 2008 (BRSA 2015: 28). The BRSA has formal relationships with the IMF, the Organisation for Economic Co-operation and Development (OECD), and the World Bank. For example, the BRSA signed a MoU with the World Bank in 2013 vis-à-vis "technical collaboration concerning emerging and developing markets" (BRSA 2015: 26). Internally, institutions like the BRSA, the Central Bank, the Treasury, the CMB and SDIF author MoUs both to promote inter-institutional co-operation and to circulate international best practice internally. However, when independent state authorities sign MoUs, the event is never simply technical in nature. Rather, financial MoUs institutionalize specific relationships of power that privilege certain social groups, such as financial capital. At the same time, such MoUs reflect prevailing political commitments to the neoliberal internationalization of the state authorities' responsibility to help to manage and stabilize a global financial process (Marois 2012: 179).

For institutional political economists, the formation of the BRSA was historically important because: (a) it should improve the performance and reliability of the banking sector; and (b) it should remove political influence (and the practical distinction between public and private bank operations) (Alper and Öniş 2003: 17). Significantly for these scholars, the transformational push came from external sources including the IMF, World Bank and the EU institutions, which would provide a sound basis and subsequent anchor of domestic reform. In other words, exogenous pressures enabled the creation of the domestic institutions needed to mediate the ebbs and flows of an increasingly finance-led capitalism, which in turn ought to help create a more virtuous cycle of accumulation. Yet neoliberal reforms in Turkey have demanded ever-increasing levels of regulation, and this has entailed the further empowerment of state institutions such as the BRSA.

The Capital Markets Board (CMB)

The CMB regulates the capital markets (securities and derivatives) in order to safeguard investments in Turkey (see http://www.cmb.gov.tr/). As the CMB is discussed in more detail in Chapter 7, only the basics of the institution will be discussed here. The main legal framework of Turkish capital markets consists of three core pieces of legislation. These include the Capital Markets Law No. 2499 of July 1981, the Decree By-Law No. 91 of October 1983 concerning securities exchanges, and the Turkish Commercial Code. Other regulations related to the capital markets include Decree No. 32 of August 1989 on "protecting the value of the Turkish currency", the Regulation concerning the establishment and operation principles of securities exchanges, the Regulation on the İSE, the Regulation concerning the establishment and operation principles of futures and options exchanges, and the Law amending the laws related to housing finance system. Hence, the CMB is the regulatory and supervisory authority in charge of securities and derivatives markets in Turkey. Its guiding mission is to "make innovative regulations, and perform supervision with the aim of ensuring fairness, efficiency and transparency in Turkish capital markets, and improving their international competitiveness" (http://www.cmb.gov.tr/). In terms of the CMB's regulatory functions, it oversees corporations with more than 250 shareholders or that trade shares on the stock exchange. The CMB also regulates Turkey's capital market institutions such as intermediary institutions (banks and brokerage firms); investment companies (including real estate investment trusts and venture capital companies); mutual funds; and a number of other institutions including settlement houses, rating institutions, independent auditors, portfolio and asset management firms, investment advisory firms, and real estate appraisal companies. Finally, its portfolio includes stock and derivatives exchanges and other markets such as precious metals exchanges.

Like the BRSA, the CMB has an important role mediating between domestic and international financial processes. The CMB has integral relations with foreign regulators and international financial institutions, including the IMF, the World Bank, the OECD and World Trade Organization, but most notably through its information exchange networks with foreign securities authorities and ties to the International Organization of Securities Commissions. Therein, and just as in banking, the EU accession process figures prominently in CMB operational guidelines. For example, the CMB is responsible for harmonization of domestic legislation relating to the free movement of capital, financial services, company law and the economic and monetary policy of the EU *acquis*. A recent relationship was formalized in 2010 with the Islamic Financial Services Board. In terms of MoUs, the CMB has signed 32 bilateral agreements regarding the sharing of information, and co-operation. Far from realizing neoliberal ideals of a 'night watchman' state, the CMB enhances and extends state institutional power.

The 2011 Financial Stability Committee

The formation of the Financial Stability Committee (FSC) in June 2011 was an important step towards the centralization of financial authority and its insulation from popular democratic oversight or influence. Officially, the FSC aims to offer a systemic approach to financial supervision in Turkey in order better to detect, manage and mitigate aggregate and systemic financial risks (IMF 2012: 26; http://www.tcmb.gov.tr/). The FSC is constituted under the office of the Deputy Prime Minister for Economic and Financial Affairs responsible for the Undersecretariat of the Treasury. The FSC members include the Undersecretary of the Treasury; the Governor of the Central Bank; the Chair of the BRSA; the Chair of the CMB; and the Chair of the SDIF. The Deputy Prime Minister can invite other ministers and public officials to the meetings if necessary. The idea is that the FSC can bridge the individual mandates of separate financial authorities in Turkey and align their policy tools. The FSC builds off and complements an earlier structure of wider financial sector representation—the Financial Sector Commission. Its members include those of the new FSC, but also from the Ministry of Finance, the Competition Authority, the Ministry of Development, the Borsa İstanbul, the BAT, and the Participation Banks Association of Turkey. Notable is the lack of popular or labour market representation. In Turkey, a key aspect of the post-crisis reproduction of neoliberalism and financialization is centralized political control and the real separation of the financial apparatus from popular and working class interests (Aydin 2013: 100; Marois and Muñoz-Martínez 2016).

The 2001 crisis served as an opportunity for domestic and international advocates to rapidly press forward with the desired neoliberal financial reforms. The incoming AKP government, then, adopted this trajectory of reform and accelerated it with the express intention of more fully integrating the Turkish financial sector into global financial markets and, by extension, to enhance the state apparatus's international regulatory capacity (Marois 2012: 179). In a sense, then, neoliberalism has been as much about liberalization as it has been about re-regulation, and this transformation has entailed a "decisive shift of power within the state itself, leading to the growing power and influence of the neoliberal wing of the Turkish economic bureaucracy and a parallel process of weakening and marginalising the statist bureaucracy" (Önis 2011: 718). Underneath this, it is possible to see the logic of financial capital as increasingly being that of the state's financial apparatus, with no direct institutional mechanisms to privilege the needs of workers in Turkish society and no democratic mechanisms for popular classes to shape the financial apparatus. This domestic transformation, in turn, feeds back into the reproduction of the neoliberal financial world market as Turkish authorities have internalized foreign best practices as their own.

Reconstituting the State's Material Financial Capacity

The contemporary financial world market requires each individual state's financial apparatus to help reproduce the global structure. For conventional approaches, this means promoting state financial apparatuses capable of effective regulation and supervision, understood in technical and economistic terms devoid of power relations, and the reduction of the state's direct presence in the economy via reduced public ownership and control of financial institutions (World Bank 2012). Yet international financial institutions also recommend that states should build up greater material capacity to intervene in markets at times of financial risk and crisis (World Bank 2013). In critical terms, this reconstitution of the state's financial apparatus under neoliberalism has to do with managing emerging finance capitalism, (or financialization, see Introduction) by building up greater material capacity to intervene and protect the interests and accumulation opportunities of capital, in particular finance capital, with little regard to privileging the needs of popular classes, workers, or democracy. This has not been a straightforward process, without contradictions. In Turkey, the process of material reconstitutions has involved reducing and restructuring material capacity through privatization processes but also increasing its material involvement in the market through public–private partnerships and the remobilization of state-owned banks for financial development. This, too, is tied to the building up of İstanbul as an international financial centre. Finally, a common element has involved the accumulation of foreign reserves as a pot of capital ready for mobilization in the interests of preserving finance capitalism.

Privatization and Financial Development

Privatization, understood technically as reducing the state's presence in the economy, in Turkey began to take root under Turgut Özal's Administration in the early 1980s (OECD 1999: 20). Laws No. 2983 (1984) and No. 3291 (1986) restructured elements of the state's legal apparatus so that policymakers could proceed with privatization. Henceforth, the Public Participation Administration (later the Privatization Administration), housed under the Prime Minister's Office, would undertake the preparation and sell-off of Turkey's state-owned enterprises (SOEs). As early as 1985, some initial privatizations took place, but these remained fairly small in scale, reflecting Turkey's gentle learning curve in this respect. At the same time, significant steps were underway to restructure major SOEs, with the goal being enhanced financial performance as preparation for eventual privatization. The government also drew in foreign expertise to inform their strategies, hiring a US investment bank to produce the 1986 Morgan Guaranty Report, which reinforced emerging neoliberal imperatives around a reduced state and enhanced market (OECD 1999: 119). The Report emphasized the need for deeper and more open financial markets, thus linking privatization to a parallel process of financial market creation. Subsequently, global privatization processes have been closely linked to financial development, both reciprocally feeding off each other (Marcelin and Mathur 2015). In Turkey, a significant turning point came via enabling re-legislation: in August 1989 Decree No. 32 under the Law of Protection of the Value of the Turkish lira completed the liberalization of capital accounts and foreign exchange operations. The government lifted the limits on the foreign assets that could be owned domestically and on foreign borrowing by Turkish banks. Moreover, foreign capital was allowed to be traded openly in corporate stocks and government securities on the İSE. This state-authored change enabled foreign financial capital to enter and purchase SOEs for sale in Turkey.

An important subsequent step came with Turkey's 1994 Privatization Law No. 4046, which sought to put privatization on more solid institutional foundations, and which is still in force today, with amendments, (Marois 2012: 103–104). Contextually, the passing of the Law occurred as Turkey's 1994 crisis unfolded (and subsequent crises in East Asia) and as state authorities adopted the April 1994 IMF stabilization programme, which called for the standard prescription of neoliberal structural adjustment policies, including accelerated privatization of SOEs. As with many neoliberal state transformation processes, the 1994 Law centralized decision-making power within the Privatization High Council, chaired by the Prime Minister, and attended by other ministers, but without formal labour union representation. Furthermore, postwar developmentalist extra-market incentives were replaced by market-based cost and price structures, as well as commercial goals (OECD 1999: 113). The 1994 Law, moreover, provided material support by establishing the Privatization Fund to help smooth the privatization process by helping to fund severance and retirement payments for redundant employees,

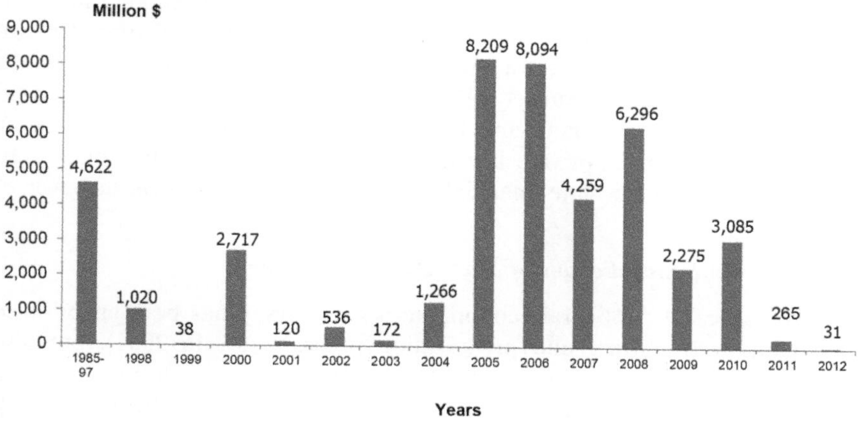

Figure 5.1 Privatisation Proceeds in Turkey, 1985–2012
Source: Privatization Administration, http://www.oib.gov.tr/index_eng.htm.

cover the debts of privatized SOEs, and/or improve the financial position of SOEs in preparation for their sale, by increasing their capital, among other things. Finally, the 1994 Law enabled the transfer of public employees to other public entities if deemed necessary. In terms of banking, the Law of 1994 reserved a special category for Ziraat Bank and Halkbank as strategic firms.

While the limited size of the İSE during the 1990s slowed the earlier sales of SOEs by public offer or flotation—as large enterprises are difficult to sell in block sales due to large capital outputs and the need for an equally large purchaser—subsequent initial public offers (IPOs) have helped to grow the İSE. This growth has facilitated more, and larger, privatizations, notably since 2005 (see Figure 5.1). Among the milestones for the İSE are the İş Bankası share sale in 1998, TÜPRAŞ in 2000 and Petrol Ofisi in 2002. Subsequently, the İSE was tested with two partial state bank IPOs in 2005 and 2007, and the Turk Telekom offering in 2008, such that it is now better able to manage larger IPOs and share volumes. Turkey's mounting capacity to handle larger privatization has been matched by the political commitment of the AKP government since coming to power in 2002, which has pursued Turkey's most aggressive privatization agenda in its history. The AKP has since boasted about both the massive increase in privatization receipts, as well as the restructuring of existing SOEs so that they operate according to financial discipline and, in doing so, generate a surplus for the government, as noted in the Ninth Development Plan 2007–2013 (SPO 2006: 27). In this way, privatization in Turkey has been quantitatively significant, insofar as the state sector has shrunk as the İSE has grown via IPOs, as well as qualitatively important, as market imperatives increasingly shape and give meaning to Turkish society and the development strategies of its remaining public enterprises. The role of the three large, remaining state-owned banks in Turkey, Ziraat Bank, Halkbank and Vakıfbank, which control about a third of total banking assets, is therefore economically and politically significant. Indeed, the future of privatization in Turkey has taken a novel direction since the formation of the Turkey Wealth Fund in August 2016, and has since concentrated numerous SOEs, including Ziraat Bank and Halkbank, within one holding institution that is governed under private law (see http://www.turkiyevarlikfonu.com.tr/EN). The effect on the state financial apparatus is yet to be seen, however.

Crisis and the Contradictions of State Banks in Turkey

The recurrence of neoliberal economic crisis in Turkey has both encouraged state bank restructuring and privatization processes (as in 2001), but also given rise to political reasons to halt bank privatization (as in 2008–09) as a means to stabilize the economy, and by extension, neoliberal financial transformation (Marois and Güngen 2016).

The 2001 crisis and subsequent May 2001 BSRP emerged out a period of intense economic and financial turbulence, much of which was generated domestically in Turkey, as in other emerging capitalist societies at the time. The crisis thus provided an opportunity to restructure, if not immediately selloff, Turkey's state-owned or public banks (Marois 2012: 169–177). In this case, restructuring began in February 2000, as the government set a new, market-based interest rate mechanism for Ziraat Bank and Halkbank designed to eliminate the banks' post-war developmentalist duty loss mechanism (essentially, their directed credit subsidies). A series of legal changes also triggered new commercialization requirements, as called for in the 1999 IMF Letter of Intent. The 2001 BSRP more aggressively and directly restructured the state-owned banks so that they began to operate much more as if they were private, profit-seeking banks (Önder and Özyıldırım 2013). For one, a Joint Board of Directors took over managerial control of Ziraat Bank and Halkbank and private sector managers were brought into the banks. The government then gave extraordinary power to the new Board to restructure the state banks for privatization. The BRSA was charged with managing state bank restructuring under the umbrella of the 2001 BSRP. To facilitate commercialization, the new managers drove down the number of state bank employees and bank branches in order to drive up profitability. Since 2002, Turkey's state-owned banks have consistently outperformed the private banks in Turkey by generating return on asset levels of around 2 per cent (which is double what most banks make in advanced capitalist societies) (see Chapter 6). This, however, would give rise to new contradictions in the context of the 2008–09 crisis, which was not instigated from within the emerging capitalist societies, but from the advanced ones, notably the USA and the United Kingdom.

By the time the 2008–09 crisis struck Turkey, two of the state-owned banks had undergone partial privatizations via IPOs. In the first instance, authorities organized a 25.18 per cent IPO for Vakıfbank in 2005, raising US $1.27 billion. In the second instance, authorities launched an IPO for Halkbank in May 2007, of which the 24.98 per cent sale earned $1.9 billion. Authorities then launched a secondary offering in November 2012, earning another $2.55 billion from the additional 23.92 per cent of shares sold (as listed shares rose to 48.90 per cent of the total). In these cases, the share sell-offs serve to internalize neoliberal profit imperatives through partial private ownership, the logic of which has been enabled through institutional restructuring intended to commercialize the banks. Yet it is significant that during the phase of AKP rule that was most politically and economically ripe for privatization to take place, only partial privatizations have occurred in the two public banks. Ziraat Bank, while officially targeted for privatization, is not undergoing any formal sale process as yet and remains fully state-owned by the Treasury (albeit now under the Turkey Wealth Fund). The three other, much smaller, state-owned development banks, Türk Eximbank (Export Credit Bank of Turkey), Türkiye Kalkınma Bankası Anonim Şirketi (Development Bank of Turkey), and İller Bank (Bank of Provinces) have not been subject to privatization and are not held within the Turkey Wealth Fund.

The debate on the effectiveness of state-owned banks is far from conclusive (Levy Yeyati et al. 2007; Marois 2013; Mazzucato and Penna 2015; Mazzucato and Penna 2017; Mazzucato and Penna 2018). Conventional neoliberal and international financial institution approaches have continued to militate on behalf of bank privatization as a means of fighting corruption and driving efficiency gains, but have nonetheless had to acknowledge the significant material capacity of state banks to lend counter-cyclically at times of crisis (World Bank 2012; Marcelin and Mathur 2015). To be sure, Turkey's state banks can and should make significant improvements in the areas of development strategy, inclusive development and democracy. Yet research on Turkey's state banks show that they can be financially efficient, support alternative inclusive development strategies, and promote an alternative public ethos that runs counter to the narrow mantra of neoliberal profit maximization (Önder and Özyıldırım 2013; Marois and Güngen 2013).

The 2008–09 crisis, in contrast to the 2001 crisis, has illustrated some of the usefulness of retaining state-owned banks within neoliberalism, given its recurrent financial instability (Griffith-Jones et al. 2016; cf.World Bank 2012). In response to the crisis in Turkey, the Central Bank doubled the exports rediscount loan limit to US$1 billion for Eximbank to help mitigate crisis impact on industry sectors (Muñoz-Martínez and Marois 2014). The loan pool widened and eligibility eased (BAT 2009: I-4). In March 2009, the capital of Eximbank increased by TL500 million. The state-owned banks remained relatively stable and highly profitable during the outbreak of crisis in late 2008 (see Chapter 6). Through such programmes as the Agricultural Credit Co-operatives scheme, Ziraat Bank was able to direct additional loans to farmers. The state commercial banks increased lending during the crisis (2008–10) from 23.8 per cent to 28.8 per cent of all loans as the private banks reduced lending from 54.5 to 51.6 percent (BAT 2015b). While generally critical of the so-called market distortions they see state banks creating, the IMF acknowledged, as did the World Bank (2012), that being state-owned helped the banks to be 'market leaders' during the post-crisis credit boom in Turkey (IMF 2012: 35).

Thus arise the contradictions of Turkey's state-owned banks. Whereas in 2001 the banks contributed to crisis (as did the private banks), in 2008–09 the state banks helped overcome crisis (as the private banks' lending contracted). In the first case, the state banks threatened neoliberal continuity, whereas in the second they helped underwrite neoliberal continuity. In this sense, the class benefits of the state banks are complicated. The support programmes and extended lending in response to the recent crisis help workers, farmers and small and medium-sized enterprises survive times of hardship. Yet at the same time, this official support legitimizes neoliberalism as a development strategy, which is not in the long-term strategic interests of workers. On balance, and without sustained political and democratic action to the contrary, the material capacity of Turkey's state banks help to sustain and legitimize continued neoliberal class rule in Turkey.

Public-Private Partnerships in Turkey: Privatization cum Financialization

The transformation of the state financial apparatus also involves the shifting ways in which public provisioning has been marketized (that is, subject to competition and financial efficiency imperatives). Prior to the 1980s, if the government delegated public services or infrastructure to the private sector this was done by concession (Özeke 2009). Concession contracts retained the privileged status and authority of the public administration and were subject to prior review by the Council of State. During the 1980s the government began to experiment with new forms of public–private partnerships (PPP), notably with the Build-Operate-Transfer (BOT) Law No. 3096, which allowed private entry into the electricity sector. The stated intention was to increase investment in infrastructure, especially in areas such as electricity, by opening it up to the private sector (in practice it was about opening up private accumulation opportunities). Then in 1994 the government introduced a new and more widespread BOT Law (No. 3996) to cover all areas of infrastructure, including energy, transportation, communication, and municipal services. In conceptual terms, PPPs can be regarded as the present privatization of future state investments.

The BOT Law and processes, like other privatization processes, were subject to legal controversies that delayed and led to the cancellation of many projects. A 1999 constitutional amendment strengthened the legal footings of the BOT process by making them subject to private law contract and, in doing so, skip over the Council of State's prior review and jurisdiction processes while maintaining the arbitration option. Presently, the BOT model is used for many new infrastructure projects, while concessions are used to transfer of operating rights to existing state-owned infrastructure facilities (such as ports).

Ongoing challenges to the PPP model in Turkey and the government's intention to solidify its legal grounds have given rise to a new PPP framework law, which will supersede and consolidate previous legislation. The public and private sectors' roles are conceived as 'equal partners', while creating a new state administrative unit to supervise and promote the model in Turkey. As of mid-2018 a general Draft PPP Law was in the process of being debated, but had not yet been passed. However, the government did pass a new PPP law in March 2013 in the health sector—the 'Law on Building and Renewal of Facilities and Procurement of Services through Public Private Partnership Model' (No. 6428).

Current investment openings with PPP includes several health projects. The National Development Plan 2007–13 emphasized that the energy sector will be opened up further to the private sector. Also, the government will pursue more of the BOT model for passenger airport terminals. In 2015 Turkey ranked second, behind Brazil, out of 139 emerging economies in PPPs, according to the World Bank's Private Participation in Infrastructure Database. In critical terms, PPPs are a way of building state capacity to provide infrastructure, but in a way that privileges private sector goals and profitability mandates. It involves a form of financialization of public provisioning, which embodies privatization of the rewards, but the socialization of the investment risks.

The Istanbul Financial Centre

The transformation of Turkey's state financial apparatus has taken a distinct turn with the government's Istanbul Financial Centre (IFC) project, set for completion in 2018 (see http://www.ifcturkey.com/). The IFC forms an integral part of President Erdoğan's intentions of increasing Turkey's regional economic and financial importance by the Republic's centenary in 2023. The 2008–09 crisis did not alter this intention, as indeed the government has accelerated the building of the IFC as one response to global financial instability. To this end, significant state restructuring efforts are envisaged, including changes in competition, tax, and financial regulation. This also includes supporting the deepening of market finance and share listings on the stock market.

To build Turkey's financial capacity, authorities have mobilized the state banks in constructing this new space of finance in Istanbul. For example, Halkbank sold US $142 million worth of shares in its real estate unit on the Borsa İstanbul to help pay for the construction of two new towers and three buildings (Bilgic 2013). When complete, Halkbank will move operations there. Likewise, Ziraat Bank will construct two large towers to headquarter its Istanbul operations there and Vakıfbank is expected to move its centre of operations to the IFC. In moves to further support the development of the IFC, the government has signalled intentions to move the Central Bank, the BRSA and the CMB to the IFC. As such, the IFC thus exemplifies how the transformation of the state has spatial dimensions, insofar as it involves constructing something materially new to support financial accumulation strategies, and that this construction means mobilizing public resources and capacity.

The Savings Deposit Insurance Fund

The material transformation of the state has entailed finding institutional means to direct public resources into the financial sector at times of crisis, in order to socialize financial risks that have gone bad (Marois 2011: 176–177). In Turkey, the government created the Savings Deposit Insurance Fund (SDIF) in 1983 amid the country's initial turn to neoliberalism. The SDIF centralized and gave stronger institutional form to foregoing institutional arrangements intended to protect depositors and manage failed banks in Turkey. In seeming contradiction to neoliberal ideals of market-based economic co-ordination, the public institution's role was to guarantee bank deposits and to rescue failed banks on behalf of the banking sector in general, thus bolstering investors' faith in Turkey's financial sector via a stronger state apparatus. To ensure this process could be managed smoothly on behalf of the interests of financial capital, and with the least possible democratic oversight, the government granted the SDIF institutional independence in 2003 (Law No. 5020) and then in 2005 the right to write new regulations (Banking Law No. 5411). The changes to the 2005 Law enhanced SDIF powers, including the ability to set the coverage and deposit limits of insured deposits (SDIF 2015: 10).

The SDIF generates revenue (which forms its financial base) from insurance premiums, fines, returns from its reserve fund, and other assorted fees. Significantly, the SDIF is entitled to borrow from capital markets and the Treasury; it may also take advances from the Central Bank and from banks' insurance premiums (SDIF 2015: 18). In 2014 deposit insurance revenues totalled US $875 million and interest income from reserves was $427 million. Budget operating expenses came to $46 million. SDIF reserves at the end of 2014 totalled some $6.9 billion. While seemingly impressive, the 2001 crisis cost $47 billion in rescue funds (including both public and private contributions), and this at a time when Turkey's banks were considerably smaller and less international than they are today. As such, SDIF reserves are modest. For this reason, the legal right of the SDIF to borrow from the government is a hugely important aspect of the contemporary financial apparatus and for the reproduction of emerging finance capitalism. By July 2003, in response to the 2001 crisis, the Treasury had injected over $28 billion into the banking sector via the SDIF (BRSA 2003: 26–27). Remarkably, at the time of the rescue, government officials understood that there was little chance of ever recuperating the socialized losses because the bad debts absorbed by the state exceeded the total wealth of the individual debtors just bailed out (BRSA 2003: 40). Again in 2008–09, the limited resources of the SDIF emerged as problematic, as the global crisis unfolded. To bolster confidence in Turkey, the AKP bypassed existing laws to offer a two-year cushion of unlimited deposit insurance directly backed by the Turkish Treasury (that is, public resources), as state authorities recognized that the SDIF had insufficient funds to finance insurance by itself. The financial transformation of the state in this case helps to restore confidence in the financial system at times of crisis, which is facilitated by state authorities building institutions capable of transferring public funds into the financial sector independently—that is, without the necessity of being democratically accountable. A tightly related aspect of the state's material capacity building, involves foreign reserve accumulation.

Turkey's Foreign Reserve Accumulation

Over the last 20 years, the foreign reserves of developing countries have grown exponentially—from US $477 billion in 1995 to $7.87 trillion by 2014 (IMF 2015). China holds the bulk of these, but, as an important emerging capitalist society, Turkish authorities have contributed. From a low of about

$20 billion prior to the 2001 crisis, Turkey's reserves exceeded $107 billion in 2014 (Figure 5.2). As a form of self-insurance against capital flight and for the protection of the domestic currency, developing countries' foreign reserves embody relationships of domination, as poorer countries pay for holding onto these pots of foreign money (cf. Rodrik 2006; Cho 2014; Labrinidis 2016). Authorities opt to socialize the costs of foreign reserve accumulation as they calculate that foreign reserves significantly bolster central bank—and by extension state—capacity to intervene as the financial lender of last resort. That is, reserve accumulation is an essential component of the state's material capacity to manage the financial instability of neoliberalism in the interests of preserving finance capitalism and capital accumulation. Foreign reserves both enable state authorities to help protect the value of financial assets in Turkey, by defending the value of the lira, but they also act as an insurance fund for foreign investors keen to be able to withdraw their investments at a moment's notice. For domestic corporations, reserves likewise enable the global mobility of capital, but also provide a large pot of available resources, should their financial operations run into difficulties and need access to foreign capital or, more dramatically, bailing out and socialization of their risks gone bad. In a more direct way than public bailouts of failed banks, reserve accumulation is a class-based institutional form by which state authorities pass on the material costs of maintaining finance capitalism to society at large through the state apparatus (Marois 2014: 309).

Growing debt levels, composed of increasingly short-term inflows, have solidified the role of reserve accumulation in contemporary risk management in Turkey, albeit in an unorthodox way. From 2010 to 2014 external debt rose from US $292 billion to $402 billion, stretching from just under 40 per cent to 50 per cent of GDP (BAT 2015: I-8). Likewise, since 2010 the proportion of

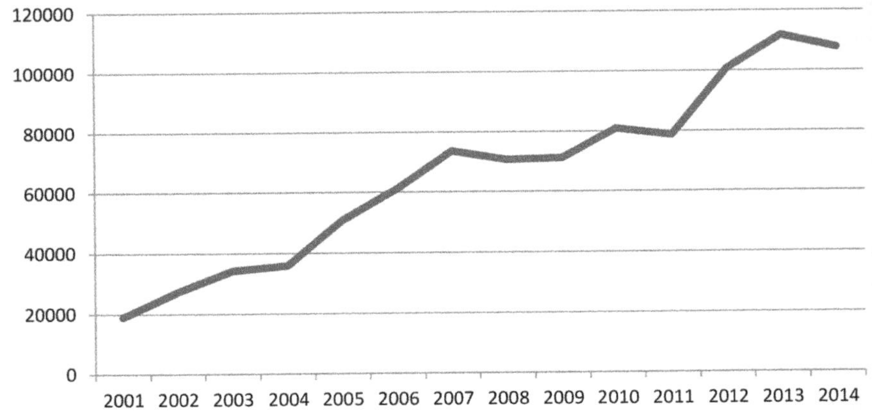

Figure 5.2 Turkey's Foreign Reserve Accumulation, US $ millions, 2001–14
Source: International Monetary Fund (2016): International Financial Statistics (Edition: January 2016). UK Data Service. DOI: http://dx.doi.org/10.5257/imf/ifs/2016–01.

short-term, hot money portfolio flows has increased to 46 percent of net capital inflows. In this context, international financial institutions deemed Turkish reserves as too modest compared with other emerging capitalist countries. In an unorthodox policy response, Turkish authorities launched the Reserve Options Mechanism (ROM) in late 2011. The intent was to stem short-term inflows, moderate domestic credit growth, and assist exchange rate and inflation volatility. Specifically, the ROM enables banks in Turkey to hold a given ratio of their Turkish lira reserve requirements in foreign currencies and gold (Alper et al. 2013: 2). Central Bank authorities affect the cost of using the ROM by adjusting the ratio of foreign currency or gold needed to cover Lira required reserve levels on a daily basis. Ideally, with high capital inflows, costs would decrease, encouraging banks to keep more required reserves in foreign currencies, increasing demand for foreign currencies, and in turn smoothing out the impact of capital inflows (Aslaner et al. 2015: 4). The ROM is thus meant to mitigate large swings in capital flows and exchange rates, easing (but not eliminating) the need for other interventions (Alper et al. 2013: 11). By mid-2014, the Central Bank had accumulated some $50 billion in reserves via the ROM. Yet the ROM has not eliminated underlying volatilities. While combined foreign reserves have grown, the gross reserves under direct Central Bank control remain relatively lower than those of other emerging capitalist countries.

Conclusion: The Financial Transformation of the State

Contrary to popular notions about neoliberal reform, in Turkey the financial transformation of the state has given rise to a more powerful and muscular state apparatus able and willing to intervene on behalf of continued financial accumulation strategies. According to political economists Ziya Önis and Ali Burak Güven, the Turkish state has "accumulated considerable institutional muscle in monetary, fiscal and financial governance as indicated by the dominance over the economic bureaucracy of large, elite organisations such as the Treasury, the TCMB [CBRT] and the BDDK [BRSA] (2011: 14). This they contrast to the state's muted response in the real sector. This Marxian account seeks not to erect a financial and real sector dichotomy, but rather to emphasize the underlying class dynamics of the financial transformation of the state. Since 2002 the AKP government has systematically undertaken financial apparatus restructuring measures in order to balance different social and class relations vis-à-vis the changing relationships of domestic and foreign investors to capital accumulation imperatives, to the benefit of finance (Muñoz-Martínez and Marois 2014). Despite momentary displays of collective will, organized labour and the popular classes have not effectively pushed for an alternative developmental trajectory to the finance-led strategy. And despite maintaining an electoral majority, the AKP has undertaken an increasingly authoritarian approach to ruling an ever-more polarized society in Turkey (Bank and Karadag 2013) and an ever-more centralized approach to the financial apparatus. Indeed, under Turkey's increasingly finance-led neoliberalism, the International Labour Organization points to a structural reduction in the adjusted labour income share in Turkey: down from about 45 per cent in the 1990s to about 33 per cent by 2013 (ILO 2015: 16). Since the 2008–09 crisis, too, authorities have reduced subsidies for staple goods and services for the working classes; increased consumption taxes, rationalized safety nets, and proceeded with market-friendly labour reform (Ortiz and Cummings 2013: 19). The effect of these reforms has been to help ensure a fiscal surplus in Turkey that in turn helps to underpin the country's creditworthiness to foreign finance. In the case of Turkey, financial restructuring has come at the expense of the people.

Note

1 For a critique of technical approaches to financial re-regulation, see Ho and Marois (forthcoming) on the crisis and China's asset management companies.

REFERENCES

Akyüz, Y. and Boratav, K. (2003) "The Making of the Turkish Financial Crisis" *World Development*, 31(9): 1549–1566.

Alper, C.E. and Z. Öniş (2003) "Financial Globalization, the Democratic Deficit, and Recurrent Crises in Emerging Markets" *Emerging Markets Finance and Trade*, 39(3): 5–26.

Aslaner, O., O. Çıplak, H. Kara and D. Küçüksaraç (2015) "Reserve Options Mechanism: Does it Work as an Automatic Stabilizer?" *Central Bank Review*, 15: 1–18.

Aydın, Z. (2013) "Global crisis, Turkey and the regulation of economic crisis" *Capital & Class* 37(1): 95–109.

Bank, A. and R. Karadag (2013)."The 'Ankara Moment': the politics of Turkey's regional power in the Middle East, 2007–11", *Third World Quarterly*, 34(2): 287–304.

BAT–Banks Association of Turkey (2009a) *Banks in Turkey*, Istanbul: BAT.

BAT–Banks Association of Turkey (2009b) *The Financial Sector and Banking System in Turkey*, Istanbul: BAT.

BAT–Banks Association of Turkey (2015a) *Banks in Turkey 2014*, Istanbul: BAT.

BAT–Banks Association of Turkey (2015b) *The Banking System in Turkey: Yearly Statistics 1959–2014*, July 2015, Istanbul: BAT.

BRSA–Banking Regulation and Supervision Agency (2015) *Banking Regulation and Supervision Agency: Information Booklet*, Ankara: BRSA.

BRSA–Banking Regulation and Supervision Agency (2002) *Banking Sector Reform: Progress Report*, July 2002, Ankara: BRSA.

BRSA–Banking Regulation and Supervision Agency (2003) *Banking Sector Restructuring Program Progress Report – (VII)*, October 2003, Ankara: BRSA.

BRSA–Banking Regulation and Supervision Agency (2009) *Financial Markets Report*, Issue 16, Ankara: BRSA.

Bedirhanoğlu, P., H. Cömert, İ. Eren, I.Erol, D. Demiröz, N. Erdem, A. R.Güngen, T. Marois, A.Topal, O.Türel, G.Yalman, E. Yeldan, and E. Voyvoda (2013)

Comparative Perspective on Financial System in the EU: Country Report on Turkey, FESSUD Studies in Financial Systems No. 11.

Bilgic, T. (2013) "Biggest Turkish IPO in Two Years to Fund Financial Center", 14 February 2013, *Bloomberg website*, Accessed 1 February 2016.

Central Bank of Turkey (2011) Financial Stability Report, May 2011, Ankara, Central Bank of Republic of Turkey.Central Bank of Turkey (2015) *Financial Stability Report*, May 2015, Vol. 20, Ankara: Central Bank of Republic of Turkey.

Cho, Y. (2014) "Making the Poor Pay for the Rich: Capital Account Liberalization and Reserve Accumulation in the Developing World", *Globalizations*, 11(6): 809–825.

General Directorate of Revenue Policies (2012) *Istanbul International Financial Center: Tax Committee*, Bulletin April 2012/2.

Griffith-Jones, S., L. Xiaoyun, and S. Spratt (2016) *The Asian Infrastructure Investment Bank: What Can It Learn From, and Perhaps Teach To, the Multilateral Development Banks?*, Institute of Development Studies Evidence Report, No. 179.

Ho, S. and T. Marois (forthcoming). "China's Asset Management Companies as State Spatial–Temporal Strategy" *The China Quarterly*.

International Labour Organization (2015) *Global Wage Report 2014/15: Wages and income inequality*, Geneva: ILO.

International Monetary Fund (2012) *Turkey: 2011 Article IV Consultation*, IMF Country Report No. 12/16.

International Monetary Fund (2015) *International Financial Statistics* (August 2015), UK Data Service.

Labrinidis, G. (2016) "Analytical Gains of Geopolitical Economy", *Research in Political Economy, 30B*: 91–123.

Levy Yeyati, E., A. Micco and U. Panizza (2007) "A reappraisal of state-owned banks", *Economia* 7(2): 209–247.

Marcelin, I. and İ. Mathur (2015) "Privatization, financial development, property rights and growth", *Journal of Banking & Finance,* 50: 528–546.

Marois, T. (2011) "Emerging Market Bank Rescues in an Era of Finance-Led Neoliberalism: A Comparison of Mexico and Turkey", *Review of International Political Economy*, 18(2): 168–196.

Marois, T. (2012) *States, Banks and Crisis: Emerging Finance Capitalism in Mexico and Turkey*, Cheltenham, Gloucestershire, UK: Edward Elgar Publishing.

Marois, T (2013) "State-owned banks and development: Dispelling mainstream myths, *Municipal Services Project Occasional Paper Series*, No 21.

Marois, T. (2018) *Towards a Green Public Bank in the Public Interest*, Geneva: UNRISD.

Marois, T. and A.R. Güngen (2013) "Reclaiming Turkey's state-owned banks", *Municipal Services Project Occasional Paper Series*, No. 22.

Marois, T. and A.R. Güngen (2016) "Credibility and Class in the Evolution of Public Banks: The Case of Turkey", *The Journal of Peasant Studies*, 43(6): 1285–1309.

Marois, T. and H. Muñoz-Martínez (2016) "Navigating the Aftermath of Crisis and Risk in Mexico and Turkey", *Research in Political Economy*, 31: 165–194.

Mazzucato, M. and P. Caetano (2015) "The Rise of Mission-Oriented State Investment Banks: The Cases of Germany's KfW and Brazil's BNDES", *SPRU Working Paper Series* (ISSN 2057–6668), University of Sussex.

Muñoz-Martínez, H. and T. Marois (2014) 'Capital Fixity and Mobility in Response to the 2008–2009 Crisis: Variegated Neoliberalism in Mexico and Turkey', *Environment and Planning D: Society and Space*, 32: 1102–1119.

Organisation for Economic Co-operation and Development (1999) *OECD Economic Surveys: Turkey 1998–1999*, Paris: OECD.

Önder, Z. and S. Özyıldırım (2010) "Banks, regional development disparity and growth: evidence from Turkey", *Cambridge Journal of Economics*, 34: 975–1000.

Önis, Z. (2006) "Varieties and Crises of Neoliberal Globalisation: Argentina, Turkeyand the IMF", *Third World Quarterly*, 27(2): 239–63.

Önis, Z. (2011) "Power, Interests and Coalitions: the political economy of mass privatisation in Turkey", *Third World Quarterly*, 32(4): 707–724.

Önis, Z. and A.B. Güven (2011) "Global Crisis, National Responses: The Political Economy of Turkish Exceptionalism", *New Political Economy*, 16(5): 585–608.

Ortiz, I. and M. Cummins (2013) "Austerity Measures in Developing Countries: Public Expenditure Trends and the Risks to Children and Women", *Feminist Economics*, 19(3): 55–81.

Özeke, H. B. (2009) "Turkey: Turkey's New PPP Law Is On The Way", 15 July 2009, *Mondaq website.*

Peck, J. and N. Theodore (2007) "Variegated capitalism", *Progress in Human Geography*, 31: 731–772.

Rodrik, D. (2006). "The Social Costs of Foreign Exchange Reserves", *International Economic Journal*, 20(3): 253–266.

Scherrer, C. (ed.) (2017) *Public Banks in the Age of Financialization: A Comparative Perspective*, Cheltenham: Edward Elgar Publishing.

SDIF–Savings Deposit Insurance Fund (2015) *Annual Report 2014*, Istanbul: SDIF.

Seabrooke, L. (2006) "The Bank for International Settlements", *New Political Economy*, 11(1): 141–149.

State Planning Organisation (2006) *Ninth Development Plan, 2007–2013*, Ankara: State Planning Organization.

World Bank (2012) *Global financial development report 2013: Rethinking the role of state in finance*, Washington, DC: World Bank.

World Bank (2013) *World Development Report 2014 Risk and Opportunity: Managing Risk for Development*, Washington, DC: World Bank.

6 The Neoliberal Restructuring of Banking in Turkey Since 2001

Thomas Marois and Ali Rıza Güngen

The neoliberal restructuring of the banks and banking sector in Turkey has been anything but linear. The first crack at opening up the predominantly bank-based, and notably state-owned, financial system to market forces was undertaken by the authoritarian post-1980s governing administration. Authorities sought to liberalize the financial sector rapidly. As with most 1980s shock therapy programmes throughout the developing world, so it was in Turkey. Advocates of economic and political reform moved aggressively to impose an idealized notion of market-oriented, neoliberal development. In Turkey, the 1982 financial crisis[1] followed immediately, and as a result financial reforms would henceforth assume a more gradual pace. This too was in step with global change. Structural adjustment in trade and industry progressed while financial reforms followed in the late 1980s and early 1990s.[2] This gave way to a well-known phase of financial shocks among the large emerging capitalist societies (including Mexico, East Asia and Brazil), which in turn gave rise to the so-called 'post-Washington Consensus' and its particularly impoverished view of the state in financial transformation.

Turkey is an especially fascinating example of contemporary neoliberal banking. Its experiences, in a sense, bracketed the financial turbulence of the 1990s: Turkey's 1994 financial crisis preceded Mexico's spectacular 1994 Tequila crisis and Turkey's dramatic 2001 crisis followed Argentina's collapse, signalling the last of the emerging capitalist society crises of that period (see Chapter 4 of this volume). Throughout Turkey's neoliberal transformation, the financial sector has remained dominated by banks (if not in isolation from a growing market-based financial sector). Moreover, bank ownership continues to be diversified between state, private domestic and foreign owners. This is not to say that significant, even structural, changes have not occurred. Indeed, there have been major quantitative and qualitative shifts since the 2001 financial crisis in Turkey.

In what follows, we draw on a Marxian-inspired historical-structural analytical framework to explore the shifts in Turkey's banking sector, albeit from a predominantly empirical basis. This approach involves a fundamental commitment to investigating and exposing the underlying exploitative and unequal social, political and economic forces shaping the reproduction of contemporary capitalist society, both within the borders of Turkey and as it is integrated into the capitalist world market. A set of core analytical premises give shape to our understanding (drawn from Hilferding 1910/1981; Marois 2012: 24–37). First, we interpret not only nation states as malleable social relations, but also individual banking institutions. We emphasize the need to look at such institutions as historically evolving within capitalism and as specific institutionalizations of social power within Turkey. A second premise sees labour is a vital category for understanding ongoing financial transformations while a third premise sees crises as constitutive of the variegated forms that contemporary finance capitalism takes. This critical political economy approach differs from contemporary neoclassical and heterodox approaches. Neoclassical economists and neoliberal advocates adopt a pre-social and ahistorical theorization of banks and states as inherently corruptible and therefore naturally prone to inefficiency and market distortions (Dinç 2005; Mishkin 2009; World Bank 2012; Calomiris and Haber 2014). Enhanced universal private property rights and better market regulation is the solution, not public ownership. Heterodox accounts distance themselves from such market fundamentalism, arguing instead for a slower pace of reform. The scope of regulation, political bargaining, and for historically accounting for country specificity is also much deeper in heterodox accounts (Alper and Öniş 2002; Önder and Özyıldırım 2013). Yet both approaches remain wedded to a better form of capitalist banking, differing over the pace and extent of regulation. Heterodox accounts, moreover, tend to idealize the role of the state in development, often overlooking exploitative and anti-labour practices within the financial sector and more broadly across developing countries. In what follows, we do not elaborate on each premise, but instead provide them to make explicit our worldview of banking transformation in Turkey.

Empirically, we draw heavily on the data from the Banks Association of Turkey (BAT), which illustrates how market-oriented reforms, particularly since the 2001 crisis, have led to higher concentrations of banking assets under private control, itself suggesting a shift in class and social power relations. As expected, Turkey's market reforms have intensified market imperatives. All the banks in Turkey—be they publicly owned, privately held, or foreign-owned—now compete to achieve above average returns. This was not always so, as public banks did not have a clear profit mandate until the 2000–01 crisis hit and privately owned domestic banks were often integrated into larger holding groups' operations (making their actual value in terms of financial returns hard to specify).

The neoliberal drive to maximize income was supported by a global expansionary phase and relative economic stability until the 2008–09 global financial crisis struck. None the less, bank profitability today remains significantly higher in Turkey than in almost all other Organisation for Economic Co-operation and Development (OECD) member countries. The political stability of one-party rule under the ever-more authoritarian yet no less neoliberal leadership of the Adalet ve Kalkınma Partisi (AKP—Justice and Development Party) underpins such banking sector prosperity. Turkish state authorities have undertaken post-crisis reforms that have institutionally restructured and internationalized the state apparatus in support of banking and finance capital (Marois 2011; see also Chapter 5). For example, state authorities ramped up the use of the Saving Deposit and Insurance Fund (SDIF) in order to take over insolvent banks and to further institutional consolidation in the banking sector. The Banking Regulation and Supervision Agency (BRSA), which was established in June 1999, undertook bank supervisory duties concerning the banking sector instead of the Treasury and the Central Bank of Republic of Turkey, which later became legally independent in 2001. Amid the 2001 crisis, the Treasury reduced the short foreign exchange positions of private commercial banks and governing authorities drew in and socialized the public banks' duty losses (official state debts held by the state banks but not compensated for by the government during the 1990s), in due course. These conjunctural political and economic developments encouraged the subsequent internalization, or drawing in, of foreign bank capital. One further element has underwritten the long-term neoliberal transformation of banking in Turkey: namely, the intensification of bank labour, through reduced staff costs and greater workplace pressures, as efficiency and profitability imperatives make their way through the workforce.

To analyze these events in banking, we explore how the financial sector in Turkey, despite significant changes in market finance (see Chapter 7), continues to be predominantly bank-based. While bank-based, all banks in Turkey, regardless of ownership category, have transformed to be aggressively market-oriented and return-driven in ways constitutive of neoliberal strategies of development in Turkey. We argue that this is not a socially neutral process: the political and economic changes have come at the expense of Turkey's working classes, but to the benefit of capital and Turkey's governing neoliberal élites.

This chapter evidences these arguments by providing data on the overall structural transformation of the banking sector. The first section briefly reviews the 2001 crisis and state-led recovery process, while the second section examines the contemporary landscape of banking in Turkey today. The third section constitutes the empirical core of this chapter. It details the ownership and control structures of Turkey's banks, forms of concentration, distribution of assets and liabilities, risks, and profitability levels. This is followed by a short conclusion.

The 2001 Crisis and Recovery of Turkish Banking

The 2001 financial crisis in Turkey is rooted in the political decisions taken since the society's post-1980s neoliberal transformation, which have generated new and escalating economic and political instabilities. Notably, the 1989 capital account opening and the 1994 financial crisis neither led to a reversal of market-oriented reforms nor to improvement in their own, neoliberal terms (Cizre and Yeldan 2005). Growing turbulence among other emerging capitalist societies (including in East Asia, Russia and Brazil) compounded instability in Turkey. This gave rise to the December 1999 disinflation programme, which was a political attempt to stabilize domestic markets by deepening liberal reforms in Turkey in ways favourable to foreign financial capital. While initially drawing in some US $12.5 billion in foreign capital, the new debts only increased the perceived risks foreign investors saw in the Turkish economy. By late 2000 a new spate of bank failures (mostly of privately owned domestic institutions, but also state banks) began to lift the veil of euphoria felt by financial capital. Capital inflows rapidly turned to outflows. Add to this the exposure of unpaid duty losses, and few financial investors were convinced their capital was safe. Turkey's squabbling political leaders exacerbated matters—an open stand-off between the Prime Minister and the President on 19 February 2001 led to $5 billion of Turkey's $20 billion in foreign reserves taking flight.

The dynamics of the 2001 crisis and recovery processes have been well explored in literature on the subject (Akyüz and Boratav, 2003; Önis 2009; Akçay and Güngen 2016: 220–224). For our purposes of understanding banking transformation in Turkey—politically, socially and economically—we can highlight three class-based responses by authorities that were intended to help overcome the crisis and to ensure continuity in Turkey's neoliberal experiment (Marois 2011: 176–182). First, Turkey's market-oriented coalition government *socialized* the accumulated debts and financial risks exposed by the crisis. Furthermore, the government brought in World Bank executive Kemal Derviş as an unelected Minister of the Economy and transferred significant governing powers to his office. Derviş quickly authored the market-oriented 'Transition to a Strong Economy' (TSE) programme and associated Banking Sector Restructuring Programme, which began by setting aside legal limits and drawing into the state apparatus (that is, socializing) the totality of the banks' losses, be they public or private. The social cost would reach US $47 billion, equalling 30 per cent of gross domestic product (GDP) in 2002, making it the most costly state-led banking rescue ever in Turkey. Of this, $22 billion covered the state banks' losses and $25 billion the private banks'.

Second, state authorities took charge of *rationalizing* the banking sector according to neoliberal precepts, variegated by Turkey's specific political economy. In brief, to protect financial capital from its own crisis-prone tendencies, the government set new restrictions, including higher capital requirements, tighter credit limits, and greater provisioning for non-performing loans (NPL). To promote a greater concentration of banking assets, authorities rewrote corporate and tax legislation to encourage bank mergers and acquisitions, as well as foreign bank entry. The once intimate links between Turkey's holding groups and their related banks, moreover, were institutionally firewalled by new regulations.[3] Eliminating some capital groups from the banking sector (Gültekin-Karakaş 2009), the restructuring aimed to put an end to the subordination of banking practices to the core holding company's wider objectives. Reform yielded tighter regulation but did not change the underlying fact that holding groups continued owning most of the banks in Turkey and that this constituted an enormously concentrated form of economic and social power. Finally, the government championed an aggressive restructuring of the still-powerful state-owned banks. While immediate privatization was off the table, given economic instability, the rapid and deep commercialization of their operations was achievable. This contributed to the consolidation of Turkey's form of neoliberalism.

Lastly, post-crisis financial transformation took a distinct turn towards the *internationalization* of the state's financial apparatus (Marois 2012: 3, 179, 205). This concept refers to how state and governing élites take charge of managing their own domestic political economy such that they contribute to protecting the global economic order in line with neoliberal principles. Internationalization thus also refers to how state elites strategically insulate the state's financial apparatus, according to international market norms, from their citizenry in general and the popular and working classes in particular. In Turkey this formal (if not substantive) separation of the political from the economic took the concrete form of enhanced independence of the Central Bank and the BRSA, with the aim of pursuing market-based policy imperatives such as price stability and inflation targeting by the Central Bank (see Chapter 5). Internationalization continued in the form of formal commitments to accession to the European Union. These crystallized in the new 2005 Banking Law, which sought to integrate more firmly the national banking system into the financial world market. The 2005 Law also firmed up financial regulation by revising the institutional framework in which the BRSA functioned (bank regulation and supervision had already been transferred from the Treasury to the BRSA in 1999) (Türel 2009: 136–142). The internationalization of the state institutionalized the new phase of market-oriented banking sector restructuring in Turkey.

It is important to signal that officials and conventional economists cite the success of these reforms. In the words of the BRSA, for example, since 2001 the banks are now successfully restructured on an operational scale, employ professional staff, and reflect a reasonable number of branches and personnel (BRSA 2010). Accordingly., the post-2001 reforms have generated more effective regulation and supervision while encouraging stronger market fundamentals in the sector (De Jonghe et al. 2012: 51–52). Indeed, many commentators now look to the 2001 reform process as vital to the relative stability of the banking sector during 2008–09. There remains, however, room for more critical analyses.

Situating the Contemporary Turkish Banking Sector

Following the 2001 financial crisis, Turkey was able to piggyback its economic recovery onto a general global upswing: annual GDP growth bounced back from -6 per cent in 2001 to 9 per cent by 2004, then averaging around 6 to 7 per cent until the 2008–09 crisis (and 4 to 6 per cent since). This phase of rapid growth displayed particular characteristics.[4] For one, it was driven by significant inflows of foreign finance capital, lured by relatively high rates of return. The capital inflows, as such, were often speculation-led and geared to benefiting from the higher rates of interest in the Turkish asset markets. This proved attractive to short-term finance capital and this, in return, supported the relative abundance of foreign exchange that in turn led to the overvaluation of the Turkish lira (TL). By 2007–08 the overvalued exchange rate was below TL1.2/US$. As Turkish society enjoyed the benefits of lower foreign exchange costs, this brought an import boom in consumption and investment goods, widening Turkey's current account deficit.

Furthermore, the post-crisis growth era has been characterized by weak employment (that is, jobless growth) and modest inflation. Unemployment rates topped 10 per cent following the 2001 crisis and were never really able to attain pre-crisis levels of around 6.5 per cent, directly impacting the poor and working classes. At the same time, however, rapid growth (and capital inflows) did not generate runaway inflation. Since 2006 the Central Bank has implemented an open inflation-targeting framework, with its current target being 5 per cent inflation of consumer prices (within a target range of 2 percentage points). While displaying a propensity for overshooting targets, inflation has generally remained under 10 per cent, and until recently hovered around 6–8 per cent following the 2008–09 crisis. Despite the positive achievements on the disinflation front, rates of interest have been slow to adjust. The real return on government debt instruments, for instance, remained above 10 per cent until 2005 and above 6 per cent until 2010. For some time this put significant pressure on authorities to meet Turkey's debt obligations. More recently, however, post-crisis fiscal austerity has led to a fiscal surplus and a slow reduction in Turkey's public debt (although private debt has skyrocketed). For the banks, however, they have tended to benefit tremendously from persistently large spreads between their borrowing and lending rates of interests, earning record levels of returns since 2001 (see below).

It is in this contemporary context that Turkey's financial services sector has expanded and changed. What is significant in the case of Turkey is that the banks maintain a major share in the financial sector overall. By the start of 2017, the banks controlled 81 per cent of the financial sector's total assets worth TL2.73 trillion or about US $776 billion (BAT 2017, I-17). Well behind the banks, the portfolio management companies account for 4 per cent and insurance companies 3 per cent, with everything from real estate investment trusts, pension funds, leasing and factoring companies comprising the remaining 12 per cent of the sector. As Chapter 7 in this collection elaborates, in some cases even these market-based financial institutions are in fact subsidiaries of the banks. The contemporary and ongoing dominance of Turkey's bank-based but market-oriented system is no anomaly (cf. Rodrigues et al. 2016). In Turkey, as in other emerging capitalist societies, it reflects the historical development of a peripheral financial system, which emerged out of the post-war period where banks played essential roles in pooling and augmenting scarce capital resources for industrialization (Marois 2012). We now turn to evidencing the empirical dynamics of the neoliberal transformation of banking in Turkey.

The Post-2001 Structure of Banking in Turkey

Bank Assets and Control

The total assets of the banking sector have expanded tremendously since 2001, from US $115 billion to over $811 billion by 2015 (BAT 2015a).[5] As a percentage of GDP this constitutes an increase from around 60 per cent to over 105 per cent of GDP (Table 6.1). While significant, these levels are well below the EU average of around 300 per cent of GDP. Relative to other emerging capitalist societies, Turkey is close to countries like Russia and India but below countries like South Korea, Brazil, South Africa and China.

Total bank loans have expanded even more dramatically: From a post-2001 crisis nadir of 17 per cent of GDP to a post-2008–09 crisis zenith of nearly 70 per cent in 2015. Deposits levels have been more varied, if showing a slow but steady increase from 2001 lows of around 35 per cent to current levels of 60 per cent of GDP. The expansion of bank assets, loans and deposits has not been matched by a corresponding increase in the number of banks since 2000–01.

Table 6.1 Total Bank Assets, Loans, and Deposits to GDP, %, 2001–14

	Bank Assets	*Loans and Receivables*	*Deposits*
2001	69.3	17.1	48.8
2002	60.7	16.1	40.6
2003	54.9	15.4	35.4
2004	54.8	18.5	35.3
2005	61.2	23.6	39.1
2006	63.9	28.8	41.2
2007	65.7	32.9	41.8
2008	74.3	38.6	47.7
2009	83.8	40.0	53.3
2010	87.5	46.3	55.9
2011	89.4	51.2	53.9
2012	91.6	54.3	54.3
2013	104.3	64.8	60.2
2014	107.9	69.1	60.4

Source: BAT 2015.

Table 6.2 Number of Commercial and Other Banks, 2000–14

	State-owned	*Private*	*Foreign*	*Under SDIF**	*Development and Investment***	*Total*
2000	4	28	18	11	18	79
2001	3	22	15	6	15	61
2002	3	20	15	2	14	54
2003	3	18	13	2	14	50
2004	3	18	13	1	13	48
2005	3	17	13	1	13	47
2006	3	14	15	1	13	46
2007	3	11	18	1	13	46
2008	3	11	17	1	13	45
2009	3	11	17	1	13	45
2010	3	11	17	1	13	45
2011	3	11	16	1	13	44
2012	3	12	16	1	13	45
2013	3	11	17	1	13	45
2014	3	11	19	1	13	47
2015	3	9	21	1	13	52
2016	3	9	21	1	13	52

Source: BAT 2015; BAT 2017; *Savings Deposit Insurance Fund; **Includes both public and private banks.

With the impact of crisis in 2000–01, a total of 18 banking institutions collapsed (Table 6.2). These included a number of small and poorly managed banks, as well as one large state-owned bank, Emlak, which was folded into the state-owned Ziraat Bank and Halkbank (as discussed below, this period also saw drastic cuts in bank branch and personnel numbers). The fallout from crisis in banking lasted until 2004–05, when the number of banks stabilized at or below 47, which was well below the 79 banking institutions in operation in 2000.

The BAT classifies the different banking institutions in Turkey according to their dominant ownership and control profile (that is, more than 50 per cent). Banks can be classified as either i) state-owned deposit banks (or 'public' banks); ii) privately owned deposit banks; iii) foreign banks; iv) banks under the SDIF; and v) development and investment banks (although they include both public and private ownership). For the sake of clarity, deposit banks may also be referred to as retail or commercial banks. In Turkey, the commercial banks may also undertake investment and development functions (and, hence, may also be referred to as universal banks) (Öztürk et al. 2010). Unlike commercial banks, the development and investment banks do not normally accept public deposits and are typically run according to particular investment strategies or are tied to certain sectors like exports, infrastructure, and so on. Ownership is varied, including three state, six private, and four foreign-owned development and investment banks. The Turkish banking sector as of the start of 2017 features six 'participation' banks or 'green' banks that operate according to Islamic principles of profit and loss sharing.[6] Ownership, too, is now both private and public as the state-owned Ziraat Bank opened a green subsidiary in 2015, followed by the foundation of the state- and *vakıf*-owned Vakıf Participation Bank in 2016. As of 2017 the deposit banks plus the Central Bank control 90 per cent of all banking sector assets; by contrast, the participation banks control 5 per cent of banking assets and the development and investment banks the remaining 5 per cent (BAT 2017: I-17).

Figure 6.1 illustrates the transformations in terms of the asset control by banks from 1988 onwards. It is worth signalling that at the time of writing—despite the rise in participation banks' control and the founding of two new state-owned participation banks—the BAT does not provide reliable data series for their asset control. The figure does include the failed banks taken over by the SDIF, whose assets are negligible since 2004, after having peaked at 8.5 per cent in 2000. Notably, one can see the decline in the ratio of assets controlled by the state banks under neoliberalism. While controlling about 45 per cent in 1990, today the state banks control about 30 per cent. By contrast, the assets of private domestic banks expanded from about 45 per cent in 1990

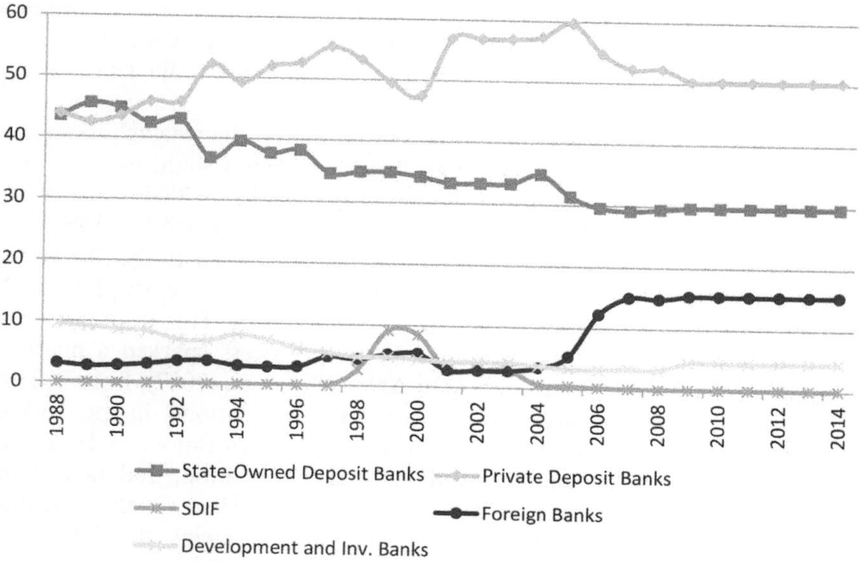

Figure 6.1 Asset Control by Banks (%, 1988–2014)
Source: BAT.

to 60 per cent within 15 years (as linked to capital account liberalization), before falling back to 50 per cent after the 2008–09 crisis. This reflects BAT data classifications, which separate banks that are owned by foreign financial capital from the private deposit banks with majority domestic shareholders. Finally, a highly significant change in asset control comes with the internalization of foreign banks. Since 2005, the rise of foreign banking in Turkey has changed the banking sector landscape in ways qualitatively more significant than the 15 per cent asset control figure represents, as will be discussed below.

The Concentrations of Bank Capital in Turkey

The contemporary banking sector in Turkey is characterized by varying forms and degrees of increased concentrations. These include ownership, asset concentration, and institutional size.

First, the ownership and control of banking assets is heavily concentrated under private control, considering both private domestic and foreign banks together control about 70 per cent of the sector. The post-war period of state bank control has long since waned under neoliberalism. Likewise, bank assets are heavily concentrated within commercial and universal banks (including green banks), with development and investment banks constituting a mere 5 per cent. While Turkey's three public development banks—Iller (Provinces) Bank, Exim (Export Import) Bank and Kalkinma (Development) Bank—have varying degrees of historical importance and expertise in development, in today's world they have relatively fewer assets and resources to promote domestic infrastructure and development projects compared with other emerging capitalist societies like China, Brazil, Mexico and India (Barone and Spratt 2015; Barone and Spratt 2017).

The banking sector's assets are also concentrated in increasingly large and predominantly private banks, although there has been a slight easing of this trend in recent years. For example, the five largest banks in 2004 controlled 63 per cent of all assets and the largest 10 banks 87 per cent (BAT 2015b, I-16). By 2015, the figures were 58 per cent and 85 per cent, respectively. The largest five include one state bank and four private banks, while the largest 10 include three state, five private, and two foreign banks. This does not minimize the fact that the 2001 crisis and recovery process sparked a phase of rapid asset concentration. According to Abbasoğlu et al. (2007), from 2001 to 2005 mergers and acquisitions (alongside some liquidations) in the Turkish banking sector experienced a phase of increasing concentration. In Turkey, as elsewhere, higher asset concentration reduced competition, and helped the banks to drive up their returns including, but not limited to, through high interest rate margins. The implication being that following the 2001 crisis Turkey's banking sector became more monopolistic in its structure. Since 2005, however, the degree of concentration or monopoly control has remained static (Macit 2012).

The Privatization and Marketization of Turkey's State-owned Banks

The trajectory of privatization in Turkey begins with Turgut Özal's administration (1983–89). In 1984 the government set out the specific aim of reducing the state's presence in the economy and of intensifying market imperatives within Turkish society. New laws created the policymaking framework and administrative arm necessary for privatizations, enabling some sell-offs by 1985. Yet the more significant changes involved the restructuring—or marketization—of major state-owned enterprises (SOEs) to enhance their financial performance by internalizing profit mandates. This was done in order to prepare the SOEs for later privatization. A subsequent milestone in the privatization process came with the passing of Decree no 32 concerning the Law of Protection of the Value of the Turkish lira (that is, capital account liberalization) in 1989. With this Council of Ministers decision the government lifted: (a) the limits on the amount of foreign assets that could be owned domestically; and (b) the limits on foreign borrowing by Turkish banks. Moreover, foreign capital was allowed to trade in company stocks and government securities in the Istanbul Stock Exchange (then named İMKB). This augmented the capacity of financial capital to enter and purchase SOEs in Turkey. Finally, to better institutionalize the legal basis of privatization, the Tansu Çiller administration (1993–96) prepared the 1994 Privatization Law No. 4046 (authored by Tezcan Yaramancı), which remains in force today with amendments (Marois 2012: 103–104). In general, the sell-offs since the 1980s have included state-owned primary industries like cement and steel, but also airports, airlines and energy suppliers. Only a few very small state banks were fully privatized. Indeed, not until 1998 did privatization receipts top US $1 billion annually (about 0.5 per cent of GDP), and this was largely from the sale of mobile phones leases and the state's 12.3 per cent share in the private domestic bank, İs Bank. Until recently the limited size and depth of the Istanbul Stock Exchange, now Bourse Istanbul, had slowed the sell-off of larger SOEs by public offer or flotation (Karataş 2001, 97–98). Furthermore, it was not until after the AKP came to power in 2002 that privatization became a clear objective of the government.

To be sure, the 2001 crisis in Turkey raised the neoliberal spectre of what to do with Turkey's powerful state-owned banks.[7] Since the late 1990s the International Monetary Fund (IMF) had been ramping up pressure on Turkey to privatize them. The December 1999 IMF Letter of Intent, for example, calls for the rapid marketization of Ziraat Bank and Halkbank (that is, to be explicitly profit-oriented) as preparation for privatization. At first glance, the crises of 2000 and 2001 seemed to provide an opportunity to complete the process. Through 2000 the coalition government eliminated the state bank duty loss mechanism and attempted to push through various rule-by-decrees and legal changes to force and/or enable bank privatizations (OECD 2001: 205–207). However, the unfolding of the 2001 crisis exposed the accumulated duty losses and poor assets forced upon the state banks during the 1990s, notably by the Çiller administration. There was now no chance, except at politically unacceptable fire-sale prices, of selling off the state banks. As such, the BSRP spearheaded state bank recapitalization and restructuring in May 2001. This entailed deep institutional changes that severely affected the historical missions of the state-owned banks to fund politically determined priority development projects. Professional private sector bankers, moreover, were appointed to head the banks. Within 18 months (June 2001 to December 2002), the number of state bank employees and bank branches were drastically reduced. While remaining state-owned in formal terms, the government's reforms *qualitatively* privatized *cum* marketized the state banks by internalizing market-based efficiency, profit-maximization, and competitive and financial imperatives.

Since the 2001 crisis the three remaining state-owned commercial banks, VakıfBank, Halkbank and Ziraat Bank, have been subject to different privatization sell-offs. For example, the third largest state bank, VakıfBank, the 'Foundations' bank, is a special case as it comes under the direction of the Vakıflar Genel Müdürlüğü (VGM—General Directorate of Foundations). VakıfBank went through several failed privatization attempts prior to the 2001 crisis. After 2001, state authorities changed Vakıf's ownership structure in preparation for an initial public offering (IPO) sale. In November 2005 an IPO of 25.2 per cent raised US $1.27 billion on the ISE, and was considered a success. As of mid-2018, the VGM retained a controlling share of 58.5 per cent. However, in 2014 the AKP government began to discuss radical restructuring plans that involved transferring all the VGM shares to the Treasury, ostensibly as a means to fully privatize the bank. The employee's pension fund, which controls the other 16 per cent of shares, would have the option of selling its shares to the Treasury. As of 2018, this had yet to occur and the plans remain highly contentious, and would likely be challenged in the Constitutional Court.

The second largest state-owned bank, Halkbank, or the 'People's' bank, continues to be majority state-owned but is placed formally under the Privatization Administration (and is therefore slated for privatization). As with VakıfBank, privatization commitments pre-date the 2001 crisis but not until March 2005 did the AKP government announce plans to have a Goldman Sachs-led consortium advise on its immediate block sale. Nearly two years later, the government passed a law clearing the way for full privatization, following the temporary suspension of Halk's sale *via* challenges in court. The National Bank of Kuwait, Spain's BBVA, Belgium's Fortis, and Turkey's Garanti and Akbank all expressed interest in a block sale, as acquiring Halk would immediately secure a market-maker position in Turkey. Yet in February 2007 authorities put an end to a block sale, opting instead for an IPO for 24.98 per cent, which were subsequently sold off in May 2007 for US $1.9 billion. Five years later, in 2012, another 23.92 per cent of Halkbank's shares were sold off on the ISE, earning some $2.5 billion—the largest share sale in Turkey's history. As such, the Privatization Administration retained control of

51.11 per cent of Halkbank. Then in August 2016 the AKP government promulgated Law No. 6741 on the 'Establishment of the Turkish Sovereign Wealth Fund Management Incorporation', forming the Turkey Wealth Fund (a sovereign wealth fund). By 2017 a range of very large state enterprises were placed within the Fund, including Halkbank and Ziraat Bank (see below). The 51.11 per cent ownership stake held by the Privatization Administration was thus transferred to the Fund. It is worth noting that while the Fund owns Halkbank (and Ziraat Bank), the Banks Association still classifies these institutions as state-owned banks (BAT 2017).

The largest of Turkey's state-owned banks, Ziraat Bank, or the 'Agricultural' bank, was until 2017 fully state-owned by the Treasury before passing to the Turkey Wealth Fund. Since at least 2001, state authorities had identified Ziraat for privatization in successive IMF Letters of Intent. The discourse around Ziraat privatization has varied considerably. Since 2002 AKP officials have differed, with some consistently arguing Ziraat must be sold (for example, former Minister and Deputy Prime Minister Ali Babacan) and with others suggesting Turkey should keep at least one state-owned bank (past BRSA president, Tevfik Bilgin). In recent years, however, Ziraat Bank, along with Halkbank and VakıfBank, have become seemingly indispensable partners in the AKP governments' new mega-project plans, for example, as key funders in the new, contentious, third Istanbul airport. As part of the new Turkey Wealth Fund, this trend is likely to accelerate, but it is unclear whether this will be in the public or private interest. The ruling AKP is also intent on mobilizing the state banks to deepen Islamic financial operations. Policymakers, too, are working to strengthen market finance, reinforce securitization and develop Islamic bond markets as part of their plans to turn Istanbul into a regional financial centre, in which regional 'participation' banks (that is, 'Islamic' banks outside of Turkish banking jargon) will be significant actors. In line with these aims, Ziraat Bank has taken on important political significance for the ruling AKP, insofar as it opened the first state-owned participation bank in May 2015. President Erdoğan praised this development in Turkish banking, challenging all three state-owned banks to increase the share of participation bank assets from the present 5 per cent to 15 or 20 per cent by 2023.[8]

In terms of the state-owned development banks, all three—Türk Eximbank (Export Credit Bank of Turkey), Türkiye Kalkınma Bankası Anonim Şirketi (Development Bank of Turkey) and Iller Bank (Bank of Provinces)—have yet to be the subject of serious privatization discussions. However, when Eximbank came into existence in 1987 (Law No. 3332) it took over the capital and assets of the State Investment Bank and transformed it into a joint stock company subject to private law. Finally, the Central Bank of Turkey is a majority state-owned institution.

While Turkey's state-owned banks seemed destined for privatization, there may be reason for pause—not least because of their inclusion in the Turkey Wealth Fund. In the wake of the 2008–09 global financial crisis, Turkish state-owned banks played an important economic (and political) role in helping smooth out the impact on Turkey by increasing lending operations (Marois and Güngen 2014). One measure involved the Central Bank doubling the exports rediscount credit limit to US $1 billion for Eximbank (to mitigate crisis impact on industry sectors). With this, the credit pool widened and eligibility eased. On 13 March 2009 the government then increased the capital of Eximbank by TL500 million. More broadly, the state-owned banks remained relatively stable and highly profitable during the crisis. The three state commercial banks increased lending significantly, helping out farmers and small tradespersons. For example, through such programmes as the Agricultural Credit Co-operatives scheme, Ziraat Bank was able to direct additional credits to farmers. The point being that even marketized state-owned banks can help to stabilize otherwise crisis-prone neoliberal strategies of development.

While generally lauded in domestic circles in Turkey, the IMF has been critical of the state-owned banks arguing that they enjoy unfair advantages over private sector banks (IMF 2012: 35). More critical scholars offer a different interpretation, suggesting that the state-owned banks helped the private banks sustain their profits, by absorbing private sector credit reductions, and in doing so help to stabilize the inherent instability of neoliberal transformation in Turkey (Marois and Güngen 2016).

The Internalization of Foreign Bank Capital

The penetration by foreign banks into Turkey increased significantly after the 2001 crisis. In particular, since 2005 Turkey has experienced growth in cross-border mergers and acquisitions in the banking sector.

One of the most notable foreign bank entries occurred when General Electric (GE) sold its shares of Garanti Bankası to the Spanish banking giant Banco Bilbao Vizcaya-Argentaria (BBVA). GE had first acquired 25.5 per cent of Garanti for US $1.6 billion in 2005. Five years later GE sold 24.9 per cent of its shares for $5.8 billion in 2010. This example, representing the second largest in merger and acquisition (M&A) deal ever in Turkey, attests to the high rates of profitability in the Turkish banking sector in comparison to its counterparts in the developed countries (Bedirhanoğlu et al. 2013: 286). Since the 2001 crisis and the establishment of the BSRP, both foreign and domestic banks have found benefit in such mergers. In another significant acquisition in 2005 Koç-UniCredito (after Koç Holding had sold 49.5 per cent of Koçbank to Unicredito) bought 57 per cent of Yapı ve Kredi for $4.6 billion.

Foreign and private domestic mergers continued. For example, in 2010 Burgan Bank of Kuwait bought Eurobank Tekfen from its Greek-Turkish partners for US $359 million. Then in 2012 Sberbank of Russia (a state-owned bank) acquired Denizbank from Dexia of Belgium for $3.8 billion. The following year the Commercial Bank of Qatar bought 71 per cent of Alternatif Bank, then in 2014 the Industrial and Commercial Bank of China bought 76 per cent of Tekstil Bankası. In minority stake purchases, Garanti Bankası sold another 15 per cent to Spain's BBVA. Then in 2012 the BRSA made an unusual move and granted operating permission for two new banks in Turkey: Odeabank of Lebanon and The Bank of Tokyo-Mitsubishi UFJ of Japan.

Three matters of note arise here. First, the internalization of foreign bank capital since 2001 has been driven by the potential to earn high returns. This is an obvious and necessary observation, given continued heterodox mythologies around banks being first and foremost in the business of intermediation. Rather, intermediation is a means of earning (high) returns on capital, at least for private corporate banks. Second, foreign bank entry has not led to a competitive renaissance in Turkey. Contrary to the aspirations of the World Bank and the IMF, foreign bank M&As did not fragment asset control or dismantle the oligopolistic structure in the private banks in Turkey. What the internalization of foreign banks has brought is greater diversification of financial products and new profitability strategies around targeting household and consumer credit—whose class-based effects see the poor and working classes directly transferring their wealth to the banks' bottom lines (Karacimen 2014). Finally, the internalization of foreign bank capital puts additional pressure on state authorities to be willing and able to protect the interests of foreign banks in Turkey—a policy recommendation that is reflected in current World Bank risk management policy advocacy reports (World Bank 2013). As such, the internationalization of bank capital globally, as internalized in Turkey, gives a qualitatively new dimension to the internationalization of the contemporary neoliberal Turkish state in terms of state–capital relations. We now turn to the data on banks' balance sheets in Turkey.

The Distribution of Bank Assets and Liabilities in Turkey

In terms of the assets held by banks in Turkey today, these are mostly composed of about one third liquid assets and of just under two thirds loans and receivables (Table 6.3). The share of loans has notably increased since 2005, while the share of liquid assets has fallen in relative terms. Fixed assets comprise 2.3 per cent of total assets. Prior to 2001 most banks, public and private, channelled funds into high-yielding government debt as opposed to corporate debt and loans or consumer credit. Accordingly, the share of government securities in total bank assets more than doubled from about 10 per cent in 1990 to 23 per cent in 1999 (Treasury, 2001: 6). After the 2001 crisis reforms, and with the government allowing generous interest rate spreads, the banks moved to increase loans over liquid assets. In Turkey, the spread between reference lending and deposit rates have reached as high as 828 basis points during the post 2008–09 crisis peak of the consumer credit boom in the first quarter of 2010. The spread fell gradually over time to 470 basis points by the first quarter of 2015. A snapshot of 2014 saw the corporate share of loans reach 70 per cent, with 30 per cent going to households (retail). Of the

Table 6.3 Balance Sheet Distribution (%), Assets and Liabilities, 2001–14

Assets					*Liabilities*			
	Liquid Assets	*Loans and Receivables*	*Permanent Assets*	*Other Assets*	*Deposits*	*Non-Deposit Funds*	*Other Liabilities*	*Shareholders' Equity*
2001	33.3	24.6	33.6	8.5	70.4	16.0	6.4	5.8
2002	56.6	26.5	8.5	8.3	67.0	14.8	6.2	10.7
2003	57.3	28.0	7.7	6.9	64.4	15.6	5.7	12.0
2004	54.4	33.7	7.2	4.8	64.4	14.8	5.8	12.9
2005	51.9	38.6	5.1	4.4	63.9	16.9	5.7	12.1
2006	50.0	45.0	3.6	1.5	64.5	18.0	5.5	9.7
2007	44.7	50.0	3.4	1.9	63.6	16.3	7.0	10.5
2008	43.7	52.0	2.8	1.5	64.2	17.7	6.4	9.9
2009	48.0	47.7	2.8	1.4	63.5	17.2	5.9	10.9
2010	43.0	52.9	2.6	1.5	63.9	16.8	5.9	11.2
2011	39.0	57.2	2.3	1.4	60.2	21.7	6.1	10.3
2012	36.7	59.2	2.5	1.6	59.3	19.8	7.5	11.7
2013	34.2	62.1	2.1	1.5	57.7	23.6	7.4	9.9
2014	32.3	64.1	2.3	1.4	56.0	24.9	7.3	10.5

Source: BAT 2015a.

corporate share, 38 per cent went to small and medium-sized enterprises (SME) in Turkey (BAT 2015a, I-18; see also Chapter 9 on SMEs).

Following the 2008–09 crisis, the credit expansion came mainly from consumer loans. Moreover, the government's response to crisis involved stimulating domestic consumption by reducing value-added tax on selected domestic goods (Muñoz-Martínez and Marois 2014: 1115). Only after the BRSA and the Central Bank intervened did consumer loan increases slow by 2012.[9] However, between 2010 and 2014 consumer loans more than doubled (BRSA 2015). Rising consumption-based loans and credit card usage have been the main mechanisms behind increased household indebtedness. As one indicator, the number of credit cards jumped after 2003, reaching 46 million in 2010 and then over 57 million in 2015. According to IMF data, household debt to GDP increased from 15.1 per cent of the GDP in 2010 to 21 per cent in 2014.

In Turkey, the banking system's liability foundation is chiefly made up of deposits. Since 2001, however, deposits have fallen from around 65 to 55 per cent of total liabilities. Compensating for this shift, non-deposit liabilities (for example, securities) have increased from about 15 per cent to about 25 per cent of the total. On average, shareholder equity has been steady, in the range of 10 to 11 per cent. Because they have been able to benefit from wide interest rate spreads and profitably to extend their loan portfolios, banks have responded favourably to the policy environment. Finally, the increase in non-deposit finance since 2011 has caused the share of deposits within total liabilities to decrease, but this also has led to a rise in the loan/deposit ratio. Banks in Turkey have been taking advantage of abundant global liquidity stemming from quantitative easing. As one policy response, whose effectiveness is yet to be determined, the Central Bank initiated the Reserve Options Mechanism in late 2011 to help stem short-term inflows, restrain domestic credit growth, and mitigate exchange rate and inflation volatility (Alper et al. 2013: 11).

As Figure 6.2 shows, since the early 1990s private domestic banks in Turkey have overcome the state-owned banks in total loans, reflecting closely their increasing size of assets. Notably until 2001–02, the share of private banks continued to outpace the state banks, regardless of asset size, as the state banks became increasingly mired in duty loss lending and were only contributing about 20 per cent of overall loans. Since then, state bank lending has increased to around 30 per cent, showing countercyclical increases amid the 2008–09 crisis, as private domestic and foreign bank lending slipped.

In Turkey, the share of foreign currency liabilities and assets displays an uneven dollarization process (Table 6.4). In the mid-1990s the share of foreign currency deposits within total deposits was over 55 per cent. During the pre-2001 crises years, liquid liabilities denominated in foreign currency increased rapidly, leading to excessive indebtedness because of the tendency of the banking system towards open positions. Borrowing from international financial markets at relatively cheaper rates, banks in Turkey financed government deficits and their target securities generated lucrative profits in the 1990s—in classic carry trade operations (Marois 2012: 123). The annual real interest rate for government securities averaged 32 per cent between 1992 and 1999 (Treasury, 2001: 3). Although converting short-term foreign liabilities into the long-term loans in domestic currency could finance growth in the economy via the banking system, maturity and currency mismatch increased the risk of crisis. In the years following the 2001 crisis, economic and political stability

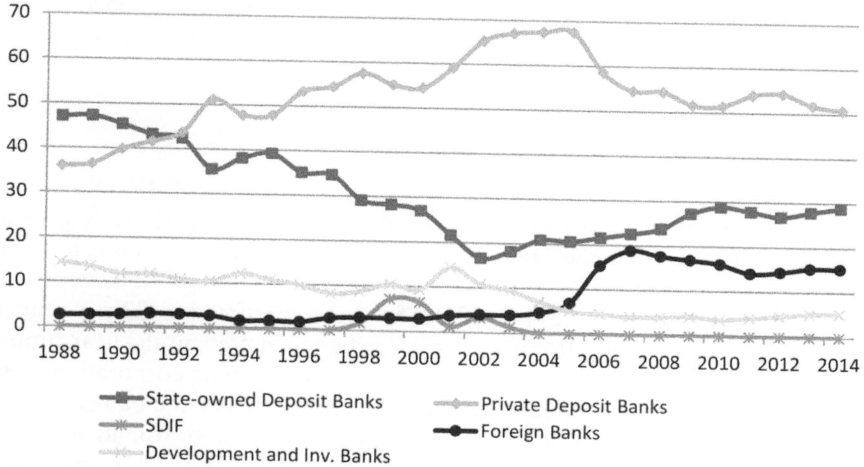

Figure 6.2 Loans by Banks (%, 1988–2014)
Source: BAT 2001; 2007; 2015b.

Table 6.4 Foreign Currency Liabilities and Assets (% of total, including Turkish currency)

	Banking System FC		*State-owned*		*Private*		*Foreign*		*Development and Investment Banks*	
Years	L	A	L	A	L	A	L	A	L	A
2001	57.5	48.1	37.2	35.5	68.6	55.1	62.9	53.6	54.6	57.4
2002	50.4	46.4	34.3	32.9	59.3	53.9	56.4	53.4	49.0	51.7
2003	43.3	39.3	27.0	25.9	52.8	47.8	50.0	43.9	41.8	45.5
2004	40.1	36.8	25.6	23.6	49.2	44.9	42.7	36.3	37.8	40.8
2005	35.7	32.3	21.1	19.2	43.2	39.0	41.7	36.8	33.5	32.3
2006	37.6	33.8	24.2	22.1	43.6	40.1	44.8	35.1	33.3	31.5
2007	33.3	28.8	21.4	19.8	38.4	35.4	39.5	24.7	29.8	24.0
2008	34.8	31.0	24.4	23.4	38.6	37.4	42.5	23.9	33.8	27.2
2009	31.7	27.2	22.3	21.4	35.6	32.3	38.0	20.5	33.9	29.7
2010	30.6	26.1	21.5	20.2	34.2	31.3	36.3	19.1	34.6	31.2
2011	36.0	30.7	25.2	24.7	40.9	35.6	37.9	23.0	43.7	37.0
2012	35.3	30.7	28.2	26.8	38.3	34.1	35.3	22.4	48.7	42.4
2013	41.2	34.7	33.4	31.6	44.1	37.4	42.8	28.0	54.5	48.3
2014	41.9	35.2	33.6	31.7	44.6	37.7	44.8	29.1	58.3	51.9

Source: BAT 2015a (L: Liabilities; A: Assets).

has led an overall decrease in foreign currency liabilities. However, foreign currency levels have jumped markedly since 2011 amid renewed global economic instability. Whereas foreign currency deposit ratios bottomed out at around a third of deposits from 2007 to 2010, by 2014 they accounted for nearly 42 per cent.

Stability and Volatility in Turkish Banking

The financial sector soundness indicators provided by the IMF (Table 6.5) provide a snapshot of the banks' financial risks in Turkey. There is general agreement that neither the open position/equity ratio nor the stagnant NPL levels are severe threats to the stability of the banking sector.[10] The depreciation of the Turkish lira in 2014 and 2015, which amounted to 23 per cent in the first nine months of 2015, however, may change matters in the near future. Further devaluation can erode equity value and push some corporations and individuals into default, thereby increase the credit risks of the banks.

Looking back, as a result of economic slowdown in and around the 2001 crisis, the banks' NPL ratio increased considerably between 1998 and 2002, not only for state banks which suffered from duty losses, but also for private banks as well. When the 2001 shock subsided, the NPL/gross loans ratio

Table 6.5 Financial Soundness Indicators for Deposit Takers in Turkey (%, 2010–15)

	2010	*2011*	*2012*	*2013*	*2014*	*2015 (Q1)*
Regulatory Capital/Risk Weighted Assets	18.97	16.55	17.89	15.28	16.28	15.50
Tier-I/Risk Weighted Assets	17.05	14.94	15.12	12.98	13.90	13.18
Provisions for NPLs/ Capital	2.36	2.48	2.96	3.15	3.51	3.79
NPLs/Gross Loans	3.49	2.58	2.74	2.64	2.74	2.73
Liquid Assets/Total Assets	55.44	49.72	50.93	47.14	53.70	55.41
Liquid Assets/Short-term Debts	79.74	72.02	76.03	72.08	77.35	79.08
FX Open Position/Capital	-0.12	-1.11	0	-3.45	-2.13	-2.80

Source: IMF database.

gradually fell to 3.5 per cent by 2007. It then rose to 5.3 per cent in 2009 due to the repercussions of the global financial crisis (BRSA 2011) before dropping back to 3.7 per cent in 2010 and declining further to 2.7 per cent in 2011.[11] Since then it has remained at around 2.8 per cent. The NPLs in consumer loans and credit cards were above average by 2015, despite the significant decline from a 2009 peak of 6 per cent (BRSA 2015). The decreases seen in NPL provision/own-funds and NPL/gross loans in comparison to the crisis years may be taken as an indication of a positive change in asset quality. However, the capital adequacy ratio of banks—that is, the ratio of regulatory capital they have, to risk-weighted assets—is in decline (see Table 6.5). The initial restructuring of the banking sector after the 2001 crisis boosted this ratio to 30 per cent. The capital adequacy ratio has been in decline for most of the years since 2003 (BRSA 2014). None the less, capital adequacy remains well above the legal 8 per cent accepted threshold. However, the ratios imply that growing credit risks will be faced by the banking sector and state regulatory authorities in the future. By extension, the chances that these risks will be socialized by state authorities, and passed onto Turkey's population, is magnified.

Bank Returns in Turkey

With the exception of the period around the 1982 crisis, banks in Turkey have shown rates of returns (as a return on assets—ROA) comparable, and generally superior, to banks found in the advanced capitalist societies—at least until the crisis began to emerge in 1999. Some key factors behind the historically high returns in Turkey included high nominal interest rates, fairly loose restrictions on related lending (lending to associated businesses within a group), and lucrative markets in government debt. From 1999 to the end of 2001, positive returns turned to dramatic losses. Since 2001, the bank restructuring and state-led recovery processes spawned a revival in profitability. By the end of 2002, banking sector returns reached 1.4 per cent—well above the average 1 per cent found in advanced capitalist societies. Over the next decade or so average ROA levels stayed in the range of 1.5 to 2.5 per cent. The increases are linked to greater loan volumes and net interest incomes obtained, which brought down the operating incomes/total incomes ratio from the peak it reached in 2002. The bankers—public, private and foreign alike—have been reluctant to reduce interest rate spreads between what they can borrow at and what they lend at. The stability of these high returns encouraged the internalization of foreign banks, as discussed above. Additionally, as we see below, dramatic cuts in operating expenses via reduced staff and branch numbers post-2001 led to reductions in overall expenses, thus driving up the bottom line at the expense of workers.

There are some interesting points to be drawn from Table 6.6. Contrary to fundamental assumptions found in conventional economics, the state-owned commercial banks (controlling about a third of the sector) have outperformed private domestic banks (the dominant player) year in and year out since 2002 (with few exceptions). Indeed, the state banks even tended to outperform the foreign banks, which are often criticized in emerging capitalist societies for

Table 6.6 Returns of Turkish Banks, 2001–14

	Private Commercial ROA	*Foreign Commercial ROA*	*State-owned Commercial ROA*	*Development and Investment (Private, foreign, and state) ROA*	*Banking System ROA*	*Banking System ROE*
2001	-4.7	7.8	0.0	3.1	-3.8	-69.9
2002	2.0	1.2	1.6	4.9	1.4	11.2
2003	2.1	2.7	2.2	4.3	2.2	15.8
2004	1.6	2.4	2.5	2.8	2.1	14.0
2005	0.6	2.5	2.3	5.3	1.4	10.6
2006	1.8	2.5	2.6	4.8	2.3	18.9
2007	2.4	2.0	2.8	4.6	2.6	19.5
2008	1.8	1.3	1.9	4.0	1.8	15.4
2009	2.4	1.9	2.6	3.7	2.4	18.3
2010	2.4	1.4	2.3	2.7	2.2	16.5
2011	1.7	1.5	1.6	2.1	1.6	13.8
2012	1.8	1.4	1.8	2.0	1.7	13.0
2013	1.6	0.6	1.6	1.6	1.4	12.8
2014	1.3	0.8	1.4	1.8	1.3	11.0

Source: BAT 2015a.

Note: ROA = return on assets.

skimming the cream (that is, taking on only premier clients) and only funding the most lucrative, safe investments. For their part, while constituting a rather small portion of the market, the investment and development banks, private and state alike, registered even higher levels of returns than all the commercial banks (although this is not uncommon). Finally, it is significant that in 2013 and 2014 bank profits across the board have fallen to their lowest levels since 2001. Ongoing political instabilities within Turkey, regional destabilization associated with Syria, and persistent global economic volatility, have all been brought to bear on the record profitability of the banks in Turkey.

Bank Branches and Employees in Turkey

In Turkey since 2001 those in control of the banks have actively managed both bank branch and employee numbers in order to enhance bank returns and/or protect market share. For example, Table 6.7 details changes in branch numbers since 2000. Evidently, the impact of the crisis in 2001 had a dramatic effect. Total branch numbers fell from over 7,800 to about 6,000 within three years. The lion's share of this contraction occurred among the state-owned banks as the BSRP sought to rationalize the state's presence in the market, according to market imperatives. Private domestic banks saw little decline or growth in their numbers until 2007–08, despite equally being at the heart of the 2001 crisis. The foreign banks, however, began to expand dramatically via mergers and acquisitions after 2004–05, expanding their branches nearly tenfold by 2008–09. As to be expected, those banks absorbed by the state apparatus (SDIF) saw their branches consolidate into a single transition bank by 2004, which is intended to wind down all operations tied to the failed banks. While few in number, the development and investment banks saw a third of their branches close amid the crisis. Yet by 2006 their branch numbers more than doubled. In general, branch numbers in Turkey have proven rather malleable by bank owners as they increase and decrease numbers in order to achieve higher returns–the banks' primary motivation under neoliberal strategies of development. This can limit so-called financial inclusion within smaller, less profitable regions or townships in Turkey, which are disproportionately affected by branch closures driven by profit imperatives. That is, the banks' competitive strategies have taken on a distinctly spatial hue. It follows that increases in branch numbers since 2005 have been intended to capture new clients and deposits, driven in part by intensified competition from foreign banks and the fact that deposits remain a core source of funding for banks in Turkey.

The changes in bank employee numbers are likewise illuminating, but for different reasons (Table 6.8). In the sector as a whole, the number of employees dropped by over 25 per cent, or from over 170,000 in 2000 to just over 123,000 workers after 2001. The change was a direct response to the crisis and state-led recovery processes. Aside from the wholesale liquidation of the SDIF banks, the most significant changes in employee numbers were in the state-owned banks. Worker numbers plummeted as part of the

Table 6.7 Number of Branches by Ownership Category

Years	*State-owned Deposit Banks*	*Privately owned Deposit Banks*	*Foreign Deposit Banks*	*Banks Under the Deposit Ins. Fund*	*Dev't and Inv. Banks*	*Total*
2000	2,834	3,783	117	1,073	30	**7,837**
2001	2,725	3,523	233	408	19	**6,908**
2002	2,019	3,659	206	203	19	**6,106**
2003	1,971	3,594	209	175	17	**5,966**
2004	2,149	3,729	209	1	18	**6,106**
2005	2,035	3,799	393	1	19	**6,247**
2006	2,149	3,582	1,072	1	45	**6,849**
2007	2,203	3,625	1,741	1	48	**7,618**
2008	2,416	4,290	2,034	1	49	**8,790**
2009	2,530	4,390	2,062	1	44	**9,027**
2010	2,744	4,582	2,096	1	42	**9,465**
2011	2,909	4,944	1,938	1	42	**9,834**
2012	3,079	5,100	2,012	1	42	**10,234**
2013	3,397	5,339	2,244	1	40	**11,021**
2014	3,500	5,455	2,226	1	41	**11,223**

Source: BAT 2015a. Note: includes foreign branches.

government's strategy to commercialise their operations by driving up profitability. While in 2000 there were over 70,000 state bank employees, by 2003 only 38,000 remained. At the same time, the government shifted the employment contracts for those remaining state bank employees so that they no longer enjoyed the benefits of being public employees, but were instead subject to private sector terms. Subsequently, as state bank profitability increased post-crisis, employee numbers began to recover, but at a growth rate below that of branch numbers. Here the strategy was to intensify labour conditions by decreasing the number of employees per branch. Employee numbers in private domestic banks fell by about 10 per cent, but grew quickly after 2003. Foreign bank employee numbers remained constant until 2005, then doubling alongside their banks' presence in the economy. Finally, development and investment bank employee numbers remained fairly constant, despite a number of closures post-crisis and despite the rapid increase in institutions after 2006. What the date reveals here, as with branch numbers, is that branches and workers numbers have been treated as highly flexible elements of underlying profitability strategies. Indeed, as the banks reopened branches in Turkey, they tended to employ about four fewer workers per branch in 2009 than in 1999. Notably, staff costs (as a percentage of the balance sheet) were cut in half, from 2.65 per cent in 1999 to a 1.35 per cent in 2009 (Marois 2012: 188).

Table 6.8 Number of Employees by Ownership Category

	State-owned	*Privately-owned*	*Foreign*	*Under SDIF*	*Development and Investment*	*Total*
2000	70,191	70,954	3,805	19,895	5,556	**170,401**
2001	56,108	64,380	5,395	6,391	5,221	**137,495**
2002	40,158	66,869	5,416	5,886	4,942	**123,271**
2003	37,994	70,614	5,481	4,518	4,642	**123,249**
2004	39,467	76,880	5,880	403	4,533	**127,163**
2005	38,046	78,806	10,610	395	4,401	**132,258**
2006	39,223	73,220	25,794	333	4,573	**143,143**
2007	41,056	75,124	36,707	325	5,322	**158,534**
2008	43,333	82,158	40,567	267	5,273	**171,598**
2009	44,856	82,270	39,676	261	5,339	**172,402**
2010	47,235	83,633	42,013	252	5,370	**178,503**
2011	50,239	89,047	37,047	243	4,842	**181,418**
2012	51,587	90,612	38,772	226	4,901	**186,098**
2013	54,466	93,365	44,159	229	5,246	**197,465**
2014	55,851	95,839	43,446	227	5,523	**200,886**

Source: BAT 2015a.

Conclusion: Banking on the Neoliberal Transformation of Finance

In the case of Turkey, there is no contradiction or confusion between the continued dominance of banks in the financial sector and that the banks are progressively more market-oriented. Regardless of ownership category, all banking institutions in Turkey are primarily responsive to profit (or positive returns) imperatives. This, of course, is not necessarily surprising for private, corporate banks. To survive, private profit-driven banks must earn returns or they will be driven out of business rapidly. Yet even here, changes have occurred as, for example, not until the 2001 crisis were the private domestic banks legally compelled to separate out their banking businesses from their wider holding groups' operational structures. More surprisingly, perhaps, the state banks have evolved into the most profitable banks of all since 2001.

The market-oriented turn of banking went hand in hand with sectoral restructuring that entailed both domestic M&As alongside the internalization of foreign financial capital. Foreign financial capital has invested heavily in the banking sector, given much higher levels of returns than those found in the advanced capitalist societies. The internalization of foreign bank capital has led to a diversification of financial products and to slow changes in bank asset control. It has not, however, changed the underlying oligopolistic structure of Turkish banking that remains heavily concentrated within a few institutions and even more heavily concentrated in the private sector, domestic and foreign. Bankers retain a heavy hand within the Turkish economy and society, and this has proved to be to their enduring benefit.

While the state-owned banks in Turkey retain a real presence, the significance of their presence is far from straightforward. Certainly after 2001 and then again after 2008–09 and to some extent after the 2016 coup attempt, state authorities benefited from the stabilizing and countercyclical abilities of the state banks, which helped to mitigate financial and economic volatility tied to Turkey's emerging finance form of capitalism. Regardless of repeated plans to fully privatize the state banks since 2001, the banks do not appear to be disappearing any time soon (although the inclusion of Ziraat Bank and Halkbank within the Turkey Wealth Fund portends change). Indeed, the transformation of these institutions into reorganized state-owned banks has distanced them from their historic and traditional mandates, which did not emphasize profit maximization until 2001. But by imitating the private banks and by aggressively reducing the number of branches and employees the state banks now earn billions in extra public revenue—which should be difficult for even the most stalwart neoliberal reformer to forego in the current climate. The future of the state-owned commercial banks is far from clear. However, increasing private and foreign bank dominance means the intensification of financial imperatives (or 'financialization') within the sector and, by extension, Turkish society. Should popular social forces seek to effect some change to Turkey's neoliberal developmental strategy, then there may be great benefit in seeking to reclaim the more social developmental functions once performed by the state banks (Marois and Güngen 2013).

Notes

1 This crisis was the result of partial interest rate liberalization in July 1980, providing room for speculative fund-raising activities by moneylenders and banks. A series of default by small financiers and banks followed the bonanza in 1982.
2 For a neoclassical view, see Mishkin 2009. For a critical view, see Kiely 2007.
3 These did not eliminate holding group banks in the sector but the reforms specified the credit limits and the limits of funds that can be invested into subsidiaries. Law no. 4672, promulgated in May 2001, reintroduced the limit of funds (repealed in 1999) which can be invested in a partnership other than a financial institution. The bank could only use 15 per cent of its equity for such a partnership and the total funds used for this purpose cannot exceed 60 per cent of bank's total equity. The law also deemed options and future contracts as credit, thereby imposing an extra limit on the funds transferable to the holding group companies by the banks. More importantly, the new BRSA regulation in June 2001 compelled the private banks to further remove banking business away from the holding groups' credit preferences. The BRSA bylaw defined qualified shareholders, members of the board of directors and the companies controlled directly or indirectly by these people as belonging to the risk group in terms of a bank's credit operations (BRSA 2002). Law no. 5411 in 2005 detailed these regulations , which made it illegal to provide cheap credit to a risk group company or person and made it compulsory to report regularly to the BRSA the credits extended to those in the risk group.
4 See Boratav and Yeldan 2006 and Bedirhanoglu et al. 2013.

5 This specific BAT resource is available for download in excel format, and provides a comprehensive and detailed empirical source for keys changes. We draw on this resource heavily in the following narrative.
6 See the Participation Banks Association of Turkey for details: http://www.tkbb.org.tr/
7 For a class analysis of the contradictions of Turkey's state-owned banks under neoliberalism, see Marois and Güngen 2016.
8 "Ziraat Participation Bank started Operations", 29 May 2015, *Istanbul Financial Centre*, available online at http://www.ifcturkey.com/view/721/ziraat-participa tion-bank-started-operations/.
9 The BRSA increased credit reserve requirements through a mandate in 2011. It imposed regulations on credit card minimum payments, raising the ratio from 20 per cent of the outstanding debt to between 22 and 35 per cent according to credit limits, and 40 per cent for at least one-year period for newcomers. The BRSA also restricted cash advances made through credit cards in 2011 (with delaying its impact to 2012) and limited the instalments in 2013. The Central Bank during the same period of time increased the cost of credits by increasing the reserve requirements and ending the interest payments to banks on the required reserves.
10 Beginning in 2002 'non-performing loans' were renamed 'loans under follow-up' and evaluated under the 'Loans' section.
11 There is a slight incongruence between the BRSA data and IMF data regarding the non-performing loans.

REFERENCES

Abbasoğlu, O.F., A.F. Aysan and A. Gunes (2007) "Concentration, Competition, Efficiency and Profitability of the Turkish Banking Sector in the Post-Crises Period," *MPRA Paper*, 5494, University Library of Munich.

Akçay, Ü. and A.R. Güngen (2016) *Finansallaşma, Borç Krizi ve Çöküş: Küresel Kapitalizmin Geleceği*, 2nd ed. Ankara: Nota Bene.

Akyüz, Y. and K. Boratav (2003) "The Making of the Turkish Financial Crisis" *World Development*, 31(9): 1549–1566

Alper, C.E. and Z. Öniş (2002) "Soft Budget Constraints, Government Ownership of Banks and Regulatory Failure: The Political Economy of the Turkish Banking System in the Post-Capital Account Liberalization Era", (February 2002). *Bogazici U, Economics Working Paper* ISS/EC 2–2.

Alper, K., K. Hakan and M. Yorukoğlu (2013) "Reserve Options Mechanism", *Central Bank Review*, Vol. 13 (January 2013): 1–14.

Barone, B. and S. Spratt (2015) *Development Banks from the BRICS*, Institute of Development Studies Evidence Report No. 111.

Boratav, K. and E. Yeldan (2006) "Turkey, 1980–2000: Financial Liberalization, Macroeconomic (In)-Stability, and Patterns of Distribution" in L. Taylor (ed.) *External Liberalization in Asia, Post-Socialist Europe and Brazil*, Oxford University Press, 417–455.

BAT–Banks Association of Turkey (2001) *Türkiye'de Bankacılık Sisteminde Rasyolar 1988–2000*, June 2001, Istanbul: BAT.

BAT–Banks Association of Turkey (2007) *Türkiye'de Bankacılık Sistemi Seçilmiş Rasyolar 2001–2006*, July 2007, Istanbul: BAT.

BAT–Banks Association of Turkey (2015a) *The Banking System in Turkey: Yearly Statistics 1959–2014*, BAT, July 2015. Istanbul: BAT.

BAT–Banks Association of Turkey (2015b) *Türkiye'de Bankacılık Sistemi Seçilmiş Rasyolar 2004–2014*, June 2015, Istanbul: BAT.

BAT–Banks Association of Turkey (2017) Banks in Turkey 2016, Istanbul: BAT.

Bedirhanoğlu, P., H. Cömert, İ. Eren, I. Erol, D. Demiröz, N. Erdem, A. R.Güngen, T. Marois, A. Topal, O. Türel, G. Yalman, E. Yeldan, and E. Voyvoda (2013) *Comparative Perspective on Financial System in the EU: Country Report on Turkey*, FESSUD Studies in Financial Systems No. 11.

BRSA–Banking Regulation and Supervision Agency (2002) *Banking Sector Reform: Progress Report*, July 2002, Ankara: BRSA.

BRSA–Banking Regulation and Supervision Agency (2010) "From Crisis to Financial Stability: Turkey Experience", *BRSA Working Paper*, Ankara: BRSA.

BRSA–Banking Regulation and Supervision Agency (2011) *Financial Markets Report*, Issue 24, December 2011, Ankara: BRSA.

BRSA–Banking Regulation and Supervision Agency (2014) *Türk Bankacılık Sektörü Genel Görünümü*, March 2014, Ankara: BRSA.

BRSA–Banking Regulation and Supervision Agency (2015) *Türk Bankacılık Sektörü Temel Göstergeleri*, June 2015, Ankara: BRSA.

Calomiris, C. W. and S. Haber (2014) *Fragile by design: banking crises, scarce credit, and political bargains*, Princeton NJ: Princeton University Press.

Cizre, Ü. and E. Yeldan (2005) "The Turkish Encounter with Neo-Liberalism: Economics and Politics in the 2000/2001 Crises", *Review of International Political Economy*, 12(3): 387–408.

De Jonghe., O., M. Disli and K. Schoors (2011) "Corporate Governance, Opaque Bank Activities, And Risk/Return Efficiency: Pre- And Post-Crisis Evidence From Turkey", *Journal of Financial Services Research*, 41(1): 51–80.

Dinç, I. S. (2005) "Politicians and banks: Political influences on government-owned banks in emerging markets", *Journal of Financial Economics*, 77: 453–479.

Gültekin-Karakaş, D. (2009) *Global Integration of Turkish Finance Capital: State, Capital and Banking Reform in Turkey*, Saarbrücken: Vdm Verlag Dr. Müller Aktiengesellschaft and Co. Kg.

Hilferding, R. (1981 [1910]) *Finance Capital. A Study of the Latest Phase of Capitalist Development*, T. Bottomore (ed.) London: Routledge and Kegan Paul.

International Monetary Fund (IMF) (2012) *Turkey: 2011 Article IV Consultation*. Country Report No. 12/16. Washington, DC: IMF.

Karacimen, E. (2014) "Financialization in Turkey: The Case of Consumer Debt", *Journal of Balkan and Near Eastern Studies*, 16(2): 161–180,

Karataş, C. (2001) "Privatization in Turkey: Implementation, Politics of Privatization and Performance Results", *Journal of International Development*, (13): 93–121.

Kiely, R. (2007) "The End of the Post-war Boom and Capitalist Restructuring", *The New Political Economy of Development: Globalization, Imperialism, Hegemony*, New York: Palgrave Macmillan, 59–76.

Macit, F. (2012) "Recent Evidence on Concentration and Competition in Turkish Banking Sector", *Theoretical and Applied Economics*, Vol. XIX, No. 8(573): 19–28.

Marois, T. (2011) "Emerging Market Bank Rescues in an Era of Finance-Led Neoliberalism: A Comparison of Mexico and Turkey", *Review of International Political Economy*, 18(2): 168–196.

Marois, T. (2012) *States, Banks and Crisis: Emerging Finance Capitalism in Mexico and Turkey*, Cheltenham, Gloucestershire, UK: Edward Elgar Publishing.

Marois, T. (2017) *How Public Banks Can Help Finance a Green and Just Energy Transformation*, Amsterdam: TNI.

Marois, T. and A. R. Güngen (2013) "Reclaiming Turkey's state-owned banks", *Municipal Services Project Occasional Paper Series*, No. 22.

Marois, T. and A. R. Güngen (2014) "Türkiye'nin Devlet Bankalarını Geri Kazanmak", *İktisat Dergisi*, 527: 54–70.

Marois, T. and A. R. Güngen (2016) "Credibility and Class in the Evolution of Public Banks: The Case of Turkey", *The Journal of Peasant Studies*, 43(6): 1285–1309.

Mishkin, F.S. (2009) "Why We Shouldn't Turn Our Backs on Financial Globalization", *IMF Staff Papers*, 56(1): 139–170.

Muñoz-Martínez, H. and T. Marois (2014) "Capital Fixity and Mobility in Response to the 2008–2009 Crisis: Variegated Neoliberalism in Mexico and Turkey", *Environment and Planning D: Society and Space*, 32: 1102–1119.

Organisation for Economic Co-operation and Development (2001) *OECD Economic Surveys: Turkey 2000–2001*, Paris: OECD.

Önder, Z. and S. Özyıldırım (2013) "Role of bank credit on local growth: Do politics and crisis matter?", *Journal of Financial Stability*, 9(1): 13–25.

Önis, Z. (2009) "Beyond the 2001 Financial Crisis: The Political Economy of the New Phase of Neo- Liberal Restructuring in Turkey" *Review of International Political Economy*, 16(3): 409–432.

Öztürk, H., D. Gultekin-Karakas, and M. Hisarciklilar (2010) "The Role of Development Banking in Promoting Industrialization in Turkey", *Région et Développement*, 32: 153–178.

Rodrigues, J., A.C. Santos and N. Teles (2016) "Semi-peripheral financialisation: the case of Portugal", *Review of International Political Economy*, 23(3): 480–510.

Treasury (2001) *Transition to Strong Economy Program*, Ankara: Undersecretary of Treasury.

Türel, O. (2009) "Türkiye Ekonomisinin Neoliberal Yapılanma Sürecinde Bankacılığın Yeniden Düzenlenmesi, 1980–2007", in M. Özuğurlu et al. (eds.) *Alpaslan Işıklı'ya Armağan*, No: 31, Ankara: Mülkiyeliler Birliği Vakfı, 131–170.

World Bank (2012) *Global financial development report 2013: Rethinking the role of state in finance*, Washington, DC: World Bank.

World Bank (2013) *World Development Report 2014 Risk and Opportunity: Managing Risk for Development*, Washington, DC: World Bank.

7 The Neoliberal Emergence of Market Finance in Turkey

Ali Rıza Güngen

Introduction

When speaking of market finance in Turkey, one needs to first recognize that private and public commercial banks dominate the financial system. Neoliberal restructuring of the economy in the 1980s and 1990s did not alter the critical role that the banks play. It is, however, also the case that the securitization of debt obligations is increasing and the use of new financial instruments for investment and risk management have started to gradually alter the landscape in the financial sector. The volume of private sector securities is growing, while the number and the significance of the activities of the non-bank financial intermediaries (NBFIs) are increasing. There are ongoing attempts to deepen financial markets and construct an accompanying regulatory framework for emergent market finance in Turkey.

This implies neither the need for a definitive characterization of Turkey's financial sector as either bank-based or market-based, nor praise of a possible shift from the former to the latter. A hybrid or variegated version is likely to emerge as a result of the deepening of financial markets, the explicit state support for development of the corporate bond market, and increases in the trading volume of the stock market. Indeed, since the 1980s official support for the deepening of the financial markets has been a permanent feature of Turkey's neoliberal governments, but it was in the aftermath of the 2001 crisis and subsequent banking sector restructuring when more decisive steps were taken. As discussed in Chapter 6, when on the brink of financial collapse, the Turkish state assumed the losses of the banks to ensure recovery of the financial sector. The 2001 Banking Sector Restructuring Programme not only socialized the losses of private banks, but also extended the support to the socialization of the exchange rate-related risks of the banking sector by the largest debt swap of modern Turkish history in June 2001. Regulatory attempts were already underway in the 1990s; however, the newly created Banking Regulation and Supervision Agency (BRSA) was faced with the crisis before being able to take precautions for restoring efficiency, as well as strengthening the sector so that a systemic threat to banking would not emerge. The financial reforms that followed the 2001 crisis altered the relations between Turkey's financial supervising authorities and consolidated government initiatives for internationalization of the regulatory framework. The state-led restructuring contributed not only to the increased concentration in the sector, but also to the increased penetration of the financial sector into the everyday lives of the Turkish people. The Turkish banking sector has benefited from higher rates of profit (see Chapter 6).

Despite a profitable and apparently robust banking sector sitting at the core of Turkey's contemporary financial system, there have been mounting concerns about creating alternative financing for corporations. A significant aspect of the post-2008 medium-term government response to crisis has been to reinforce securitization and strengthen market finance. On the one hand, this turn to market finance in Turkey can be seen as spillover from intensified international financial integration and as contiguous with Turkey's post-1980s pattern of economic internationalization. On the other, the emergence of market finance has been mediated by domestic forces, such that the babysteps taken have not yet radically changed the financial architecture in Turkey.

This chapter will chart the emergence of market finance in Turkey. It will analyze Turkey's capital market institutions, processes of financial deepening and the role of NBFIs in the post-2001 period. I will argue that market finance has been relatively insignificant compared to the role of banks such that the Turkish financial sector should still be grasped as dominated by banks. In addition, however, there are significant social and economic forces pushing for financial market deepening and the creation of alternative financing mechanisms in Turkey. Therein, the Turkish state plays a vital role, impacting heavily upon the forms financial deepening take and the emergence of market finance. In this understanding I define the *financialization of the state* in Turkey as involving the internalization of financial imperatives by the state and the neoliberal restructuring of the state with reference to financial norms, reflecting itself not only in fiscal policy and debt management, but also monetary policy and financial regulation (Güngen 2014). This entails parallel processes of *internationalization* of the state's financial apparatus, or when state authorities institutionalize international financial reforms and thereby internalize financial imperatives in ways that also move the state's financial apparatus further away from popular control and political debate (Marois 2011). Analysis of the data and the regulatory initiatives suggest that the capital market developments should be grasped by taking into consideration state intervention and restructuring. It is worth recalling that while the system remains dominated by banks, there is a strong possibility for secular growth of market finance in Turkey. This, as is recognized in literature on the subject, does not necessarily lead to stable growth and the fair distribution of wealth. Rather, market finance seeks to increase prospects for securitization and enable new mechanisms for the benefit of financial sector, arguably to drive overall economic growth and development (Mishkin 2009).

I will develop the argument in the following four sections. The second section will chart the structure of the Turkish financial sector and outstanding securities. It will explain the size of the assets of NBFIs and the developments in bond and equity markets as well. The third section will discuss the impact of financial flows on gross domestic product (GDP) growth and document the financial intermediation activity and the growth of the financial sector with reference to the increased level of financial integration. The fourth section will provide an examination of post-2001 attempts to construct a regulatory framework not only in order to deepen market finance in Turkey, but also to adopt measures to minimize the threat of systemic risk. The conclusion will summarize the main findings and underline the fact that neoliberal market finance has progressed some way in Turkey in the last decade, the legal framework has been revisited, and state restructuring implies the suppression of alternatives alongside the explicit support to the financial sector.

Structure of the Financial Sector, NBFIs and Market Developments

The intertwining of the NBFIs with the oligopolistic structure of the Turkish banking sector impacts back upon the development of the NBFIs. The structure of the financial sector is complex, given ongoing restructuring, but the trends and the course of development can be elaborated through an analysis of data.

While banking sector assets and Central Bank of the Republic of Turkey assets have comprised about 85 to 90 per cent of all the assets in the financial sector throughout the post-2001 period, some NBFIs and their financial portfolios are intimately related to banking sector operations. Some financial market institutions, such as those in factoring and leasing, are dominated by the subsidiaries of commercial banks in Turkey. There are ramifications as the close relations between financial actors find their reflection in regulatory distinctions that are often difficult to grasp. For example, although the term 'market finance' implies all non-bank financial operations, it is necessary to consider the specificities of the Turkish financial sector and analyze NBFI portfolios, operations and their supervision in detail. This section will first clarify the institutions and then analyze the non-bank financial sector with reference to the structure and size of its securities. I will focus on the size of market finance and the composition of the outstanding securities, as well as analyze the corporate bond and equity markets.

The structure of the financial sector can be explained with reference to regulatory distinctions. In the supervision of market finance institutions there is a tripartite regulatory structure, which will be also dealt with below. The non-bank financial sector authorities include the BRSA, Treasury and the Capital Market Board (CMB). As banking institutions dominate, the BRSA as banking regulator has an overarching role in the supervision of the financial system in general. Furthermore, BRSA supervision extends to NBFIs such as factoring companies, financial leasing companies, finance companies (which are specialized in mortgage finance, consumption and vehicle finance), financial holding companies[1] and asset management companies. The

Table 7.1 NBFIs (Institutions and Funds) Under the Supervision of the CMB

Institution	*Definition*	*Further explanation*
Intermediary Institutions	Non-bank intermediaries operating in capital markets	Financial intermediaries specialized in securities investment
Portfolio Management Companies	Companies that manage portfolios of institutional and individual investors.	As joint-stock corporations, they act as the agents of their clients in the financial market
Real Estate Appraisal Companies	Institutions which employ appraisers to determine values of real estates, components of the real estates and real estate projects	As joint-stock corporations, they work for minimization of risks related to the value of the real estate
Portfolio Depositary Institutions	Takasbank, intermediary institutions and banks can assume the role of a depository institution for registering the financial assets of collective investment schemes	Financial assets are deposited to the licensed institutions for keeping the track
Independent Auditing Firms	Firms that provide auditing services in line with the regulatory framework	Auditing for meeting legal requirements and keeping investor trust in balance sheets
Rating Agencies	Agencies which provide credit ratings and/or corporate governance ratings	Licensed by CMB, their ratings provide information on creditworthiness and risks of market actors.
Funds/Investment Companies	*Definition*	*Further Explanation*
Mutual Funds	Funds that collect money from the public in return of participation certificates and invest in securities and precious metal	Composition of portfolio may differ, some provide guaranteed returns, some invest into other funds
Pension Funds	Funds established by the pension companies	Investing the collected premiums into fixed-income and flexible securities
Exchange Traded Funds	Funds for managing a portfolio with principles of risk diversification and fiduciary ownership, whose shares are traded on the stock exchange	Authorized participants directly participate in the creation and redemption process
Hedge Funds	Funds in which the qualified investors participate	Exempt from bylaw regulations, uses more complex portfolio management techniques
Foreign Mutual Funds	Funds registered abroad	

Institution	*Definition*	*Further explanation*
Venture Capital Mutual Funds	Collective investment schemes, directing issued capital toward venture capital investments	Issue and purchase borrowing instruments, participate in the management of entrepreneur company
Real Estate Mutual Funds	Collective investment schemes bringing together investors and real estate owners	Deal with securitization within real estate sector, provide liquidity to large scale real estate
Securities Investment Trusts	Investment companies managing portfolios composed of capital market instruments, gold and other precious metals	As joint-stock corporations they issue shares, quoted, traded and priced at stock exchange
Real Estate Investment Trusts	Investment companies managing portfolios composed of real estates, real estate based projects and capital market instruments based on real estates.	Shares listed on BIST, invest in specific areas or help the realization of real estate projects
Venture Capital Investment Trusts	Investment companies managing portfolios composed of venture capital investments	Shares also listed on BIST

Source: CMB 2013; 2014 and monthly bulletins.

Note: CMB annual reports include additional terminology for funds. The reports also provide subcategories for mutual funds (securities investment funds) according to the bylaws and the composition of their portfolios; such as protected funds, ME.ds funds and liquid funds. The table provides a simplification by addressing these as mutual funds (see Bedirhanoğluet et al. 2013 for previous configuration).

Undersecretariat of the Treasury, by contrast, supervises insurance, reinsurance and pension companies. While the former two provide service in life and non-life branches, the latter collect the premiums for future pension payments. In these sectors, too, bank subsidiaries have been active.

The CMB is the main state authority in market finance, supervising all the remaining institutions functioning in the capital markets. Moreover, the CMB regulates the capital market operations of the banks in Turkey. The NBFIs under CMB supervision include intermediary institutions, portfolio management companies, real estate appraisal companies, portfolio depository institutions, funds, investment trusts (also known as investment companies), independent auditing firms and rating agencies.[2] As a result of the new Capital Market Law promulgated in December 2012 (No. 6362) and the ensuing regulatory attempts, the CMB reorganized and redefined investment funds and companies in 2013 and 2014 (see Table 7.1).

The number of funds and trusts increased significantly in the post-2001 period, but the number of intermediary institutions decreased slightly. The volume of NBFI portfolio values (documented below) and the stock market capitalization of investment trusts continued to grow in accordance with GDP growth during the same period, but stagnated in recent years. The aforementioned reorganization by the CMB came after the introduction of the Capital Market Law, which was justified with reference to the need for meeting the demands of financial actors and addressing the dynamism in the market. This was another step in the process of financial market deepening in neoliberal Turkey. While succeeding former law no. 2499, the new Capital Market Law was a response, on the one hand, to the growing operations of the NBFIs and, on the other, to the need of the policymakers having a 'market regulatory text' on which they can rely for flexible and depoliticized decision-making in the forthcoming years.[3] Aiming to strengthen the financial apparatus, capital market regulation also exemplified the internalization of financial imperatives, aiming to turn the state's financial apparatus into an enabling actor.

Size and Assets of the Non-bank Financial Sector

In Turkey there were 62 financial factoring companies and 26 financial leasing companies (at the end of 2016), according to Financial Institutions Association (FKB) data, and 14 finance companies and 16 asset management companies, according to the BRSA data. The reason BRSA supervises these institutions stems from the role of bank subsidiaries in the respective sectors.

All four types of financial companies have operations that are gradually increasing (but nonetheless constitute a miniscule volume of assets in relation to the financial sector as a whole). Therein the 14 companies that are bank subsidiaries have a factoring market share more than 50 per cent with assets worth of TL11.3 billion (TurkRating 2014). In financial leasing, the bank subsidiaries control almost 85 per cent of the market, and leasing is effectively a bank service in Turkey (Deloitte 2015).

In terms of services offered in Turkey, the factoring companies mainly service the textile, construction and metal works sectors with increases seen in the energy sector. The sector has seen growth, too, stemming from demand by the many small and medium enterprises in the Turkish economy. By contrast the leasing sector, according to the volume of contracts, is split between manufacturing and services sectors, with respective shares of 45 per cent and 49 per cent. Construction occupies the lion's share (almost 44 per cent) within the services sector (FKB 2014).

It is impossible to have reliable time series data for the profit rates of NBFIs under the supervision of BRSA.[4] Return on assets ratios of factoring and leasing companies and the assets of finance companies and asset management companies, however may give information about the dynamism of these sectors. The factoring companies remain relatively more profitable compared to the financial leasing companies. While the return on assets for leasing was 3.8 per cent in 2009, it dropped to 1.8 per cent in 2013. Factoring companies, by contrast, earned 3.3 per cent in 2013. Their combined total profits; however, amounted to less than 4 per cent of total banking sector profits in the same year (FKB 2014) The removal of tax advantages for leasing in 2007 hurt returns (Deloitte 2015), as did the impact of the global financial crisis on Turkey in 2009 (FKB 2014). The recent return on asset measures are not accessible for finance companies in Turkey, which earn profits through mortgage and vehicle loans, as well as through some insurance services. The assets of finance companies reached TL32.7 billion in total at the end of 2016 and net profits of factoring, leasing and finance companies continue to grow (FKB 2017). The asset management companies buy non-performing loans at a highly discounted rate, then restructure the debt and try to collect the money in due course. While risky, it can be extremely lucrative. The principal value of total loans managed by them amounted to TL21 billion in 2015.[5]

There were 60 active insurance, reinsurance and pension companies in Turkey at the end of 2015. Of these, 36 were non-life and four were life insurance companies. There was only one reinsurance company and 19 pension companies (Treasury ISB 2015). In their attempt to boost domestic savings, cited by the International Monetary Fund (IMF) as a key weakness in the Turkish economy, state authorities started a cash support scheme in 2012. The state contributes up to 25 per cent of premiums paid to private pension funds for long-term savers. In 2013, state support reached TL 1.15 billion, with the volume of the premiums increasing by 15 per cent in real terms (TSB 2013).[6] By April 2018 the state's contribution had reached to TL10.4 billion with some 6.9 million participants.[7] In this way, the government played the role of market-maker by explicitly supporting private pension growth. By the end of 2017, pension company assets exceeded TL148 billion.[8]

The effect has become evident as the portfolio values of securities investment and pension funds have grown. Table 7.2 provides an overview of a number of capital market development indicators. For example, real estate investment company assets increased more than threefold in 2010, arguably as a result of the capital inflows and the interest rate declines which boosted the housing sector. The portfolio value of pension funds increased by 50 per cent in 2012, reflecting the role of state support. The increase in domestic savings via the Turkish pension system has created a profitable niche for both commercial banks (and subsidiaries) and pension funds, which invest the new pools of money in financial instruments. Despite such rapid growth, the portfolio value of these NBFIs was around 9 per cent of Turkish GDP in recent years, compared to 3.5 per cent in 2001.

The changes in portfolio values and NBFI assets should be read together with the gradual, structural transformation of outstanding securities in Turkey (Figure 7.1). Public debt obligations have always occupied a significant place in the debt-led emergence of neoliberalism in Turkey. For more than three decades public debt has offered a significant field of profitable investment, despite the end of the infamous public debt trap in Turkey since the 2001 crisis. The variegated neoliberal emergence of market finance in Turkey, in other words, did not lead to a fast-growing private securities market; instead, public

Table 7.2 Selected Indicators of Turkish Capital Markets, US $ billion (2001–17)

	Portfolio Value of Mutual Funds	*Portfolio Value of Pension Funds*	*Net Assets Value of Invest-ment Trusts*	*Portfolio Valueof Real Estate Invest-ment Trusts*	*Market Capitalization of Venture Capital Investment Trusts*	*Portfolio Management Companies (Managed Values)*
2001	3.3	-	0.08	0.6	0.005	1.9
2002	5.7	-	0.08	0.6	0.002	3.5
2003	14.2	-	0.1	0.8	0.002	12.7
2004	18.2	0.2	0.2	1	0.06	18.1
2005	21.8	0.9	0.3	1.6	0.06	22.3
2006	15.6	1.9	0.3	1.7	0.06	18.2
2007	22.5	3.8	0.5	3.3	0.04	26.6
2008	15.8	3.9	0.3	2.8	0.03	20.2
2009	19.9	6.1	0.4	3.1	0.05	26.6
2010	21.6	7.8	0.4	11.1	0.1	30.3
2011	15.9	7.5	0.3	6.2	0.4	25.1
2012	17.1	11.3	0.4	8.8	0.4	31.5
2013	14.1	12.3	0.2	8.7	0.5	30.3
2014	14.3	16.2	0.1	9.4	0.6	35
2015	12.7	16.4	0.1	7.2	0.4	33.6
2016	14.5	19.4	0.1	7.0	0.3	34.6
2017	14.3	21.0	0.1	7.1	0.7	41.8

Source: CMB monthly statistics.

Note: There is a slight incongruence between annual reports and monthly statistics. Monthly statistics from 2017 and 2018 are preferred to have the latest data. Portfolio values of mutual funds include those of the foreign funds, which remain negligible throughout the period. There is no data for pension funds in 2001–03 and market capitalization of venture capital investment trusts are derived from monthly statistics.

securities still constitute about three-quarters of all debt securities. The ratio of net total of private sector securities to net value of total securities stock revolves around 40 per cent in recent years.

Judged by the size of NBFI assets and portfolio values, Turkey has witnessed substantive growth in market finance since the 2001 crisis. The slowly increasing share of private sector in total outstanding securities supports this claim. None the less, quantitative growth has neither manifested as structural transformation nor qualitative break with the past in Turkey. Similarly, research suggests there has been no radical shift in foreign portfolio investors' appetite for Turkey's financial markets (cf. Heinemann 2014). The data on corporate bond markets and the equity markets further supports the claim that market finance in Turkey is emergent, not triumphant.

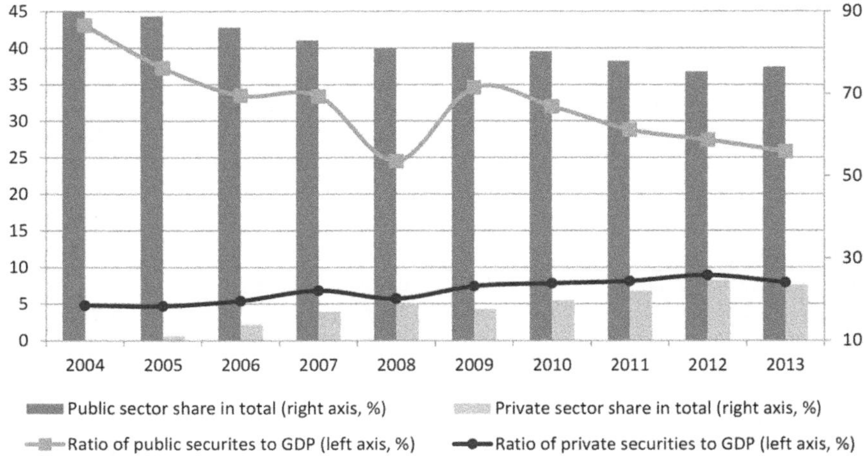

Figure 7.1 Outstanding Debt Securities (by nominal values, 2004–13)
Note: Investment funds are not included in CMB outstanding securities data for private securities. Portfolio composition of investment funds composed mainly of public debt securities until 2009. Since then, the share of public debt and reverse repo in investment fund portfolios are in a decline and the share of 'other' composed of mainly private securities rose from 1.4 per cent in 2009 to 36.5 per cent by 2013. The ratios to GDP are calculated on the basis of the new GDP series in current prices, by TurkStat.
Source: CMB annual reports.

Developments in the Corporate Bond Market and Stock Market

Not until after 2005, and with the enactment of new regulations supportive of alternative market-based financing, did the issuances of Turkish private sector securities increase (Table 7.3). To be sure, the corporate bond market emerged in the late 1980s and early 1990s, but effectively died in the subsequent years and bank loans remained dominant in corporate sector financing. The share of corporate bonds and commercial papers in the sources of funds of non-financial sector amounted to 6.8 per cent in 1987 and 1988, but declined to 1.2 per cent in 1993 (Sak 1995). Turkish corporations gave up on issuing bonds for two main reasons (cf. Ergüneş 2008; Güngen 2014). First, the withholding tax rates made it less preferable to invest in corporate bonds, while the high-yielding government debt instruments ensured constant flows of money into this area. The second reason, albeit less discussed, involves the organizational structures of finance capital and holding groups. In Turkey (as in other emerging capitalist economies), the private commercial banks were typically part of a larger holding group.[9] By extending related credits through their associated bank, the holding groups had the internal capacity to fund their own commercial and industrial operations for much of the 20th century. The 2001 crisis began to change matters, as authorities erected a firewall between the formal holding groups' and associated banks' operations (to help prevent a repeat of the crisis) (Marois 2012: 170; see also Chapter 6 in this volume). Yet not until after state authorities re-regulated the sector via tax amendments in 2006 and 2007 and new regulations that lowered costs and simplified issuances did bonds start to become a source of corporate finance. It should also be added that the commercial banks are still the most active players in the shallow corporate bond market. For example, of more than TL4 billion corporate bond issuance in the first four months of 2011, more than 98 per cent of the offerings belonged to banks and the remaining share belonged to a factoring company (Kökden 2011). Bond issuance by non-financial corporations has started to increase in recent years, although bank dominance continues. On the investor side, there is no such concentration as the penetration of financial institutions further into everyday life has led to an increase in the number of individual investors who use their savings to enter the bond and bills market. Despite a 17 per cent decline in the number of investors in the market of private sector debt instruments in 2014 compared with the previous year, more than 90 per cent of investors in 2014 were private individuals (TSPB 2015: 51).

The combined impacts of crisis and re-regulation spurring the Turkish non-financial corporations' search for alternative sources of funds in the last decade have given rise to higher private sector foreign exchange debt levels. Triggering some official concern, state authorities pointed to domestic Islamic financial institutions as a potential remedy to over-exposure to foreign liquidity risks. Following the Ninth Development Plan (2007–13), Turkish authorities provided tax exemptions for *sukuk* issues (bonds that do not offer

Table 7.3 Outstanding Private Securities (excluding shares, 2006–17, TL million)

	Corporate Bonds	*Commercial Papers*	*Asset-Backed Securities*	*Bank Bills*	*Warrants*
2006	120	-	-	-	-
2007	140	230	-	-	-
2008	240	320	-	-	-
2009	360	100	-	56	-
2010	1,281	105	-	1,495	20
2011	4,221	100	573	9,672	58
2012	9,526	734	1,605	17,848	60
2013	14,420	-	2,163	22,160	131
2014	18,954	-	2,395	26,279	115
2015	19,395	-	1,941	27,549	228
2016	18,754	-	2,055	30,776	253
2017	19,178	-	1,849	44,245	425

Source: CMB monthly statistics.

interest-based returns, but a share of tangible assets and derived future profit, according to Islamic rules). The annual volume of *sukuk* issuance exceeded US $4 billion by 2014 and is dominated by so-called 'participation banks' (the local term for Islamic banks in Turkey) (Lackmann 2014).

Just as the corporate bond market is characterized by a slow pace of growth and is dominated by relatively few corporations (World Bank 2012), so too is this largely true for the stock market (TCMA 2015). In 2012 financial authorities changed the name of the Istanbul Stock Exchange to the Borsa İstanbul (BIST), whose capitalization has been volatile in the post-2001 period (see Figure 7.2).[10] By 2014 the BIST trading volume had reached US $370 billion (TSPB 2015) as the stock market capitalization-to-GDP ratio hit 27 per cent—well behind those of other emerging capitalist economies such as South Korea and South Africa (86 and 266 per cent, respectively). The bond trading volume was $287 billion in 2014. However, trade has mostly focused on public securities, as noted above.

In Turkey both the corporate bond market and stock market show contemporary signs of enhanced activity and growing interest by non-financial corporations. Market finance mechanisms, however, have not reached to the desired level set by policymakers and, indeed, expected by many after more than three decades of neoliberal, market-oriented transformation. This is not to say that Turkey's level of international financial integration, domestic financial market development, and overall quantity of financial flows are of little significance for the economy as a whole. On the contrary, such market-oriented, finance-led reforms in the post-2001 period have consolidated the

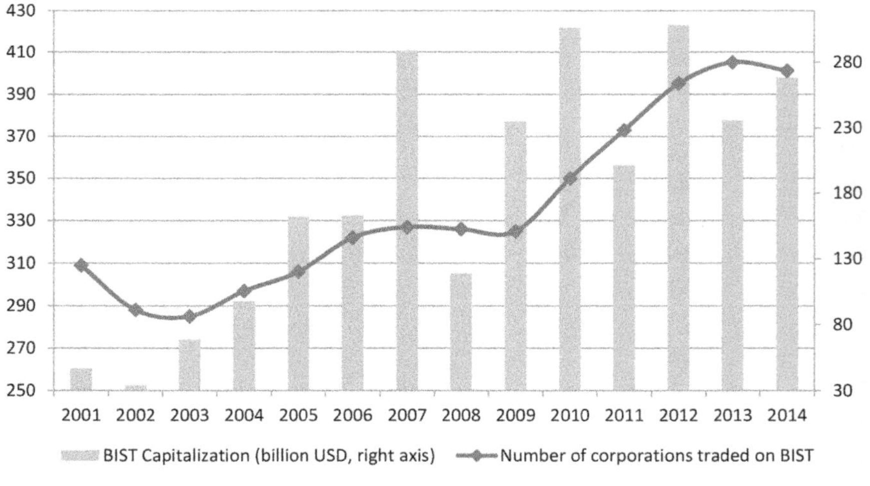

Figure 7.2 Number of Corporations Traded on BIST and Capitalization (US $ billion, 2001–14)
Source: CMB Annual Reports.

political and economic significance of financial capital in Turkish society (Marois 2011; BSB 2012).

Importance of Financial Flows and Growth of Financial Activity Revisited

As elaborated on in Chapter 3, governing élites set the Turkish economy on a new finance-oriented path following capital account liberalization in 1989. The influx of capital inflows boosted the economy for a brief time, but subsequently led to imbalances and instabilities. As the current account balance worsened, either the erosion of creditworthiness due to macroeconomic imbalances or the fragility of the banking sector triggered outflows and economic busts, as witnessed in 1994 and 2000–01. Figure 7.3 illustrates a striking parallel between net financial flows and GDP growth in post-2001 Turkey. Notably, the 2008–09 financial crisis, which erupted in the advanced capitalist countries, generated rapid outflows from Turkey, as from other emerging capitalist economies. Significantly, central bank authorities in the advanced capitalist economies created massive amounts of money via quantitative easing from 2009 onwards. In search of higher returns, these funds created in the core developed economies made their way into the periphery, renewing capital inflows into developing economies such as Turkey. This resulted in a significant increase of foreign exchange borrowing by the private sector, and credit expansion in Turkey (Orhangazi and Özgür 2015).

Whereas Figure 7.3 indicates the quantitative importance of the financial inflows, the *quality* of the inflows also matters. As Central Bank Chair in 2014, Erdem Başçı (2014) recognized, the aftermath of the 2008–09 financial crisis has dramatically increased the share of portfolio investment, i.e. 'hot

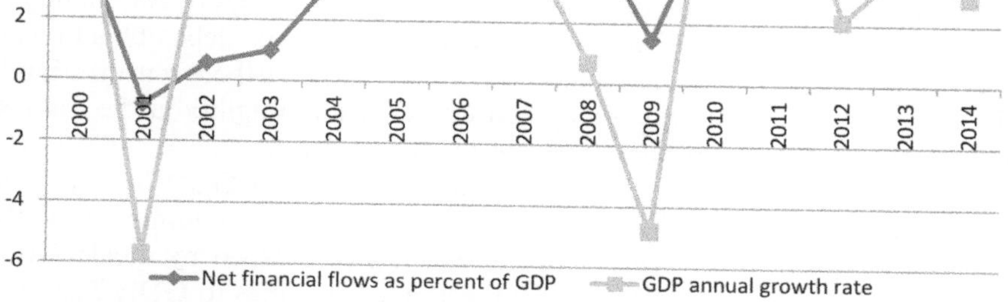

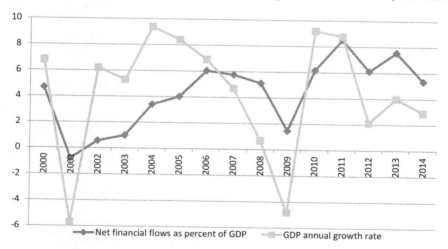

Figure 7.3 Net Financial Flows and Annual GDP Growth in Turkey (%, 2000–14)
Source: CBT (Balance of Payments, Fifth Handbook), IMF World Economic Outlook data.

money' flows as a source of current account deficit financing in Turkey. In contrast to more stable long-term and foreign direct investment, volatile short-term inflows characterized the post-2008 period, giving rise to concerns among Turkish policymakers and technocrats (CBRT 2011: 9–12). Indeed, all IMF Article IV papers since 2010 have cited Turkey's financial short-termism as a significant concern. The associated domestic credit boom forced Turkish authorities to attempt to contain increasing consumption expenditure, but to little avail. The Central Bank also employed interest rate increases (a wide interest rate corridor) and pushed up the reserve requirements of banks to stem the tide. None the less, authorities are seeking a delicate balance as relatively meagre domestic growth since 2012 has been dependent on domestic demand.To promote capital inflows, interest rates must be kept at high levels, which would stifle the domestic demand in the medium term, as well as result in economic activities losing pace. Falling interest rates provide an incentive for domestic consumption, but it will result in further depreciation of the Turkish lira, which lost 20.5 per cent of its value against the US dollar in the first 18 months of the state of emergency (from mid-2016 to early 2018). Depreciation of the lira also meant an increased burden for corporations that were heavily indebted in foreign currencies.

The Turkish Capital Markets Association (TCMA), whose members include banks and NBFIs such as portfolio management companies and investment companies, emphasizes the need to continue the efforts for financial deepening (TSPB 2015). A deepened financial market, however, does not automatically bring more savings into the equation. Again, if IMF warnings are any indicator, domestic savings have improved little to none despite the indicated post-2001 financial growth patterns. Turkish policymakers launched the official financial inclusion campaign in 2014 to address the issue. The state strategy document portrays households as risk-absorbing units, and details the road map for increasing the use of financial services (FİK 2014). Given the real wage squeeze,[11] financial inclusion will arguably lead to more indebted households (Güngen 2018). The campaign may also reinforce securitization of debt obligations. The asset-backed securities market had dried up in the mid-1990s, as issuance costs outweighed the usefulness of its existence. After the change of legislation in 2007 and a series of communiqués that started to be issued from 2008, the securitization of debt obligations is increasing. Since then the CMB has paved the way for further securitization.[12] Therefore, financial deepening may end up in causing fragility in the market, creating a Turkish sub-prime market in the medium term.

Increasing the contribution of the financial sector to GDP has been an objective of neoliberal policymakers for a long time. In economic terms, the growing significance of financial operations can be grasped by a calculation of the contribution of the financial and insurance activities to GDP. The ratio of financial intermediation activity to GDP provides a snapshot of growth in the financial sector in comparison to other sectors as well. According to the data from the Ministry of Development, the ratio of financial and insurance activities to GDP jumped to its highest ratio before the 2001 crisis, but declined rapidly in the early 2000s. The new data series used by TurkStat do not include the ratios for the years before 1998 and it is not meaningful (because of the different method of calculation) to compare using data from the 1987 series. None the less, it is reasonable to suggest that based on current prices, the ratio of financial intermediation activity to GDP grew from an average of around 2 per cent in the 1980s to around 3.5 per cent on average in the last decade (Türel 2009), with dramatic increases during the economic crisis years. The data imply that financial intermediation activity gained importance relative to the first decades of neoliberalism (Türel 2009). Policy-makers point out that the mentioned growth needs to be supported and accelerated. According to the 64th Government Programme, the ratio will reach 6.5 per cent (in current prices) by the end of 2018 (T.C. Başbakanlık 2015).

In the aftermath of the 2001 crisis and in response to the monetary policy of the Central Bank and the exchange rate policy of state authorities, an appreciating Turkish lira provided the opportunity for companies to benefit from exchange rate operations. This strategy has been confirmed by the head of the Istanbul Chamber of Industry in 2007 (Türel 2009). Non-financial corporations not only benefited from Turkish lira appreciation between 2002 and 2007, but also increased their income from financial operations significantly in 2014, raising the ratio of income from non-operating activities to overall annual income to 50.3 per cent (data is for the largest 500 manufacturing companies in Turkey). Accordingly, some of the largest non-financial corporations henceforth preferred investing in foreign exchange assets to compensate for lower profits in manufacturing (Sönmez 2015).

Corporations are not permitted to issue hard currency bonds in domestic market (Linhardt 2015) and borrowing in US dollars was preferable for non-financial corporations, given the relatively overvalued Turkish lira until 2014–15. Going to international bond markets or selling private placements, however, led eventually to greater foreign debt exposure for non-financial corporations, and led to the warnings of the Central Bank (CBRT 2013; 2014). The rapid depreciation of the Turkish lira in 2015, resulted in a highly indebted real sector, triggering wider economic instabilities (IMF 2014). Despite the success of Adalet ve Kalkınma Partisi (AKP—Justice and Development Party) in avoiding an economic slump after the 2016 coup attempt, financing deficit and diversifying the tools to meet the needs remained a problem. The government's emphasis on the growth of financial sector did not bring new sources of funding for non-financial corporations. Balance of payments risk and portfolio outflows, as well as the state of emergency, led to the huge currency depreciation of 2016–18.

Post-2001 Regulations for the Non-bank Financial Sector

Turkey has undertaken a plethora of regulatory initiatives since the 2001 crisis in ways constitutive of its emergent, variegated form of market finance. This

Table 7.4 Ratio of Financial and Insurance Activities to GDP (in 1998 prices and current prices, %, 1998–2014)

	1998	*1999*	*2000*	*2001*	*2002*	*2003*	*2004*	*2005*	*2006*	*2007*	*2008*	*2009*	*2010*	*2011*	*2012*	*2013*	*2014*
1998 prices	7.6	8.4	8.2	10.0	8.9	8.0	8.3	8.7	9.3	9.8	10.6	12.1	11.8	11.9	12.0	12.7	13.2
Current prices	7.6	10.2	7.0	8.6	4.4	3.4	3.3	2.8	2.9	3.2	3.5	4.5	3.7	3.1	3.3	3.3	3.0

Source: Economic and Social Indicators, Ministry of Development.

strengthening of state capacity has involved building domestic regulatory and institutional capacity in such ways that the institutional apparatus was also internationalized according to international (most often US or EU) standards. In this process, the Turkish regulatory framework for market finance has maintained its tripartite form, as discussed above. Governance within this tripartite arrangement has adopted a so-called depoliticized decision-making framework. It has been repeatedly underlined by policymakers and the regulatory authorities that the main target was to set international regulatory standards and compose a framework derived from best practices (CMB 2013). The supervisory distinctions are maintained not because of the failure of imitating a pre-existing regulatory model, but rather due to the fact that policymakers find these useful for backing up depoliticized decision-making procedures. State supervisory authorities tend to respond to financial market developments via directives, detailed communiqués and risk management without having to resort to a politically accountable debate, either at the parliamentary or civil society level. By various mechanisms, from tax exemptions to incentives, and from the redefinition of non-bank institutions to directives and communiqués for supporting the profitability and enhanced transactions in the sector, state authorities renewed their emphasis on the deepening of the market finance in the aftermath of 2008–09 international financial crisis. In other words, Turkish policymakers explicitly supported non-bank financial institutions and intermediaries by regulatory initiatives, the results of which will be seen in the near future.

Some illustrations help substantiate this point. In the leasing and factoring sector, major state interventions targeted tax rates and sell and lease-backs conditions. In the post-2001 period in general, the removal of tax advantages for the leasing sector has affected the volume of contracts. A flat tax rate of 1 per cent provided an implicit subsidy to the leasing sector until it was replaced in 2007, with the higher tax rates differing according to the leased goods in question. Legal changes reintroduced tax exemptions and discounts to a great extent in both 2008 and 2011 (Deloitte 2015). The major initiative in the leasing sector has been the designation of financial leasing and factoring sector in detail, the promotion of sell and lease-backs *via* law no. 6361 promulgated in December 2012, and also the tax exemptions for lease-backs provided by law no. 6495 promulgated in August 2013. The insurance sector, on the other hand, had its framing law promulgated in June 2007 (law no. 5684). Considerable support to the insurance sector was given by the new law on pension funds and savings introduced in June 2012 (law no. 6327, which significantly revised law no. 4632 of 2001). The major target was to boost long-term savings by the state's cash support for future pensioners,which can amount to 25 per cent of the premium paid.[13]

Law no. 6362, namely the Capital Market Law, was also promulgated in December 2012. The new Law was justified with the need for providing support to capital market development and the aim was explicitly written in order "to maintain the development and functioning of capital market in a reliable, transparent, effective, stable, fair and competitive milieu" and "regulate and supervise the capital market for protecting the investor rights and interests" (TBMM Plan Bütçe Komisyonu 2012). The preparation of the law benefited from pre-accession assistance programme of the EU and the law has been another attempt to increase the compatibility of the Turkish financial market legislation with EU regulations. More importantly, the law set standards for financial reports and auditing activity, regulated the financial market infrastructure institutions related to clearing and custody operations, composed the legal framework for trade repositories, transformed the union of financial market intermediaries into a new body with more self-regulatory power, enabled the expansion of mortgage institutions, and updated the punishments for crimes regarding financial activities, in line with EU regulations.

The Capital Market Law's content reflected the wider neoliberal orientation of Turkey's economy. Notably, the Law provided the general framework in which autonomous regulatory institutions will respond to market developments and the demands of investors. In the ensuing years, secondary regulations gained importance in maintaining this logic and more deeply institutionalizing it. The CMB issued numerous by-laws, directives and communiqués to more closely approximate the market-based regulatory framework of the EU and other international standards.[14] Ali Babacan, then Deputy Prime Minister in charge of the Economy, defined the notable aspect of the regulatory efforts as enhancing the capacity for the management of systemic risks.[15] Far from being an *en vogue* example of institutional entrepreneurship, Turkey's efforts reflect the internalization of post-global crisis international financial imperatives. As a cumulative indication, the World Bank's 2014 World Development Report is titled 'Risk and Opportunity: Managing Risk for Development'. In Turkey, this narrative was repeated in post-2008 debates and official reports. The underlying logic was notable even before the promulgation of the Law in late 2012, in the establishment of the Financial Stability Committee (FSC) in charge of observing the international risks and co-ordinating the responses to financial market volatility. Initially, an *ad hoc* committee meeting held frequently from 2011 onwards, the FSC (comprising the Central Bank, Treasury, BRSA, CMB and SDIF representatives) consolidated its place and impacted upon the action plans and institutional agendas of its component regulatory authorities. Policymakers portray the FSC as the body in which macro-prudential measures for economic management are discussed and decided. Indeed, some critics suggest that it has become a closed circle of technocrats and policymakers with no form of transparency at all.

Alongside the internalization of international best practices into the Turkish state apparatus, ruling AKP cadres have also promoted Istanbul as a regional and international financial centre (CMB 2014. The High Planning Council approved the Istanbul International Financial Centre Strategy (IFC) in 2009. According to the IFC, Istanbul will become first a regional financial centre, which necessitates the development of participation banks and Islamic finance. Combined with financial infrastructure development and the diversity of financial services, Istanbul is expected to turn into a global hub in the near future. In accordance with the strategy, the CMB (a member of the Islamic Financial Services Board from 2010 onwards), signed a technical assistance agreement with the Islamic Development Bank in 2012. In order to increase Turkey's market share in global Islamic financial markets, state authorities also decided to use the state-owned banks. Notably, authorities founded Turkey's first state-owned participation bank in 2015 as a subsidiary of Ziraat Bank, the oldest and largest state-owned bank in Turkey. VakıfBank, the third biggest commercial state bank followed suit in 2016. Ruling AKP policymakers portray the foundation of new participation banks as a major step for the deepening of Islamic bond markets in Turkey.

The CMB portrayed 2013 as 'a hectic year' because of the re-formation of the basic framework of NBFI operations and numerous amendments via secondary regulations (CMB 2013: x). The Board defined 2014 as "the year when legal and structural transformation of the Turkish capital markets which has been initiated in the previous year has been completed" (CMB 2014: x). The impact of these regulations, both in terms of profitability and the strength of the claims for the creation of an exemplary and developed legal framework, can be assessed only in the coming years. Suffice it to say that the nature of state re-regulation has not been class-neutral and financial transformation has tended to benefit financial capital directly by tax exemptions, cash support schemes, and most notably the further removal of policymaking bodies from popular control.

Conclusion

The neoliberal emergence and transformation of market finance in Turkey continues, and does so in ways mediated by the specificity of Turkish society and the country's integration into global financial markets. That said, the last decade or more of AKP rule symbolizes the apex of market finance advocacy. Policymakers and financial sector representatives alike have repeatedly emphasized the centrality of non-bank finance and alternative financing mechanisms. As the official agent of change, the ruling AKP organized supportive campaigns, set about restructuring the state apparatus, revisited the legal framework, and strengthened the so-called depoliticized decision-making processes. There are signs that capital market reforms will result in the further growth of financial assets and increased penetration of the financial sector into society. The trading volume of securities, however, is small, and a considerable number of people, notably women and the younger generations, have yet to access financial services. The long-term effects of political efforts and legal changes are yet to be fully realized, either economically or politically. However, the global consensus is that financial globalization will bring with it greater volatility and risk.[16] Consequently, state authorities must be better prepared to manage crisis as and when it hits. Indeed, that capacity is the *sine qua non* of contemporary internationalized, emerging capitalist states.

The social and class power of finance capital, re-institutionalized by the process of state restructuring and internalized within the state apparatus, suppresses alternatives to capitalist financial imperatives. According to the hegemonic point of view in Turkey, financial stability relied on this re-institutionalization, also named as a further step in the implementation of structural reforms.[17] It also meant subordination to neoliberal discipline, and suppressing threats (such as the collective rights of labour and its organizational power) to the economic and political power of financial capital. The neoliberal emergence of market finance in Turkey proceeds along the lines promoted by AKP cadres, but it has not led to stable growth and the fair distribution of wealth. The increased prospects for securitization and new mechanisms mainly benefit financial capital and it is questionable whether policymakers will reap their expected benefits, such as increased savings and more developed financial markets with higher liquidity and better opportunities for investors.

Notes

1 Law no. 5411, promulgated in 2005, defined financial holding companies as the companies whose more than half of the affiliates are financial and/or credit institutions. Another condition, determined in the 2006 bylaw by BRSA is that more than half of the paid-up capital of the holding company should be allocated to financial institutions.

2 As of 2013, there were 41 banks operating in Turkish capital market, intermediating the sale and purchase of capital market instruments, though none of the banks (commercial and investment) had licences for leveraged purchases and margin trading or short-selling (CMB 2013: 115). The major activities of investment and commercial banks in the Turkish capital market, besides the sale and purchase of capital market instruments, have been the purchase and sale of derivatives and repo transactions.

3 This has been explicitly stated in the 2012 report of the Commission for Planning and Budgeting of the National Assembly, which explained the motives and the targets of the law before submitting it for legislators' discussion (see TBMM Plan Bütçe Komisyonu 2012).

4 The data for the profitability of the NBFIs in Turkey is not continuous and comparable. In addition, many of the regulations for non-bank sector took place in the aftermath of the 2008–09 crisis, which make it difficult to assess their impact on profitability. It is possible to claim, however, that banking sector profitability exceeded the average ratios in many advanced capitalist countries throughout the post-2001 period (see BAT 2002–13; Also see Chapter 6 in this collection).

5 Dünya Gazetesi (8 August 2015) "Varlık yönetim şirketleri elektrik, su, gaz ve telekom borcuna da talip", http://goo.gl/X4qFTt, retrieved 18 August 2015.

6 Official statistics by the Insurance Association of Turkey provide the nominal growth as well as the real growth deflated in accordance with the consumer price index.

7 Pension Monitoring Center constantly updates the basic indicators and the number of participants on behalf of Turkish Treasury. The data can be accessed via https://www.egm.org.tr/bilgi-merkezi/istatistikler/bes-istatistikleri/bes-ozet-verileri/.

8 Related data and the consolidated balance sheets can be accessed via http://www.tsb.org.tr/bilancolar.aspx?pageID=910.

9 By the term finance capital, I refer to the conglomerates that exercise a significant degree of control on both the money capital and productive capital. For the development of finance capital in Turkey, see Öztürk 2010, see also Chapters 2 and 3 in this volume.

10 The move was more than a change of the name. The status of the stock exchange has also been changed from a state-owned body established by Decree no. 91 in 1983 to a "private legal entity" in 2012 by Law no. 6362. In fact, the World Bank had been advising the privatisation of the stock exchange to ensure its commercial viability in the long term (see World Bank 2003).

11 The decline in the real wages after the 2001 financial crisis of Turkey has not been compensated. Data from Turkish Ministry of Development, 2014 Economic Indicators reveal that real wages in the manufacturing sector declined also in the aftermath of the global financial crisis and then reached to their 2007 level in 2013.

12 CMB reorganized the investment funds after the promulgation of Capital Market Law no. 6362. In 2014, the Board found the legal infrastructure for real estate investment funds (communiqué no. 28871) and regulated mortgage finance institutions (communiqué no 29063), both of which use securitization for liquidity provision.

13 These reforms did not extend to the foundation of an independent supervisory authority as expected by the EU. Arguably, the Insurance Supervision Council of the Treasury was conceived to have the expertise and found sufficient by policymakers despite the EU expectations. Founded in 1959 and functioning as a relatively autonomous body under the Ministry of Commerce, the Council was transferred to the Treasury in 1994. The political regime and the names of various ministries have been changed in Turkey in mid-2018. This council was transferred to the Ministry of Finance and Treasury in 2018.

14 There has been numerous secondary regulations by CMB before 2013 as well. The importance of post-2012 regulations reside in their scope and the reconstruction of the functioning frame as a whole. The list of the legal changes and secondary regulations can be accessed via CMB website (CMB 2015).

15 www.bloomberght.com, (31 December 2012) "Babacan yeni Sermaye Piyasası Kanunu'nu değerlendirdi", http://goo.gl/GGAHFS, retrieved 14 August 2015.

16 The idea of macroprudential regulation has formed the core of consensus in the post-2008 period (Baker 2013). For international financial institutions, state authorities should take macroprudential measures to minimize risks against the background of increasing complexity of financial systems (see FSB, IMF and BIS 2011).

17 This perspective is most notable in the researchers from new institutional economics camp. Accordingly, the "lower quality growth" experienced by Turkey remain partly because the structural reforms staggered and the JDP governments failed in strengthening market-supporting institutions in the post-2008 period (see Acemoğlu and Üçer 2015).

REFERENCES

Acemoğlu, D. and M. Üçer (2015) "The Ups and Downs of Turkish Growth, 2002–2015: Political Dynamics, the European Union and the Institutional Slide", *National Bureau of Economic Research Working Paper Series*, No. 21608.

Baker, A. (2013) "The New Political Economy of the Macroprudential Ideational Shift", *New Political Economy*, 18(1): 112–139.

BAT–Banks Association of Turkey (2002–13) *Banks in Turkey*, Istanbul: BAT.

Başçı, E. (2014) "TCMB Plan ve Bütçe Komisyonu Sunumu", 17 December 2014, *CBRT website*, Accessed 9 September 2015.

Bedirhanoğlu, P., H. Cömert, İ. Eren, I. Erol, D. Demiröz, N. Erdem, A. R. Güngen, T. Marois, A. Topal, O. Türel, G. Yalman, E. Yeldan, and E. Voyvoda (2013) *Comparative Perspective on Financial System in the EU: Country Report on Turkey*, FESSUD Studies in Financial Systems No. 11.

BSB–Bağımsız Sosyal Bilimciler (2012) *IMF Gözetiminde 10 Uzun Yıl (1998–2008): Farklı Hükumetler Tek Siyaset*, Istanbul: Yordam.

CBRT–Central Bank of Republic of Turkey (2011) *Financial Stability Report (May, 2011)*, Ankara: CBRT.

CBRT–Central Bank of Republic of Turkey (2013) *Financial Stability Report (May, 2013)*, Ankara: CBRT.

CBRT–Central Bank of Republic of Turkey (2014) *Financial Stability Report (May, 2014)*, Ankara: CBRT.

CMB–Capital Market Board (2001–14) *Annual Reports*, Ankara: CMB.

CMB–Capital Market Board (2015) "Sermaye Piyasası ile İlgili Mevzuat Değişiklikleri (2006–2015)", *CMB website*, Accessed 10 August 2015.

Deloitte (2015) *Türkiye leasing sektörü: Sürdürülebilir büyüme yolunda adımlar*, Istanbul: Deloitte Türkiye.

Ergüneş, N. (2008) *Bankalar, Birikim, Yolsuzluk: 1980 Sonrası Türkiye'de Bankacılık Sektörü*, Istanbul: Sosyal Araştırmalar Vakfı.

FİK–Finansal İstikrar Komitesi (2014) *Finansal Erişim, Finansal Eğitim, Finansal Tüketicinin Korunması Stratejisive Eylem Planları*, June 2014, Ankara, *CMB website*, Accessed 13 November 2014.

FKB–Finansal Kurumlar Birliği (2014) *Finansal Kiralama Sektörü Özet İşlemler Raporu, 31 December 2014*, Ankara: FKB.

FKB–Finansal Kurumlar Birliği (2017) *Finansal Kurumlar Birliği 2016 Faaliyet Raporu*, Ankara: FKB

FSB, IMF and BIS – Financial Stability Board, International Monetary Fund and Bank for International Settlements (2011) *Macroprudential Policy Tools and Frameworks: Progress Report to the G-20*, Washington ,DC: IMF.

Güngen, A. R. (2014) "Hazine Müsteşarlığı ve Borç Yönetimi: Finansallaşma Sürecinde Bir Kurumun Dönüşümü", *Amme İdaresi Dergisi*, 47(1): 1–21.

Güngen, A. R. (2018) "Financial Inclusion and Policy Making: Strategy, Campaigns and Microcredit *a la Turca*", *New Political Economy, 23(3)*: 331-347.

Heinemann, T. (2014) "Relational geographies of emerging market finance: The rise of Turkey and the global financial crisis of 2007", *European and Urban Regional Studies*, (2014): 1–17.

International Monetary Fund (IMF) (2014) *2014 Article IV Consultation*, IMF Country Report No. 14/329. Washington, DC: IMF.

Kökden, M. (2011) "Turkey Domestic Corporate Bond Markets", *Corporate Bond Market in Turkey: Priorities and Challenges Meeting*, 26 April 2011, Capital Market Board of Turkey and the World Bank Group, Istanbul, Turkey.

Lackmann, B. G. (2014) "The Six Key Countries Driving Global Islamic Finance Growth", *Nomura Journal of Capital Markets*, Autumn 2014, 6(2): 1–28

Linhardt, S. (2015) "Turkey's corporate embark on search for capital", 1 September 2015, *The Banker*, Accessed 23 September 2015.

Marois, T. (2011) "Emerging market bank rescues in an era of finance-led neoliberalism: A Comparison of Mexico and Turkey", *Review of International Political Economy*, 18(2): 168–196.

Marois, T. (2012) *States, Banks and Crisis: Emerging Finance Capitalism in Mexico and Turkey*, Cheltenham: Edward Elgar.

Mishkin, F. S. (2009) "Why We Shouldn't Turn Our Backs on Financial Globalization", *IMF Staff Papers*, 56(1): 139–170.

Orhangazi, Ö. and G. Özgür (2015) "Capital flows, finance-led growth and fragility in the age of global liquidity and quantitative easing: The case of Turkey", *PERI Working Paper*, No, 397, Umass-Amherst.

Öztürk, Ö. (2010) *Türkiye'de Büyük Sermaye Grupları: Finans Kapitalin Oluşumu ve Gelişimi*, Istanbul: SAV.

Sak, G. (1995) "The Istanbul Stock Exchange and the Corporate Sector: Reflections on Turkey's Financial Liberalization Process", *Development of Financial Markets in the Arab Countries, Iran and Turkey*, proceedings of workshop organized by ERF–Economic Research Forum for the Arab Countries, Iran and Turkey, Beirut 15–16 July 1994.

Sönmez, M. (2015) "Karlar Azalıyor, Ücretlere Baskı Artıyor", *Sanayinin Sorunları ve Analizleri XIII. TMMOB Makina Mühendisleri Odası Bülten*, December 2015: 210.

TBMM Plan Bütçe Komisyonu (2012) *Sermaye Piyasası Kanunu Tasarısı ile Plan ve Bütçe Komisyonu Raporu (1/638)*, Ankara: TBMM.

T.C. Başbakanlık (2015) *64. Hükümet Programı*, 25 November 2015, Ankara: T.C. Başbakanlık.

TCMA–Turkish Capital Markets Association (2015) *Turkish Capital Markets*, June 2015, Istanbul: TCMA.

Treasury ISB–Undersecretariat of Treasury Insurance Supervision Board (2015) *Annual Report About Insurance and Individual Pension Activities*, Ankara: Undersecretariat of the Treasury.

TSPB–Türkiye Sermaye Piyasaları Birliği (2015) *Türkiye Sermaye Piyasası 2014*, Istanbul: TSPB.

TSB–Türkiye Sigorta Birliği (2013) *Faaliyet Raporu*, Istanbul: TSB.

TurkRating (2014) *Faktoring Sektör Raporu*, Haziran 2014, Istanbul: TurkRating.

Türel, O. (2009) "Türkiye Ekonomisinin Neoliberal Yapılanma Sürecinde Bankacılığın Yeniden Düzenlenmesi, 1980–2007", in M. Özuğurlu et al. (eds.) *Alpaslan Işıklı'ya Armağan*, No: 31, Ankara: Mülkiyeliler Birliği Vakfı, 131–170.

World Bank (2003) *Non-Bank Financial Institutions and Capital Markets in Turkey*, Washington, DC: World Bank.

World Bank (2012) *Turkey Corporate Bond Market Development: Priorities and Challenges (Report no 66711-TR)*, Washington, DC: World Bank.

8 The Turkish Corporate Sector in the Era of Financialization: Profitability and M&As

Demir Demiröz and Nilgün Erdem

Introduction

Although Turkish financial markets are not fully developed, financial liberalization in Turkey has produced some of the results that were anticipated by authors of literature on the subject of financialization. On the one hand, the importance of financial channels as a source of income has grown since the 1980s. On the other, the pace of mergers and acquisitions (M&A) has rapidly increased, especially since 2005, demonstrating that businesses in Turkey have themselves become more tradable entities. In this sense, not only was Krippner's observation that "*nonfinancial* firms have themselves become increasingly dependent on financial activities as sources of revenue" (Krippner 2011: 28) valid for Turkey; at the same time, capital itself (in the sense of ownership titles of a business enterprise and as different from capital goods) became vendible—as observed in the establishment of the centralized stock market in Turkey (the Borsa İstanbul), or in the growing magnitude of M&A activity, which took place outside of the stock exchange.

This chapter focuses on financial earnings and M&As as two facets of the financialization of the corporate sector in Turkey. The first section presents the ratio of non-operating income to balance sheet profits to demonstrate the significance of financial earnings for the Turkish 'real sector'. The second section describes basic quantitative features of the emergent Turkish M&A market, assesses its magnitude in relation to the Turkish economy, specifies its sectoral composition, and discusses monopoly power as the motivating force behind the top M&As. The third section concentrates on telecommunications and banking to demonstrate that regulatory changes were a facilitating factor opening the way for M&As. The background of the Türk Telekom privatization and restructuring in the banking sector is described in detail to demonstrate how several elements of neoliberal restructuring such as liberalization and the re-regulation of industries, the removal of majority ownership restrictions on foreign capital, and the adoption of international arbitration principles, laid the foundation for M&As at a historical juncture in which several of Turkey's macroeconomic indicators were viewed positively.

Profitability of the Non-Financial Sector in Turkey

Due to the liberalization of the current account in 1980 and of the capital account in 1989, the structure of the Turkish economy has become largely dependent on external capital flows. In order to ensure capital inflows, since 2000s regulations on both direct and financial capital movements have been implemented. External borrowing from international financial institutions and from other nation states has mostly been replaced by capital inflows through 'integrated' international private capital markets, thanks to the elimination of capital controls. These steps therefore enabled such borrower–lender relationships that made high speculative earnings possible.

The debt-driven financial expansion required that the investment environment had to be designed in order to eliminate financial risks that finance capital may face. Creditors should be somehow 'insured' against these risks, and potential market losses should mostly be transferred to others by government guarantees of private sector foreign debt.

After the enactment of financial liberalization measures, the behaviour of economic actors in Turkey changed. To obtain short-term high revenues, they preferred increasingly speculative financial investment. This contributed to the conditions that laid the groundwork for financial crises.

The Composition of Incomes in the Non-financial Sector

We use two data sets to assess the dominance of financial activities on the real sector: i) from the top 500 industrial firms in Turkey, obtainable from the records of the İstanbul Chamber of Industry (ICI); and ii) from a large sample of corporate sector accounts kept by the Central Bank of the Republic of Turkey.

To show the dominance of financial activities in the economy, we can examine *incomes through non-industrial activities* of the 'The Top Five Hundred Industrial Companies' of the ICI. The account called *Income and profit from other operations* includes dividend income from affiliates, dividend income from subsidiaries, interest income, commission income, provisions no longer required, profit on sale of marketable securities, exchange gains, rediscount income, and others. It should be noted that these accounting items, which comprise 'other income' in Table 8.1 are incomes from non-industrial activities, but they exclude state subsidies. In the crisis years, we notice that their income from non-industrial activities—mainly interest income—increased substantially during 1993 to 1994, and 2000 to 2001. After 2003, because of greater fiscal discipline, these firms did not enjoy high real interest earnings from government bonds.

For example, after the liberalization of interest rates in 1980, interest rates rose excessively and interest rate spreads widened.[1] The high interest rate for borrowing, in turn, greatly increased the costs for firms, operating on low shareholders' equity but relying heavily on loans. After the liberalization of interest rates, the share of interest payments in the value added of the private

Table 8.1 Income of Top 500 Industrial Companies in Turkey from Non-Industrial Activities and its Share in the Net Balance Sheet Profit (Pre-Tax),TL, 1982–2014

	Other Income (1)	*Change (%)*	*Net Balance Sheet Profit (2)*	*Change (%)*	*1/2 (%)*
1982	18,439		120,558		15.3
1983	37,783	104.9	192,819	59.9	19.6
1984	65,888	74.4	316,573	64.2	20.8
1985	104,501	58.6	433,462	36.9	24.1
1986	204,558	95.7	663,879	53.2	30.8
1987	285,321	39.5	1,593,763	140.1	17.9
1988	632,251	121.6	2,494,087	56.5	25.3
1989	1,299,144	105.5	4,189,118	68.0	31.0
1990	2,224,648	71.2	6,679,368	59.4	33.3
1991	3,721,504	67.3	7,282,288	9.0	51.1
1992	7,794,368	109.4	20,052,423	175.4	38.9
1993	17,548,778	125.1	43,093,652	114.9	40.7
1994	57,694,649	228.8	105,587,224	145	54.6
1995	96,191,958	66.7	206,857,875	95.9	46.5
1996	195,948,193	103.7	370,418,929	79.1	52.9
1997	407,054,079	107.7	771,761,381	108.3	52.7
1998	699,577,134	71.9	797,402,394	3.3	87.7
1999	1,577,329,277	125.5	720,405,946	-9.7	219.0
2000	1,760,163,086	11.6	1,538,333,855	113.5	114.4
2001	4,645,687,973	163.9	718,029,004	-53.3	647.0
2002	4,833,432,876	4.0	4,269,008,132	494.5	113.2
2003	5,016,304,190	3.8	6,985,609,668	63.6	71.8
2004	3,557,069,000	-29.1	9,087,928,518	30.1	39.1
2005	3,048,142,484	-14.3	8,236,526,584	-9.4	37.0
2006	3,380,665,053	10.9	12,855,752,414	56.1	26.3
2007	6,124,524,780	81.2	17,223,034,088	34.0	35.6
2008	3,793,360,109	-38.1	10,317,558,781	-40.1	36.8
2009	5,686,581,323	49.9	12,852,111,028	24.6	44.2
2010	5,980,685,439	5.2	17,453,114,853	35.8	34.3
2011	4,277,422,708	-28.5	18,828,305,331	7.9	22.7
2012	8,380,646,242	95.6	21,325,259,558	13.5	39.3
2013	5,141,416,921	-38.7	17,576,443,067	-17.6	29.3
2014	11,887,303,520	131.2	27,502,537,512	56.5	43.2

Source: İstanbul Chamber of Industry.

institutions doubled, exceeding the share of wages (Akyüz 1991: 5). During the period of 1986–88, the share of interest in the value added of the top-500 industrial firms was also higher than the share of wages (Türel 1993: 148–155).

Additionally, in the crisis year of 2001, the share of interest payments in the value added of the large firms was above 90 per cent and this ratio for the large private firms was also substantially above the share of wages (ICI 2007: 53). While the interest payment share of top 500 private industrial enterprises declined after 2001, their debt did not decrease between 2002 and 2014 (ICI 2015). Because of capital inflows, the domestic currency appreciated so much that foreign borrowing became attractive. Therefore, in order to reduce production costs, the real sector, especially large enterprises, preferred borrowing externally instead of borrowing domestically. The quantities borrowed from abroad consistently exceeded domestic credit for the private sector throughout the 2000s. At the end of 2014, the private sector owed US $275 billion, which represented two-thirds of the total foreign debt of Turkey. This figure was $50 billion at the beginning of 2000s and it represented only one-third of the foreign debt. For example, while the foreign debt stock of non-financial enterprises was $33 billion in 2003, this figure reached $118 billion by 2014. Within the private sector, non-financial enterprises accounted for 56 per cent of the aggregate increase of private external debt during the period of 2002–2014 and 70.1 per cent of the total stock of private debt in 2014.[2] Research by the credit ratings agency Moody's on Turkish corporate firms showed that the country's rated corporate firms have 90 per cent of their debt denominated in foreign currency (UNCTAD 2014: 3). For this reason, the corporate sector has been highly vulnerable to foreign exchange risks.

The Share of Non-Operating Income in Profits between 1982 and 2014

Profitability in industry has three widely used definitions: Sales profitability = balance sheet profit/sales proceeds; return on equity capital = balance sheet profit/equity capital; return on assets = balance sheet profit/total assets (ICI 2015: 52). To evaluate the profitability of firms in different aspects, the calculations of return on sales, return on assets and return on equity are important. While sales profitability is an indicator of the efficiency of industrial activities, return on equity capital and return on assets show the earnings yield on their investment.

After the privatization of public enterprises between 1980 and 2012, the number of state-owned firms in the top 500 firms decreased from 100 to 13. Hence it can be said that the aggregate profitability ratios of our sample mostly cover the private sector.[3]

Note: Sales profitability = balance sheet profit/Sales proceeds x 100; return on equity capital = balance sheet profit/equity capital x 100; return on net assets = balance sheet profit/total assets x 100.

The profitability ratios of the top500 industrial firms during 1982 to 2014 are given in Figure 8.1. Over the medium term, the various measures of profits move in a fairly similar manner.[4] These figures are also mainly in line with economic fluctuations.

To obtain a better understanding of financialization, financial incomes in addition to profitability figures in non-financial sector should be analyzed. In Turkey, it is not possible to measure precisely the percentage of financial

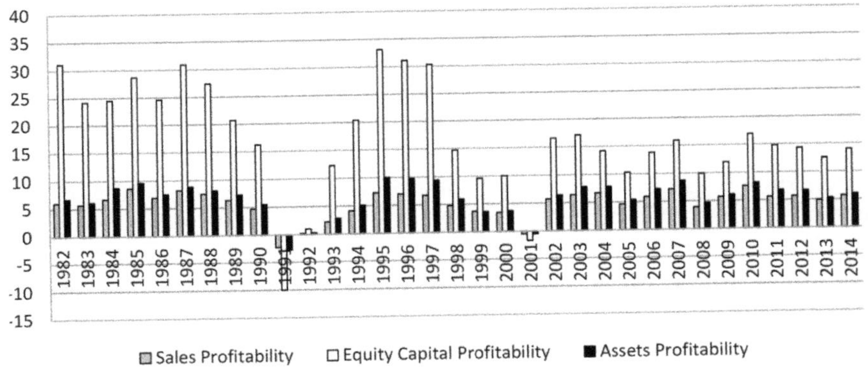

Figure 8.1 Aggregate Profitability of the Top 500 Industrial Firms Affiliated to the ICI, % (1982–2014)

Source: *İstanbul Sanayi Odası Dergisi* (*Journal of the İstanbul Chamber of Industry*) (ICI 2015:52, 54). For the full series, see previous issues of *Journal of the İstanbul Chamber of Industry*, titled *Turkey's Top 500 Industrial Firms.*

profits within the total profits from the available data. Therefore, we use non-operating incomes over net profit/loss of non-financial establishments as a proxy measure for financial earnings.

To assess the extent of financial activities in the industrial sector, the non-operating incomes of the top 500 industrial firms as a proportion of their net balance sheet profit may be examined (Figure 8.2). According to the data, private industrial firms were attracted by non-industrial activities and these activities became the norm during the 1990s and 2000s.

The non-operating income/pre-tax profit ratio in Figure 8.2 indicates that the economic interest of industrialists shifted to more profitable activities other than industrial production in the 1990s.[5] Demir (2009) also shows that operating profitability[6] declined from 25 per cent in 1994 to less than 4 per cent in 2003.

Dramatic increases in the crisis years left aside, these figures indicate that the non-operating income/pre-tax profit ratio was around 50 per cent in the first half of the 1990s and rapidly increased from 1997 to 2001, then decreased considerably in the post-crisis period (Figure 8.2). Increasing aggregate demand during a boom period, such as between 2002 and 2007, thanks to high foreign capital inflows, might lead to a rise in fixed investments to a certain degree. But in 2009, the non-operating income/pre-tax profit ratio exceeded 40 per cent, while the government had to increase interest rates in the domestic market following foreign capital outflows.

In the crisis years of 1993–94 and 2000–01, income from non-industrial activities increased substantially. The annual change in income from non-industrial activities were, respectively, 228.8 per cent and 163.9 per cent. For example, the ratio of financial revenues to net profits before tax among the

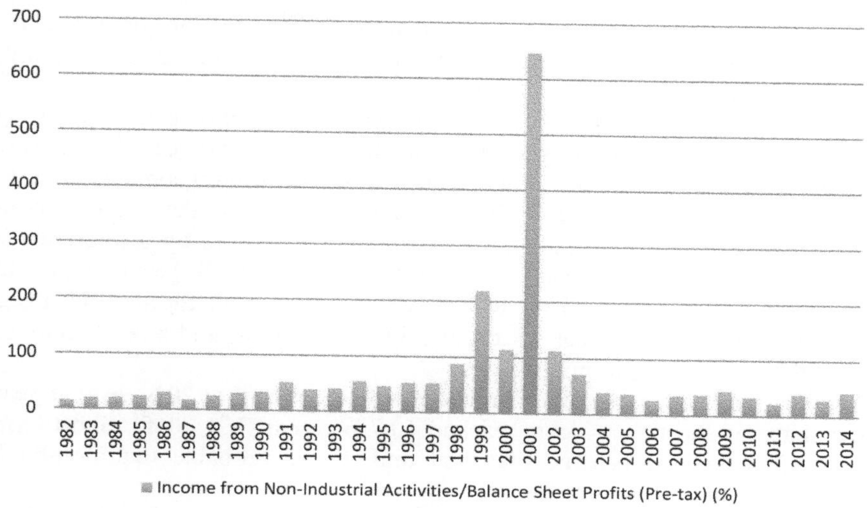

Figure 8.2 The Ratio of Income from Non-Industrial Activities to Balance Sheet Profits (Top 500 Industrial Firms, 1982–2014)
Source: *İstanbul Sanayi Odası Dergisi* (*Journal of the İstanbul Chamber of Industry*) (ICI 2015: 62). For the full series, see previous issues of *Journal of the İstanbul Chamber of Industry*, titled "Turkey's Top 500 Industrial Firms".

top500 industrial firms increased from about 33 per cent in 1990 to 219 per cent in 1999. In the 1990s the public sector borrowing requirement was high and the domestic borrowing policy created high interest gains to private firms, especially large enterprises. Therefore, Boratav, Yeldan and Köse (2000) emphasized that the firms acted partly as institutional rentiers.

In the 2001 crisis, the non-operating income/pre-tax profit ratio rose to 647 per cent; in this period interest rates were too high and profits decreased sharply. One likely factor explaining this rise is that firms took advantage of the high real interest environment and preferred to finance public deficits (Boratav 2007: 200).

In summary, the fact that industrial firms generated significant portions of their profits from predominantly financial activities, and lending to the government at high interest rates, clearly had a negative impact on investment performance. Contrary to the theory of 'financial pressure', domestic savings moved away from fixed capital investment toward speculative financial investment in Turkey. Rittenberg (1991), Akyüz (1990), Balkan and Yeldan (2002) indicated that in Turkey after liberalization, high interest rates resulted in a downward slide of the investment function, with a negative impact on fixed capital formation.

Financial incomes can be also examined in specific sectors. To do that, we reorganize the Company Accounts statistics of the Central Bank[7] into five main economic sectors (namely: manufacturing, services, construction, energy and agriculture) from 1998 to 2010. Figure 8.3 illustrates the share of operating income and non-operating income as a share of total income firms in non-financial sectors.[8]

As an important indicator of financialization, the ratio of non-operating income to total income of institutions in these sectors has recorded striking values. The findings point to high levels of non-operating income in services, construction and energy. For the manufacturing sector, the ratio of non-operating income to total income approach to the ratio of operating income to total income. Non-financial firms substantially increased their foreign debt due to high domestic interest rates. It was observed that the top 500 firms operated with high debt/net asset and debt/equity ratios, and a large share of their debts was short-term.

While the debt/equity ratio climbed to 132.4 per cent in 2014, in that year the share of short-term debts reached 60.7 per cent (ICI 2015). Short-term external borrowing became prevalent and it was probable that non-bank sources of funding also increased.

The empirical findings suggest that firms in the real sector take into account alternative investment opportunities in financial markets when making their decisions on physical investment. Accordingly, rather than investing in long-term *fixed investment*, these firms may choose to invest in *short-term financial instruments.*

When the profit rates of the top 500 industrial firms are compared with those that can be inferred from the Central Bank data set, they are not in full accord. Moreover, because of the problems of definitional discrepancies and reliability concerning various sources of data, it cannot be definitively argued that profits in the financial sector are systematically over and above those in non-financial sectors—a hypothesis that is often associated with arguments on financialization.

The Turkish M&A Market in the 2000s

There are diverse reasons why businesses engage in M&As. According to the United Nations Conference on Trade and Development (UNCTAD), one reason is speed: Assets like distribution and supplier networks, marketing, brand names, licences, and research and development take time to develop. When businesses enter a new market geographically or sector-wise, M&As allow them to takeover these assets rapidly (UNCTAD 2000: 140). Furthermore, M&As are preferable to new investments precisely because they avoid the creation of new capacity. Businesses are in search of market share and monopoly power. To enter a market without adding new production capacity is a less risky strategy (Nitzan and Bichler 2011: 330), especially if the market outlook is slack. In the case of horizontal M&As, taking over a competitor's market share and intangible assets strengthens the market position of the acquiring firm, cutting price competition in the market and adding to

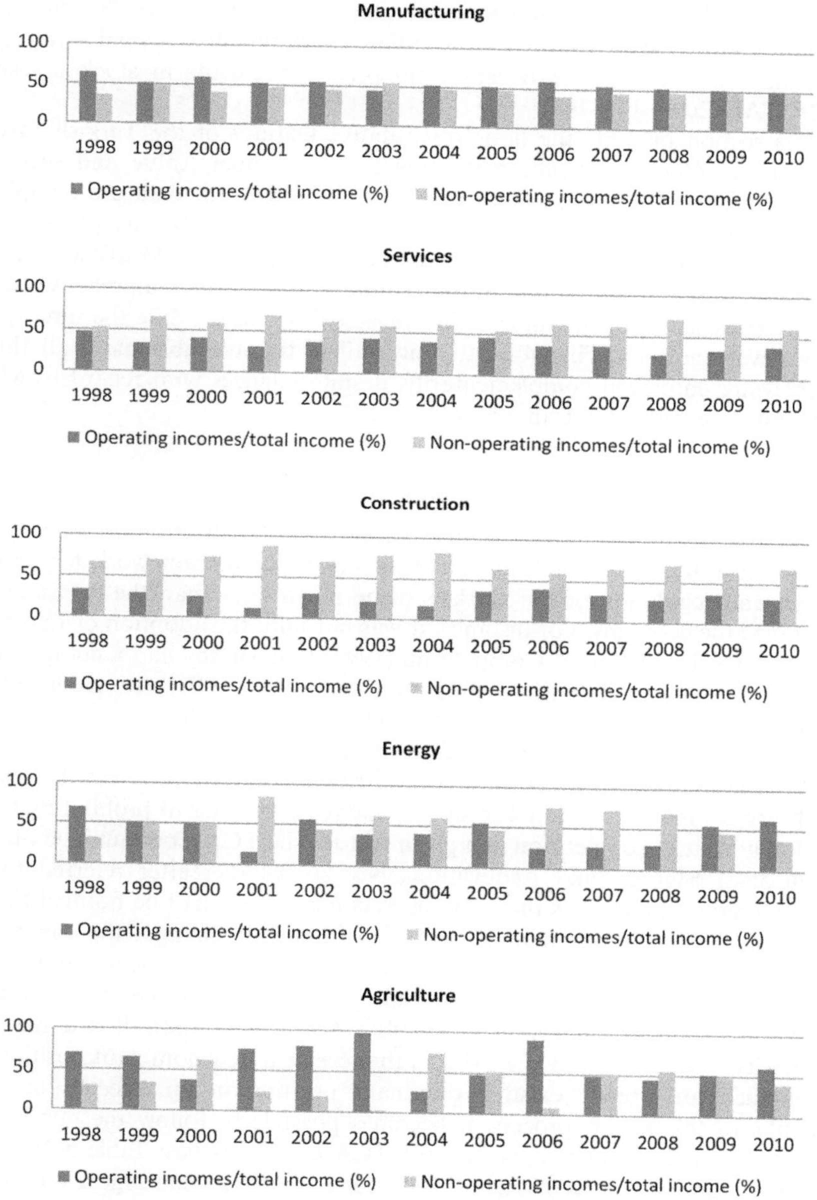

Figure 8.3 Operating Income and Non-operating Income as Share of Total Income (%)
Note: Data adjusted for inflation in 2004.
Source: Central Bank of the Republic of Turkey, authors' calculations.

earnings. Other motivations behind conducting M&As are to benefit from economies of scale by attaining greater size, to obtain efficiency gains through creating synergies, and to benefit from price movements in stock markets (UNCTAD 2000: 143–144).

This section presents the basic quantitative features of the Turkish M&A market. As official statistics pertaining to the number, value and sectoral composition of M&As are not readily available, relevant data are compiled from three different sources: the Turkish Competition Authority (TCA), the management consultancy firm Ernst & Young (EY), and the DealWatch deals database. Moves from the first of these sources to the last, comprehensiveness and/or consistency of the information revealed increases, while the time span they cover shortens. Therefore, to fully utilize the available data, all three sources are employed complementarily, despite nuances with regard to what they count as an M&A transaction.

Number and Value of M&As in Turkey

A peculiar feature of the post-1980 economic liberalization experience in Turkey was that the establishment of an institutional framework for supervision and regulation of the markets came much later than the decisions to liberalize the economy. For instance, it was not until the adoption of Law No. 4054 on the Protection of Competition (1994) that Turkey had a competition law; even then, the Turkish Competition Authority (TCA)—an independent regulator established to perform the duties given by this law—had to be awaited until 1997 for the law's enforcement.

A basic duty of the TCA is to control M&As that are to affect the goods and services markets within Turkey's boundaries, in order to prohibit mergers that may restrict competition in a given sector. The TCA Communiqué on the Control of Mergers and Acquisitions No. 2010/4 (hereafter referred to as Communiqué) establishes that a business combination shall be notified to the TCA on the conditions that i) the deal permanently changes the control of business entities that are involved in the transaction (which leaves out intra-group transactions); and ii) the pecuniary magnitude of the transaction is above the specified turnover thresholds[9]. The Competition Board has the authority to deny clearance to M&As that create a new dominant position or strengthen an already existing dominant position in an affected market. Thanks to this review process, it becomes possible to follow the number of M&As from the applications that the TCA concludes (see Table 8.2). As a corollary, any portrayal of the pre-1998 period becomes contingent on efforts that bring M&A data together in a piecemeal manner[10].

The TCA uses the term M&As generically, to cover privatizations and joint ventures as well as mergers and acquisitions; because from in its view, all four types of transaction are forms of business combination that require controlling. To delineate the differences among these types, the following definitions can be useful: Acquisitions are activities by which the buyer either takes complete control of a target firm, or purchases enough of a target firm's equity to acquire a share in the control of it. In this sense, privatizations are a subset of acquisitions by which the state transfers the controlling rights over a state-owned asset to the buyer. Mergers combine under a new legal entity ownership structures of the uniting firms, in agreed proportions. Whereas in joint ventures, without ceasing their own formal existence, parties contribute equity to a firm for the pursuit of a specific objective (such as developing new technology, or entry into a new market).

Given the available data, acquisitions stand out as the most common practice in Turkey. Acquisitions grew steadily from 56 in 1999 to 122 in 2005, peaking at 209 in 2008 before falling back to 130 in 2014. Four factors help explain the general rise in acquisitions. First, Turkey's improving economic prospects, as reflected by sovereign risk indicators, boosted foreign investors' confidence for investing in Turkey. According to an International Monetary Fund (IMF) working paper, Turkey's 1-year credit default swap (CDS) spread, which can be taken as an indicator of sovereign risk, fell sharply—by 1,000 basis points (bps)—between mid-2002 and 2003, and gradually declined thereafter until the end of 2005 to as low as 30 bps (Keller, Kunzel, Souto 2007: 11–12)[12]. In addition, Turkey's growing domestic market led businesses

Table 8.2 Number of Mergers and Acquisitions Concluded, 1998–2014[11]

	Mergers	*Acquisitions*	*Joint Ventures*	*Privatizations*	*Total*
1998	n.a	n.a	n.a	n.a	52
1999	5	56	5	2	68
2000	13	70	11	6	100
2001	6	73	7	0	86
2002	14	83	6	0	103
2003	7	76	9	14	106
2004	7	88	8	19	122
2005	5	122	8	35	170
2006	4	138	23	21	186
2007	6	193	22	11	232
2008	3	209	20	23	255
2009	4	128	12	2	146
2010	3	202	5	66	276
2011	3	168	68	14	253
2012	1	190	91	21	303
2013	1	125	68	19	213
2014	4	130	63	18	215

Source: Data compiled from TCA Annual Reports.

Note: n.a. = data not available.

that want to operate within the region to choose Turkey as a hub for their operations (EY 2015: 7). This too attracted acquisitions by foreign investors. Domestically, major Turkish business groups conducted refocusing strategies: they sold some branches of their operations that were not profitable enough, while purchasing others. Lastly, the number of privatizations in Turkey increased after 2003; some domestic business groups profitably resold the privatized assets to foreign capital, either partially or fully.

Table 8.2 illustrates that the level of merger activity has not been very significant, and remains so. This is because of holding companies' characteristics in Turkey. They are owned either by certain families, or individual capitalists. Given the holding group structure, there is little incentive to merge existing concerns under a single, jointly controlled business entity. Mergers are typically between two foreign owners. A close inspection of Competition Board decisions retrievable from the TCA Decisions Database, verifies this point. Out of 59 mergers whose files were accessed for the period of 2002–14, a total of 33 were between two foreign owners, one deal was between foreign and domestic owners, and only five deals were between Turkish owners. The remaining 20 were not considered mergers by the TCA standards as they were intra-group transactions.

Joint ventures, such as acquisitions, have shown a significant increase, especially since 2006. In Turkey, foreign companies tend to use joint ventures to form business partnerships and consortiums with domestic companies and other foreign companies. The increase in joint ventures can therefore be seen in tandem with the rise in the number of foreign companies and internationalization of Turkish capital. According to the Ministry of the Economy, the number of companies with foreign capital participation in Turkey was 6,511 at the end of June 2003. This number had risen to 41,528 by the end of 2014—an increase of more than five times in 11 years (Ministry of the Economy 2015: 7).

As the TCA started to record the transaction values of M&As only from 2013, one must turn to alternative sources to make observations about the increase in the financial value of M&As. Annual reports published by the Turkish office of multinational auditing and consulting firm EY are specifically on M&As in Turkey. Tables 8.3 and 8.4 compile data from 13 of these reports[13] to provide insight into the value and composition of M&As. As EY and the TCA adopt different sets of accounting rules[14], a mismatch between the two sources is inevitable regarding the number of M&As reported. However, as the two series correlate with each other in general, reasons for any discrepancies are not discussed here. Furthermore, it must be noted that not all deal values are disclosed to the public. Table 8.3 shows that the proportion of disclosed to undisclosed deals recorded in the EY Reports decline over time. The decline in this ratio causes the gap between the disclosed values and the EY's estimate for total deal values to widen in certain years. This is a disadvantage while interpreting the figures in Tables 8.3 and 8.4.

Table 8.3 Number and Value of Deals

	Total Number of Deals (A+B)	*Deals by Foreign Investors (%)*	*Disclosed Number of Deals (A)*	*Undisclosed Number of Deals (B)*	*Disclosed Deal Value (US $ billion) (C)*	*Estimated Deal Value (US $ billion)*	*Average Deal Size (US $ million) (C/A)*
2002	54	35	34	20	0.6	n.a	18
2003	80	25	54	26	1.4	n.a	26
2004	91	20	67	24	2.5	2.6	37
2005	164	37	93	71	30.3	31.0	326
2006	154	54	96	58	18.3	19.2	191
2007	182	51	135	47	25.5	26.7	189
2008	171	58	92	79	16.3	18.5	177
2009	116	47	51	65	3.9	5.7	76
2010	232	40	125	107	14.3	18	114
2011	264	45	149	115	11.5	14	100
2012	314	41	130	184	17.4	24	134
2013	336	34	135	201	13.7	20	102
2014	318	37	130	188	17.7	22	136

Source: Data compiled from Ernst & Young *Mergers and Acquisitions Turkey* Reports.

Note: Data for 2010 and 2012 were corrected by the authors in order to exclude the cancelled privatization tenders, which were large in size. The value of these tenders were US $12.1 billion (eight electricity and one gas distribution firm) in 2010 and $5.7 billion (highways and bridges deals) in 2012.

According to Table 8.3, the number of M&As gradually grew, from 54 in 2002 to 318 in 2014. Domestic and foreign owners were both active in the market. The number of deals by foreign investors exceeded the number of deals by domestic investors in 2006, 2007 and 2008. In terms of transaction values, total disclosed deals were weak but rising before an unprecedented take-off occurred in 2005. The high level of activity lasted for four years until it came to an abrupt stop in 2009 because of the global financial crisis. However, momentum was quickly restored and has settled at around a total disclosed value of US $15 billion per year since then. Furthermore, the average deal size contracted in time, due to the fact that there were fewer extremely valuable targets for acquisition. It is worth noting that the Turkish M&A market is largely comprised of smaller deals, and the majority of transactions are below $50 million each. As a result, last time the size of the average deal was as high as $150 million was 2008.

Without privatizations, the growth of transaction values in the Turkish M&As market would have remained much less significant. The share of privatizations in total disclosed values was substantial from 2002 to 2014 except in two years (see Table 8.4). Continuity in privatization figures is a manifestation of the fact that the ruling party, the Adalet ve Kalkınma Partisi (AKP—Justice and Development Party), has executed an uncompromising

Table 8.4 Shares of Foreign and Financial Investors and Privatizations

	Disclosed Deal Value (US $ billion)	*Privatizations (US $ billion)*	*Share of Ownership as a % of the Disclosed Deal Value*			
			Private Sector Deals (%)	*Privatizations (%)*	*Foreign Investors (%)*	*Financial Investors (%)*
2002	0.6	0.0	96	4	40	n.a
2003	1.4	0.8	41	59	36	10
2004	2.5	1.2	54	46	14	3
2005	30.3	21.8	28	72	57	5
2006	18.3	0.2	99	1	90	11
2007	25.5	11.2	56	44	66	7
2008	16.3	7.0	57	43	74	15
2009	3.9	1.8	54	46	39	5
2010	14.3	3.4	76	24	69	2
2011	11.5	3.2	72	28	56	6
2012	17.4	6.8	61	39	54	4
2013	13.7	8.4	39	61	24	4
2014	17.7	11.0	38	62	26	2

Source: Data compiled from Ernst & Young *Mergers and Acquisitions Turkey* Reports.

Figures in Table 8.3 and 8.4 cover privatizations made through the transfer of operating rights (TOR) method. As the term suggests, by TOR, the government sells the operating rights of an income-generating asset in its possession to the highest bidder for a limited time. Another type of deal that is covered under privatizations is the sale of assets in the Savings Deposit Insurance Fund (SDIF) portfolio. The government had stripped the owners of the failed banks of their conglomerates in the aftermath of the Turkish economic crisis of 2001–02. The SDIF sold these conglomerates piece by piece to compensate for the tremendous US $30.4 billion burden that bank failures had placed on the Treasury (SDIF 2013: 309).

privatization policy. Besides being an important source of revenue, this policy worked to i) diminish the bargaining power of state economic enterprise (SEE) employees (who were among the most organized segments of the working class) and restrain real wage increases; ii) reduce the public sector borrowing requirement and bring down inflation; and iii) transferring to private hands hundreds of public assets, large and small, among which were several SEEs that had the most income-generation capacity among all firms in Turkey. In this sense, privatization figures in Table 8.4 signify that the AKP's privatization policy went far beyond that of a financial tool. In fact, it worked strategically to gain the consent of major business groups, foreign investors, and international creditors, by reassuring them that the government was up to the task of neoliberal restructuring that was expected from it.

Foreign investors were responsible for 57 per cent of the disclosed value for the whole period, which corresponded to a transaction volume of US $99 billion in total. Peak years in the total disclosed value were also the years in which the foreign investors' share dominated. As an explanation for these observations, growing foreign investor confidence in Turkish economy was

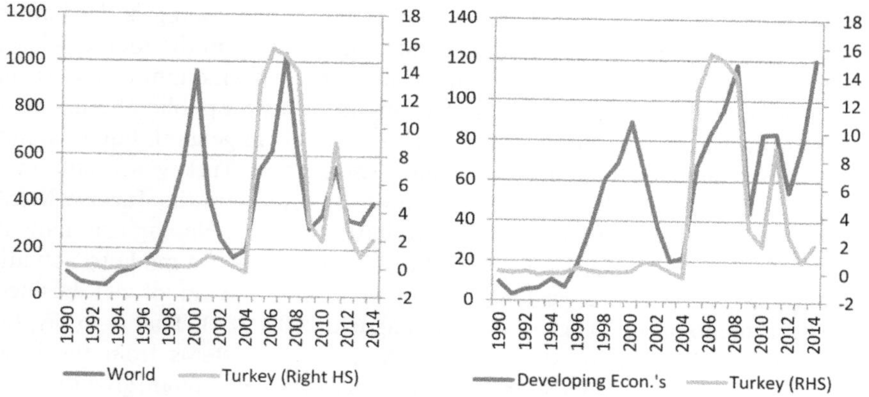

Figure 8.4 Net Value of Cross-Border M&As by Region/Economy of Seller (US $ billion)

Source: *UNCTAD World Investment Report 2015*: Annex Table 3, pp.A11-A12. For the full series, see the annex table in UNCTAD World Investment Report website, titled 'Web Table 9. Value of cross-border M&As by region/economy of seller, 1990–2014'.

already mentioned. A rise in the so-called 'global risk appetite' was a complementary factor. According to the Bank for International Settlements (BIS), international bank credit (banks' cross-border credits) in all currencies that were extended to non-banks and banks grew incessantly from 2003 to the 2008 collapse (CGFS 2011: 9). Such growth in global liquidity, which is indicative of an expansion in the business activity, was conducive to M&As. Furthermore, UNCTAD data shows that the gross value of cross-border M&As recorded worldwide more than quadrupled in the 2003–07 period (UNCTAD 2015: 15). This suggests that foreign investors' interest in the Turkish assets was part of a global trend in the expansion of cross-border M&As.

Figure 8.4 illustrates this point more clearly. It compares the value of cross-border M&A sales in Turkey with those globally and in developing economies on a net basis[15]. As the figure shows, a new global wave of cross-border M&As started around the mid-1990s, with the first thrust coming from the deals in developing economies. Turkey was not a part of the wave at this stage. Until 2005, net values of cross-border M&A sales recorded for Turkey were close to zero and even negative in 2004 (see the scale on the right hand side). Therefore, it is possible to assert that Turkey joined the cross-border M&A wave rather abruptly only a decade after its start. Additionally, Figure 8.4 illustrates that since 2005, the net value of cross-border M&A sales in Turkey closely correlated with the world in general. However, it is also apparent that Turkey started to lag behind since 2010. Turkey's divergence in recent years is even more apparent when the comparison is made with developing economies. While net M&A sales in developing economies recovered from the 2009 slump, the trend remained downward in Turkey.

Returning to Table 8.4, a final point that needs mentioning is the limited share of financial investors, such as private equity funds, in the total disclosed value. Private equity funds buy or invest in a firm with the aim of increasing its value in the shortterm and then of selling it through a public offering or to another investor with a profit margin. This requires, in general, liquid capital and stable financial markets. As capital markets in Turkey are still in a developing stage, the rarity of financial investor activity in the Turkish M&A market is congruent with an observation that Ferraz and Hamaguchi made in the context of developing countries: "Most transactions are made to actually acquire assets, in the expectancy of an increasing stream of net business profits in the long run" (Ferraz and Hamaguchi 2002: 384). That is to say, the expected benefit from most of the M&As in Turkey stems from the basic features of Turkey's goods and services markets (e.g. their growth, geographical positioning, or oligopolistic character) as opposed to making capital gains in the equity market.

Significance of the Turkish M&A Market

Notwithstanding their insights, two problems make the data provided by EY Reports unsuitable for further purposes. These are i) EY Reports do not correct for deals that have failed after having been announced; and ii) sectoral categories in EY Reports change from year to year, making the sectoral breakdown of M&As impossible to watch consistently over time. The first correction is necessary to find the annual value of deals that are actually closed. Once this is made, comparisons with other realized magnitudes in the economy may be more reliable. The second correction is important for presenting the M&A sectoral composition systematically.

To deal with both issues, Emerging Markets Information System (EMIS) database is useful although it covers a shorter time span than EY Reports. By narrowing down the M&As that are listed in this database to the deals whose status is completed and whose target country is Turkey, a new time series that shows the value of closed M&As from 2005 to 2014 is obtained. As in EY Reports, this series only includes deals with disclosed values, and excludes outbound transactions.

To assess the significance of M&As within the economy, the newly obtained series is then juxtaposed with the gross fixed capital formation (GFCF) in Turkey (see Table 8.5). GFCF measures the amount spent in the economy on domestic physical assets such as machinery and construction. In this sense, GFCF is a rough estimate of investment expenditures that create new production capacity or infrastructure in the country. The ratio of M&As to GFCF, therefore, indicates how much business capital is invested in buying existing production capacity instead of building it from scratch. This is a ratio that Nitzan and Bichler call the 'buy-to-build indicator' (2009: 338).

The calculation in the last row of Table 8.5 suggests that, for every dollar that was allocated to GFCF in Turkish economy from 2005 to 2014, about 10

Table 8.5 M&As as percentage of Gross Fixed Capital Formation (GFCF)

	2005	*2006*	*2007*	*2008*	*2009*	*2010*	*2011*	*2012*	*2013*	*2014*	*2005–14*
M&As: Total Deal Value (US $ billion)	41.0	19.0	27.2	22.8	6.3	15.2	13.7	21.0	15.1	18.2	**199.5**
GFCF (US $ billion)	133.6	158.5	189.9	205.2	144.2	192.0	233.7	238.8	271.2	269.9	**2,036.9**
M&As/ GFCF (%)	30.7	12.0	14.3	11.1	4.4	7.9	5.9	8.8	5.6	6.7	**9.8**

Source: To calculate GFCF, Turkey's GDP in current US dollars is divided by the share of GFCF in GDP. Thereby, GFCF in current US dollars is obtained. GDP in current US dollars and GFCF as a percentage of GDP are taken from World Bank Database, World Development Indicators, Series Codes NY.GDP.MKTP.CD and NE.GDI.FTOT.ZS, respectively. The series are consistent with the revision TurkStat made in Turkey's system of national accounts in 2016. For M&As, the DealWatch database in Emerging Markets Information System is used (see text for explanations).

Note: Corrections are made to omit transactions in which the target company's operation is only marginally related to Turkey.

cents worth of M&As took place on average (a buy-to-build ratio of 9.8 per cent)[16]. A comparison of this estimate with the USA and United Kingdom is possible for a similar time span (2005–12). When the raw data that Francis provides are used to calculate an average buy-to-build ratio for these two countries, the results are 50.2 per cent and 29.4 per cent, respectively (Francis 2013: 63, footnote 1). Therefore, while Turkey's buy-to-build ratio may appear small when compared with the USA and the United Kingdom, the fact that it has reached this point starting from miniscule levels highlights the emergence of Turkish M&A market, which partly overlaps but is in no way confined to the centralized stock exchange in Turkey, the Borsa İstanbul.

Sectoral Overview of M&As

To see the sectoral composition of M&As, the data drawn from the EMIS database is categorized according to the North American Industry Classification System (NAICS). Then, each sector's intra-sectoral sum is divided by the total deal value recorded in a particular year. Table 8.6 presents the results of this calculation in percentage points. Figures cover only domestic and inbound cross-border deals. In terms of the sectoral composition of M&As, the highest sectoral shares on average belong to the finance and insurance (24.5%), manufacturing (18.8 per cent), and utilities (15.5 per cent) sectors from 2005 to 2014. Information, transportation, and retail trade sectors also lead in certain years.

The Turkish finance and insurance sector stands out as the top choice for European, US, Russian and Middle Eastern investors. For some domestic business groups, which had picked up the valuable sections of troubled banks'

Table 8.6 Sectoral Breakdown of M&As (% Shares of Total Deal Values)

Sectors (NAICS)	*2005*	*2006*	*2007*	*2008*	*2009*	*2010*	*2011*	*2012*	*2013*	*2014*	*2005–2014*
Mining	0.6	0.4	0.0	0.5	8.7	3.4	2.4	0.9	0.6	0.4	**1.1**
Utilities	0.4	1.4	3.0	19.0	27.8	18.1	5.1	44.2	34.4	27.9	**15.5**
Construction	0.0	0.0	1.0	2.6	0.2	0.0	0.8	1.6	0.7	2.6	**0.9**
Manufacturing	26.1	15.7	21.0	19.4	28.4	5.9	36.8	11.6	12.8	9.8	**18.8**
Wholesale & Retail Trade	1.5	11.5	3.7	25.0	3.3	13.5	18.3	5.3	5.6	6.4	**8.7**
Transportation & Warehousing	10.0	3.0	29.9	2.3	6.1	3.0	7.3	6.8	8.7	17.6	**10.6**
Information	36.9	8.9	5.0	0.6	2.0	2.0	3.7	1.3	4.9	9.9	**11.0**
Finance & Insurance	21.7	55.3	28.5	12.5	10.8	45.5	4.9	20.5	20.2	18.0	**24.5**
Real Estate & Leasing Services	0.5	2.2	2.6	2.6	3.9	4.4	3.6	3.1	4.7	3.5	**2.7**
Hospitals & Healthcare	0.1	0.0	2.2	1.0	3.1	0.0	12.0	0.4	0.8	0.2	**1.5**
Hotels & Restaurants	1.4	1.2	1.4	0.4	4.0	2.5	0.6	0.4	2.6	1.9	**1.4**
Others	0.6	0.5	1.7	14.2	1.5	1.8	4.5	3.9	4.0	1.8	**3.4**
Total	100	100	100	100	100	100	100	100	100	100	100
Total Deal Value (US $ billion)	41.0	19.0	27.2	22.8	6.3	15.2	13.7	21.0	15.1	18.2	199,5

Source: Data compiled from Emerging Markets Information System (EMIS), DealWatch Database.

Notes: Sums may not equal to 100 because of rounding. Notes for the Table 8.5 apply.

portfolios following the 2001 financial crisis, or which had acquired privatized state banks in the 1990s, very lucrative exit opportunities became available in banking. The newly formed domestic-foreign banking partnerships, on the other hand, provided domestic banks with the foreign expertise and linkages needed to effectively enter the financial world market, while also strengthening their capital structure. In the insurance sector, the decade-long downward profitability trend, which started around 2003 in non-life branches (Insurance Supervision Board 2015: 28), triggered a wave of acquisitions. As late as 2009, the prominent businessperson Güler Sabancı said that she expected further consolidation in the industry.[17] Allianz, AXA, Eureko, Mapfre, Zurich, Sompo Japan, Groupama, Metlife and Aegeas were among the largest buyers in life and non-life branches. Sellers were mostly domestic banks, which had operations in these branches. Since 2005, the total value of M&As in the insurance sector reached US $5.6 billion, while in commercial banking it was $37.5 billion.

According to reports by the High Audit Committee of Turkey, the number of employees in the SEEs in manufacturing industry decreased from 122,000 in 2001 to 26,000 by the end of 2013 (High Audit Committee of Turkey 2009:

54; 2014: 43) indicating that throughout the 2000s, many of the state-owned firms in the manufacturing sector were privatized. ERDEMİR (iron and steel), TÜPRAŞ (oil refining), PETKİM (petrochemical products), TEKEL (liquor and cigarettes), aluminium, fertilizer, cement and sugar production assets were among the most notable ones. From 2005 to 2014, privatizations in the manufacturing sector totalled US $9.5 billion. However, this comprised only a quarter of the total value of manufacturing deals recorded in this period, the remaining 75 per cent being private sector deals. The largest private sector deals spread to a wide range of sub-sectors such as cable manufacturing, pharmaceuticals, electrical equipment, sugar and confectionary, and soft drinks.

The utilities transactions seen in the power, gas and water sectors, by contrast, were mostly the result of privatizations. Here, the privatization of electricity and gas distribution networks went hand in hand with the sales of hydroelectric and thermal power plants. In several cases, the transfer of the operating rights of nearby coal/lignite mining fields and harbour operations were also included to the privatization of thermal power plants. Buyers were predominantly domestic business groups whose main lines of activity (apart from Sabancı Holding) were construction, trade or manufacturing. As a result of these privatizations, sizeable private energy companies such as Enerjisa and Zorlu Enerji were created in a time span of no longer than a decade. The total value of privatizations in utilities amounted to US $21.6 billion, which made 69 per cent of the sector total.

Sporadic increases observable in the shares of transportation and information sectors in 2005, 2007 and 2014 can again be explained by privatizations. In these years, the government privatized, via the TOR method, five airports, namely, İstanbul Atatürk, İstanbul Sabiha Gökçen, Antalya, Milas-Bodrum and Dalaman, which operated as hubs for most of Turkey's tourist traffic. Total amount of privatization revenue collected was US $11 billion. Privatization auctions for these airports were especially attractive to international investors, who either formed consortia with domestic companies, or later acquired the controlling stake in the winning domestic company, as in the deal between TAV Airports and Aéroports de Paris in 2012. Also in 2005, the government privatized Türk Telekom, the state monopoly in fixed-line telephone services, and sold Cem Uzan's sequestrated mobile telecommunications company, Telsim, to international bidders.

Other privatizations and private sector deals in the transportation and information sectors were scattered throughout the period. For instance, İstanbul Metropolitan Municipality sold the operating rights of its ferry company (İDO), which operated in the Sea of Marmara. Via similar methods, the government privatised a dozen ports, harbours and marinas along Turkey's coastlines. In the media sector, several newspapers, and radio and television broadcasting channels, which were transferred to the SDIF after the 2001 economic crisis, were sold to domestic holding groups. The largest among these media channels, Sabah-ATV Group, was sold for US $1.1 billion through a controversial tender process where pro-government Çalık Holding was the only participant. On the side of private sector deals, five television channels and four newspapers changed private hands—some of them more than once—in line with government's intention to dominate the Turkish media. The remainder of the transaction volume in the information sector came mostly from the transfer of shares in wireless telecommunication companies, Turkcell and Avea. The most significant private deal in the transportation sector was the sale of a Turkish deep sea freight transportation company, UN Ro-Ro, to an American private equity fund, KKR, in 2007 for $1.3 billion.

Largest M&As and Monopoly Power

Table 8.7 summarizes information pertaining to the highest value M&As in Turkey. Minority stake purchases denote acquisitions by which the buyer gains less than a 50 per cent voting right in the management of the company. The top M&As are clustered around certain sectors. In privatizations these are telecommunications, manufacturing, transportation and utilities, whereas banking is the sector of choice within the top private sector deals. It is notable that all the deals in the latter category were conducted by foreign investors.

A common feature of these deals is the high degree of monopoly power that they conferred on the buyers. One way to approach the issue of monopoly power is to refer to market concentration ratios. For instance, experts in TCA's research department employ market concentration ratios, especially the Herfindahl-Hirschman Index (HHI), for their structure-conduct-performance analysis of the Turkish manufacturing industry (Korkut, Sesli and Kalkan 2014: 10). Therein, they hold to the idea that a concentrated market structure allows firms to pursue cost-plus pricing strategies, which translate into higher performance and profits (2014: 7). Therefore, concentration ratios may help demonstrate the relationship between the high level of prices paid for the top target firms on the one hand, and the oligopolistic markets in which they operate commanding significant market shares on the other.

The Turkish Statistical Institute (TurkStat) calculates two types of indicators of market concentration. The four-firm concentration ratio (CR_4) denotes the market share of four largest firms in the industry based on their sales. According to the TurkStat classification, $100>CR_4>70$, $70>CR_4>50$, and $50>CR_4>30$ are considered to represent 'very high', 'high' and 'medium concentration ratios, respectively. These classifications signify the degree to which an industry is likely to be oligopolistic in character, i.e. open to domination by the largest firms. The second indicator, HHI, is calculated by calculating the square roots of the market share of each firm which operate in the same industry. HHI is considered to be a more sensitive measure of concentration as it takes into account the monopoly power of each firm with respect to other firms in the market. This means that it is possible that an industry with a 'high' CR_4 ratio can be considered unconcentrated due to its low HHI.[18]

Table 8.7 Top M&As with a Disclosed Value ≥ US $2 Billion

Target	*Value, US $ billion*	*Buyer*	*Country of Buyer*	*Industry*	*Year*
A. Privatizations					
Türk Telekom (TTAŞ)	6.56	Oger Telecom	Saudi Arabia	Wired Telecommunications	2005
Telsim	4.55	Vodafone	United Kingdom	Wireless Telecommunications	2005
TÜPRAŞ	4.14	Koç Holding	Turkey	Petroleum Refineries	2005
Antalya Airport	3.50	Fraport AG, IC Holding	Germany, Turkey	Transportation	2007
İstanbul Atatürk Airport	3.00	Tepe-Akfen Venture (TAV Airports)	Turkey	Transportation	2005
İddaa	3.00	Çukurova Holding, Intralot	Turkey, Greece	Sports Betting	2008
ERDEMİR	2.77	OYAK Group	Turkey	Iron & Steel	2006
İstanbul Sabiha Gökçen Airport	2.60	Malaysia Airport Hold. GMR Infra., Limak,	Malaysia, India, Turkey	Transportation	2007
Seyitömer Thermal Power Plant (TPP)	2.45	Çelikler İnşaat	Turkey	Electricity Generation	2012
PETKİM	2.04	Socar & Turcas	Azerbaijan, Turkey	Petrochemicals	2007
Boğaziçi Electricity Distribution	1.96	Limak-Cengiz-Kolin Consortium	Turkey	Electricity Distribution	2012
B. Acquisitions					
Garanti Bankası	5.80	BBVA	Spain	Financial Services	2010
Yapı Kredi Bankası	4.60	Koç Holding, UniCredito	Turkey, Italy	Financial Services	2005
Denizbank	3.78	Sberbank	Russia	Financial Services	2012
Migros	2.90	BC Partners**	United Kingdom	Supermarkets (Organised Retail)	2008
Finansbank	2.77	National Bank of Greece	Greece	Financial Services	2006
OYAK Bank*	2.67	ING Bank	Netherlands	Financial Services	2007
Garanti Bankası	2.47	BBVA	Spain	Financial Services	2014
Denizbank*	2.44	Dexia Bank	Belgium	Financial Services	2006
Mey İçki* (TEKEL)	2.10	Diageo	United Kingdom	Alcoholic Beverages	2011
Enerjisa	1.96	E.ON SE	Germany	Electricity Generation and Distribution	2012
C. Minority Stake Purchases					
Turkcell	3.33	Alfa Telecom	Russia	Wireless Telecommunications	2005
Akbank	3.10	Citibank	USA	Financial Services	2006

Note: Outbound cross-border transactions are not included.

*A resale after privatization. **Private Equity Firm.

The US Department of Justice and the Federal Trade Commission set the HHI thresholds for 'highly concentrated' and 'moderately concentrated' markets to 1>HHI>0.25 and 0.25>HHI> 0.15, respectively (US Department of Justice 2010: 19).

Table 8.8 shows TurkStat's CR_4 and HHI calculations for the industrial classes where the top M&As were conducted (except in banking and organised retail where the data is inapplicable or absent). HHI figures demonstrate beyond doubt that privatisations in the concentrated industrial sectors involved the transfer of large chunks of market share to private control, which amounted to in certain cases, making incumbent business groups private monopolies in their business segments such as in Türk Telekom or TÜPRAŞ deals. Among private sector deals, Turkcell, Migros and Mey İçki were market leaders when they were sold. Turkcell is still the largest mobile phone operator (ITCA 2015: 38) and one of the most profitable companies in Turkey. Migros was the largest deal closed by a private equity firm in the Turkish market.[19] With this deal, BC Partners, obtained the biggest fast-moving consumer goods retailer in Turkey as of 2008 (Erdoğan et al. 2012: 6). Mey İçki currently owns a 76 per cent share in the Turkish liquor market, according to the Euromonitor database.

Furthermore, the top deals that are categorized as belonging to 'unconcentrated' industrial sectors in Table 8.8 share a similar feature.

Table 8.8 Concentration Ratios in the Top M&As Industries

Industrial Classes (Four-digit) (NACE Rev. 2)	CR_4 *(2013)*	*HHI (2013)*
Wired Telecommunications	95.2% (Very High)	0.69 (Highly Concentrated)
Wireless Telecommunications	93.9% (Very High)	0.38 (Highly Concentrated)
Manufacture of Refined Petroleum Products	93.3% (Very High)	0.84 (Highly Concentrated)
Distilling, Rectifying, and Blending of Spirits	95.5% (Very High)	0.64 (Highly Concentrated)
Gambling and Betting Activities	86.2% (Very High)	0.48 (Highly Concentrated)
Service Activities Incidental to Air Transportation	69.7% (High)	0.17 (Moderately Concentrated)
Distribution of Electricity	41.9% (Medium)	0.07 (Unconcentrated)
Production of Electricity	38.5% (Medium)	0.07 (Unconcentrated)
Manufacture of Basic Iron, Steel, and Ferro-Alloys	36.8% (Medium)	0.05 (Unconcentrated)

Source: Concentration in Industry and Service Sectors (TurkStat).

Several shortcomings related to the measurement of concentration ratios account for their low HHI values, and these are easy to specify. One shortcoming is that TurkStat measures concentration ratios on a nationwide scale, whereas in certain markets there are regional oligopolies. For instance, distribution of electricity is a case in point. In each of Turkey's 21 privatized electricity distribution regions, the right to function as the supplier of electricity to clients who are not eligible as 'free consumers'[20] belongs to a single company. Considering that the ratio of 'free consumers' as of 2014 ranged between 2 per cent and 15 per cent (in electricity consumption terms) for different distribution regions (EMRA 2015: 24), it is evident each distribution company has been operating as a strong regional oligopoly.

Another shortcoming is that in Turkey, the very broadly defined industrial sectors often cause concentration ratios for certain products to be underestimated. For instance, the steel producer ERDEMİR, which was privatized in 2005, currently commands a 40 per cent domestic market share in flat steel, according to a sector report (Deniz 2014: 7). However, the industrial activity it belongs to—manufacture of basic iron, steel and ferroalloys—is not specific enough to account for this fact. Finally, as for the privatization of the Seyitömer thermal power plant, it can be said that the 600 megawatt capacity of the plant corresponded to just 1.1 per cent of Turkey's overall installed capacity in electricity production as of 2012, but the price paid included the operating licence of the state-owned lignite fields in the province, as well as the plant itself.[21]

The target banks among the top M&As, i.e., Garanti Bankası, Akbank, Yapı Kredi, Koçbank, Denizbank, Finansbank, and Oyakbank, were also among Turkey's largest private banks, and they remain so over a decade later[22]. The reason for foreign banks' interest in buying Turkish banks had partly to do with 'monopoly rents' arising from the uncompetitive environment of banking in Turkey (Repková and Stavárek 2014: 638). As the ratios in Table 8.9 show, the Turkish banking sector became more concentrated in the first decade of 2000s. Similarly, a Banks Association of Turkey study, calculating HHIs for the same indicators, stated that by 2005 the Turkish banking sector had reached the boundary of a strong oligopolistic structure (Arıcan et al. 2011: 143).

In summary, domestic and foreign business groups were eager to buy up pieces of these oligopolistic markets with high concentration ratios because of the profitability advantages they rendered. Yet oligopoly in itself is no guarantor of successful returns. Rather, it should be borne in mind that a long period of economic and institutional restructuring was necessary before the political and economic conditions were ripe for these transactions to be realized fruitfully. The telecommunications and banking sectors are good examples where regulatory change was a pre-condition for the realization of M&As.

Table 8.9 Concentration in the Turkish Banking Sector, 1995–2014

	Number of Banks	*Ratio of Assets of the Top 8 Banks to Total Bank Assets*	*Ratio of Credits of the Top 8 Banks to Total Bank Credits*	*Ratio of Deposits of the Top 8 Banks to Total Bank Deposits*
1995	68	63.9%	63.9%	69.8%
2000	79	63.3%	63.8%	65.9%
2002	54	75.7%	67.6%	79.2%
2005	47	79.5%	71.8%	84.6%
2011	44	80.7%	79.6%	84.8%
2014	47	78.4%	77.4%	81.6%

Source: Data compiled from The Banks Association of Turkey, authors' calculations.

Note: As of year end for each representative year.

Regulatory Restructuring and M&As in Telecommunications and Banking

The previous section suggested that the Turkish M&A market in the 2000s owed its significance to the value of transactions that were realized mainly in the form of acquisitions and privatizations. This section examines different aspects that made these transactions possible. First, the importance of changes in Turkey's legal and regulatory frameworks is demonstrated by focusing on the privatization of Türk Telekom in the Turkish telecommunications sector. The privatization of Türk Telekom signified the transfer of a service that had hitherto been publicly provided by a state monopoly, to a foreign private company. In this sense, it imposed on governing authorities several of the reforms that were required for the completion of such a transaction: i.e., i) preparing a solid legal and institutional base for privatizations; ii) making reforms to secure foreign investors' property rights; and iii) re-regulating the telecommunications sector as a preparation for the post-privatization period. A second aspect that made M&As possible, namely improvement in Turkey's economic and monetary conditions, is explained through acquisitions in the banking sector. Regulatory restructuring had as much importance in banking as in telecommunications, but in addition, M&As in banking were market-induced. The high profitability of the Turkish banking sector relative to their Organisation for Economic Co-operation and Development (OECD) counterparts stands out as the factor that led foreign financial institutions to acquire banks in Turkey.

Telecommunications

In 1994, pro-market reform authorities, guided by an intention to privatize telecommunications, separated telephone services from the General Directorate of PTT (Posts, Telegraph and Telephone) of the Ministry of Transport. This led to the creation of Türk Telekomünikasyon A.Ş. (Türk Telekom or

TTAŞ) as a joint stock company and a state economic enterprise with monopoly over the fixed-line telephone services (Atiyas 2005: 5). The authorities also allowed two private companies, Turkcell and Telsim, to function in the mobile telecommunications market in 1994. Until 2001, TTAŞ was kept out of the mobile market.

Privatization policy was subject to strong opposition and public scrutiny in the 1990s and 2000s. In this sense, privatization of TTAŞ was part of the political and ideological struggle, which tested governments' power and willingness to make neoliberal market reforms. As the TTAŞ privatization dragged on for more than a decade, the successful execution of TTAŞ transaction has gained a wider significance for the future of other privatizations, as well as for the prestige of pro-market reform parties pressing for them.

In 1993, 1994 and 1995[23], the Constitutional Court defeated three initial attempts to privatise TTAŞ at their very outset. Fulfilling the legal requirements that the Constitutional Court imposed proved to be a time-consuming challenge for the governing authorities. Therefore, privatization of TTAŞ, like other important privatizations, had to wait for the changes in legal and administrative frameworks. The first step was to prepare a clearer legal basis for privatizations. Methods to be implemented in privatizations were specified in a coherent manner for the first time, with the enactment of Privatization Law No. 4046 in 1994. In 1999, a comprehensive amendment was made in the Constitution that concerned i) the provision of public services by private parties; and ii) the resolution of disputes arising from private parties' contracts with the state. Inscribing these revisions to the Constitution undermined a strategy that political parties that opposed privatizations had hitherto successfully pursued—namely to use the legal system as a defence mechanism against privatizations.

Second, an amendment to Article 125 of the Constitution opened the door for international arbitration as an alternative method of dispute resolution in Turkey. With this amendment, foreign investors who made concession contracts with the state for the provision of public services were offered the option to bypass national courts in resolving the disputes that concerned the terms of their contracts. Furthermore, an amendment to Article 155 of the Constitution restricted the duty of the Council of State in relation to concession contracts. Instead of examining them, the Council of State would henceforth give its non-binding opinion on these contracts within two months.

A third step that the authorities took, was to reform the telecommunications sector. In 2000, Law No. 4502 was enacted, which transformed TTAŞ into a company that operated purely according to the private law and ceased its status as a state economic enterprise. The same law also decided the termination of the company's monopoly in fixed-line services by the end of 2003 (OECD 2002: 9), and established the Telecommunications Authority (TA) "as the first sector-specific independent regulatory body in Turkey" (OECD 2002: 15). The TA was vested with powers such as issuing secondary legislation, monitoring tariffs, investigating anti-competitive practices, and imposing fines.

Two tenders opened in June and December 2000 for the block sale of 20 per cent and 33.5 per cent of TTAŞ shares, respectively, both failed because there were no tender applications from foreign investors. Meanwhile, the economic crisis of 2000–01 broke out in Turkey. Urgently in need of funds, the Turkish government conceded to the 'accelerated and complete' privatization of TTAŞ, which was asserted by the IMF as a prerequisite for releasing a new tranche of credit allocated to Turkey's 'rescue package' (OECD 2002: 9). This concession set off another round of restructuring in Turkey's legal framework—this time under the pressure of economic crisis and of the IMF—that i) allowed foreign control in TTAŞ; and ii) assured foreign investors about the security of their property rights in Turkey.

In transferring the majority control in a strategic asset such as TTAŞ to private investors, national security concerns were an obstacle. Law No. 4673, which was enacted in May 2001, made several arrangements to deal with these concerns. In general terms, it authorized the TA to take measures for the provision of telecommunication services in line with the necessities of national security. More concretely, the law identified a single 'golden share' that is distinct from the shares open to privatization in TTAŞ, and attached to the golden share special rights with specific reference to the protection of national interests. The golden share would be represented by one member in the board of directors and appointed by the Ministry of Transport. Next, it prescribed the operations of satellite services to be divested from the company. Finally, it restricted the maximum foreign ownership in TTAŞ to 45 per cent of the shares while permitting the complete sale of the company to private investors (except for the golden share). These arrangements were important in the sense that when TTAŞ was actually privatized in 2005, the Constitutional Court rejected the appeal for cancellation of the transaction on the basis that it has found regulations in the telecommunications sector sufficiently in place.[24]

Another issue that apparently put off foreign investors was about the protection of their contractual rights. A disadvantage of the existing framework of arbitration in Turkey was that arbitral awards, i.e., judgments by arbitration tribunals, could be appealed on the basis of Turkey's Code of Civil Procedure (CCP). In line with commitments made to the IMF, authorities enacted the International Arbitration Law No. 4686 (IAL) in June 2001. The IAL determined the rules and procedures to be followed in the arbitration proceedings seated in Turkey, and application of CCP to the arbitration proceedings was ceased. The IAL also generalized arbitration, on a consensual basis, to nearly all business contracts that had a 'foreign element', not confining it to disputes which involved the state. Also, the international arbitration standards adopted by the IAL liberalized the arbitration processes as much as possible from the intervention by state courts (Bilgen Özeke 2005: 68).

The privatization process of TTAŞ restarted a year after the 2002 general elections that had swept the AKP to power. In 2003, the cabinet approved the privatization of a minimum of 51 per cent of the company through a block sale. However, for the purchaser to be a foreign investor in such a transaction, a new regulation was necessary. Law No. 5189, enacted in 2004, abrogated the clause[25] that put a 45 per cent upper limit on foreign ownership in TTAŞ. As a preparation for the post-privatization period, Law No. 5369 on the Provision of Universal Service was enacted in 2005. It aimed to guarantee the provision of basic telecommunications services at reasonable prices even at locations where it is 'financially challenging'[26] for operators to provide.

Finally, privatization of TTAŞ was concluded in November 2005 through the signing of a share sale agreement and a concession contract. A total of 55 per cent of TTAŞ and the right to provide telecommunications services for 21 years were transferred to Oger Telecom (of Saudi Arabia) in return for US $6.5 billion[27]. The buyer was the newly found subsidiary of the construction-based company Saudi Oger, which had no former experience in the fixed-line telephone business. Amid criticisms, the authorities rejoiced in the event: As in the words of the then president of the Privatization Administration, privatization of TTAŞ was a "flagship transaction that will have a material impact on the perception of the country by the international community", and it "increased confidence in the government's commitment to the privatisation programme at large" (Kilci, 2005: 36).

The market share of TTAŞ show that the liberalization of ownership in the telecommunications sector had limited success in creating effective competition in fixed-line telephone services in Turkey. As of late 2015, the share of TTAŞ in local calls was 85 per cent, and in inter-province and international calls the ratios were 56 per cent and 68 per cent, respectively (ITCA 2015: 37–38)[28]. As a result, TTAŞ collected 83 per cent of all the telephone services revenues generated by the fixed-line operators (ITCA 2015: 35). However, it may be argued that the state of competition in the telecommunications sector is more complex than TTAŞ's market share in the fixed-line segment would suggest. The decline in the number of fixed-line subscribers from 19 million in 2005 to 11.6 million in 2015. indicated apparently that for some consumers, mobile services were a substitute for fixed-line services. In mobile services, three companies are currently in business. These are Turkcell (owned by Çukurova Holding and TeliaSonera), Vodafone and Avea (a subsidiary of TTAŞ). Turkcell is the market leader with 48 per cent of subscribers. Vodafone's and Avea's market shares are 29 per cent and 23 per cent, respectively (ITCA 2015: 61). Among the telecommunications sector companies, TTAŞ and Turkcell report huge profits by Turkey's standards. Their consolidated financial reports show that their after-tax net profits in 2014 were US $845 million and $617 million, respectively. On the other hand, Vodafone Turkey started to report a profit only since 2013, and Avea has continued to report a loss, which was $340 million in 2014 (ITCA 2015: 20).

Banking

Historically, the banking sector in Turkey has been characterized by both public and private domestic bank ownership, alongside smaller foreign banks, and this remained so until the late 1990s (Marois 2012). The impact of the 2001 financial crisis, however, would trigger substantial regulatory and ownership changes across the sector. As discussed in Chapter 5, the government announced the 2001 Banking Sector Restructuring Programme (BSRP) in response to the crisis. The crisis and recovery process itself entailed processes wherein a number of mostly private banks with weak capital structures and loan portfolios were eliminated or consolidated into other banks. Furthermore, institutional reforms restricted once-common lending practices for banks held within holding groups (that is, crony practices of related lending within the group).

Once the financial crisis started, a total of 12 banks, whose sizes ranged from small to medium had to be eventually transferred to the SDIF for reasons of illiquidity, insolvency and/or misuse of bank resources (see Table 8.10). Thus, the number of banks seized since November 1998 has reached a total of 19.

SDIF's preferred method of resolving the transferred banks was to put up their assets for sale in various forms, encouraging private banks to acquire their assets on a selective basis. Their remaining unsold assets were concurrently merged with the other transferred banks. Finally, all unsold banks/assets were transferred to a single bank, Bayındırbank (later renamed Birleşik Fon Bankası—Joint Fund Bank), whose resolution process continues. Thus, the financial burden of collecting bad debts was left with the public.[29]

The BSRP entailed important re-regulation of the banking system processes. For example, non-financial subsidiaries that appeared in holding banks' balance sheets were transferred to parent holdings; non-banking financial services that were disconnected to banks were consolidated around them; and small-scale banks were discarded by merging them with larger banks. As a result, the system evolved from a convoluted structure toward one in which each conglomerate conducted its financial services through a single bank. An amendment made in 2001 to the then current Banks Law No. 4389 also facilitated bank consolidations by exempting M&As in the banking sector from the TCA's review process[30]. Part of this restructuring is observable in Table 8.11, which shows merger activity by Turkish conglomerates in banking. As it shows, holdings like Koç, Sabancı, Doğuş, and Fiba reduced the number of banks they owned in Turkey to one, and İş Bankası merged the two development and investment banks it controlled.

However, this was not simplification for its own sake. As argued elsewhere, post-crisis restructuring led to the internationalization of the state, that is, the convergence in domestic regulatory practices according to internationally recognized best practices (Marois 2011: 180). This helped to create an ideal regulative environment for foreign capital to invest in the Turkish banking sector. Conglomerates like Koç Holding, Çolakoğlu Group, Doğuş Holding and Sabancı Holding used this opportunity to attract foreign investment into their banks and to strengthen their capital structures (see Table 8.12) (Gültekin-Karakaş 2009: 359–362). Others that shied away from competition under

Table 8.10 Resolution of the Banks Transferred to the SDIF

Bank	*Date of Transfer to the SDIF*	*Date of Sale or Transfer*	*Buyer*	*Percentage of Balance Sheet Sold*	*Process for the Unsold Accounts*
Bank Ekspress	12.11.1998	30.06.2001	Tekfen Bank	51	Transferred to Etibank
Egebank	21.12.1999	10.08.2001	OYAK Bank	32	Transferred to Etibank, Kentbank, and the SDIF
Sümerbank	21.12.1999				
Yaşarbank	21.12.1999				
Yurtbank	21.12.1999				
Bank Kapital	27.10.2000				
Ulusal Bank	28.02.2001				
Demirbank	06.12.2000	30.10.2001	HSBC	33	Transferred to Bayındırbank, Bank 2000, and the SDIF
Sitebank	09.07.2001	21.12.2001	Novabank	62	Transferred to Bayındırbank
Tarişbank	09.07.2001	21.10.2002	Denizbank	88	Transferred to Bayındırbank and the SDIF
Pamukbank	18.06.2002	12.11.2004	Halkbank	100	-
Interbank	07.01.1999	02.07.2001	-	-	Transferred to Etibank
Esbank	21.12.1999				
Etibank	27.10.2000	05.04.2002	-	-	Transferred to Bayındırbank
İktisat Bankası	15.03.2001	20.03.2001			
Kentbank	09.07.2001	05.04.2002			
EGS Bank	09.07.2001	18.01.2002			
Toprakbank	30.11.2001	30.09.2002			
Bayındırbank	09.07.2001	-	-	-	Resolution continues

Source: Savings Deposit Insurance Fund (SDIF), *Bank Resolution Experience of the SDIF* (SDIF 2013: 270–272).

re-regulation sold their small-sized banks such as Dışbank, Tekfenbank, MNG Bank and Türkiye Finans, to foreign banks.

In addition, monetary developments in Turkish economy created the ideal market conditions for bank profitability, which induced foreign bank entries. During eight years following the 2001 financial crisis, Turkey had gone through a disinflationary process that brought down interest rates to the levels that were unseen in the post-1980 Turkish economy. To illustrate, the overnight interbank rate, which indicates the minimum rate of return on money available in the market, declined from 59 per cent to 5 per cent (when measured in quarterly averages) from the first quarter of 2002 to the first quarter of 2012. The lasting downward trend of the overnight interbank rate starting from 2001 is clearly observable in Figure 8.5 below. Moreover, despite the decline in interest rates, the Turkish lira did not depreciate against the US

Table 8.11 Selected Mergers in the Banking Sector

	Banks Merged	*Title After Merger*	*Market Share Before Merger (%)*	*Market Share After Merger (%)*	*Conglomerate*
31.08.2001	Körfezbank and Osmanlı Bankası	Osmanlı Bankası	2.22	3.19	Doğuş Holding
14.12.2001	Osmanlı Bankası and Garanti Bankası	Garanti Bankası	6.12	9.54	
29.03.2002	Sınai Yatırım Bankası and T. Sınai Kalkınma Bankası	T. Sınai Kalkınma Bankası (TSKB)	0.40	0.75	İş Bankası
03.04.2003	Fibabank and Finansbank	Finansbank	2.32	2.52	Fiba Group
19.09.2005	Ak Uluslararası Bankası and Akbank	Akbank	13.25	13.35	Sabancı Holding
02.10.2006	Koçbank and Yapı ve Kredi Bankası	Yapı ve Kredi Bankası	6.10	10.08	Koç Holding

Source: Compiled and calculated from statistics of the Banks Association of Turkey.

Note: Quarterly balance sheets that immediately follow the merger date are used to calculate the after-merger ratio (as percentage of total banking assets).

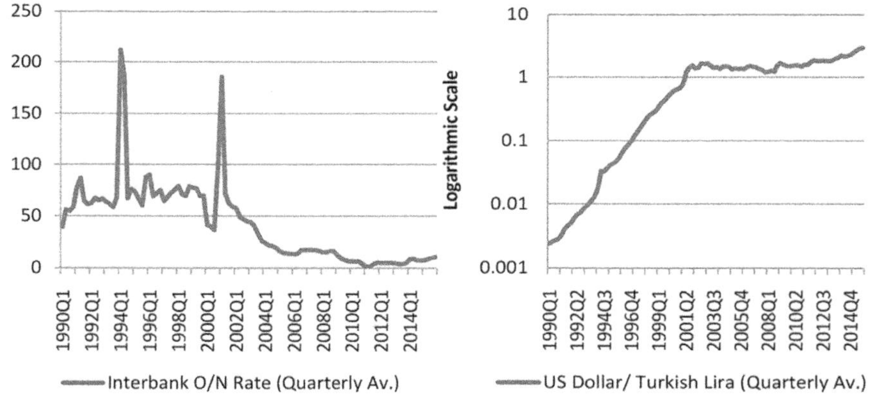

Figure 8.5 Interbank Overnight Rate (Turkey) and US $/TL Exchange rate
Source: CBRT, Electronic Data Delivery System. For interbank overnight Rate (weighted average), series code TP.PY.P06.ON; for US $/TL (the new TL conversion made), series code TP.DK.USD.S.EF.YTL.

Table 8.12 M&As by Foreign Financial Institutions in the Banking Sector, 2002–14 (US $ billion)

Target	*Value*	*Stake (%)*	*Buyer*	*Country of Buyer*	*Seller*	*Year*
A. Acquisitions						
Koçbank	0.24	50	UniCredito	Italy	Koç Holding	2002
Türk Ekonomi Bankası	0.22	42	BNP Paribas	France	Çolakoğlu Metalurji	2004
Dış Ticaret Bankası (Dışbank)	1.14	89	Fortis Bank	Belgium, Netherlands	Doğan Holding	2005
Yapı ve Kredi Bankası	4.60	57	Koçbank	Turkey, Italy	Çukurova Holding	2005
C Yatırım ve Kalkınma B. (renamed BankPozitif)	0.13	58	Bank Hapoalim	Israel	Cıngıllı Holding	2005
Garanti Bankası	1.56	26	GE Consumer Finance	USA	Doğuş Holding	2005
Finansbank	2.77	46	National Bank of Greece	Greece	Fiba Group	2006
Tekfenbank	0.18	70	EFG Eurobank	Greece	Tekfen Holding	2006
Denizbank	2.44	75	Dexia Bank	Belgium	Zorlu Holding	2006
MNG Bank (renamed Turkland Bank)	0.16	91	Arab Bank, Bank Med	Jordan, Lebanon	Mehmet Nazif Günal	2006
OYAK Bank	2.67	100	ING Bank	Netherlands	OYAK	2007
Türkiye Finans Katılım Bankası (Türkiye Finans)	1.08	60	National Commercial Bank	Saudi Arabia	Yıldız Holding, Boydak Group	2007
Eurobank Tekfen	0.36	99	Burgan Bank	Kuwait	Eurobank Ergasias	2010
Garanti Bankası	5.80	25	BBVA	Spain	Doğuş Holding, GE Capital	2010
Denizbank	3.78	100	Sberbank	Russian Federation	Dexia Bank	2012
AlternatifBank	0.42	71	Commercial Bank of Qatar	Qatar	Anadolu Endüstri H.	2013
Tekstil Bankası	0.32	76	Ind. and Comm. Bank of China	China	GSD Holding	2014
Garanti Bankası	2.47	15	BBVA	Spain	Doğuş Holding	2014
B. Minority Stake Purchases						
Akbank	3.10	20	Citibank	USA	Sabancı Holding	2006
Şekerbank	0.26	34	TuranAlem Securities	Kazakhstan	Şekerbank VPF*	2006
Turkish Bank	0.16	40	National Bank of Kuwait	Kuwait	Özyol Holding	2007
C. Mergers						
Türk Ekonomi Bankası	n.a	n.app.	Fortis Bank (Turkey Branch)	n.a.	n.app.	2010

Source: Compiled from Emerging Markets Information System (EMIS), DealWatch Database.

Note: *Şekerbank Voluntary Pension Fund (VPF); n.a. = not available.

dollar as fast as it did in the 1990s. In fact, as Figure 8.5 shows, after years of the lira's speedy depreciation, the dollar/lira rate fluctuated inside the 1.2–1.6 band between 2002 and 2011.

The stability, and at times, nominal revaluation, of the Turkish lira, in combination with falling inflation and interest rates, laid the groundwork for market conditions that led to an increase in bank profits. First, a gradually declining interest rate expanded the capitalized value of all income-bearing assets, including bank assets, almost with no effort. Meanwhile, bank liabilities, instead of financing government debt, were now channelled to the private sector and household loans (OECD 2011: 593–594). Turkish public and private banks saw an opportunity to generate new sources of returns, benefitting especially from Turkey's low level of household indebtedness. Thereby, the creation of a debt-financed, domestic consumption-led growth in the economy also improved bank profits (see Chapter 5).

Keen to take advantage of this promising market conjuncture, several important foreign financial institutions acquired controlling stakes in Turkey's largest banks. As Table 8.12 shows, UniCredito, BNP Paribas, General Electric, Citibank and BBVA were in this group. Others, such as Fortis, Dexia, ING and the National Bank of Greece preferred completely to disenfranchise the former owners, and they found ready sellers as a consequence of inflated asset values. As a result of foreign bank penetration to the Turkish banking sector, the diversity of financial products in the banking sector increased (see Chapter 6), and several prominent domestic holding groups like Tekfen, Doğan, Zorlu, Anadolu, OYAK, Yıldız and Boydak withdrew from banking for good.

Conclusion

The ratio of non-operating income to after-tax profits of the top 500 industrial firms in Turkey increased throughout the 1980s and 1990s, reaching extremely high levels between 1999 and 2002 before settling around 35 per cent. Main sources of these non-operating incomes were interest incomes and foreign exchange gains. When the Central Bank's Company Accounts statistics were investigated for the 1998–2010 period, it was observed that the level of non-operating income was almost as high as operating income in manufacturing and more than operating income in the services and construction sectors. These findings support the conclusion that financial liberalization in Turkey has shifted the conditions in which non-financial sector activities take place toward the pursuit of financial earnings.

For the period 2005–14, around US $199 billion worth of M&As were recorded, which approximately corresponded to one-tenth of all the Turkish economy's gross fixed capital formation for the period. This chapter argued that this level of activity pointed to the emergence of the Turkish M&A market to be understood as a facet of financialization in Turkey. Some characteristics of this market were: i) acquisitions were the major form of deals; ii)

M&As in financial services, manufacturing, and utilities made up 59 per cent of the total deal value; iii) average M&A deal size was around $130 million; iv) top M&As involved an exchange of large chunks of market share; and v) foreign and domestic buyers, and privatizations and private sector deals, were equally salient, while private equity funds played a marginal role.

A number of factors were underlined to explain the significance of foreign investors and privatisations in M&A transactions. The year 2005 signalled an upsurge in the wave of cross-border M&As globally, which remained strong towards developing economies even after the global financial crisis began. Turkey did join this new wave because in contrast to the mid-1990s, the Turkish market, following a two-decade-long neoliberal regulatory restructuring, was finally open for large-scale M&As. Certain aspects of this restructuring were detailed in the third section of this chapter in relation to the Türk Telekom privatization. Under the AKP government, Turkey implemented a thorough privatization programme that resulted in selling-off its blue-chip assets. Privatizations in telecommunications, petroleum refining, petrochemicals, liquor, steel manufacturing, and electricity distribution enabled the incumbent domestic and foreign buyers to corner these oligopolistic markets. Thereby, a core objective that the transnational corporations might have expected from globalization was accomplished. Furthermore, Turkey's macroeconomic conjuncture helped M&As. Turkey's rapid economic growth, stagnant real wages, normalizing inflation and interest rates, and stable (at times, appreciating) currency promised high returns to capital, and inflated the asset values in the economy, implying lucrative entry and exit opportunities in the M&A market for the period in question. As discussed in the third section, the Turkish banking sector was among the beneficiaries of and the contributors to this rapid expansion period. High profitability of the Turkish banks, especially in comparison to bank profitability in several European countries, and the new bank regulations that were put in place, encouraged foreign entry to this sector. Most of this entry took the form of acquisitions and placed banking at the forefront of the Turkish M&A market, with the highest transaction volumes.

Notes

1 In a reported case where the interest rate on a deposit was 58 per cent, the cost of credit to a client could reach 105 per cent; and where the interest rate on a deposit was 80 per cent, the interest rate for borrowing reached 151 per cent (Sönmez, 1992: 33).

2 Data are accessible via www.tcmb.org.tr.

3 The spectacular fall in profit rates in 1992–93 is intimately related with the major losses of state economic enterprises within the sample in these years. Otherwise, profit rates generally tend to be lower during the crisis periods (i.e. 1994 and 2000–01).

4 For this period, average rates of sales profitability is calculated as 6.6 per cent in the private and 4.3 per cent in the public sector. The public sector registered higher profitability rates than private sector in the years 1985, 1986, 2002, 2003, 2004, 2008, 2009 and 2010. "The most striking result was obtained in 1991 with the

lowest rate of −12 per cent. The relevant figure was −10.1 per cent in 1992. However, there are certain reasons for these results. Turkish Electricity Company (TEK) which comes the second after Tüpraş in the ranking based on sales from production started to take part in questionnaires 1985. Furthermore, TEKEL which would only submit certain data up to that date, started to send full statements for the survey. In 1990 the share of TEK in public sector was 16 per cent according to sales from production and 20 per cent according to net value added. The developments in TEK have always affected the state of public sector. TEK made profit only in 1985 and 1986 and since then has claimed losses for each year" (Özmucur, 1993: 113).

5 "When the value added created by company is calculated, the pre-tax balance sheet profit is not directly included as factor income. If income generated through non-industrial activities is included in total profit, it is subtracted from balance-sheet profit, which gives us profit as share of national income. And this figure is then included in the value added as factor income" (ICI 1993: 59).

6 Operating profitability is defined as ratio of operating profits (which are net sales minus cost of goods sold minus operating expenses) to net sales (Demir, 2009: 322).

7 The Company Accounts (CA) statistics of the Central Bank of the Republic of Turkey are based on firms' non-consolidated balance sheets and income tables that are reported to the Turkish Revenue Administration. Only firms with positive loan balance vis-à-vis the financial sector enter the statistics. Each CA volume covers a three-year period; therefore, a firm's financial tables for three consecutive years must be available in the Central Bank system for it to be included in the statistics. These criteria and other updates give rise to differences among the CA volumes regarding the number of firms and the sectoral divisions. For example, for the period of 2008–10, balance sheets of 8,576 firms were compiled into 16 main and 30 sub-sectors whereas, for 2006–08, data included 13 main and 26 sub-sectors from only 7,352 firms. Here, to obtain a time-series that covers 1998–2010, we simply reorganise the data into five main sectors, i.e., manufacturing, services, construction, energy, and agriculture, and calculate the ratios of operating incomes and non-operating incomes in total incomes. Operating incomes are sales profits minus operating costs. Non-operating incomes mainly consist of interest incomes and exchange gains. Total income is operating plus non-operating incomes. We are thankful to Zafer Barış Gül for his valuable comments and suggestions on the CA statistics.

8 Caution must be exercised in comparing the Company Accounts (CA) statistics with the ICI's top 500 industrial firms records. The ICI records, although nationwide, are based on information obtained by questionnaires filled out by the firms. It is not possible to say which top 500 firms are included in the CA statistics in which years, or whether they are covered at all unless the CA volume makes it explicit. The top 500 industrial firms include electricity generation companies whereas the manufacturing sector in the CA statistics does not.

9 Before the Communiqué was in effect, a market share threshold was also applied as a criterion of notification; however, the market share basis of notification was repealed in the new communiqué. For further information on the historical development of Turkey's primary and secondary competition legislation, see Öz (2013).

10 For such an effort, see Akdoğu (2011: 140).

11 Table 8.2 draws the number of M&As from various TCA Annual Reports (2008: 82; 2010: 56; 2015: 50). Still, it needs stressing that figures in Table 8.2 do not represent the total number of 'closed' (completed) deals in Turkey. First, they do not cover deals that do not fulfil the conditions set by the Communiqué. However, if an 'out of scope' transaction had nonetheless been notified to the TCA, as has been occasionally done, it enters into the figures. Second, there are deals that the TCA denied clearance and those that were stopped following the TCA clearance.

Table 8.2 does not check for these refused applications or cancelled deals. Third, outbound deals, i.e., foreign M&As executed by firms located in Turkey, too, require notification and are included. Fourth, M&As in the banking sector have been made exempt from the TCA control since 2001. All these factors reduce the suitableness of the official TCA data to reflect the exact number of M&As closed in Turkey annually.

12 Data since 2006 are accessible via www.datagrapple.com. For comparison with pre-2006, if the period from October 2008 to July 2009 (in which the global economic crisis made a serious impact on Turkey's CDS) is overlooked, it is possible say that Turkey's 1-year CDS spread never passed 200 bps between 2006 and 2014.

13 Upon the request of authors, EY's İstanbul Office kindly shared eight annual reports for years from 2002 to 2009, which were inaccessible via the website.

14 For information on the basis of preparation of EY Reports, see EY (2015: 32).

15 The difference with the gross basis being that the net value of cross-border M&A sales takes into account foreign firms' divestments in a host economy. When a foreign firm sells its operation in the host economy, this transaction raises the gross value of M&As, but decreases the net value of M&As.

16 It can be reminded that this estimate (9.8 per cent) reflects only transactions with disclosed transaction values, and that general government investment expenditures are included in the GFCF. A disadvantage of the newly estimated national income series (base year 2009) published by TurkStat is that the private sector component of the GFCF cannot be observed separately. There is also an ongoing discussion among economists that TurkStat overestimates the GFCF due to its change of methodology in valuing construction. The upshot being that the ratio of M&As to GFCF may be higher in reality.

17 Radikal (5 September 2009) 'Sigortada birleşmeler yaşanabilir'. http://goo.gl/QdZEkK.

18 E.g., consider a hypothetical market in which 4 firms share equally 68 per cent of the market (each with 17 per cent market share) and the remaining 32 per cent market share is divided equally among 32 firms (each with 1 per cent). The CR_4 for this market is 68 per cent, which signifies high concentration in the market. Whereas the HHI gives $4(0.17)^2 + 32(0.01)^2 = 0.1188$, which says this is an unconcentrated market.

19 For a list of top M&As by private equity firms, see Bedirhanoğlu et al. (2013: 295).

20 A client, whose electricity consumption is above a legally identified limit, is eligible to become a "free consumer". For more information, see Bahçe and Taymaz (2008: 1605).

21 For the transaction details, see *Official Gazette* (19 March 2013). http://goo.gl/Ou34zY.

22 Koçbank merged with Yapı Kredi, and Oyakbank became ING Bank.

23 These court cases pertain to the Statutory Decree No. 509 (and its authorizing law), Law No. 4000 (certain clauses), and Law No. 4107, respectively (Atiyas 2009: 112).

24 For this decision, see Constitutional Court Decision 2005/104 in *Official Gazette* (21 September 2006).

25 Additional Article 17 (clause 3) of Law No. 406.

26 Article 1, Law No. 5369. For more on universal service in Turkey, see Oğuz (2013).

27 In 2008, another 15 per cent of TTAŞ shares were privatised through initial public offering in Borsa İstanbul, this time raising US $2.4 billion. 30 per cent of the company is still owned by the Undersecretariat of the Treasury.

28 Information Technologies and Communications Authority (ITCA) replaced the Telecommunications Authority (TA) in 2008.

29 To clarify the status of these transactions in relation to the value of M&As that were presented in the previous section, in principle, amalgamations carried out by

the SDIF to restructure banks are excluded from Tables 8.3 and 8.4 whereas the sales made by the SDIF to private parties are covered by them. This is issue does not interfere with our comments since transactions of large value (Demirbank and Sitebank) were realised prior to 2002 and the EY Reports do not go back as far to include them. None the less, the importance of these takeovers is obvious when the prices involved in their re-sale to foreign banks are considered (e.g., OYAK Bank and Denizbank deals in Table 8.12).

30 This exception continues to be in force in the Banking Law No. 5411 (Article 19), despite criticism from the OECD (Öz 2015: 79).

REFERENCES

Akdoğu, E. (2011) "Türkiye'de 1988–2008 Döneminde Firma Birleşmeleri, Birleşme Dalgaları ve Genel Tablo", *Muhasebe ve Finansman Dergisi,* 52: 137–152.

Akyüz, Y. (1990) "Financial System and Policies in Turkey in the 1980s", in *The Political Economy of Turkey: Debt, Adjustment and Sustainability*, T. Arıcanlı and D. Rodrik (eds.). London: Palgrave Macmillan, 98–131.

Akyüz, Y. (1991) "Trade and Finance: Some Policy Dilemmas", *Unpublished seminar*, Antalya.

Arıcan, E., B. T. Yücememiş, M.E. Karabay and G. Işıl (2011) *Türk Bankacılık Sektöründe Ölçek Ekonomileri, Pazar Hakimiyeti ve Rekabet Gücü, Maliyet Etkinliği ve Ölçek Ekonomilerine İlişkin Ekonometrik Bir Uygulama*. İstanbul: Türkiye Bankalar Birliği.

Atiyas, I. (2005) *Regulation and Competition in Turkish Telecommunications Industry*, Ankara: TEPAV.

Atiyas, I. (2009) "Recent Privatization Experience of Turkey: A Reappraisal", in Z. Öniş and F. Şenses (eds.) *Turkey and the Global Economy: Neo-liberal restructuring and integration in the post-crisis era*, New York: Routledge, 101–122.

Bahçe, S. and E. Taymaz (2008) "The impact of electricity market liberalization in Turkey 'Free consumer' and distributional monopoly cases", *Energy Economics* 30: 1603–1624.

Balkan, E. and E. Yeldan (2002) "Peripheral Development under Financial Liberalization. The Turkish Experience", in E. Balkan and S. Savran (eds.) *The Ravages of Neoliberalism: Economy, Society and Gender in Turkey*, New York: Nova Science, 39–54.

Bedirhanoğlu, P., H. Cömert, İ. Eren, I. Erol, D. Demiröz, N. Erdem, A. R.Güngen, T. Marois, A. Topal, O.Türel, G. Yalman, E. Yeldan, and E. Voyvoda (2013) *Comparative Perspective on Financial System in the EU: Country Report on Turkey*, FESSUD Studies in Financial Systems No. 11.

Bilgen Özeke, H. (2005) "New law renews investors' faith in arbitration", *International Financial Law Review*, 3: 68.

Boratav, K. (2007) *Türkiye İktisat Tarihi 1908–2005*. İstanbul: İmge Yayınevi.

Boratav, K., E. Yeldan and A. Köse (2000) "Globalization, Distribution, and Social Policy: Turkey: 1980–1998", *CEPA Working Paper Series*, No 20, Center for Economic Policy Analysis, New School University.

CGFS–Committee on the Global Financial System (2011) "Global Liquidity–Concept, Measurement and Policy Implications", *Bank of International Settlements*, CGFS Paper No. 45.

Demir, F. (2009) "Financial liberalization, private investment and portfolio choice: Financialization of real sectors in emerging markets", *Journal of Development Economics*, 88(2): 314–324.

Deniz, G. (2014) *Global Slowdown Hits Pricing Outlook!* Iron & Steel Sector (December 17), İstanbul: Yatırım Finansman Securities, Retrieved from Emerging Markets Information Service (EMIS) Database on 20 August 2015.

EMRA–Energy Market Regulatory Authority (2015) *Elektrik Piyasası 2014 Yılı Piyasa Gelişim Raporu*, Ankara: T.C. Enerji Piyasası Düzenleme Kurumu.

Erdoğan, T., M. B. Akkaya, N. Ünübol, E. İnce, and S. Işık (2012) *Türkiye Hızlı Tüketim Malları (HTM) Perkakendeciliği Sektör İncelemesi Nihai Raporu*, Ankara: Rekabet Kurumu,

EY–Ernst &Young (2015) *Mergers and Acquisitions Report Turkey 2014*. İstanbul: EY Turkey.

Ferraz, J. C. and N. Hamaguchi (2002) "Introduction: M&A and Privatization in Developing Countries", *The Developing Economies*, 40(4): 383–399.

Francis, J. A. (2013) "The Buy-to-Build Indicator: New Estimates for Britain and the United States", *Review of Capital as Power*, 1(1): 63–72.

Gültekin-Karakaş, D. (2009) *Hem Hasımız Hem Hısımız Türkiye Finans Kapitalinin Dönüşümü ve Banka Reformu*. İstanbul: İletişim Yayınları.

High Audit Committee (2009) *Genel Rapor 2001–2005*, Ankara: T.C. Başbakanlık Yüksek Denetleme Kurulu.

High Audit Committee (2014) *Kamu İşletmeleri 2013 Yılı Genel Raporu*, Ankara: T.C. Sayıştay Başkanlığı.

ICI–İstanbul Chamber of Industry (2015) "Türkiye'nin 500 Büyük Sanayi Kuruluşu 2014", *İstanbul Sanayi Odası Dergisi*, Özel Sayı.

ICI–İstanbul Chamber of Industry (2007) "Türkiye'nin 500 Büyük Sanayi Kuruluşu 2006", *İstanbul Sanayi Odası Dergisi*, 497.

ICI–İstanbul Chamber of Industry (1993) "Türkiye'nin 500 Büyük Sanayi Kuruluşu" *İstanbul Sanayi Odası Dergisi*, 330.

Insurance and Supervision Board (2015) *Annual Report about Insurance and Individual Pension Activities 2014*, Ankara: Republic of Turkey Prime Ministry Undersecretariat of Treasury.

ITCA–Information Technologies and Communication Authority (2015) *Türkiye Elektronik Haberleşme Sektörü Üç Aylık Pazar Verileri Raporu, 2015 Yılı 3.Çeyrek*, Ankara: Bilgi Teknolojileri ve İletişim Kurumu.

Keller, C., P. Kunzel and M. Souto (2007) "Measuring Sovereign Risk in Turkey: An Application of the Contingent Claims Approach", *International Monetary Fund Working Paper*, WP/07/233, Washington, DC, International Monetary Fund.

Kilci, M. (2005) "Kick-starting the sell-off", *MEED Middle East Economic Digest*, 49 (39): 36–37.

Korkut, D .Ş., E. Sesli, and E. Kalkan (2014) "Türkiye İmalat Sanayiinde Yapı-Davranış-Performans Analizi: 2003–2008", *Rekabet Dergisi*, 15(3): 3–36.

Krippner, G. R. (2011) *Capitalizing on Crisis: The Political Origins of the Rise of Finance*. Cambridge, Massachusetts: Harvard University Press.

Marois, T. (2011) "Emerging Market Bank Rescues in an Era of Finance-Led Neoliberalism: A Comparison of Mexico and Turkey", *Review of International Political Economy*, 18(2): 168–196.

Marois, T. (2012) *States, Banks and Crisis: Emerging Finance Capitalism in Mexico and Turkey*. Cheltenham: Edward Elgar Publishing.

Ministry of the Economy (2015) *Uluslararası Doğrudan Yatırım Verileri Bülteni*, Ankara: T.C. Ekonomi Bakanlığı.

Nitzan, J. and S. Bichler (2009) *Capital as Power: A Study of Order and Creorder*, New York: Routledge.

Organisation for Economic Co-operation and Development (OECD) (2002) *Regulatory Reform in Turkey: Regulatory Reform in the Telecommunications Industry*, Paris: OECD.

Organisation for Economic Co-operation and Development (OECD) (2011) *Bank Profitability: Financial Statements of Banks 2010: OECD Banking Statistics*, Paris: OECD.

Oğuz, F. (2013) Universal Service in Turkey: Recent developments and a critical assessment. *Telecommunications Policy*, 37: 13–23.

Öz, G. (2013) "Competition Law in Turkey from Association to Accession", in B. Akçay and Ş. Akipek (eds.) *Turkey's Integration into the European Union: Legal Dimension*, Plymouth: Lexington Books, 51–72.

Öz, G. (2015) *Avrupa Birliği ve Türk Rekabet Hukukunun Bankacılık Alanında Uygulanması*. Ankara: Yetkin Yayınları.

Özmucur, S. (1993) Türkiye'nin 500 Büyük Firmasının Finans Yapısı. *İstanbul Sanayi Odası Dergisi*, 330.

Repková, I. and D. Stavárek (2014) "Concentration and Competition in the Banking Sector of Turkey", *Amfiteatru Economic*, 16(36): 625–640.

Rittenberg, L. (1991) "Investment Spending and Interest Rate Policy: the Case of Financial Liberalization in Turkey", *The Journal of Development Studies*, 27(2): 151–167.

SDIF–Savings Deposit Insurance Fund (2013) *Bank Resolution Experience of the SDIF*, İstanbul: Savings Deposit Insurance Fund.

Sönmez, M. (1992) *Türkiye'de Holdingler Kırk Haramiler*, İstanbul: ArkadasYayınları.

TCA–Turkish Competition Authority (2008) *9. Yıllık Rapor 2007 Yılı*. Ankara: Rekabet Kurumu.

TCA–Turkish Competition Authority (2010) *11. Yıllık Rapor 2009*, Ankara: Rekabet Kurumu

TCA–Turkish Competition Authority (2015) *16. Yıllık Rapor 2014*, Ankara: Rekabet Kurumu.

Türel, O. (1993) "1980–1992 Döneminde Türkiye'de Finansal Yapı ve Politikalar", in O. Türel and İ. Önder (eds.) *Türkiye'de Kamu Maliyesi, Finansal Yapı ve Politikalar*, İstanbul: Tarih Vakfı Yurt Yayınları, 119–174.

UNCTAD–United Nations Conference on Trade and Development (2000) *World Investment Report 2000–Cross-border Mergers and Acquisitions and Development*, Geneva: United Nations.

UNCTAD–United Nations Conference on Trade and Development (2014) "The Recent Turmoil in Emerging Economies", *UNCTAD Policy Briefs*, No. 29.

UNCTAD–United Nations Conference on Trade and Development (2015) *World Investment Report 2015–Reforming International Investment Governance*, Geneva: United Nations.

US Department of Justice and the Federal Trade Commission (2010) *Horizontal Merger Guidelines*, 19 August 2010, Washington, DC: Federal Trade Commission.

9 The State, Crisis and Transformation of Small and Medium-sized Enterprise Finance in Turkey

Aylin Topal

Small and medium-sized enterprises (SMEs) still constitute the backbone of the Turkish economy in the neoliberal era. According to the latest TurkStat data[1], in 2014 SMEs accounted for 99.8 per cent of the total enterprises in Turkey, 73.5 per cent of total employment, 54.1 per cent of wages, 62 per cent of total sales turnover, 53.5 per cent of total value-added, 55 per cent of gross investment and 55.1 per cent of total exports. Yet as the McKinsey Global Institute (MGI) (2003) and the OECD (2014) reports suggest, it is the 'dual structure' of large and small enterprises in Turkey that constitutes a 'growth constraint' (cf. MGI 2003: 39), as small enterprises dominate the employment market with their low average labour productivity (OECD 2014: 84). However, it is also possible to evaluate such a 'dual structure' with its productivity-enhancing effects through consortia, franchising and subcontracting that organically connect SMEs to large enterprises (cf. Taymaz 2009). Through these common practices, Turkish SMEs set the wage index for the whole sector in which they operate across different enterprise sizes. As greater profit shares are directly dependent on the wage index in the economy, the employment capacity of the Turkish SMEs has a cost-saving effect for a given sector across different size levels. Therefore, it would not be an overstatement to assert that as Turkish SMEs have cut the costs of production, this in turn has increased the competitiveness of Turkish capital and facilitated new patterns of competitive integration of large enterprises into international markets. However, the challenges of SMEs to remain competitive are many. One recurrent theme has been the problem of accessible and affordable finance.

This chapter explains the impact of Turkey's financial transformation since the 1980s on domestic SMEs. As is common in bank-based emerging markets like Turkey, SMEs have faced difficulties in accessing sources of sustainable finance with the transition to neoliberalism. During the 1990s, governments responded with new public credit mechanisms for SMEs. Then in the 2000s, private banks in Turkey saw SME finance as an increasingly appealing source of returns. This chapter argues that in order to integrate the SMEs into their sectoral networks, the Turkish state, as the risk-taker of last resort, provided financial support for the SMEs. Increasing state support for SMEs is not incompatible with the modalities of a neoliberal capital accumulation strategy. Since the transformation of the banking sector is part and parcel of the transformation of the whole economy, private banks seemed to orient themselves towards opening up new sources of finance for SMEs, provided that the public resources would be made available for strengthening financial credentials and accounting capabilities. Furthermore, this analysis brings to the fore the state as a nodal regulatory agency enabling interpenetration of capital and its overall circulation in the economy. This argument will be laid out in four sections. The first section briefly pictures the formation of the Turkish business community in the post-war era until the 1980s. The second section discusses the initial adjustment attempt of SME finance through Turkey's transition to neoliberalism from the early 1980s to 2001. The third section focuses on the emergence of innovative SMEs finance sources channelled through public and private resources in the post-2001 period. The fourth section focuses on the impact of the 2008 crisis on SME finance. Finally, the fifth section takes stock of these policies by evaluating the available Central Bank of the Republic of Turkey dataset of manufacturing sector balance sheets across firms of different sizes.

Structural and Institutional Differentiation of the Turkish Business Community in the Post-War Era

Post-war policies shaped the business community in line with the concentration and centralization tendencies of capital. While these policies aimed at Turkey's integration into the global economy, the concomitant capital accumulation brought about the dominance of family-controlled holding groups.[2] Credits extended by the Industrial Development Bank of Turkey, which was established in June 1950, helped the establishment and development of enterprises in a wide range of manufacturing activities. These horizontally diversified enterprises benefited from incentive policies enacted by the state during a period of balance of payments difficulties (Yalman 2009: 267). Moreover, increasing state investments favoured private firms as nominated state contractors in infrastructure and construction activities (Buğra 1994). These private firms had evolved into holding groups following the enactment of the 1958 Banking Law and the subsequent changes in taxation legislation, which in turn enabled them to access sources of finance to help boost their investments in new growth industries (see Chapter 2 in this volume).

In the background of the emergence of holding groups and the strengthening of large corporations, institutional differentiation of the Turkish business community was taking place. The 1950 Law of Chambers led to the creation of a hierarchical business association, the Union of Chambers and Commodity Exchanges (TOBB), as the legal organization for all industrial and, predominantly, commercial firms, of which they were obliged to become members.[3] However, while TOBB had represented all business interests on paper, the interests of holding groups and large corporates started to conflict with Turkey's smaller enterprises towards the late 1960s. The conflict emerged over the direction of Turkey's import-substitution industrialization policies, as the holding groups had a degree of flexibility to shift between different domains of activity (for example, banking, manufacturing, foreign trade, tourism, construction) in accordance with the changing priorities of macroeconomic policies. As Fernand Braudel (1982: 433) aptly describes, this specific institutional form of capital brings a relatively higher adaptation capacity, namely, "to slip at a moment's notice from one form or sector to another, in times of crisis or of pronounced decline in profit rates". In 1971 the large holding groups united under the umbrella of a voluntary employers' union, Turkish Industry and Business Association (TÜSİAD). In its own words, TÜSİAD emerged as a "reaction of the business world to the non-functioning and crisis-generating closed economy system".[4] This employers' union has since become the most effective organization in co-ordinating and directing the whole business community in defining the crisis of the late 1970s and setting the new direction of the economy in transition to neoliberalism.

For much of the early 20th century, development experts believed SMEs hindered the process of economic development with their "informal labor relations" and "pre-modern technologies"; yet, by the 1980s international organizations and policymakers started to acknowledge the vitality of SMEs (Taymaz 1997: 41). In the post-war period, import-substitution industrialization favoured large-scale production for the advantage entailed in the economies of scale (Özar 2007: 245). SMEs thus attracted little attention as rapid industrialization strategies meant facilitating the corporate sector in general and holding groups in particular. However, in the midst of new economic processes and of the global crisis of the late 1970s, a clear sea change in the evaluation of SMEs appeared. Expansion of global production chains, and the subsequent relocation of manufacturing activities internationally to jurisdictions with lower costs, brought SMEs to the fore (Özar 2007: 245). SMEs were increasingly becoming an integrated part of rotation and valorization of capital both nationally and internationally. It was in those years that the United Nations Industrial Development Organization underlined the significance of industrial subcontracting through SMEs for a smoother path to industrialization; the International Labour Organization defined SMEs as a potential engine for attaining self-sustained economic growth; and the World Bank emphasized the role of SMEs to create income and employment for the poor in urban areas (UNIDO 1974; ILO 1976; World Bank 1978).

However, the global debt crisis of the 1980s caused a tightening in the domestic market and drying up of available credits in Turkey. Many Turkish SMEs that lacked the capacity to produce for the export market, opted to exit. Meanwhile, Turkish holding groups sought to acquire these assets, including by putting adverts in Turkish newspapers calling for SMEs to sell them their operations (Sönmez 1982: 110–111). Turkey's economy began a prolonged phase of capital centralization and concentration within the holding groups, although this would not necessarily eliminate Turkey's numerous SME producers.

SMEs and Financial Adjustments in the 1980s and 1990s

As an important portion of capital and capitalist enterprises, SMEs had to be defined and distinguished from others. For the first time, Turkey's Fourth Five-Year Development Plan (1979–83) mentioned the term 'small industry' separately from the traditional terms of 'tradesmen' and 'craftsmen' (Sarıaslan 1994: 169). However, until 2005 SMEs were classified differently by various organizations, which is also an important factor behind the lack of availability of reliable data on Turkish SMEs. In October 2005 a single definition was ratified by a Council of Ministers' Decree No. 2005/9617, based on the number of employees (Micro: 0–9; Small: 10–49; Medium: 50–249), the size of their annual balance sheet and turnover. Although the criteria for the classification were aligned to the European Union (EU) definition, the limits for the annual balance sheet and turnover were reduced significantly in the Micro, Small and Medium-Size definition relative to the size of the Turkish market. Later in November 2012, the Council of Ministers raised the annual balance sheet and turnover criteria to expand the portion of the enterprises eligible to receive SME-specific supports (see Table 9.1).

Although holding groups and large firms appear to form the most important segment of Turkey's export-oriented industry, the State Planning Agency considered the well-being of Turkish SMEs "as a sign of economic stability as they continued to employ a significantly large amount of the workforce" (DPT 1984: 156). Turkey's Fifth Five Year Development Plan (1985–89) suggested that SMEs attempt to link themselves to large enterprises as subcontractors. The Plan also sets the objective of enhanced financial supports for SMEs through the state-owned Halkbank (DPT 1984: 3, 34). Similarly, the government programme in 1989 noted that SMEs are like the cement needed to consolidate workers and capital, and they thus should be financially supported to boost export capacities.[6] The Sixth Five-Year Development Plan (1990–94) stated the need to improve the financial profile of the SMEs and increase the availability of loans for them without collateral requirements (DPT 1989: 308).

Turkey's Development Plans embodied two additional policy changes that favoured SME expansion. First, in 1990, the government merged two existing, but by then ineffective institutions, the Small Industry Development Organisation (KÜSGET, founded in 1983) and the Industrial Training and Development Centre (SEGEM, founded in 1978). These two became the now powerful Small and Medium Enterprises Development Organisation (KOSGEB), which functions as a major instrument for the execution of SME-specific policies.[7] Second, in 1991 the government established the Credit Guarantee Fund (KGF) with the mission to support SMEs that have limited access to bank loans for lack of collateral. The KGF was established not simply to increase the number of firms accessing bank loans, but to offer more medium- and long-term credits and to increase the loan limits available to SMEs.

The credit guarantee schemes are presented as a key policy tool to address the SME financing gap. In Europe especially, a network of local, regional and sectoral credit guarantee institutions were being formed through the 1990s (cf. OECD 2013: 8). The establishment of the KGF in Turkey was motivated by a Technical Co-operation Agreement co-signed by German and Turkish governments in 1993 to undertake a project entitled 'Assistance in the Establishment of a Loan Guarantee Fund for Small and Medium-Sized Industrial Firms'. "Within the scope of promotion for small and medium-sized industries", the two governments "shall co-operate on the establishment of a loan guarantee fund in selected regions in a two-year pilot phase" (*Official Gazette*, 14 July 1993 no: 21637: 11–12). The German government agreed to employ experts to assist the organization and structure the guarantee fund, workflow organization, and staff training on how to process an application for loan guarantees. The first shareholders of KGF included TOBB (with a 50.99 per cent share), the Confederation of Turkish Tradesmen and Craftsmen (TESK) (with 0.43 per cent), the Free Entrepreneurs and Managers Foundation of Turkey (TOSYÖV) (with 0.01 per cent), and the Vocational Education and Supporting of the Small-Scale Industry Foundation (MEKSA) (with 0.01 per cent). In 1995 KOSGEB entered the partnership followed by Halkbank in March 1996. At the end of the term of the co-operation agreement with Germany, the project seemed to have lost its initial motivation and remained low-profile until 2003.

With the completion of the Customs Union with the EU in 1996, many agree that Turkey's SMEs bore the burden of the initial shock of economic opening and increased competition (OECD 2004: 9). While consecutive Turkish governments promised to help improve SMEs' productivity, international competitiveness, and thus their access to credit, the policies remained insufficient to meet the objectives. By the eve of Customs Union with the EU, 71 per cent of SMEs had yet to access any credit from the banks due to their low level of collateral, despite their declared need for additional funding

Table 9.1 Definitional difference of Micro, Small and Medium-Sized Firms between Turkey and the EU

Criteria			*Size*		
			Micro	*Small*	*Medium*
Annual balance sheet	Turkey (TL)	2005	≤1 Million	≤5 Million	≤25 Million
		2012	≤1 Million	≤8 Million	≤40 Million
	EU (Euro)		≤2 Million	≤10 Million	≤43 Million
Annual turnover	Turkey (TL)	2005	≤1 Million	≤5 Million	≤25 Million
		2012	≤1 Million	≤8 Million	≤40 Million
	EU (Euro)		≤ 2 Million	≤10 Million	≤50 Million

Source: Author's own compilation based on two information sites footnoted below[5].

(Sarıaslan 1996). Arguably in response to SME credit access problems, the government of the time favoured SMEs in the Seventh Five-Year Development Plan (1995–99). After emphasizing their potential to generate jobs, the plan underlined that KOSGEB had not been sufficiently successful in accomplishing its given mission (Müftüoğlu 2009: 13). Thus, the institutional capacity of KOSGEB had to be strengthened (DPT 1995). The Plan also proposed alternative SME financial support and an enhanced credit guarantee fund to ease the shock of implementation of the Customs Union.

In the late 1990s, Turkey's public banks provided new alternative financial resources for the SMEs. Although venture capital (also known as equity participation) practices are typically carried out by financial intermediary companies, in the Turkish context the state-owned banks would emerge as the first risk-takers. Because of the information asymmetry that exists between the SMEs in need of finance and the potential lenders, the venture capital was initially called risk capital. A number of new financial institutions were established in order to supply capital to new or existing firms. These new intermediary institutions would also provide SMEs with assistance in strategy setting and networking, thereby precluding the highrisk of default. To serve such a purpose, two institutions with the support of public banks were established. Vakıf Risk Capital Investment Partnership Company was established in 1996 by VakıfBank, and Partnership to KOBİ Investment, was established in 1999 with the co-financing of TOBB, Halkbank, KOSGEB, TESK and 16 Chambers of Industry and Trade. However, as noted on the official website of the KOBİ Investment Inc. "due to several economic crises and political instabilities" these companies were "unable to become fully operational." Similar to the KGF above, these companies would become active in the field of venture capital after 2003, once "the economical [sic] and political stability was established" according to the prevailing perception.[8]

Throughout the 1990s, the private banks had been mostly catering to the corporate sector, along with public debt. In particular, major private banks affiliated with holding groups financed their own groups (that is, engaged in related lending). In 1988, of the ten Turkish banks comprising about 80 per cent of the total assets of deposit banks, four were state banks, four were holding banks, one was owned and managed by its employee pension fund (Turkish Trade Bank), and the last one was İşBank.[9] Several other holding groups entered the banking sector, while several have since formed joint ventures with foreign trade and investments banks (cf. Buğra 1994: 183). While corporate firms were able to access credit, given their links to private banks, SME finance, albeit insufficient, was predominantly provided by the public banks. As the government of the time refused to compensate the public banks for the losses incurred due to this subsidized lending, the public banks began to accumulate unpaid duty losses, which became a source of risk in Turkey's neoliberal and financial transformation processes (Marois 2012: 175; see also Chapter 6).

The Aftermath of the 2000–01 Crisis and the AKP Period: The Boost for Innovative Financial Instruments

The overwhelming dependence of the Turkish economy on short-term capital flows in the 1990s posed a threat to political as well as economic stability. Although export promotion policies in the 1980s were implemented with a competitive exchange rate policy, the 1989 capital account liberalization required a reversal of this policy, resulting in high real interest rates and an appreciated domestic currency. Increasing financial inflows otherwise known as 'hot money' flows became the main remedy for the soaring public sector borrowing requirement. Meanwhile, volatile and speculative financial flows trapped the Turkish economy within the newly emerging financial global cycles and exogenous pressures on exchange rates.

Such a defenceless financial market against volatile flows of foreign capital rendered the pegged-exchange rate regime unsustainable. According to a letter of intent written by the Ministry of State for Economic Affairs and the Governor of the Central Bank addressed to the Managing Director of the International Monetary Fund (IMF), dated 9 December 1999:

> [s]peculative and arbitrage activities have attracted more and more resources, and have distorted the working of financial markets and institutions.... Moreover high real interest rates, together with a weak fiscal primary position have pushed public finances onto an unsustainable path. Public sector debt- including the so-called duty losses of state banks and the net asset position of the central bank- is projected to increase from 44 percent of GNP at end-1998 to 58 percent of GNP at end-1999. This leaves Turkey vulnerable to swings in international financial markets' confidence."[10]

Soon enough, the acknowledged macroeconomic instability brought a series of severe economic-cum-political crisis starting in November 2000. With severe liquidity shortage in the domestic markets, the government requested to access the Supplementary Reserve Facility from the IMF. The request was granted to calm down the markets. When a dispute between the Prime Minister and the President was exposed, the Central Bank had to sell its foreign reserves to counteract skyrocketing short-term interest rate above 5,000 percent. The government was forced to declare to end the pegged exchange rate and let the exchange rate float (Yeldan 2001).

The Transition to a Strong Economy Programme of 2001, which was put together in the wake of this severe crisis, aimed to enhance the capacity of the Turkish financial system. Along with the switch to a floating exchange rate, the resilience against external shocks would be increased with stringent institutional supervisory mechanisms. New state regulatory capacities helped to mitigate risk perceptions of both the public and private banks (Marois 2012: 170). To attain these objectives, the government set new higher capital requirements, and clearer loan limits for Turkish banks, and more stringent conditions for mergers and acquisitions. Finally, changes rendered the use of public banks to absorb official duty losses without compensation from the government obsolete.

In line with Turkey's new more stringent financial discipline, the government changed Ziraat Bank's and Halkbank's mandate so that they must be profitable, which in turn made it more difficult for the SMEs to access cheap public bank loans. At the same time, the government raised the spectre of the privatization of Ziraat Bank and Halkbank, further constraining banks' cash management. In response, the two banks increased their loan interest rates.[11] Although these two banks still remained public as of 2018, they have been restructured as increasingly market-oriented and this has altered the scope of their traditional developmental activities.

In the immediate aftermath of the 2000–01 crisis, while public banks were to be rolled back to help manage unemployment levels, new support programmes for SMEs through 'innovative' financial instruments would be advanced. Although there were certain institutional innovations in the late 1990s, as already mentioned above, in opening new financial channels for SMEs, they remained relatively inactive until 2003. That is to say, the development of non-traditional financial instruments had been lagging behind the demand for increased availability of financial resources for SMEs.

The electoral triumph of the Adalet ve Kalkınma Partisi (AKP—Justice and Development Party) in the November 2002 elections formed Turkey's first single-party government since 1991. Turkish business circles and international financial markets in general responded positively. As economic analysis released by Merrill Lynch clearly pointed out "the arrival of a single-party government would strengthen Turkey's economic balances".[12] And the new governing party did not disappoint these expectations. It proved to be a suitable actor that could accelerate the process of neoliberal transformation, progressively lifting the institutional barriers to financialization and privatization from 2003 onwards.

At the same time, the AKP government echoed both the EU and Organisation for Economic Co-operation and Development (OECD) standpoints, with an emphasis on its commitment to boost competitiveness and the capabilities of the SMEs. Furthermore, government authorities emphasized that new export markets for the SMEs would be explored. In order to facilitate SMEs' access to finance, the AKP Government Programme, the Eighth Five Year (2000–05), the Ninth (2007–13)[13] and the Tenth (2014–18) Development Plans called for improved 'innovative' financial instruments. In these texts, the KGF, venture capital and start-up capital, which could be considered as a form of venture capital, were mentioned in a more emphasized fashion than in the Seventh Five-Year Development Plan. The 2002 Regular Report on Turkey's Progress Towards Accession to the EU included an SME action plan among the short-term priorities, which also required harmonization of the SME definition.[14] Turkey's SME Strategy and Action Programme, which it signed with the EU in November 2003, aimed to increase the efficiency and international competitiveness of Turkey's SMEs. In line with these policy frameworks, successive AKP governments increased the role of the state in revitalizing already existing financial institutions that would provide the SMEs with 'innovative' instruments. Furthermore, the AKP government also launched new subsidy programmes for the SMEs in 2003, a significant one of which was the purchase of capital equipment with a series of tax incentives and offsets for SMEs (OECD 2004: 15).

Concomitantly, the Transition to a Strong Economy Programme became a turning point in terms of net financial flows, which has had important implications on bank credit. Notably, perceptions of high-risk real investments tailed off. Consequently, foreign portfolio flows and major privatization deals ballooned after 2001. Increasing global liquidity, coupled with decreasing interest rates in the major developed countries, have been the major external factors behind this surge. As will be discussed later, booming foreign capital flows would also impact corporate balance sheets after 2004.

From 2003 onwards, private banks turned increasingly to SME finance. More concretely, the KGF was revitalized as 18 new private banks agreed to sign protocols. With this new resource, the KGF as an intermediary body collectively assumed the risk of SME entering the financial arena with the backing of a public guarantee. According to the protocol between the banks and the KGF, when a bank receives a credit application from an SME, it examines the application according to its regular procedures. If the bank deems the application appropriate but finds the collateral of the firm unsatisfactory, it sends the application file to the KGF. Then, if the KGF decides to be the guarantor for the loan, the firm receives the credit from the bank with the collateral guaranteed by the KGF. The guarantee of the KGF could not exceed 80 per cent of the credit amount and the maximum term of credit was eight years. In return for its collateral provision, the KGF charges a commission fee that is equivalent to between 2.0 per cent and 4.0 per cent of the guarantee amount for each year.[15] Currently, the official priorities of the KGF are to support young and female entrepreneurs, to promote innovative investments, to promote high-tech SMEs, to support exports, to increase the rate of employment, and to contribute to regional development.

Sharing the risk of new and existing SMEs has become an investment opportunity for financial intermediaries with the support by the public banks. The first risk capital company, VakıfBank Risk Co. was renamed as VakıfBank Venture Capital Co. in 2004. In the author's interview with one of the KOSGEB directors, the preference of the venture capital over risk capital in the related legislation was explained with regards to negative connotation of the concept of 'risk' as opposed to the rather positive meaning of 'venture'. In 2003, the Treasury allocated lump sum funds to be provided to the SMEs through equity participation funds. In 2003, the name of the Partnership to KOBI Investment Inc. was changed to KOBI Venture Capital Investment Trust (in short, KOBI Inc.) and the Trust became active from 2004.[16] The

Istanbul Venture Capital Initiative, founded in 2007, has become "the first dedicated fund of funds [€160 million] and co-investment programme" structured as "a public-private partnership that aims to serve as a catalyst for the development of the private equity business."[17]

Again in 2003, KOSGEB underwent significant institutional restructuring, which triggered substantial growth in membership. Most importantly, in 2003 KOSGEB started providing financial support for SMEs. A large portion of the KOSGEB budget was allocated to the Credit Interest Support Programme, according to which KOSGEB pays the interest of the borrowed loan while the SME is responsible for the principal of the credit. Through this interest rate support on bank loans, SMEs have been able to access loans at below market rates or even at a zero interest rate, through banks as intermediaries. Thus, KOSGEB has become the central public institution to catalyze the financial 'inclusion' of SMEs, while shouldering the risk of the process of the interpenetration of different types of capital.

The Post-2008 Era and Augmented Public Funds for SMEs

In the post-2008 era, as the banking sector tended to retain higher provisions, state authorities increased supports for SMEs. In 2009, Turkey accepted the Basel II criteria. The new restrictions tied to Basel II are said to discriminate against SMEs while favouring larger corporate firms (Aras 2007). Credits tied to SMEs would be ranked lower in quality, and hence deemed at higher risk of default due to the weaker financial structure of SMEs. Under these more

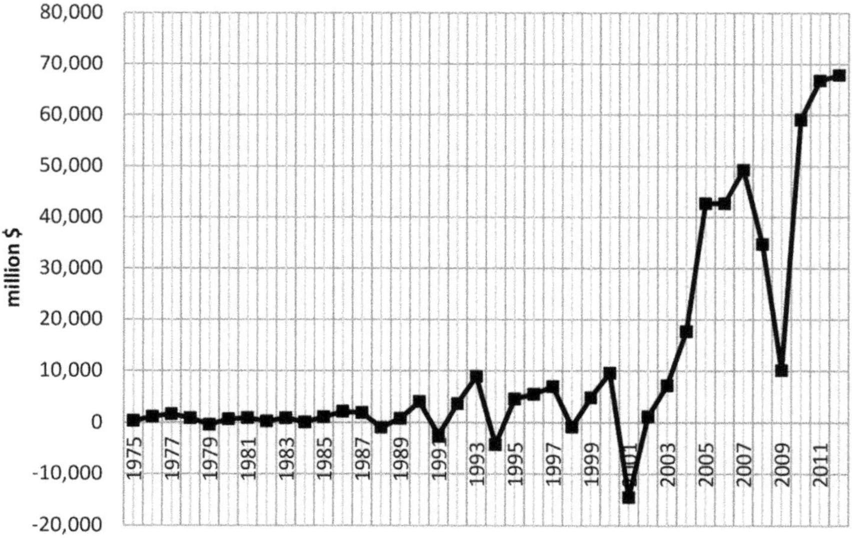

Figure 9.1 Capital inflows, 1975–2011
Source: CBRT, WB.

stringent conditions, SMEs that qualify for loans would none the less pay higher rates of interest. As Table 9.2 shows, SME loan defaults as a percentage of total loans since 2008 have soared, particularly in 2009, before recovering in the following years. The AKP government sought to mitigate the adverse impact of the crisis on SMEs through alternative credit mechanisms. For this aim, the Treasury granted a fund of US $1 billion to the KGF in October 2009. The debtors that had not had any repayment difficulties until 30 June 2008, yet would not be able to be make repayments after then, would be eligible to have their debts restructured. This debt restructuring was made possible by guarantee of the KGF up to 75 per cent of the total debt (Tuvay 2009). Since 2009, when the KOSGEB Law (no. 5891) was amended to combine all SMEs in the different sectors, the number of firms benefitting from these alternative resources have increased several-fold. With similar intentions, the definition of SMEs was expanded in 2012 with regards to annual budget and turnover. Consequently, while only 400 firms were registered with KOSGEB in 2002, by 2012 this number totalled 700,000.[18]

The new financial resources have also been rescaled at both sub- and supranational levels. At the sub-national level, regional development agencies have initiated several support programmes for SMEs since 2009. These decentralized development agencies periodically call for projects from SMEs. The successful ones are granted 25 per cent to 50 per cent of the overall cost of the investment. In addition to these grants, development agencies initiated interest rate support programmes in which they can provide loans to the selected SMEs with zero and low rates of interest. At the supranational level, the European Investment Bank (EIB), the Undersecretariat of the Treasury and its banking partners signed a loan agreement in June 2009. An EIB loan for SMEs was concluded with the Industrial Development Bank of Turkey, Turkish Development Bank (TKB)[19] and VakıfBank for a total amount of €400million. The EIB also entered into a loan agreement in support of SME lending with Halkbank, signing a first €150 million tranche of a total facility of € 300 million.[20]

As Table 9.3 shows, although the percentage allocation fluctuates around the same rates, the total amount of loans extended to SMEs has increased significantly. When total bank loans are examined in Table 9.4 with regards to the different SME sizes, it is seen that medium-sized firms have increased their share in total SMEs.

Sources of Net Funds in Liabilities in Manufacturing Sector

Despite the unreliability of SME datasets in Turkey, existing Central Bank balance sheet datasets on Turkish manufacturing sector provide some insight into the financial structure of the manufacturing sector across different-sized firms. Notwithstanding that, it should be noted that these datasets do not cover the sector completely, but include the firms that respond to a voluntary annual survey of the Central Bank. Therefore, the number of firms in this dataset tends to vary each year, along with the structure of their balance sheet.

The Central Bank dataset reveals the evolution of the structure of liabilities across different-sized enterprises in the sector. To begin with, the share of current/short-term liabilities on the balance sheet increases as the size of firm decreases. This shows that access to long-term credit is still relatively more difficult for smaller enterprises. Notwithstanding, short-term trade loans for small size firms have significantly decreased since 1996, which signals that they have changed the borrowing option from within the sector towards banking sector options albeit insufficient. Furthermore, the rate of increase of the share of long-term liabilities of small and medium-size firms is unambiguously higher than large firms. This suggests that long-term borrowing options for medium-sized and small firms have been made available since 2000.

The impact of the 2000–01 crisis and banking regulations is reflected in the structure of liabilities. The share of bank financing, both short- and long-term, fell significantly from 2000 to 2004. Short-term bank loans in particular have been low both for corporate firms and SMEs, while SMEs' access to short-term bank loans appears to have been curtailed more than that of larger firms in manufacturing. Short-term bank loans granted to small and medium-sized manufacturing firms dropped by 8.8 and 6.4 percentage points between 2000 and 2004, respectively, while the same figure for large firms was 5.3 percentage points. Both short- and long-term bank loans then started to increase incrementally each year until the 2008 crisis, when they fell significantly. Despite fluctuations, bank financing of small and medium-sized firms shows an increasing trend since 2009.

A parallel trend appearing in liabilities can be observed in the share of equity finance on the balance sheet of manufacturing firms. Equity finance increased from 37.1 per cent in 2002 to 52.7 per cent in 2004, while it dropped by 8.2 percentage points between 2004 and 2008. In 2009 it increased by 3.7 percentage points, reaching 48.2 per cent. Small firms in particular were forced to increase their equity until 2009, despite their high losses. Since 2009, equity has shown a slightly decreasing trend again in all firms in the

Table 9.2 Percentage Allocation of Total Default Loans (2008-2017)

Recipient	*2008*	*2009*	*2010*	*2011*	*2012*	*2013*	*2014*	*2015*	*2016*	*2017*
Corporate	35.7	31.8	35	36.8	39.1	36.7	36.1	29.2	31.0	31.7
SME	28.6	31.8	30	26.3	30.4	30.0	30.6	33.3	37.9	39.7
Household	28.6	36.4	35	36.8	34.8	33.3	33.3	35.4	35.1	28.6
Default Loans (TL billion)	14	22	20	19	23	30	36	48	58	63

Source: Banking Regulation and Supervision Agency https://www.bddk.org.tr/WebSitesi/turkce/Raporlar/TBSGG/13810tbs_temel_gostergeler.pdfhttps://www.bddk.org.tr/WebSitesi/turkce/Raporlar/TBSGG/16430tbs_temel_gtergeler_doc_turkce.pdf.

manufacturing sector. Considering the fall of the share of trade loans in liabilities, the manufacturing sector in general, and small and medium-sized firms in particular, appear to have integrated into the banking sector since 2009.

Conclusion

Although the configuration of the particular balance of internal forces is necessarily situated within the international context, the forces of various forms and fractions of capital should be taken into account in coming to terms with the historically specific characteristics of financialization in Turkey. Taking into account the specific characteristic of the Turkish business community—that is, the dominance of family- controlled conglomerates undertaking or *holding* its business in diversified sectors—effective analyses of the transformation of Turkish financial system and the impact of such a transformation on the real sector require a particular emphasis on the size of the enterprise in question. Therefore, in this chapter, small and medium-sized enterprises have been examined as a lynchpin of the differentiation between the financial and non-financial sectors.

While the globally dominant form of internationalization of capital is shaped cardinally by finance capital, such transformation takes place within national contexts set by state policies. Therefore, as Jessop (1983) succinctly puts it, the accumulation of capital is realized in the context of a changing balance of intra- as well as inter-class forces while the state comes to play an important role in reproducing the overall circuit of capital. More concretely, while finance capital has secured its interest in the neoliberal era, the immediate interests of the other fractions, such as SMEs were to be advanced by the exercise of state power via selective state policies. Furthermore, it could also be argued that the pursuit of SMEs' interests has been conducted within the margins of manoeuvre of the dominant accumulation strategy, as they have been central actors in the overall neoliberal restructuring, particularly since 1990.

Thus, the financing of SMEs required explicit state support in order to enable the private banking sector to service the SMEs. Since the 1980s, Turkish governments have attempted to set the equilibrium of compromise among the fractions of the capitalist class. More concretely since the early 2000s, successive AKP governments have crafted strategies deemed appropriate for the continued valorization of SMEs in order to unify different moments in the circuit of capital. Expansion of public sector credit mechanisms in support of the SMEs could reveal the state's role in the allocation of money capital as a mechanism for the socialization of risk. This then entails a political commitment on the part of the government to continue with the neoliberal strategies of development, especially given the political significance of SMEs as an electoral constituency. From this perspective, it would not be surprising to observe that Turkish SMEs were able to articulate their own

Table 9.3 Percentage Allocation of Total Bank Loans, 2006–September 2017

Loan Recipient	*2006*	*2007*	*2008*	*2009*	*2010*	*2011*	*2012*	*2013*	*2014*	*2015*	*2016*	*2017 (sept)*
Households	31.8	33.5	32.1	33.4	33.1	32.8	33.5	31.7	29.9	25.9	24.2	23.8
SMEs	27.2	26.8	23.0	21.2	23.9	23.9	25.1	25.9	26.8	26.2	24.3	25.0
Corporate Sector	41.0	39.7	44.9	45.4	43.0	43.3	41.4	42.4	44.4	47.9	51.5	51.3
Total Bank Loans (TL billion)	219	286	367	393	526	683	795	1.047	1.241	1.485	1.734	1.994

https://www.bddk.org.tr/WebSitesi/turkce/Raporlar/TBSGG/16430tbs_temel_gtergeler_doc_turkce.pdf.

Table 9.4 Percentage Distribution of Total Bank Loans by Size, 2006–September 2017

Size of Group	*2006*	*2007*	*2008*	*2009*	*2010*	*2011*	*2012*	*2013*	*2014*	*2015*	*2016*	*2017(sept)*
Micro	40.2	37.5	39.1	35.1	32.5	33.7	27.0	26.1	26.4	25.4	26.1	25.5
Small	30.2	31.2	26.4	26.5	27.2	26.4	31.5	31.5	33.3	34.1	33.3	32.7
Medium	29.5	31.4	34.5	38.4	40.3	39.9	41.5	42.4	40.0	40.0	40.6	41.6
Total Loans (TL billion)	60	77	85	83	125	163	200	271	333	389	421	498

https://www.bddk.org.tr/WebSitesi/turkce/Raporlar/TBSGG/16430tbs_temel_gtergeler_doc_turkce.pdf.

Table 9.5 Sources of Net Funds in Liabilities of the Manufacturing Sector, % (1996–2016)

Liabilities	*1996*	*2000*	*2002*	*2004*	*2006*	*2008*	*2009*	*2010*	*2011*	*2012*	*2013*	*2014*	*2015*	*2016*
Current Liabilities	49.5	48.7	43.9	35.1	36.8	39.2	35.8	38.5	41.0	40.3	41.0	39.8.	41.1	43.5
Short-Term Loans	16.2	18.3	14.4	11.1	13.0	16.6	13.1	13.9	15.3	15.3	16.3	15.6	15.7	16.4
Short-Term Bank Loans	13.7	15.5	12.4	9.9	11.3	14.0	10.4	11.3	12.5	12.5	13.1	12.1	12.1	13.0
Other[21]	2.5	2.8	1.9	1.3	1.7	2.4	2.7	2.6	2.8	2.8	3.3	3.5	3.6	3.5
Short-Term Trade Loans	16.7	16.9	18.2	15.0	15.1	13.8	13.9	15.3	16.5	15.3	15.5	14.9	15.2	15.5
Other[22]	16.5	10.8	11.3	8.9	8.7	8.8	8.7	9.3	9.6	9.7	9.2	9.3	10.2	11.5
Long-Term Liabilities	12.8	15.6	19.0	12.2	13.4	16.3	16.0	16.0	17.0	18.0	20.7	22.5	23.5	22.6
Long-Term Loans	8.9	10.0	12.1	7.9	9.8	12.6	11.9	12.3	13.3	14.2	16.6	18.1	19.3	18.1
Long-Term Bank Loans	8.6	9.8	11.9	7.1	8.9	11.7	11.0	11.4	12.3	12.7	14.1	15.1	16.4	15.3
Other Long-Term Loans[23]	0.2	0.2	0.2	0.8	0.8	0.9	0.8	0.9	0.9	1.5	2.5	3.0	2.9	2.7
Other[24]	3.7	5.5	7.0	4.4	3.7	3.8	4.1	3.8	3.7	3.9	4.0	4.4	4.1	4.4
Equity	37.7	35.8	37.1	52.7	49.8	44.5	48.2	45.2	42.0	41.6	38.3	37.7	35.4	33.9
Paid-up Capital	15.1	15.1	18.7	51.8	38.8	33.2	34.0	30.9	28.5	26.6	23.2	21.6	20.4	18.8
Capital and Profit Reserves	19.3	22.1	20.8	21.3	12.2	12.4	14.3	13.1	12.0	12.6	11.5	11.5	11.2	10.8
Profits	3.3	-1.4	-2.4	-13.0	-1.2	-1.1	-0.2	1.3	3.4	2.4	3.5	4.6	3.9	4.4

Source: Author's own calculation based on the CBRT sectoral balance sheet data.

Table 9.6 Sources of Net Funds in Liabilities of Small Manufacturing Sector, % (1996–2016)

Liabilities	*1996*	*2000*	*2002*	*2004*	*2006*	*2008*	*2009*	*2010*	*2011*	*2012*	*2013*	*2014*	*2015*	*2016*
Current Liabilities	59.7	61.6	44.4	35.0	46.9	41.6	36.9	37.8	41.2	49.3	49.6	47.5	49.1	48.2
Short-Term Loans	18.8	20.5	14.2	11.0	16.5	17.9	13.4	14.4	15.8	17.3	18.7	17.9	17.9	16.5
Short-Term Bank Loans	17.6	19.3	13.4	10.5	15.3	16.7	12.4	13.3	14.3	16.1	17.2	16.9	16.7	15.1
Other[25]	1.2	1.2	0.8	0.5	1.3	1.2	1.0	1.2	1.5	1.2	1.4	1.0	1.2	1.5
Short-Term Trade Loans	21.6	19.7	17.8	13.4	17.0	12.6	12.1	12.1	13.0	15.7	15.0	13.7	13.2	13.8
Other[26]	19.4	21.7	12.3	10.6	13.4	11.0	11.4	11.3	12.9	16.1	15.9	15.9	18.1	17.9
Long-Term Liabilities	9.0	12.0	22.1	13.7	11.1	17.0	13.3	15.0	19.0	17.2	20.2	23.2	25.1	26.5
Long-Term Loans	5.2	7.7	14.4	8.8	8.5	14.3	9.8	11.9	13.7	14.4	17.0	20.6	22.3	23.0
Long-Term Bank Loans	5.0	7.5	14.1	8.3	7.4	13.1	9.0	11.2	12.9	13.6	16.2	19.7	21.4	22.1
Other Long-Term Loans[27]	0.2	0.1	0.3	0.5	1.1	1.2	0.9	0.7	0.8	0.8	0.8	1	0.9	0.9
Other[28]	3.9	4.2	6.6	4.9	6.4	2.7	3.5	3.1	5.2	2.8	3.2	2.6	2.8	3.5
Equity	31.3	26.1	33.5	51.3	42.0	41.5	49.7	47.2	39.9	33.6	30.2	29.3	25.8	25.3
Paid-up Capital	17.8	19.2	23.8	71.7	48.9	44.9	41.5	40.3	46.1	28.1	25.3	24.1	22.8	23.0
Capital and Profit Reserves	14.4	19.5	19.2	8.7	8.1	8.8	18.8	16.8	7.6	6.6	6.7	5.9	4.7	6.1
Profits	-1.0	-2.6	-9.5	-27.9	-15.5	-12.3	-10.7	-10.0	-13.8	-1.1	-1.9	-0.8	-1.8	-3.9

Source: Author's own calculation based on the CBRT sectoral balance sheet data.

Table 9.7 Sources of Net Funds in Liabilities of Medium-Sized Manufacturing Sector, % (1996–2016)

Liabilities	*1996*	*2000*	*2002*	*2004*	*2006*	*2008*	*2009*	*2010*	*2011*	*2012*	*2013*	*2014*	*2015*	*2016*
Current Liabilities	51.5	50.4	45.9	37.4	44.1	44.9	39.8	42.6	44.8	44.8	44.9	45.6	46.0	46.2
Short-Term Loans	21.0	21.3	17.0	13.7	17.0	19.4	15.1	16.4	17.4	17.4	18.5	20.5	19.4	19.7
Short-Term Bank Loans	20.0	19.1	15.2	12.7	15.5	17.7	13.3	14.8	15.9	15.7	16.5	17.8	17.2	17.3
Other[29]	1.1	2.2	1.9	1.1	1.5	1.7	1.8	1.5	1.5	1.7	2.1	2.7	2.1	2.3
Short-Term Trade Loans	16.9	18.0	18.4	15.1	17.2	15.2	15.1	16.4	16.8	16.2	16.0	15.0	15.9	15.4
Other[30]	13.1	11.2	10.4	8.7	10.0	10.2	9.6	9.8	10.6	11.1	10.3	10.1	10.7	11.1
Long-Term Liabilities	11.5	15.8	15.0	11.1	13.7	15.8	14.8	14.7	16.3	15.8	19.3	21.0	21.5	22.0
Long-Term Loans	7.2	10.3	9.6	7.4	10.4	12.8	11.8	12.0	13.4	13.2	16.3	17.3	18.8	19.1
Long-Term Bank Loans	7.0	10.2	9.5	6.7	8.8	11.1	10.2	10.5	11.6	12.0	14.8	15.6	17.3	17.6
Other Long-Term Loans[31]	0.2	0.1	0.1	0.7	1.6	1.7	1.5	1.6	1.9	1.2	1.5	1.7	1.5	1.5
Other[32]	4.3	5.6	5.4	3.6	3.3	2.9	3.0	2.7	2.9	2.5	3.1	3.7	2.7	2.9
Equity	37.4	33.8	39.1	51.5	42.2	39.3	45.4	42.7	38.9	39.4	35.8	33.4	32.5	31.8
Paid-up Capital	16.8	16.8	22.3	62.1	39.7	35.7	34.6	32.2	29.8	29.3	26.0	22.7	21.7	20.1
Capital and Profit Reserves	18.4	21.4	20.9	9.9	7.6	8.8	10.7	9.4	9.7	7.8	7.5	7.2	8.0	9.0
Profits	2.2	-4.4	-4.1	-20.4	-5.0	-5.1	0.0	1.0	-0.7	2.3	2.3	3.6	3.0	2.8

Source: Author's own calculation based on the CBRT sectoral balance sheet data.

Table 9.8 Sources of Net Funds in Liabilities of Large Manufacturing Sector, % (1996–2016)

Liabilities	*1996*	*2000*	*2002*	*2004*	*2006*	*2008*	*2009*	*2010*	*2011*	*2012*	*2013*	*2014*	*2015*	*2016*
Current Liabilities	47.8	44.3	43.1	34.2	33.8	37.4	34.8	37.7	40.2	38.4	39.3	37.8	39.2	42.6
Short-Term Loans	14.1	15.5	13.4	10.2	11.5	15.7	12.7	13.3	14.8	14.6	15.6	14.4	14.7	15.8
Short-Term Bank Loans	10.8	12.3	11.3	8.7	9.7	12.8	9.6	10.3	11.6	11.5	11.9	10.5	10.5	12.0
Other[33]	3.2	3.2	2.1	1.5	1.8	2.9	3.1	3.0	3.1	3.1	3.7	3.9	4.2	3.6
Short-Term Trade Loans	16.1	16.8	18.2	15.1	14.4	13.6	13.9	15.4	16.7	15.1	15.4	15.0	15.2	15.7
Other[34]	17.6	12.1	11.5	8.9	7.8	8.0	8.2	9.0	8.7	8.8	8.4	8.4	9.2	11.1
Long-Term Liabilities	13.7	15.6	20.1	12.5	13.6	16.4	16.5	16.4	16.9	18.6	21.0	22.8	23.8	22.4
Long-Term Loans	9.9	10.1	12.6	7.9	9.7	12.4	12.1	12.4	13.3	14.4	16.7	18.1	19.1	17.5
Long-Term Bank Loans	9.7	9.9	12.5	7.1	9.1	11.7	11.4	11.6	12.4	12.8	13.8	14.6	15.7	14.3
Other Long-Term Loans[35]	0.3	0.2	0.1	0.8	0.6	0.7	0.6	0.8	0.9	1.6	2.8	3.4	3.4	3.2
Other[36]	3.8	5.5	7.5	4.5	3.9	4.0	4.5	4.0	2.6	4.2	4.3	4.7	4.7	4.8
Equity	38.5	40.1	36.9	53.4	52.6	46.3	48.7	45.9	42.9	43.0	39.7	39.4	37.0	35.0
Paid-up Capital	14.1	15.1	16.7	44.9	37.6	31.4	33.2	29.8	26.6	25.9	22.4	21.1	19.9	18.1
Capital and Profit Reserves	20.2	22.4	21.0	16.2	13.9	13.8	14.7	13.6	13.0	14.2	13.0	12.9	12.6	11.4
Profits	4.2	2.7	-0.9	-7.6	1.2	1.1	0.8	2.4	3.0	2.8	4.2	5.4	4.6	5.6

Source: Author's own calculation based on the CBRT sectoral balance sheet data.

economic interest within those of capital in general, as they are considered one of the primary support bases for the continuation of AKP rule over the last decade and a half.

It is, in this respect, important to note that as the country was moving towards a crucial constitutional referendum on 16 April 2017, which eventually changed the country's government system from parliamentarianism to executive presidency, the government took a series of decisive actions to ease SMEs' access to finance. In November 2016 the government announced that it would increase the fund for KGF from US $550 million to $6.8 billion dollars and the KGF guarantee has been raised to 85 per cent by a Decree (no: 677). Finally, in late March 2017 on the eve of the referendum, the Treasury and the KGF signed a protocol for a new credit guarantee system for SMEs, with export capacities and foreign exchange acquisition transactions that would provide the Treasury guarantee up to 100 per cent. Moreover, the amount of capital provided by the Treasury as compensation for non-performing loans was increased to $6.66 billion dollars (Şimşek 2017). These credits were named, very tellingly, as "breather loans". While providing a breathing space for suffocating SMEs, these policies are risking to increase the budget deficit, leading to a major crisis in the public finances (Sönmez 2017). During the first half of 2018, on the eve of the early national elections in June, there have been new KGF funds and KOSGEB supports made available for SMEs. The Prime Minister has also announced a possible definitional change of SMEs (increasing the annual budget and turnover from TL40 million to TL125 million) so that many more enterprises would enjoy these lucrative incentives.[37]

From this analysis it is plausible to conclude that, not only because of the economic significance of the SMEs to the overall economy and its competitiveness in the world market, but also for reasons of political expediency, state authorities will continue to socialize part of the risks involved in financing SMEs.

Notes

1 http://www.turkstat.gov.tr/PreHaberBultenleri.do?id=21540(Accessed 22 May 2018).

2 The word 'holding' is used for these conglomerates, although this foreign word is not used in Turkish otherwise. In this chapter, they will be referred to as 'holding groups'.

3 Additionally, the 1964 Law of Tradesmen and Craftsmen enabled the Ottoman Guild System, Akhism, to evolve into Confederation of Turkish Tradesmen and Craftsmen (TESK-*Türkiye Esnaf ve Sanatkarları Konfederasyonu*). Members of TESK was engaging in more traditional form of micro and small businesses such as grocery stores, carpentry, shoe-making, taxi drivers, auto repairs, dry cleaning among others (Sarıarslan 1994: 169).

4 http://www.tusiad.org/tusiad/history/tusiad-retro/.

5 http://www.resmigazete.gov.tr/eskiler/2005/11/20051118-5.htm. http://ec.europa.eu/growth/smes/business-friendly-environment/sme-definition_en.

6 https://www.tbmm.gov.tr/hukumetler/HP47.htm.

7 ibid.
8 http://kobias.com.tr/web/en/history.html.
9 See Chapter 2 for the details for the characterization the İşBank as a conglomerate without a holding structure.
10 https://www.imf.org/external/np/loi/1999/120999.htm.
11 http://www.yoikk.gov.tr/dosya/up/eng/SME%20strategy%20and%20action%20plan.pdf.
12 *Turkish Press Review*, "Turkey's Single-Party Government Will Lend Hope", Merrill Lynch, http://www.hri.org/news/turkey/trkpr/2002/02-11-07.trkpr.html (Accessed 25 March 2016).
13 After the completion of the Eighth Five-Year Development Plan, the term of the Ninth plan was extended to seven years. The term of the Tenth Development is also five years.
14 http://ec.europa.eu/enlargement/pdf/turkey/npaa_2003/IV-16_en.pdf.
15 http://www.kgf.com.tr/eng/3nasilbasvurulur.htm.
16 http://kobias.com.tr/kobiportal/en/history.html.
17 http://www.bsec-organization.org/aoc/smes/Pages/AnnexIV-ActionPlanWGSMEs-annexes-combined.pdf Accessed: 2 April 2016.
18 http://www.kosgeb.gov.tr.
19 TKB is a state development bank that aims to provide financial support for development projects in the less developed regions.
20 In addition to these two agreements, a third agreement of worth €335 million between the EIB and the Treasury was signed in support of public sector research activity. http://www.eib.org/projects/press/2009/2009-102-eib-supports-small-businesses-and-research-in-turkey-with-record-loans-of-eur-900-million.htm.
21 Until 2004, this figure was calculated as the sum of current maturities of long-term credits and accrued interest and other short-term loans. Since 2004, balance sheets include a new item: loans on leasing payables.
22 Total sum of other short term loans, advance payments, contract progress costs, taxes and other liabilities payable, provision for liabilities and expenses, short-term deferred income and expense accruals, and other short-term liabilities.
23 Since 2004, this figure includes leasing payables minus deferred lease interest payables. The rise in this figure is due to the addition of the leasing payments.
24 Total sum of trade credits, other long term loans, advance payments, provision for other liabilities and expenses, long-term deferred income and expense accruals, and other long-term liabilities.
25 Until 2004, this figure was calculated as the sum of current maturities of long-term credits and accrued interest and other short-term loans. Since 2004, balance sheets include a new item: loans on leasing payables.
26 Total sum of other short term loans, advance payments, contract progress costs, taxes and other liabilities payable, provision for liabilities and expenses, short-term deferred income and expense accruals, and other short-term liabilities.
27 Since 2004, this figure includes leasing payables minus deferred lease interest payables. The rise in this figure is due to the addition of the leasing payments.
28 Total sum of trade credits, other long-term loans, advance payments, provision for other liabilities and expenses, long-term deferred income and expense accruals, and other long-term liabilities.
29 Until 2004, this figure was calculated as the sum of current maturities of long-term credits and accrued interest and other short-term loans. Since 2004, balance sheets include a new item: loans on leasing payables.
30 Total sum of other short-term loans, advance payments, contract progress costs, taxes and other liabilities payable, provision for liabilities and expenses, short-term deferred income and expense accruals, and other short-term liabilities.

31 Since 2004, this figure includes leasing payables minus deferred lease interest payables. The rise in this figure is due to the addition of the leasing payments.
32 Total sum of trade credits, other long-term loans, advance payments, provision for other liabilities and expenses, long-term deferred income and expense accruals, and other long-term liabilities.
33 Until 2004, this figure was calculated as the sum of current maturities of long-term credits and accrued interest and other short-term loans. Since 2004, balance sheets include a new item: loans on leasing payables.
34 Total sum of other short-term loans, advance payments, contract progress costs, taxes and other liabilities payable, provision for liabilities and expenses, short-term deferred income and expense accruals, and other short-term liabilities.
35 Since 2004, this figure includes leasing payables minus deferred lease interest payables. The rise in this figure is due to the addition of the leasing payments.
36 Total sum of trade credits, other long-term loans, advance payments, provision for other liabilities and expenses, long-term deferred income and expense accruals, and other long-term liabilities.
37 https://www.dailysabah.com/economy/2018/03/02/turkish-govt-announces-new-support-program-for-smes.

REFERENCES

Aras, G. (2007) *BASEL II Sürecinde Kobiler Için Yol Haritası*, Deloitte: CEO/CFO Series.

Braudel, F. (1985) *Civilization and Capitalism: The Wheels of Commerce (Vol. II)*, Berkeley, Los Angeles: University of California Press.

Buğra, A. (1994) *State and Business in Modern Turkey: A Comparative Study*, Albany: State University of New York Press.

DPT (1984) *Beşinci Beş Yıllık Kalkınma Planı 1985–1989*, Publication no: 1974, Ankara: DPT Müsteşarlığı

DPT (1989) *Altıncı Beş Yıllık Kalkınma Planı 1990–1994*, Publication no: 2174, Ankara: DPT Müsteşarlığı.

DPT (1995) *Yedinci Beş Yıllık Kalkınma Planı 1996–2000*, DPT website, Accessed 22 May 2018.

International Labour Organization (1976) *World Employment Programme: Research in Retrospect and Prospect*, Geneva: ILO.

Jessop, B. (1983) "Accumulation strategies, state forms, and hegemonic projects", *Kapitalistate*, 10: 89–111.

Marois, T. (2012) *States, Banks and Crisis: Emerging Finance Capitalism in Mexico and Turkey*, Cheltenham, Gloucestershire, UK: Edward Elgar.

McKinsey Global Institute (2003) *Making the Productivity and Growth Breakthrough*, Istanbul: McKinsey and Co.

Müftüoğlu, T. (2009) *SME Support Policies in Turkey after 1990: Review, Evaluation and Suggestions*, Agence Française de Développement, mimeo.

Organisation for Economic Co-operation and Development (2004) *Small and Medium-Sized Enterprises in Turkey: Issues and Policies*. Paris: OECD.

Organisation for Economic Co-operation and Development (2013) *SME and Entrepreneurship Financing: The Role of Credit Guarantee Schemes and Mutual Guarantee Societies in supporting finance for small and medium-sized enterprises*, CFE/SME (2012)1/FINAL, OECD Public Official Document.

Organisation for Economic Co-operation and Development (2014) *OECD Economics Surveys: Turkey 2014*, Paris: OECD.
Özar, Ş. (2007) "The Neo-Liberal Paradigm and Small Enterprises: Accumulation by Dispossession in the Case of Turkey", in A.H. Köse and F. Şenses (eds.), *Neoliberal Globalization as New Imperialism*, New York: Nova Science Publisher, 245–258.
Sarıaslan, H. (1994) *Küçük ve Orta Ölçekli İşletmelerin Finansal Sorunları: Çözüm İçin Bir Finansal Paket Önerisi*, Ankara: TOBB.
Sarıaslan, H. (1996) *Türkiye Ekonomisinde Küçük ve Orta Ölçekli İşletmeler: İmalat Sanayi İşletmelerinde Sorunlarve Yeni Stratejiler*, Ankara: TOBB.
Şimşek, M. (2017) "Turkey: Credit Guarantee System Protocol Signed". *Anadolu Agency*, 21 March 2017, Anadolu Agency website, Accessed 4 May 2017.
Sönmez, M. (1982) *Türkiye Ekonomisinde Bunalım: 12 Eylül Sonrasının Ekonomi Politiği II*, İstanbul: Belge.
Sönmez, M. (2017) "Turkey's AKP Scrambles to Contain Crisis Ahead of Key Vote" Al-Monitor, 18 February 2017, Al Monitor website, Accessed 4 May 2017.
Taymaz, E. (1997) *Small and Medium-sized Industry in Turkey*, Ankara: State Institute of Statistics.
Taymaz, E. (2009) "Informality and Productivity Differentials Between Formal and Informal Firms in Turkey", *METU ERC Working Papers in Economics*, 09/01.
Tuvay, B. (2009) "KGF'den KOBİ'lere Yeni Can Suyu", *KOBİ Girişim*, October 2009: 8–12.
UNIDO (1974) *Subcontracting for Modernizing Economies*, New York: UN.
World Bank (1978) *Employment and Development of Small Enterprises*, Washington, DC: The World Bank.
Yalman, G. (2009) *Transition to Neoliberalism: The Case of Turkey in the 1980s*, İstanbul: Bilgi University Press.
Yeldan, E. (2001). "On the IMF-Directed Disinflation Program in Turkey: A Program for Stabilization and Austerity or a Recipe for Impoverishment and Financial Chaos?" SSRN website, Accessed 22 May 2018.

10 Financial Transformation and Housing Finance in Turkey

Işıl Erol

Introduction: The Real Estate Sector in Turkey

Since the adoption of import-substitution industrialization as development strategy from the 1960s onwards in Turkey, the construction industry has been considered as an engine of economic growth. With the reorientation of economic policies since the 1980 stabilization programme, the construction industry has been assigned a new role as part of the export-oriented growth strategy as Turkish contractors have expanded their activities abroad, especially in the Middle East and North Africa. Meanwhile, within the domestic economy, the construction industry assumed a new saliency with the foundation of the Housing and Public Partnership Directorate in 1984 and its subsequent separation into the Public Participation Administration and the Housing Development Administration (TOKI) in 1990.

Like most other developing countries, Turkey has been experiencing premature deindustrialization processes that have been accelerated by the Adalet ve Kalkınma Partisi (AKP—Justice and Development Party) government after the 2001 economic crisis.[1] In other words, Turkey is rapidly becoming a service sector-based economy without having fully industrialized, which is a result of Turkey's post-1980s neoliberal economic policies and subsequent financialization processes tied to wider financial globalization (Rodrik 2015). The urban policy consequences of premature de-industrialization have been the creation of a 'new' middle-income class—*the urban rich*, who take risks, demand and consume a lot—and the commodification of cities and urban spaces by the AKP government through a radical change in urban legislation and city building. Consequently, within the region, including the Eastern Europe, Middle East and Russia, Turkey has been one of the fastest-developing real estate markets since 2002. Large-scale housing projects with shopping malls and office developments emerged in big cities. Likewise, the Turkish housing market and its financing have experienced significant changes over the last decade. These changes have given rise to three main dynamics: the need for affordable housing for low-income households; the increased entry of global investors into the Turkish real estate market; and legislative reforms.

Turkey has a population of approximately 82 million, which has grown over the last five years at an average annual rate of 1.5 per cent and which represents the 19th largest population in the world. The population increase and the high migration from rural to urban areas over the last 30 years resulted in exponentially rising demand for urban land and housing in urban areas, particularly among low and middle-income groups. This situation has led to an affordability problem for these groups, which are unable to purchase or rent a dwelling, and also to the increase in squatter housing neighbourhoods (*gecekondu*), which do not satisfy either sustainability or liveability conditions. Accordingly, social housing is a key issue in Turkey. Currently, TOKI has the duty to provide affordable housing for low-income households. However, TOKI is still far from achieving its mandated objectives as the population's needs are extremely diverse and funding sources are limited. Since the foundation of the TOKI, it has been undertaking numerous projects of mass housing and landscaping; TOKI has gained significant momentum since the AKP government came to power in 2002.[2]

While failing to respond to the need for affordable housing, the Turkish real estate market has become a rising star in the region. This is a result of economic growth in Turkey, favourable demographics, the continuing urbanization processes, and the neoliberal urban policies adopted by the AKP government. These dynamics have increased the stakes of global investors in the Turkish real estate market. According to a report titled *Emerging Trends in Real Estate Europe*, prepared jointly by PriceWaterhouseCoopers and the Urban Land Institute, Istanbul is ranked as the most attractive investment market in Europe. In this report, it is noted that in the 'Existing Property Performance', 'New Property Acquisitions', and 'Development Prospects' categories, Istanbul is followed by Munich, Warsaw, Berlin and Stockholm. Moreover, according to a survey conducted by the Association of Foreign Investors in Real Estate, Turkey ranks as the third most attractive real estate investment destination among the emerging countries in 2012.[3]

Most recently, essential legislative reforms, introduced in line with the European Union (EU) harmonization process, have made investing in the real estate market easier and more profitable than ever. The amendments to the Land Registry Law, the Housing Finance Law[4], and the redrafting of Tax Laws are designed to improve the competitiveness of the Turkish real estate sector in the global market. Specifically, in May 2012 the Turkish Parliament passed the Law on the Transformation of Areas under Natural Disaster Risk (Law No. 6306) and enacted certain amendments for Article 35 and 36 of the Land Registry Law No 2644, which redefined rules of reciprocity and substantially eased foreign investment restrictions in Turkey. The 2012 Urban Transformation Law authorized public sector involvement in urban regeneration processes. This involved an initial estimation of about 6.5 million dwelling units seen to be at risk of natural disaster risk. Additionally, the newly amended Reciprocity Law (May 2012) substantially eased foreign investment restrictions in Turkey. Accordingly, European and especially Gulf-based property investors, have turned their attention not only to the Istanbul real estate market, but also to other Anatolian cities, including Ankara, Izmir, Antalya, Bursa and Mersin.

This chapter first discusses the share of the real estate sector in the Turkish economy over the period from 2000 to 2014. Significant increases in demand for Turkish real estate have resulted in a substantial amount of construction in the country. Hence, Turkey has one of the highest volumes of housing production in Europe. The chapter, secondly, analyzes housing production and housing policies with the help of statistical data and demonstrates that the Turkish housing market operates under highly competitive conditions without much regulation, nor many incentives. Finally, the chapter reviews the housing finance system in Turkey and points out that in recent years, mortgage loans and the real estate investment trusts (REITs) have been the new financial instruments that have linked the Turkish economy strongly into international (especially EU-based) financial markets. Additionally, the role of the state in the housing sector has changed with its direct involvement in the production and financing of housing, especially after 2002. The development of a mortgage market, and the emergence and rapid growth of the REIT sector will be discussed in the last part of the chapter.

The Real Estate Sector and Economic Growth

This sub-section discusses the share of real estate sector and construction activities in the Turkish economy over the past 15 years. Figure 10.1 displays the share of the real estate market: namely, the construction sector, and real estate, renting and business activities, in gross domestic product (GDP) between Q4 2000 and Q4 2014. Over the last decade, real estate market had 10.5 per cent to 11.5 per cent share of GDP. As of the end of 2014 the construction sector-to-GDP ratio was 6.0 per cent, while the real estate, renting and business activities-to-GDP ratio was 4.6 per cent.

Currently, the construction industry is the sixth largest economic sector in Turkey, based on its value added to GDP, and employs 7.4 per cent of the total labour force. Figure 10.2 displays the real growth rate of the construction industry in conjunction with the fluctuations in real GDP growth rate between 1999 and 2014. After the 2001 financial crisis, Turkey's economy moved full-speed ahead, except for a temporary reversal in 2009 during the global financial crisis. Real GDP growth had been significantly negative in the past three financial crises of 1999, 2001 and 2008−09. It is evident that the 1999 and 2001 financial crises in Turkey and the recent global financial crisis in 2008–09 directly resulted in negative growth rates in the construction sector as well. Specifically, the growth of the construction industry declined by −3.1 per cent in 1999, −17.4 per cent in 2001 and by −16.1 per cent in 2009. It can be concluded that during periods of accelerated economic growth (2002–07 and 2010–11), construction output grows at a faster rate than the economy as a whole, but during periods of stagnation (2001 and 2008–09), the construction industry is the first to suffer.

A recent study by Erol and Unal (2015) investigates the causal relationship between construction investments and economic growth in Turkey from Q1 1998 to Q4 2014 and concludes that economic growth in Turkey has preceded construction activities with lags of between two and four quarters, but not vice versa during 1998–2014. The authors argue that, unlike the widespread belief that construction plays a crucial role in Turkey's economic growth the construction industry is not a driver of economic growth but a follower of fluctuations in the macro-economy. However, sub-sample analysis of the study reveals that the causal relationship between economic growth and construction investments varies noticeably across the sub-periods in the national economy, and that the substantial expansion in the construction sector has contributed to economic growth over the last five years. The low interest rate environment, with the help of radical changes in urban legislation and construction project in cities, boosted the construction industry, which resulted in economic growth in the sub-period of 2010–14.

In the following subsections, recent developments in the Turkish real estate market will be examined with a focus on i) housing production and housing policies; and ii) the housing finance system in Turkey.

Housing Production and Housing Policies in Turkey

In terms of housing production, Turkey is one of the most active real estate markets in Europe. Annual housing starts have numbered between 500,000–600,000 dwelling units in most years during the last two decades in Turkey, and reached 1 million in 2014. Culturally and socially, home ownership is among the most popular forms of investment and Turkish households generally prefer to be homeowners rather than tenants.

This section looks at housing production in Turkey by analyzing the statistical data on i) the number of housing starts and housing units with occupancy permits; and ii) the number of housing starts by producer type. Firstly, there are two main statistics, which provide an overall picture of housing production in Turkey: housing starts and occupancy permits. 'Housing starts' is an economic indicator that reflects the number of privately owned new housing units on which construction has been started in a given period of time. Occupancy permits are documents indicating that a building inspector is satisfied that the completed building work is suitable for occupation.[5] Secondly, the data on housing production actors includes the relative shares of the public sector, private sector, and construction co-operatives in the total number of construction permits, and will be examined later in this chapter.

The first data on construction permits show that annual housing starts began to rise in 1990, exceeded 500,000 dwelling units in 1993, and remained over that level during the following two years, as shown in Figure 10.3. A decline in housing starts began in 1996 and continued until 2002, when

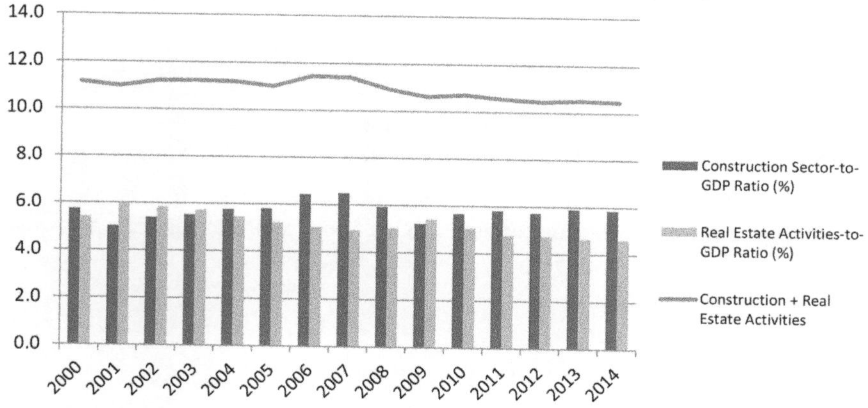

Figure 10.1 The Share of Real Estate Market in GDP, Q4 2000–Q4 2014
Source: Turkish Statistical Institute, www.turkstat.gov.tr.

housing starts fell as low as 161,920 dwelling units. This fall was due to a number of factors: the destructive earthquake that hit the north-western regions of Turkey in 1999; the new building regulations that followed the earthquake; and a period of economic crises from 1999 to 2002. Housing recovery began in 2003. Housing starts reached over 500,000 again in 2005, hitting 600,387 in 2006, then remained over 500,000 during the global financial crisis of 2008–09. In 2010 housing starts reached 907,451. But this was due to enlarged geographical coverage of building regulations, up from 19 to cover all 81 provinces. As the new regulations involved additional costs, many house-builders aimed to avoid those costs by obtaining construction permits prior to the regulations taking force in their provinces (Türel and Koç 2015). None the less, construction permits peaked at 1,019,730 dwellings at the end of 2014.

Secondly, occupancy permits began to increase considerably in 1986 and exceeded 250,000 dwelling units in 1989, as shown in Figure 10.4, which displays the occupancy permits issued in terms of dwelling units between 1970 and 2014. Between 1990 and 2001, occupancy permits grew from 215,613 to 277,056 dwellings. The 2001 financial crisis in Turkey affected the construction sector significantly; as such, the number of occupancy permits issued declined to 161,491, 162,908, and 164,994 dwelling units in 2002, 2003 and 2004, respectively. The recovery began in 2005 and occupancy permits increased from nearly 250,000 dwellings in that year to 556,331 dwellings by 2012. By 2014 the number of occupancy permits issued had reached 767,401 dwellings.

When housing production is examined in terms of producer groups, the public sector, the private sector, and construction co-operatives appear as the three main actors. Figure 10.5 displays the percentage shares of three housing

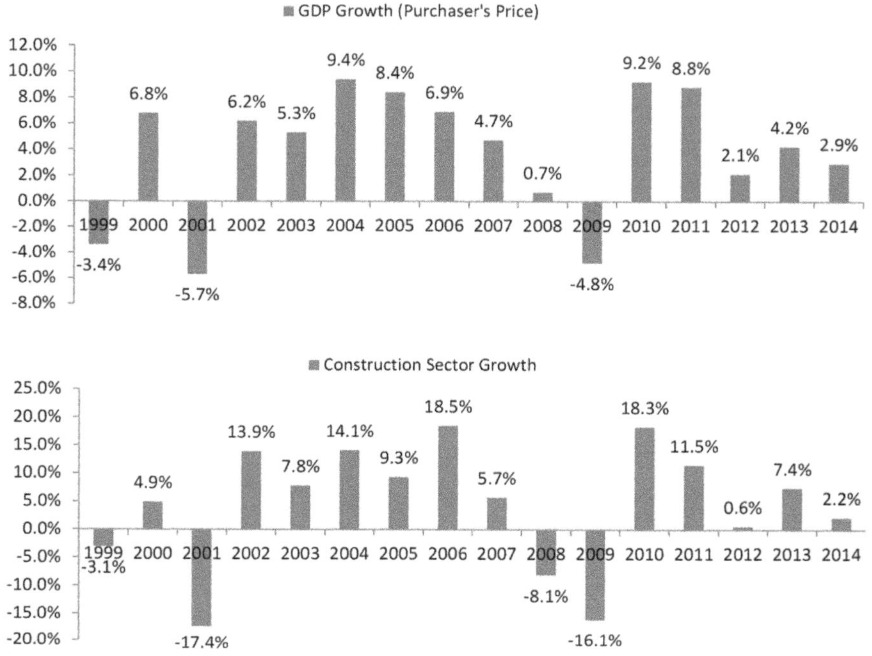

Figure 10.2 Real Growth Rate in Construction Activities and GDP
Source: TUIK: Gross Domestic Product in constant prices by type of economic activity, NACE Rev. 2, in 1998 basic prices.

producer groups in terms of construction permits for housing starts between 1995 and 2014. Clearly, the private sector has the leading part in housing starts with shares ranging between 84 per cent to 94 per cent between 2001 and 2014. During the same period, public sector producers have shares between 3 per cent and 6 per cent of total housing starts. The share of construction co-operatives declined from 22 per cent in 1998 to just 1.7 per cent by 2014. As shown in Figure 10.3 above, housing starts began to increase substantially in 2004. This rise appears to be mainly due to the significant increases in housing starts by the private sector, which reached 102,802 units in 2005.

The private sector in residential building had been dominated by small-capital builders who produce mostly apartments on single parcels of land. However, in recent years moderate-to-large capital domestic builders and even global construction companies have increased their share in total housing production as they produce housing on large tracts of land with many on-site amenities, including parking, sports facilities and the means to operate private security guards. Many of these properties are in the form of gated communities and targeted at upper-income groups (Türel and Koç 2015). Consequently, the share of the private sector in total housing starts has increased steadily from 78.5 per cent in 2000 to 94.0 per cent by 2014. The rise in the share of the private sector has been at the expense of co-operatives, which are regarded as non-profit producers, together with the public sector.

Construction co-operatives in Turkey have produced housing for their members (shareholders) since the mid-1930s. Co-operative members acquire dwellings in freehold ownership status after construction is finished, and then the co-operative is dissolved. Contrary to their counterparts in many European countries, co-operatives in Turkey are not permitted to produce social rented housing. Co-operatives have been supported by local and central governments in the forms of allocation of loans from public funds at lower than market interest rates; the sale of land developed by local or central government agencies usually at lower than market prices; and the supply of infrastructure to co-operative housing projects without much concern for recovering investment costs (Türel 2010).

Co-operative housing starts have been decreasing since 1993, and fell to just 1,591 buildings in 2011, from 28,714 buildings in 1997—the lowest level since 1990. Their share was about 22.0 per cent in 1997–98, but fell to just 1.7 per cent by 2014. The end of public loans for co-operative starts coincides with this decline. With the increasing dominance of the private sector in housing supply, co-operatives have been facing great difficulties in finding land at affordable prices, as they are in increasing competition in the land market with the private sector. Co-operatives are also in competition with the public sector, which is the other non-profit housing producer in Turkey. Except for in 2009, the public sector had a higher share in housing starts than co-operatives during 2008–14 (see Figure 10.5).

The number of housing starts or construction permits of the three groups of housing producers in terms of the market value are presented in Figure

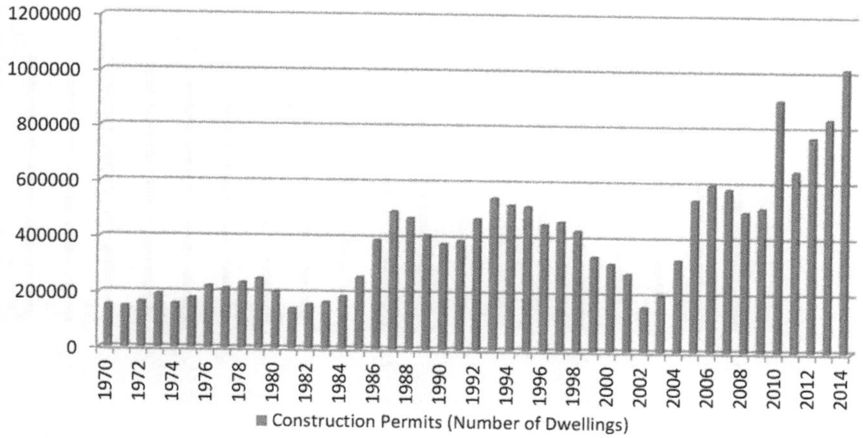

Figure 10.3 Construction Permits (Number of Dwellings), 1970–2014
Source: Turkish Statistical Institute, www.turkstat.gov.tr.

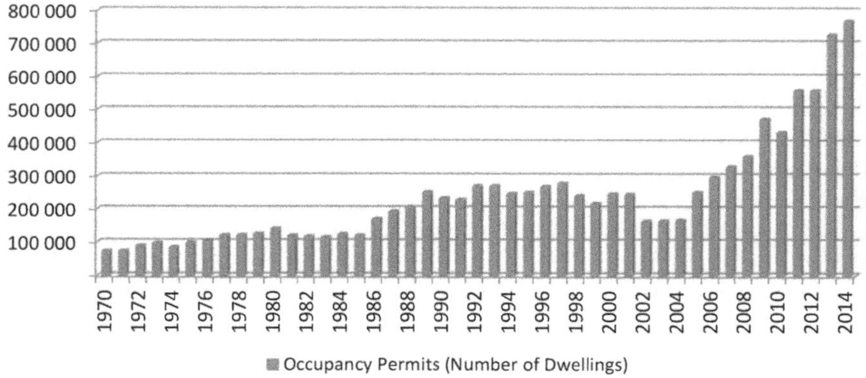

Figure 10.4 Occupancy Permits (Number of Dwellings), 1970–2014
Source: Turkish Statistical Institute, www.turkstat.gov.tr.

10.6. Once again, the private sector has the leading share in the market value of housing starts, at between 70 per cent and 86 per cent of the total value of housing starts. Public sector producers enjoyed their highest share, of 17.7 per cent, in 2012, but their share declined to 14.8 per cent in 2013 and 11.9 per cent in 2014. The share of construction co-operatives was around 20 per cent in the late 1990s, but declined to under 2 per cent by 2014.

Indeed, high levels of housing production have occurred without noticeable policies addressed to the demand side or supply side of the housing market. This implies that housing markets in Turkey operate under highly competitive conditions, without much regulation by central and local governments. However, one of the outcomes of the less regulated housing market is the great

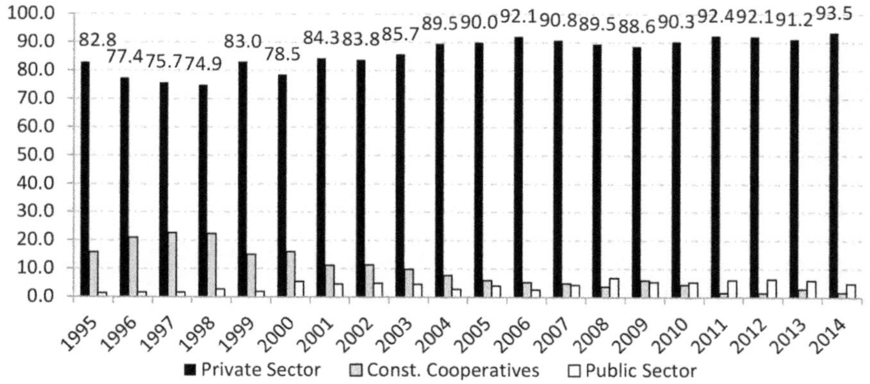

Figure 10.5 Share of Three Housing Producer Groups in Construction Permits Issued (Number of Units), 1995–2014, %
Source: Turkish Statistical Institute, www.turkstat.gov.tr, annual construction statistics.

variation of housing starts between different provinces in Turkey. In certain provinces supply falls far short of demand, whereas authorized housing production comfortably meets local needs in several other provinces (Türel and Koç 2015).

Housing policies are classified as: i) demand-side housing market policies; ii) supply-side housing market policies; and iii) intervention policies the in housing market, especially when housing policy was in its infancy.

Demand-side Housing Market Policies

In the historical development of housing policies in Turkey, the provision of housing loans from public funds at below market interest rates has been the most important demand-side policy. The Social Security Institution (SSI) began to finance co-operative housing by 1950 at a fixed annual interest rate of between 4 per cent and 5 per cent. As many as 233,000 dwelling units were built using SSI loans during 1950–84. However, the funds used lost value as inflation was often much higher than the mortgage interest rates. The SSI had to stop providing finance in 1984, and a new organization attached to the Prime Ministry, called the Housing Development Administration (TOKI), emerged.

The state founded TOKI to meet housing demand and to develop the housing construction sector. TOKI, working through its loan originator banks of Emlak Bank, Pamuk Bank, and VakıfBank, has funded over 500,000 housing construction loans and over 250,000 long-term mortgage loans since its foundation until the 1990s (Erol and Patel 2004). An implicit interest rate subsidy for TOKI-provided loans was one of the most important demand-side market policies. During 1984–89 fixed mortgage interest rates were set between 15 per cent and 25 per cent, while the inflation rate ranged between 29 per cent and 69 per cent. Consequently, 500,000 dwelling units that were financed by TOKI during that period enjoyed substantial amounts of unintended interest subsidies. The implicit interest rate subsidy decreased, after the interest rate of loans issued by TOKI were indexed to the rate of wage increases in the public sector in 1989. Hence, selling TOKI-produced housing with as much as 85 per cent loan-to-value loans, at interest rates indexed to the public sector wage increase became the primary demand-side housing policy targeted at average-to-lower-income households. However the value of TOKI's assets continued to decrease, as most of its income was allocated to the National Budget by 1993[6] and the rate of the public sector wage increase remained below the level of inflation during the years of economic crisis, and did not recover until much later (Türel and Koç 2015).

In the early 2000s, the housing loan market began to grow significantly, mainly as a result of a compulsory change in the investment policies of commercial banks. Until the late 1990s the government was borrowing at high rates of interest, and banks were able to earn high income by investing in government bonds (as discussed in Chapters 5 and 6). However, as the supply

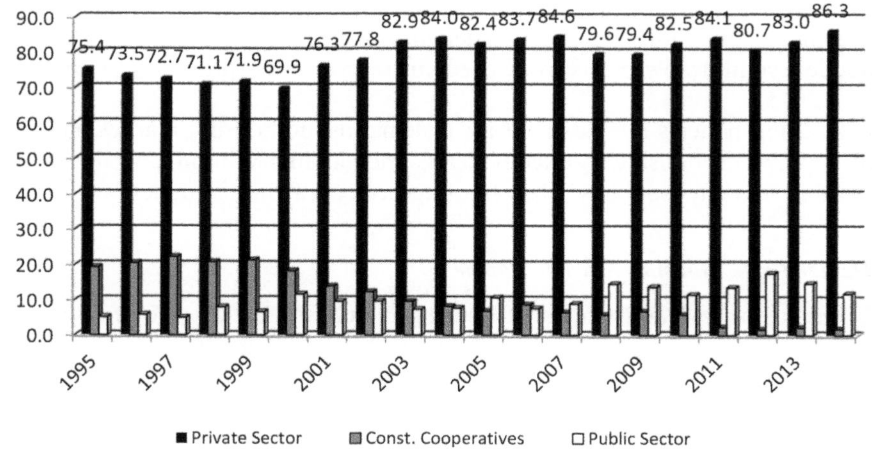

Figure 10.6 Share of Three Housing Producer Groups in Construction Permits (Market Value of Dwellings) 1995–2014, %

Source: Turkish Statistical Institute, www.turkstat.gov.tr, annual construction statistics.

of high-income government bonds dried up, banks moved into housing loans as an alternative source of income. The market value of housing loans jumped from TL70.1 billion (US $290.8 million) in 1997 to TL248.4 billion in 2000 and TL273.6 billion ($1.6 billion) by March 2004. Emlak Bank and Vakıf-Bank, which had been the main loan originators of TOKI since the mid-1980s, were still the dominant players (although Emlak Bank ceased operations in 2001) in the mortgage market.[7] These two state-owned banks dominated the housing finance market between the mid-1980s and mid-1990s with between 87 per cent and 97.3 per cent of the total mortgage market value in their portfolios. TOKI lost its monopoly as a housing finance institution because of the decreasing value of its fund under the weight of interest rate subsidies, and its mortgage products with very low loan-to-value ratios (Erol and Patel 2004).

Commercial banks have greatly increased their involvement in mortgage loans and became the primary source of mortgage loans by 2004 with the fall of inflation and mortgage interest rates. Since the new Housing Finance Law of March 2007, banks have been able to operate in mortgage finance in safer conditions and people now have greater options in making decisions for mortgage loans, which will be explored in the next section in detail.

The governments that came to power after 2002 began reducing new mortgage loans by TOKI and stopped them altogether in 2005. Co-operatives had been the main beneficiaries of the TOKI loans that were paid with the progress of construction. Indeed, out of 1,051,000 TOKI-produced dwelling units that were financed between 1984 and 2005, 944,000 were co-operative housing units (Türel and Koç 2015). Currently, the annual mortgage interest rates of commercial banks are about twice as high as the rates applied by TOKI. There are no subsidies for households for mortgage loan interest payments, if they own the house for personal use.

It is important to note that the provision of subsidies for moderate-to-low-income families living in rental accommodation, which is a well-known demand-side policy that is implemented in many countries, has not come on the agenda of governments until now. Rental subsidies were put into effect only as a limited support measure for civil servants.

Supply-side Housing Market Policies

Among the supply-side housing policies, housing production by TOKI on publicly-owned land has been the most important measure during the last decade. Since 2003, housing starts by TOKI have reached 537,000 dwelling units, which was about 11 per cent of the national starts during the same period (Türel 2012). Almost all TOKI-produced housing is in the form of multi-storey apartments, and their prices are generally below the market rate. All dwelling units produced by TOKI are sold to first time home-buyers.

Supporting co-operatives' owner-occupied housing was the most important supply-side policy by the middle of the 1930s. Co-operatives did not pay value-added tax (VAT) for a long time and currently they pay only 1 per cent VAT on the cost of construction of their dwellings by outside contractors. From 1966 to the end of 2011 co-operative housing starts reached 2.7 million units, which made up about 18 per cent of total starts (Türel and Koç 2015). Since 2002 government support for co-operative housing has significantly decreased, and the share of co-operative housing starts fell below 10 per cent by 2003 and fell to just 1.7 per cent by 2014.

An important supply-oriented policy was introduced by the enactment of the Building Amnesty Law in 1984, with the aim of managing the transformation of unauthorized housing. The Law defines the process and required conditions of regularization and transformation of unauthorized built dwelling units. In recent years TOKI, in co-operation with Turkish municipalities, has been involved in the transformation of settlements that could not be transformed through the market process, in accordance with the Building Amnesty Law. In the finished projects, one- or two-storey structures have been replaced by multi-storey apartments.

Housing Market Interventions

Rent controls are the primary direct housing market intervention in Turkey. They have been implemented on the decisions of the Appeals Court, based on the maximum annual rate of the increase in rents, as this had not been regulated by any law until that point. In 2000 the maximum rent increase was determined by the Law No. 4531 as 25 per cent for only that year, as was recommended by the International Monetary Fund in parallel to their economic stabilization programme. The recent Turkish Code of Obligations (February 2011) specifies that rents can be increased as much as the rate of increase in the 'Producers Price Index' during the preceding 12 months.

To conclude, housing markets in Turkey operate under highly competitive conditions, without much regulation or incentives. With the exception of direct provision of housing by the TOKI, mostly for moderate-to-lower-income households, there is not any effective policy that attempts to support low-income households in terms of housing acquisition and consumption. The transformation of unauthorized housing units where many lower-income households live as tenants, further reduces the supply of affordable housing for such households. A solution to the affordability problem in the absence of demand-side policies comes within the housing market, as housing is supplied at highly differentiated prices in spatially differentiated sub-markets of cities.

The Housing Finance System in Turkey

The sources of housing finance are both institutional and non-institutional in Turkey. While co-operative housing and equity sharing agreements are the non-institutional financing alternatives, project debt financing, housing loans (mortgages) and real estate investment trusts (REITs) are the institutional financing instruments. Furthermore, the changing role of the state with the direct involvement in financing development projects, through the transformation of TOKI, has also been an effective alternative financing model since 2002, when the AKP government came to power.

Housing co-operatives are legal entities established to provide their members with residential flats or houses. These entities are traditionally one of the most favoured methods of acquiring a property among Turkish citizens, particularly among the middle-income part of society. Equity-sharing agreements are also widely used in Turkey. In this arrangement, the landowner offers his or her land to the contractor in return for a portion of the equity interest (for example, in return for half of the flats in apartments that will be built in the development). In project debt financing, the project developer applies to a financial institution, which agrees to provide a secured loan of appropriate maturity and terms.

As noted above, since 2002 the state has been directly involved in financing real estate development projects through TOKI, which has been generating a particular model—called revenue-sharing for housing production—in order to meet the objectives of the government's housing production agenda. This model is based on the production of housing units on TOKI-owned lands in co-operation with the private sector (developers and contractors) and sharing the sales revenue of the project with the shareholder firm. The shareholder meets all the investment costs, except for land, as this is provided by TOKI at the beginning of the investment period. Having the land at no cost, getting procurement procedure and the necessary legal permissions in the shortest term under TOKI's public guarantee, the shareholder firms have the advantage of high marketing and sales capabilities.

The peculiarity of housing production by TOKI is not only limited to its housing provision model, but also the size of its land stock, which was approximately 118,000,000 square metres at December 2012, which can be used for any purposes by TOKI. Since 2002, TOKI has produced 640,726 housing units involving 540,216 (85.4 per cent of the total) units of affordable housing. The shares of affordable housing varies, from 22.9 per cent for the low-income and poor housing group, 40.6 per cent for low- and middle-income households, 15.1 per cent for the regeneration of squatter housing, 6 per cent for disaster recovery housing and 0.9 per cent for village-agriculture housing. The rest of housing production, totalling 14.6 per cent, was allocated to luxury housing as part of a revenue-sharing model to cross-subsidize affordable housing. The affordable housing units vary between 65 square metres and 87 square metres, with 12 per cent of the value of a unit put down as collateral, on a 15-year loan.

Hence, since 2002 the role of the state in the housing sector has changed, with its direct involvement in the production and financing of housing. The state has participated in large-scale mass housing projects through its agency, TOKI. Despite the increasing role of the state in housing finance, the most rapidly growing sources of financing in recent years have been housing loans or mortgages, and the newly emerging REIT sector.

Indeed, mortgage loans and REITs are the new financial instruments that have linked Turkey strongly into international (especially EU-based) financial markets. The Housing Finance Law of March 2007, Law No. 5582, introduced the mortgage system and envisaged the possibility of the eventual securitization of mortgages. Hence, long-term fixed rate borrowing became, for the first time ever, an available financing option for potential homeowners in Turkey. The main target of the mortgage system is thought to be middle-income households (Erol and Tırtıroğlu 2008) Moreover, due to the government's declining domestic debt requirement, investors have started to seek alternative investment opportunities within a reasonable risk class, including mortgage-backed securities defined within this Law. The legal foundation of the Turkish REIT structure, put in place in 1995, was designed by the Capital Market Board of Turkey, and the 'Principles Communiqué Pertaining to Real Estate Investment Trusts' was published on 22 July 1995. The following sections will provide detailed discussions on the development of the mortgage market and the REIT market in Turkey, respectively.

The Development of the Mortgage Market

Despite the historically high demand for real estate assets, a well-organized and developed mortgage market did not exist in Turkey until the early 2000s. The absence of an efficient mortgage market was mainly due to persistently high inflation, the inability of the banks to fund mortgages from their deposit base, and the lack of standardization within the title and appraisal systems.[8]

The measures, taken after the crisis of 2000–01, have been effective in suppressing inflation, building investor confidence and attracting substantial and indeed record amounts of foreign investments, notwithstanding the drawbacks highlighted above. The recent improvements in the Turkish economy, especially the drop in the inflation rate, have led the government to work on a draft of regulatory changes that would facilitate the legal environment for the establishment of the mortgage system. The efforts for the development of the mortgage system have attracted the construction sector and the related financial sectors. The result was an increase in the construction of the new housing units, development of the mortgage products, and a significant decline in mortgage interest rates (Erol and Çetinkaya 2009). Eventually, the Turkish Parliament ratified the Housing Finance Law in 2007.

Due to recent improvements in Turkish economy, especially between 2002 and 2007, Turkey experienced strong growth in the outstanding mortgage debt. The share of housing loans, which had been less than 1.0 per cent of GDP before 2004, had increased to 6.1 per cent by the end of 2013. In 2005, in an attempt to identify the share of housing loans within the total consumer loans, the Banking Regulation and Supervision Agency (BRSA) started to classify consumer loans as i) car loans; ii) housing loans; iii) personal loans; and iv) other loans. Figure 10.7 shows the distribution of consumer loans in terms of the 'outstanding loan balances' between 1997 and 2014. After 2004, housing loan and personal loan balances were considerably higher than car loans. More specifically, the housing loan balance increased from TL2.4 billion in 2004 to approximately TL115 billion by 2014. The personal loan balance increased from TL9.4 billion in 2005 to TL95.5 billion in 2014. Lastly, the car loan balance had reached approximately TL6 billion by the end of 2014. It is important to note that unlike some Central European countries, the level of housing loans in Turkey was not large enough in 2008–09 to cause any instability or risk to the Turkish banking system (see Karacimen 2014, for a detailed discussion on the relationship between labour market dynamics and consumer credit in Turkey).

The percentage share of the housing loan balance in total outstanding consumer loans is displayed in Figure 10.8. Housing loans or mortgages represented only 9.7 per cent of overall consumer loan value in 2003, whereas as of the end of 2014 housing loans had a share of 44.1 per cent. Between 2005 and 2014 the outstanding housing loan balance ranged between 44 per cent and 49 per cent of the overall consumer loan portfolio. Although housing loans have a substantial share within total consumer loans, they comprise a considerably lower share in overall banking sector credit. More specifically, except for the year 2010, housing loans have only a 10 per cent share in total banking sector credit (see Figure 10.9). In 2010 the share of housing loans peaked at up to 23 per cent of total banking sector credit.

Analyzing the Turkish mortgage market from the perspective of lenders, it can be observed that mortgage loans are almost entirely extended by the deposit banks. In other words, development and investment banks do not have any role in mortgage origination in Turkey. As the mortgage market is mainly funded through saving deposits, the mortgage debt-to-GDP ratio is low in Turkey. As seen from Figure 10.10, privately owned deposit banks have the largest share in mortgage lending. Between 2005 and 2014, the share of privately owned deposit banks in overall mortgage lending ranged between 46 per cent and 68 per cent. Except in 2007, the share of foreign deposit banks has been considerably lower than the share of state-owned deposit banks in overall mortgage lending. In 2007, the shares of state-owned banks and foreign banks have been more or less the same—that is, around 26 per cent. After 2007, the share of state-owned banks increased gradually, from 26.4 per cent in 2007 to 33.5 per cent in 2014, while the share of foreign banks declined from 26.1 per cent in 2007 to 14.2 per cent in 2014 (Figure 10.10).

Examination of the percentage shares of individual banks in mortgage lending activity indicates that the top 10 deposit banks, which are at the top of the list of banks according to total asset size, are also the top 10 banks in mortgage lending, although not in the same order. No foreign bank features in the list of the top 10 mortgage lenders. Hence, the big players in the Turkish mortgage market are the largest domestic deposit banks and they leave no place for foreign banks in the housing finance sector.

Deposit banks extend loans to borrowers who wish to purchase a single-family detached/semi-detached/apartment unit. While lenders generally rely on the appraisal company's determination of the eligibility of the property subject to transaction, some lenders have their own staff to do the appraisal work. Currently, Turkish banks offer a variety of mortgage products including TL-denominated fixed-rate, adjustable-rate, and graduated payment mortgages and US dollar- and euro-denominated mortgages, of which the most popular products are fixed-rate mortgages with either 60 to 120-month contract maturity. The prevailing mortgage interest rates for 10-year maturity loans ranged from 1.15 per cent to 1.50 per cent in April 2018.

In terms of insurance policies, hazard and earthquake insurance is required by all lenders. This has been a requirement since 1999 and is provided by Turkish Catastrophe Insurance Pool (TCIP). The TCIP takes the first loss position and private insurers take the second loss position. The annual premiums due to the TCIP are collected by private insurance companies from homeowners and then forwarded to the TCIP. Earthquake insurance rates are not fixed. They are determined according to the type of dwelling and the earthquake zone it is in. Most lenders also require a life insurance policy that would remain in effect over the term of the mortgage. Such a policy would help to cover the full repayment of the loan in the event of the borrower's death. Borrowers are required to renew their policy annually (at least during the term of the loan). Mortgage default insurance products are not prevalent in Turkey.[9] Existing sectoral studies suggest that there is no urgent need for

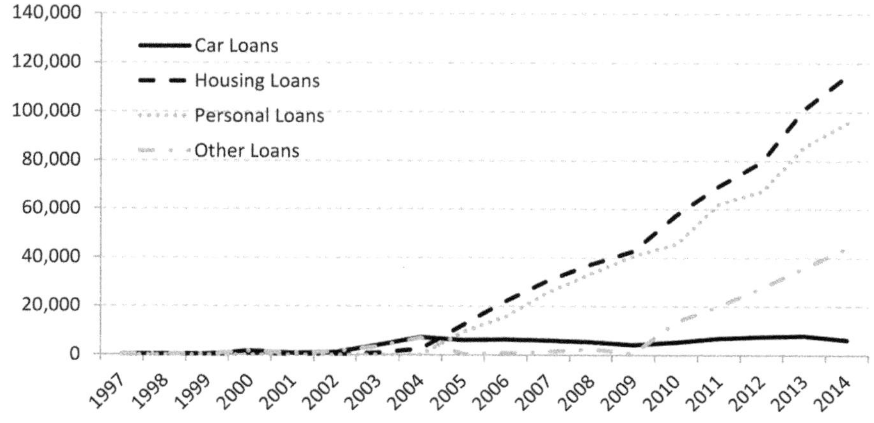

Figure 10.7 Outstanding Loan Balances, TL Million, 1997–2014
Source: Banks Association of Turkey, www.tbb.org.tr.

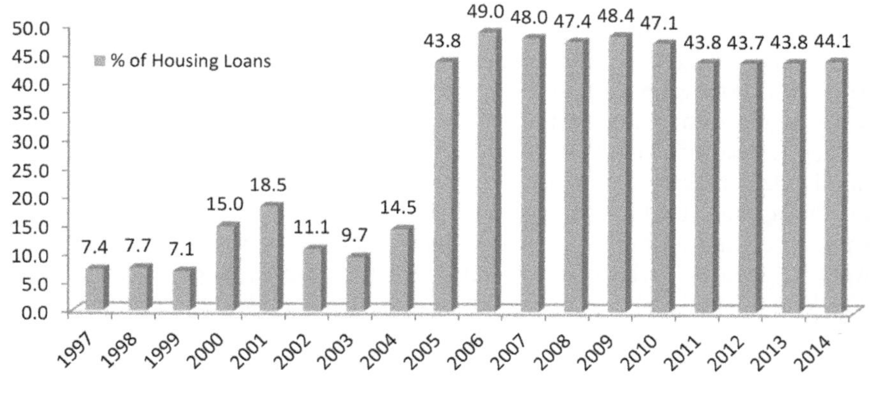

Figure 10.8 Share of Housing Loans in Total Consumer Loans (Outstanding Loan Balances), 1997–2014, %
Source: Banks Association of Turkey, www.tbb.org.tr.

mortgage insurance, as this will increase the cost of funds for borrowers (Erol and Çetinkaya 2009).

The 2007 Housing Finance Law and Secondary Market for Mortgages

The Housing Finance Law of March 2007 modified the Foreclosure and Bankruptcy Law, Capital Markets Law, Consumer Protection Law, Financial Leasing Law, Mass Housing Law and some Tax Laws. Moreover two bye-laws (Serial III, No 33–34 by the Capital Markets Board—CMB) were put

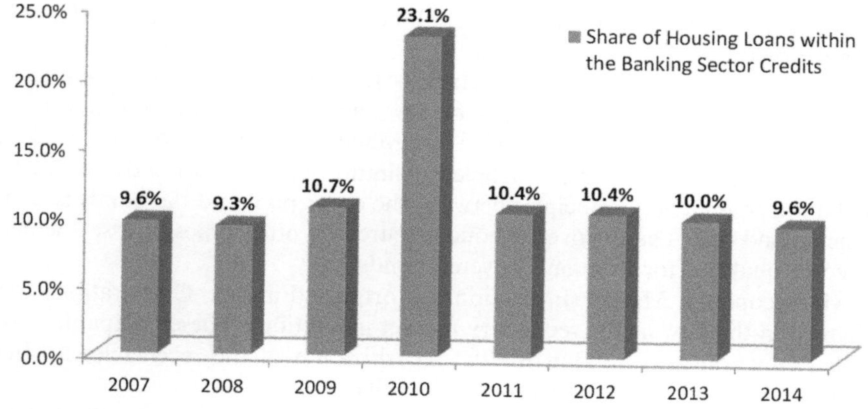

Figure 10.9 Share of Housing Loans in Total Overall Banking Sector Credit (Outstanding Loan Balances), 2007–2014, %

Source: Banks Association of Turkey, www.tbb.org.tr.

into effect for covered debt instruments (covered bonds) and securitization instruments (asset-backed and mortgage-backed securities).

The following issues are defined within the 2007 Housing Finance Law (Teker 2007):

i) Housing Finance and Primary Mortgage Lenders: According to the 2007 Housing Finance Law, housing finance covers loans for home-buying purposes (houses under construction are also included), home equity loans, loans extended for refinance, and home ownership through leasing. The primary lenders are banks that lend or lease directly to the customer for the purposes of housing finance, as well as leasing companies and consumer finance companies specializing in mortgage lending as non-bank mortgage companies. Mortgage companies are subject to the approval and licensing of the BRSA.

ii) Less Time to Foreclose: Due to high inflation and rapidly increasing real estate prices, defaulted borrowers tend to use every legal right they have to delay the legal foreclosure process, as the penalties and objection fees remain below the equity value they have earned as value of their property has increased. With the amendments in the Foreclosure Law, the foreclosure process is shortened.

iii) Real Estate Appraisal Services: The aim was to make sure that properties held by publicly owned companies and real estate investment trusts (REITs) are valued properly.

iv) Consumer Protection: In the past, consumer finance companies were unable to extend home loans to consumers, as homes were excluded from the definition of consumer goods. This law has amended that definition in order to enable consumer finance companies to act as mortgage lenders (subject to BRSA approval). Lenders who were not able to extend variable and adjustable rate mortgages in the past will now be able to do so,under the new regulations.

v) Mortgage-backed Capital Market Instruments: The new Housing Finance Law introduces two types of new capital market instruments to be issued by 'housing finance funds', i.e. covered bonds and mortgage-backed securities. The first one is the detailed definition of covered bonds and identification of matching principles between the cover pool and the bonds issued. The second one is asset covered bonds secured by other types of assets which are not qualified for mortgage covered bonds.

vi) Secondary Market Institutions: Mortgage Finance Corporations are defined in the Law as the secondary market institutions. These companies can either function as a conduit for the securitization of the receivables arising from housing finance and/or provide liquidity.

vii) Introduction of New Tax Incentives: These incentives are expected to decrease the overall operational costs of funding mortgage loans through capital markets with secondary market instruments. Some of these incentives include stamp duty and other types of transaction tax exemption.

The BRSA became a member to Financial Stability Board (FSB) in April 2009. The FSB released its Principles for Sound Residential Mortgage Underwriting Practices on 18 April 2012. According to the Board, the recommendations issued are intended to address "problems arising from poorly underwritten residential mortgages, which contributed significantly to the global financial crisis." As the crisis demonstrated, the consequences of weak underwriting practices in one country can affect the global economy through securitisation of those poorly underwritten mortgages. As such, it

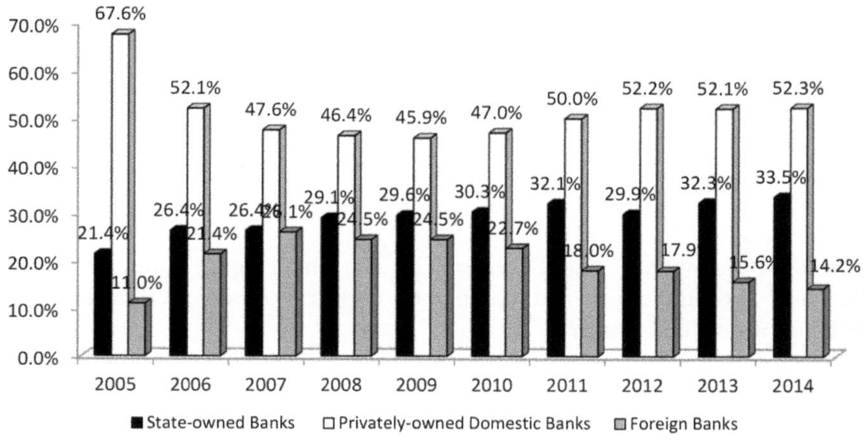

Figure 10.10 Share of State-owned, Privately Owned and Foreign Deposit Banks in Overall Mortgage Lending, 2005–14, %

Source: Banks Association of Turkey, www.tbb.org.tr.

says, "it is important to have sound underwriting practices at the point at which a mortgage loan is originally made."[10]

It is important to note that although secondary mortgage market legislation came into force in 2007 with the new Housing Finance Law, only a few transactions in this market have occurred. Indeed, there are a number of internal and external problems limiting the growth of the Turkish mortgage market. Firstly, issuances of Turkish Treasury still have low credit ratings from external credit assessment institutions. Therefore, most of the secondary market products to be issued in Turkey would not get high rating grades and this in turn limits the potential growth of the secondary market, and hence the primary market. Secondly, several governmental institutions such as the CMB, BRSA, Central Bank and the Undersecretariat of Treasury have explicit or implicit responsibilities regarding the development of the mortgage market. This multi-agency regulatory infrastructure may create co-ordination problems. Thirdly, although the banking sector has shown robust growth in the past decade, capital markets are lagging behind. This is another reason limiting the product variability and volume of the secondary market, and hence the primary market. Lastly, unlike their European counterparts, mortgage lenders in Turkey are almost all deposit banks and not investment banks, and finance mortgage loans through their savings deposit base. Although the target market for mortgage lending is assumed to be middle-income households, families with some amount of wealth accumulated for down-payment can become eligible to take mortgage loans to achieve homeownership. As lenders have to bear high risks caused by a mortgage–savings duration mismatch, they target families with low-risk and high-income profiles. Thus, a wide segment of the families are left underserved (Kutlukaya and Erol 2015).

The Emergence and Rapid Growth of Real Estate Investment Trusts (REITs)

Real estate investment trusts (REITs) are publicly listed real estate companies that mainly invest in real properties, such as retail, industry, residential and office real estate. The REIT sector has been a valuable source of housing finance that has been used in conjunction with other institutional funding sources to help the financing owner-occupied housing in Turkey. The introduction and ongoing growth of REITs represent one of the most visible and important recent changes in the Turkish economy.

Turkish REITs operate under statutory requirements that visibly differentiate these entities from their counterparts in other countries. The legal foundation of the Turkish REIT[11] structure, put in place in 1995, is considerably different and more complex than those observed elsewhere and predates those in Singapore, Japan, France and the United Kingdom. Erol and Tirtiroğlu (2011) highlight the unique aspects of Turkish REITs. In particular, this legal foundation i) exempts Turkish REITs from paying corporate taxes, but lets them enjoy complete freedom in their dividend policy choices; ii) mandates concentrated ownership of a leader entrepreneur, usually a founding financial institution; and iii) allows REITs to build considerably more diversified asset portfolios than their counterparts elsewhere.

As of December 2014, there were 31 REITs that traded publicly on the Borsa İstanbul (BIST) with a total market capitalization of TL42,059 million (US $18,104 million) and an overall portfolio value of TL21,981 million ($9,462 million). The total market capitalization of BIST companies in December 2014 was TL627,365 million ($269,800 million), of which the REIT sector made up 6.7 per cent of the total(www.cmb.gov.tr).

Entry into the sector, mergers and acquisitions, and joint venture agreements are currently ongoing processes. Turkish REITs can and do engage in a variety of activities. For the purposes of generating capital gains or earning rental income, REITs can i) purchase and sell real estate; ii) lease real estate from third parties and rent them in return to generate rental income; iii) purchase and sell capital market tools and make reverse repo transactions with such tools; iv) buy land in order to carry out real estate development projects; and v) purchase foreign real estate on the condition of obtaining ownership and investment in real estate-backed foreign marketable securities and of not exceeding 10 per cent of the value of the REIT portfolio (Erol and Tirtiroğlu 2011). According to Article 5 of the 1998 Communiqué, REITs may be founded i) for a specific period to realize a certain project; ii) for a specific or unlimited period to invest in specific areas; and iii) for a specific or unlimited period without any limitation of objectives. All Turkish REITs are of the third type, so they are not limited by a certain product type or geographic location, but are still bound by the general principles set by the CMB. Currently, REITs must invest a minimum of 50 per cent of their portfolios in real estate and real estate-backed securities. Earlier, this ratio was 75 per cent (Article 27 of the 1998 Communiqué). This reduction has given them further flexibility to construct a more diversified portfolio with short- and long-term fixed income securities (Erol and Tirtiroğlu 2011).

Evidently, the Emlak Konut REIT stands out as the industry leader, with the highest market value of approximately TL10.5 billion (see Table 10.1). Specifically, the market value is the number of shares outstanding multiplied by the closing price per share on 31 December 2014. Emlak Konut is a state-owned REIT and the major shareholder is TOKI. Hence, the land portfolio of TOKI and its implicit power in parliament in ratification of laws makes Emlak Konut REIT not only the leader in the REIT market, but also a monopoly, as it is an associated state institution to the TOKI.

Table 10.1 reveals that the largest ten REITs predominantly invest in real properties. Except for Vakıf REIT (another state-owned REIT), Sinpas REIT and Emlak Konut REIT, the remaining companies principally invest in real estate with shares of between 75 per cent and 97 per cent in their portfolios.

Finally, statistical data published by BIST show that REIT initial public offerings (IPOs) have dominated the Turkish IPO market in recent years. More specifically, Table 10.2 shows comparative summary statistics for REIT and non-REIT IPOs since 2006 and highlights the vibrancy and importance of REIT IPOs and the real estate sector in Turkey. Although the number of REIT IPOs each year in Table 10.2a is considerably less than that of non-REIT IPOs, the US dollar volume of REIT IPOs per year is considerably larger than that of non-REIT IPOs, especially between 2010 and 2014. For example, the US dollar volume of six REIT IPOs was equivalent to 54.5 per cent of the US dollar volume of 28 IPOs in 2010.

Table 10.2b shows, between 2010 and 2013, REITs' i) names; ii) IPO US dollar volumes; iii) percentage share of the top five IPOs; and iv) pertinent ranking in the top five IPOs. REIT IPOs show strong rankings. The top five IPOs (REIT and non-REIT combined) represented 78 per cent, 71.5 per cent, 74.3 per cent, and 93.7 per cent of the total dollar volume during this period, respectively. Other statistical data show that the share of the total funds of REIT IPOs, in the overall total funds raised in the top ten IPOs, on BIST is 52.3 per cent between 2010 and June 2014. Thus, a clear picture of the dominance of REIT IPOs in the Turkish IPO market in recent years has emerged (Erol et al. 2016).

Hence, as a result of the increasing significance of financial flows and investments in the national economy and the neoliberal and finance-led restructuring of the state's institutional apparatus, sources of housing finance are increasingly becoming institutional in Turkey. Project debt financing, housing loans (mortgages), covered debt instruments, asset-backed and mortgage-backed securities, and REITs are the new financial instruments that have linked Turkey strongly into international—especially EU-based—financial markets.

Table 10.1 Top Ten REIT companies in Turkey as of Q4 2014 (share of real estate investments in REIT portfolios and market value)

Rank	*Name of the company*	*Share of real estate investments in the asset portfolio, %*	*Market value (TL)*
1	Emlak Konut REIT	60.15	10,488,000,000
2	Torunlar REIT	75.37	1,730,000,000
3	Sinpaş REIT	59.52	1,248,000,000
4	Iş REIT	86.20	972,972,000
5	Doğuş REIT	92.17	972,450,903
6	Yeni Gimat REIT	97.17	927,360,000
7	Halk REIT	87.96	844,459,000
8	Akmerkez REIT	75.62	604,794,720
9	Vakıf REIT	27.88	575,395,017
10	Saf REIT	87.05	558,559,051

Source: Capital Markets Board of Turkey, 31 December 2014.

Conclusion

Turkey is rapidly becoming a service economy without having had a proper experience of industrialization, as a result of neoliberal economic policies followed by governments since the mid-1980s, and the rapid financialization process through deepening of financial globalization (Rodrik 2015). Since the 2000s there has been a significant change in the mode of integration of the Turkish economy into the global capitalist order, and since the election of the AKP government in 2002, the financialization-led process has intensified. One of the most notable urban policy consequences of the financialization process has been the commodification of cities and urban spaces by the AKP government through a radical change in urban legislation and city building. In other words, the spatial outcome of rapid financialization in the economy has been a substantial amount of construction all over the country, and Turkey has had one of the highest volumes of housing production in Europe during the past decade.

The economic policies of the AKP government have supported the construction industry as the engine of economic growth. However, the construction industry was fragile and highly volatile during 1998–2014. Throughout the years of accelerated growth in 2002–07 and 2010–11, construction output increased at a faster rate than the economy as a whole, but in the periods of stagnation in 2001 and 2008–09, the construction industry was the first to suffer. During 2010–14 the Turkish economy experienced high levels of foreign capital inflows and the lowest level of interest rates since the mid-1990s. The low interest rate environment not only reduced the cost of financing, but also increased the availability of housing loans, resulting in a significant amount of construction in the country. The growth in the construction industry delivered the largest contribution to real GDP growth in 2010 and 2011. Furthermore, in May 2012 two laws regarding the construction sector were ratified by the Turkish parliament. The Law on the Transformation of

Table 10.2a Share of REIT IPOs Within the Overall IPO Market in Turkey Since 2006

	Total Number of non-REIT IPOs	*Total Number of REIT IPOs*	*Total Funds Raised (US $)*	*Funds Raised by REITs (US $)*	*Share of REIT IPOs,%*
2006–09	27	2	6,112,637,038	389,846,835	6.38
2010	22	6	2,104,017,741	1,146,436,801	54.49
2011	25	2	826,488,497	202,595,189	24.51
2012	16	1	303,431,651	55,670,600	18.35
2013	7	3	676,550,309	217,057,511	32.08
2014	5	1	50,344,763	8,892,169	17.66

Table 10.2b Size of REIT IPOs in the Overall IPO Market in Turkey, 2010–13

	REIT	*Total funds raised (US $)*	*% Share in the top 5 IPOs*	*Rank in the top 5 IPOs in each year*
2010	Emlak Konut GYO	722,519,975	44.18	1
2010	Torunlar GYO	288,827,127	17.66	3
2010			Total: 61.84	
2011	Kiler GYO	121,949,503	20.64	2
2011	Akfen GYO	80,645,686	13.65	3
2011			Total: 34.28	
2012	Ozak GYO	55,670,600	Total: 24.70	2
2013	Halk GYO	141,683,168	22.33	2
2013	Panora GYO	55,729,706	8.79	3
2013			Total: 31.12	

Source: Borsa İstanbul, IPO Data: http://www.borsaistanbul.com/en/data/data/ipo-data, accessed 20 October 2014.

Areas under Natural Disaster Risk authorized public sector involvement in the urban transformation process with an initial estimate of 6.5 million dwelling units in zones at risk of natural disaster (principally from earthquakes). In the same year, the Turkish parliament also enacted certain amendments of Articles 35 and 36 of the Land Registry Law No. 2644, which redefined rules of reciprocity and substantially eased foreign investment restrictions, and foreign property investors have subsequently turned their attention to the Turkish real estate market. Consequently, within the region including Eastern Europe, the Middle East and Russia, Turkey has been one of the region's fastest developing real estate markets.

This study has revealed that financialization shapes the housing sector, as new financial instruments and funding sources, such as mortgage loans, covered bonds, asset-backed and mortgage-backed securities, and REITs have an increasing role in the financial sector. These new financial instruments have linked the Turkish economy strongly into international (especially EU-based) financial markets. Furthermore, the changing role of the state and its direct involvement in financing development projects, through the transformation of TOKI, has also been an effective alternative financing model since 2002, when the AKP government came to power. The state has also participated in large-scale mass housing projects through its agency, TOKI. Despite the increasing role of the state in housing finance, the most rapidly growing sources of financing in recent years have been housing loans (via the mortgage market) and the REIT sector.

Due to the recent improvements in the national economy, especially between the years 2002 and 2007, Turkey experienced strong growth in the mortgage loans (albeit off a low base). Although housing loans have a substantial share of total consumer loans, they have considerably lower shares in the overall volume of banking sector credit. This is mainly because, unlike their European and US counterparts, mortgage lenders in Turkey are almost all deposit banks. As investment banks do not have any role in mortgage origination, the mortgage market is mainly funded through the saving deposits base and the mortgage debt-to-GDP ratio is very low in Turkey. In 2007 the secondary mortgage market legislation came into force with the new Housing Finance Law.[12] None the less, only a small number of transactions in this market have taken place so far, due to internal and external problems limiting the growth of the Turkish mortgage market. The Turkish REIT market, another promptly growing source of housing financing, predates those in developed economies such as Japan, France and the UK. REITs provide a substantial amount of corporate funding from institutional investors in a well-structured market environment, and also bring transparency to the real estate sector. The Turkish REIT market is a small market with approximately 7 per cent of total stock market capitalization; however, it is growing rapidly and has played a dominant role in stock market IPOs in recent years. The main problem with the REIT sector is that the market has a monopolistic structure, in which the industry leader Emlak Konut REIT is owned by the state and its major shareholder is the state housing agency, TOKI. The Emlak Konut REIT enjoys a monopoly position in the REIT market by being very powerful in the ratification of laws regarding urban legislation and city building in general, and REITs in particular.

To conclude, capital market instruments such as mortgage loans, mortgage-backed securities and REITs have been growing as new alternative sources of housing finance in Turkey. However, these instruments and markets either have small shares in the financial sector of the economy (including mortgage loans and mortgage-backed securities) or have monopolistic and/or inefficient market structures, as in the case of REITs. If the growth of housing sector becomes more heavily dependent upon the direct support of state in the near future, this dependence may easily produce cleavages between different socio-economic groups, as well as urban spatial segregation.

Notes

1 According to Rodrik (2015), as developed economies have substituted away from manufacturing towards services, so too have developing countries. Such sectoral change may be premature for economies that never fully industrialised in the first place. Thus, deindustrialisation process in the developing countries is appropriately called premature since it means that many (if not most) developing nations are becoming service sector-based economies without having had a proper experience of industrialization.

2 From 1960s to the mid-1990s, the housing finance system was supported mainly by three institutional organizations: Social Security Institutions, Governmental Institutions (Housing Development Administration (or TOKI) and Ministry of

Resettlement and Construction), and Commercial Banks. Workers' social security fund, the leading mortgage lender of the market between the 1960s and the mid-1980s, was replaced by TOKI with its three loan originator banks from the mid-1980s to the 1990s. TOKI, working through its loan originator banks of Emlak Bank, Pamuk Bank and VakıfBank has funded over 500,000 housing construction loans and over 250,000 long-term mortgage loans since its foundation until the mid-1990s (Erol and Patel 2004).

3 ISPA, http://www.invest.gov.tr/en-US/sectors/Pages/RealEstate.aspx.

4 The Law Amending the Laws Related to Housing Finance No. 5582 (March 2007).

5 The construction permit and occupant permit are certificates which must be given by municipalities for projects to be constructed within the boundaries of municipalities, by industrial zone district offices within the boundaries of industrial zones, free trade zone offices within the boundaries of free trade zones, and must be given by governorships (Directories of Public Works and Settlement) if construction is outside the boundaries of municipalities, before any construction begins, according to Article 21 of Construction Law No. 3194, www.turkstat.gov.tr.

6 The Mass Housing Fund was allocated to (or defined under) the government's national budget in 1993. Hence, between 1993 and 2003 the funding sources of TOKI declined significantly, and the institution diverged considerably from its main function of producing housing during this period.

7 Since public banks could not fulfill their banking functions in the 2001 banking crisis period, with a new law the status of Emlak Bankası (with other state-owned banks of Ziraat Bankası, Halk Bank) was converted to corporation and they have been subjected to the provisions of the Banks Act and commercial code.

8 See Erol and Patel (2005) for failed attempts to introduce mortgages during the high inflation era.

9 Recently, a number of banks, (Finansbank, İş Bank and VakıfBank) have started to ask for mortgage payment protection insurance from the borrowers in the case of being unemployed or injured. The insurance policy generally pays up to six monthly payments to the bank. However, this product is different from mortgage default insurance that is widely used in the US and British mortgage markets.

10 FSB Issues Principles for Sound Mortgage Underwriting, 18 April 2012. The principles span the following areas, some of which proved to be particularly weak during the global financial crisis: i) Effective verification of income and other financial information; ii) Reasonable debt service coverage; iii) Appropriate loan-to-value ratios; iv) Effective collateral management; and v) Prudent use of mortgage insurance.

11 The Turkish acronym for REIT is GYO (Gayrimenkul Yatırım Ortaklığı). These entities, although they are labelled REITs, are considered to be a hybrid of Real Estate Investment Trusts and Real Estate Operating Companies structures.

12 Along with the primary mortgage market rules, the Housing Finance Law of March 2007 also defines the derivatives market for mortgages loans (the covered bonds, securitization tools of asset-backed and mortgage-backed securities) as the secondary mortgage market in the country.

REFERENCES

Erol, I. (2016) "Construction, Mortgage Market Development and Economic Growth in Turkey", T.A. Raymond, O. Franklin, E. Ochieng and M. Vida (eds.), *Real Estate, Construction and Economic Development in Emerging Market Economies*, New York: Routledge, 37–64.

Erol, I. and O. Çetinkaya (2009) "Originating Long-Term Fixed-Rate Mortgages In Developing Economies: New Evidence from Turkey", *METU Studies in Development*, 36: 325–362.

Erol, I. and D. Tirtiroğlu (2008) "The Inflation-Hedging Properties of Turkish REITs." *Applied Economics*, 40(20): 2671–2696.

Erol, I. and D. Tirtiroğlu (2011) "Concentrated Ownership, No Dividend Payout Requirement and Capital Structure of REITs: Evidence from Turkey", *The Journal of Real Estate Finance and Economics*, 43(1): 174–204.

Erol, I., D. Tirtiroğlu and E. Tirtiroğlu (2016) "Evolution of Noise and Pricing Reversals: Comparative Evidence from REIT and Non-REIT IPOs", Unpublished paper under revision for publication.

Erol, I. and K. Patel (2004) "Housing Policy and Mortgage Finance in Turkey During the Late 1990s Inflationary Period," *International Real Estate Review*, 7(1): 98–120.

Erol, I. and K. Patel (2005) "Default Risk of Wage-Indexed Payment Mortgage (WIPM) Contract in Turkey", *Journal of Housing Economics*, 14(3): 271–293.

Erol, I. and U. Unal (2015) "Role of Construction Sector in Economic Growth: New Evidence from Turkey", *Munich Personal RePEc Archive*, December 2015, Paper no. 68263.

Karacimen, E. (2014) "Interlinkages between credit, debt and the labour market: Evidence from Turkey", *Cambridge Journal of Economics*, 39(3): 751–767.

Kutlukaya, M. and I. Erol (2015) "Analysis of Cross-country Variations in the Depth of European Mortgage Markets", *Journal of Housing and the Built Environment*, 31 (3): 513–543.

Rodrik, D. (2015) "Premature Deindustrialisation in the Developing World", Vox, CEPR's Policy Portal, 12 February 2015.

Teker, B. (2007) "The New Turkish Mortgage Law", *Turkey Real Estate Book 2007*, Hague: Rep–Real Estate Publishers B.V., 230–233.

Türel, A. (2010) "Development and the Present State of Housing Production by Housebuilding Co-operatives in Turkey" *Cambridge Centre for Housing and Planning Research Conference*, 16–17 September 2010, King's College, Cambridge, UK.

Türel, A. and H. Koç (2008) "Türkiye'de İllere Göre Konut Üretiminin Farklılaşmasının Arsa Arzıile İlişkisi", in S. Kayasü, O. Işık, N. Uzun and E. Kamacı (eds.) *Gecekondu, Dönüşüm, Kent*, Ankara: METU Faculty of Architecture Publications, 243–262.

Türel, A. and H. Koç (2015) "Housing Production Under Less-Regulated Market Conditions in Turkey", *Journal of Housing and Built Environment*, 30: 53–68.

11 Restricted But Significant: Financialization of Households and Retail Banking Activities in Turkey

İpek Eren Vural

The contemporary financialization of capitalism is characterized by extraordinary growth in the scope of financial markets into economic and social spheres that had previously remained beyond their reach (Fine 2012; Bryan and Rafferty 2014). One manifestation of this trend is the penetration of commercial banks and other financial actors into the daily lives of the masses as sources of new profits, as well as the growing reliance of households on commercial banks to meet their basic needs (Lapavitsas 2009). This has been observed in the growth of retail banking activities by commercial banks, coupled with rising household debt.

This chapter will trace the evolving nature of the relationship between commercial banks and individuals/households and highlight four of its characteristics in Turkey. First, in the 2000s there has been significant growth in the retail activities of commercial banks, together with substantial growth in household debt. In fact it has been noted that household borrowing has been central for sustaining consumption power and economic growth in Turkey throughout the 2000s (Aydın et. al. 2015; Orhangazi and Özgür 2015; Becker 2016). Second, rising household debt and a growing reliance on consumer credit have not been class-neutral processes. On the contrary, they have disproportionately affected the lower social classes, and performed a wage substitution effect at the expense of increasing transfers from these classes to the finance sector (Karaçimen 2015). The first part of this chapter will highlight these issues and discuss various regulatory measures introduced by the state to encourage, mediate or contain credit use by households.

Third, rising household reliance on credit has been partly underpinned by the effects of the short-term capital-led growth model and the associated neoliberal policies on the Turkish labour market. The second part of the chapter reiterates research findings that analyze the effects of this growth model, such as wage suppression, low rates of employment, declining labour force participation, and high levels of unemployment, which fuel increasing household debt.

Fourth, despite growth in retail banking activities of commercial banks, and rising household debt in Turkey during the 2000s, there are prominent social and spatial inequalities in access to and use of financial services across Turkey. The third part of the chapter will analyze these inequalities.

Financialization, the Short-term Capital-led Growth Model, and the Surge in Retail Banking Activities

Financialization literature frequently refers to the changing functions of the commercial banks during the era of financialization, and in particular the growth in their retail banking activities (Lapavitsas 2009). This involves the growth in their lending and credit activities to households, as opposed to the predominance of commercial credit in earlier decades.

In Turkey, commercial banks' activities have varied across different phases of the process of financialization in the economy. The growth of retail banking activities became prominent in the second phase of financialization starting in the 2000s, while in the first phase during the 1990s, commercial bank lending was primarily directed towards financing government debt (Bakır and Öniş 2010; Ertürk 2003).

The onset of this first phase of financialization in the Turkish economy was marked by the liberalization of the capital account in 1989. Since then, the different economic growth models that emerged in Turkey have been characterized by their dependence on capital inflows—mostly short-term in nature—which have been widely used to finance chronically high current account deficits in the economy (Orhangazi and Özgür 2015). Throughout the 1990s, short-term capital inflows were prominent in financing large public debts (ibid). The government debt market, and the high-interest Treasury bonds that were issued to finance public debt, became the primary mediums in developing the financialization of the economy (Ertürk 2003). Fully liberalized capital accounts allowed inflows of short-term capital to invest in high-interest Treasury bonds. During this period, commercial banks raised funds from both domestic and international markets, and lent predominantly to the government through investment in low-risk, high-interest Treasury bonds, often at the expense of private sector investments that were deprived of credit (Ertürk, 2003; Ergüneş 2009). This trend was clearly reflected in the composition of total bank assets. During 1990–99 the share of government bonds within total bank assets increased from 10 per cent to 23 per cent, while the share of loans to the private sector declined from 36 per cent to 24 per cent (Turkish Treasury 2001, cited in Ertürk 2003: 196). This earlier phase of financialization in the Turkish economy was interrupted by two major crises, the first in 1994, and then again in 2001, both of which were triggered by sudden outflows of short-term capital (see Chapter 4 in this volume).

Monetary and structural adjustment policies adopted after the 2001 crisis marked the onset of a new phase in the financialization of the economy characterized by a debt-driven and consumption-based growth model (Yeldan 2007; Bakır and Öniş 2010, Akçay 2015). Dependence on capital inflows was again the central component of the growth model. Tight monetary and fiscal policies implemented during 2002–07 included inflation-targeting programmes to maintain price stability, and high interest rates both to keep inflation low and to attract foreign capital inflows (Bakır and Öniş 2010). Unlike the first phase of financialization in the 1990s, during this second phase the debt shifted from the public sector onto the private sector and capital inflows were used to sustain growing private rather than public debt (Orhangazi and Özgür 2015; Becker 2016). Private sector debt consisted of foreign debt issued by commercial banks and non-financial private corporations (Bakır and Öniş 2010; Ergüneş 2009; Yeldan2007: 10) on the one hand, and household debt on the other (see below for more details). Higher domestic real interest rates encouraged foreign borrowing by both the commercial banks, and non-financial private corporations, and increased their foreign indebtedness (Bakır and Öniş 2010). Restrictive fiscal policies, which reduced public debt, encouraged profit-seeking commercial banks to expand their lending towards households (TBB 2008). Simultaneously, inflation-targeting policies implemented by the Central Bank restricted real wage growth (Yeldan 2007), and contributed to greater reliance by households on personal loans (Akçay 2015; Karaçimen 2015). The ensuing growth in household borrowing and indebtedness was an essential element that sustained consumption and economic growth throughout the 2000s (Aydın et. al. 2015; Orhangazi and Özgür 2015).

Against this background, during the second phase of financialization in the Turkish economy, there was a significant upsurge in retail banking activities of commercial banks. Developments triggered by this trend included i) significant growth in the share of personal loans within total bank loans; ii) rising household debt; and iii) diffusion of consumer loans among the lower income brackets. Each one of these components is analyzed below.

Growing Share of Personal Loans within Total Bank Loans

Since 2000 there has been significant growth in the lending activities of commercial banks. The share of loans within total bank assets increased from a low point of 22 per cent in 2001—the year of financial crisis—to 59 per cent in 2012 (Şahbaz and İnkaya 2014: 73). As can be seen from Table 11.1, during the same period personal loans (defined by the Banking Regulation and Supervisory Agency of Turkey, to include credit card loans, and consumer loans, such as housing, car, and generalpurpose loans) became one of the fastest-growing sectors within the banking system (BRSA 2011b: 28). Their share within total loans provided by commercial banks increased from 15.7 per cent in 2002 to 33.5 per cent in 2012. The share of personal loans (i.e. consumption and credit card loans) as a proportion of gross domestic product (GDP), which stood at an average of 1.9 per cent during 1998–2002, increased to 7.0 per cent during 2003–07, before climbing to 17.3 per cent during 2008–14 (Karaçimen 2015 cited in BSB 2015: 168). Growth in personal loans within total bank assets continued in the aftermath of the global financial crisis, rising from 16 per cent in 2008 to 19 per cent in 2013 (Selimler 2015: 143).

As can be seen from Table 11.1 above, with the exception of automotive loans, all types of personal loans recorded significant growth over the 2000s. Credit card expenditure constituted a major driver in the phenomenal growth of personal loans. During 2000–06, the share of credit card loans within total bank loans increased from 6.8 per cent to 10 per cent. As such, they became one of the most important markets for the banking sector. From 2007 onwards, credit card loans underwent a gradual but steady decline, falling to a level of 6 per cent in 2014. Meanwhile, consumption loans recorded significant growth, rising from 19 per cent of total bank loans in 2005to 23 per cent in 2014. Growth within the components of consumption loans varied depending on the sector. While automotive loans showed a continuous decline, the share of housing loans increased from 8 per cent of total bank loans in 2005 to 11 per cent in 2007, and since then has stabilized at around 10 to 11 per cent. More spectacular growth was observed in the general purpose component of personal loans, which almost doubled from 6.7 per cent of total bank loans in 2005, to 12 per cent in 2014.

The rapid growth in personal loans spurred the introduction of various macroeconomic measures to arrest their dramatic growth. Such measures were strengthened especially in the aftermath of the 2007 global financial crisis, as a new policy approach that emphasized the necessity of complementing price stability with macroeconomic and financial stability gained significance among economic governance circles, including the Banking Regulation and Supervision Agency, and the Central Bank of the Republic of Turkey. Initial macroeconomic measures implemented towards this end targeted credit card loans and were sporadic in nature. Introduced in 2008, they aimed to reduce credit supply by raising the risk weightings of credit card loans. Partly influenced by these measures, and partly constrained by the effects of the global financial crisis, credit card expenditure during 2007–11 recorded a declining trend, whereby its share in total bank loans declined from 9.7 per cent to 8.0 per cent. (BRSA 2011b: 33; Table 11.1). Starting with 2010, the explicit goal of the new policy approach was announced as complementing inflation targeting with measures that reduce the impacts of capital flows on foreign exchange rates (see below) and credit. In this context, controlling credit growth was seen as an essential component to maintain financial stability (Alper et al. 2013: 342). A bulk of new macroeconomic measures followed in October 2013, and February 2014 aiming to restrict both the supply of and demand for loans. These measures include, raising consumer credit risk weightings, adjusting credit lines with income, suspending credit card usage and line expansion in case of defaults, and restricting the use of instalments in credit card expenditures. According to the Central Bank of Turkey, these measures were successful in restricting the growth of consumer loans (CBRT 2014b: 72) Credit card expenditure did indeed decline from TL84 billion in 2013 to TL74 billion in 2014. As noted below, however, this fall has been more than offset by the growth in other components of consumer loans, such as general purpose loans. As of June 2015, the share of personal loans within total bank loans had declined to 27 per cent from high of 33.5 per cent in 2012 (cf. BRSA 2015; and Table 11.1). Despite such a decline, personal loans continue to constitute the second largest sector of lending by the banking sector, behind commercial loans (which constitute 47 per cent of total bank loans) and ahead of loans for small and medium-sized enterprises (26 per cent) (BRSA 2015).

Developments in payment technologies in Turkey during the 2000s have been an important component underpinning credit growth. The phenomenal expansion in the number of credit cards issued by commercial banks, as well as the numbers of automated teller machines (ATM) and point of sale (POS) machines reveals not only the extent to which commercial banks extended their retail banking activities in the second decade of the 21st century, but also the extent to which their financial activities penetrated the lives of ordinary people. The growth rate of the numbers of credit cards during 2001–11 was 265 per cent. (BRSA 2011a: 61). Given the fact that over the same period, the employed population increased by only five per cent, this significant growth reveals not only the aggressive strategies of commercial banks in increasing their market share and profit rates, but also the changes in the consumption patterns of ordinary individuals (BRSA 2011a: 61). The total number of credit cards in circulation reached 58 million in 2015, while the credit card transaction volume reached TL543 billion (Inter Bank Card Center 2015). The growth in the number of credit cards is paralleled by the growth in the number of ATMs and POS stations. The cumulative annual average growth rate in the numbers of ATMs during 2005–15 was 12 per cent, while the corresponding growth rate in the number of POS stations during the same period was 7 per cent.

Rising Household Debt

Paralleling the increase in lending activities by commercial banks to the private households, there has been an upsurge in the reliance of households on personal loans. In developed economies, growth in housing loans and mortgages has been the most important driver of household debt. In Turkey, housing loans have also been one of the fastest-growing components within personal loans (CBRT 2014a: 47) and serve as the engine of a booming construction sector. Table 11.1 illustrates that housing loans increased from 2005 onwards, following the extension of repayment periods, and interest rate reductions in 2004. While in mid-2004 the average monthly interest rates on housing loans was 2.4 per cent, at the end of 2005 this had fallen to 0.99 per cent (BRSA 2006, cited in BSB 2015: 172). The ratio of housing loans to total GDP increased from 2 per cent in 2005 to 7 per cent in 2013 (CBRT 2014a: 47). The share of total bank loans provided by the commercial banks increased from 8.4 per cent in 2005 to 10.9 per cent in 2011 (see Table 11.1).

Table 11.1 Personal Loans as Share of Total Bank Loans, %

% of Total Bank Loans	*2000*	*2002*	*2003*	*2005*	*2006*	*2007*	*2008*	*2009*	*2010*	*2011*	*2012*	*2013*	*2014*
Commercial						40	45.1	45.7	43.3	43.3	41.4	42.4	44.4
Small and Medium-sized Enterprises						26.8	23	21.2	23.8	23.9	25.2	25.9	26.8
Personal	21.3	15.7	20	30.5	31.6	33.3	31.9	33.1	32.8	32.8	33.5	31.7	28.7
Credit Cards	6.8	9.1	10.9	11.4	10	9.7	9.3	9.3	8.3	8.1	9.1	8	6
House				8.4	10.6	11.4	10.6	11.4	11.6	10.9	10.8	10.6	10.1
Automotive				4.2	3.1	2.2	1.5	1.1	1.1	1.1	1	0.9	0.6
General purpose				6.7	7.6	10.7	10.5	11.2	11.9	12.7	12.6	12.3	12

Source: BSRA, 2015:12; 2010:18; 2011b:18; 2007:94; 2006:97; 2006:87; 2007:94, 2004a:47, 2004b, Central Bank of the Republic of Turkey, FSR 2011.

Their share declined slightly thereafter and stabilized at around 10 per cent in 2014. Growth in housing loans was also vibrant in the aftermath of the global financial crisis.

However, housing loans do not have the largest share within personal loans. As opposed to developed economies, where credit growth was primarily fuelled by housing loans (Stockhammer 2010: 5; Catte et al. 2004), in Turkey loans for immediate consumption needs have a larger share within personal loans. This can be traced to the growth of the general purpose component of personal loans, which consists of loans taken by individuals for professional goals, or for education, holidays, and food and clothing requirements (CBRT 2005: 19). The share of general purpose loans within total loans provided by commercial banks almost doubled, from 6.7 per cent in 2005 to 12 per cent in 2014 (see Table 11.1). It has been suggested that part of the demand for housing loans shifted towards general purpose loans following the introduction in 2011 of a restriction on the loan-to-value ratio of housing loans (CBRT 2014b: 70). The restriction, which requires that the mortgage amount cannot exceed 75 per cent of the value of the appraised property, may well account for the 1 per cent rise in the share of general purpose loans within total bank loans during 2011–12. However, an even stronger diversion in consumer borrowing towards general purpose loans was generated following the introduction in February 2014 of further governmental measures to restrict credit card loans. Hence, the recent decline in credit card expenditure referred to above, was more than offset by an increase in general purpose loans, which rose from TL129 billion in 2013 to 149 billion in 2014. As of June 2015, while credit card expenditure renewed its increasing trend and reached TL75 billion, general purpose loans rose further to TL155 billion (BRSA 2015; CBRT 2015: 12). This data, together with the discussion on the supply of consumer loans among lower-income groups in the next section, support arguments that subordinate classes in Turkey increasingly rely on consumer loans to meet their consumption needs and to reproduce their labour power (cf. Karaçimen 2015).

Recent government measures to counter economic stagnation that followed the failed coup d'état attempt in 2016 also point out to the centrality of household borrowing for consumption and growth. Amid the rising unemployment and stagnant economic growth, in September 2016 the earlier policies that had been introduced to contain credit growth were reversed. New measures were introduced that aimed to further stimulate credit growth. Hence, the loan-to-value ratio for housing loans, noted above, has increased from 75 per cent to 80 per cent, while the monthlyinstalment limits on credit card spending and cash withdrawals have increased from nine to 12 months. Moreover, the maturity cap for generalpurpose loans has been raised from 36 months to 48 months, and the restructuring of the current balance on performing general purpose loans was allowed, with maturities up to 72 months (CBRT 2016: 42). Credit growth ensuing from these measures is expected to energize hitherto stagnating economic activity.

Greater reliance by households on bank credit as a means to finance consumption has been coupled with sharp increases in household debt. Household debt, expressed as the share within household disposable income of credit card and consumption loan debts, has been increasing rapidly since 2003. The ratio of credit card and consumer loan debt to household disposable income increased continuously, from 7.5 per cent in 2003 to 55 per cent of disposable household income in 2013 (Table 11.2). The ratio of household debt to GDP has also been rising, from 7.9 per cent in 2005 to 13.6 per cent in 2008, and further to 15.4 per cent in 2009 (CBRT 2009: 30; CBRT 2010: 19). As of June 2013, the ratio of household debt to GDP had reached 22.9 per cent (CBRT 2013: 54).

The debt service burden of households is an important indicator of the transfer of income from households to the banking sector in the age of financialization. (Barba and Pivetti 2009; Lapavitsas 2009; Bakır and Öniş 2010). In Turkey, the share of interest payments within household disposable income grew from 2.1 per cent in 2003 to 5.4 per cent in 2013 (Table 11.2; Karaçimen 2015).

In addition to rising debt, there are also prominent difficulties in the repayment of personal loans. In the aftermath of the financial crisis, in 2009 and 2010 the share of personal loans within total non-performing loans (NPL) rose from 31 per cent to 37 per cent, outperforming the non-performance in other loan types, such as commercial loans and small-and medium-sized enterprise (SME) loans. Declining since then, it fell behind the share of commercial NPLs, and stood at 33 per cent as of 2013. The non-performance ratio for personal loans likewise climbed to 6 per cent in 2009, but has been in decline since then. As of March 2014, the ratio of non-performance for personal loans was 3.2 per cent, which was still higher than the other available loans types, such as loans to SMEs (3.1 per cent), and commercial enterprises (2.4 per cent) (BRSA 2014: 18). Credit cards have the highest non-performing ratio within personal loans; standing at 5.4 per cent in 2013, while general purpose loans have the second highest ratio, standing at 3.1 per cent (Selimler 2015: 144). Housing loans, on the other hand, have the lowest non-performance ratio within both personal loans and all other loan types, standing at 0.6 per cent in 2013 (ibid).

Despite the rising share of consumer loans in Turkey, foreign exchange and interest rate risks associated with these loans have been regulated. To begin with, interest rate risks of consumer loans have been lower in Turkey because of a policy of fixed as opposed to volatile interest rates on consumer loans, with the exception of housing loans where interest rates were indexed to changes in the Consumer Price Index. (CBRT 2009: 30). Moreover, compared with some Eastern European and Baltic States, such as Hungary, Poland, Latvia, Estonia and Lithuania (CBRT 2009: 30), the share of foreign currency loans within consumer loans was limited. Even before the crisis, in 2006 the share of foreign currency loans within total consumer loans was modest, standing at 4 per cent, while the share of foreign currency housing loans within total housing loans was 6.5 per cent. At the onset of the crisis, in 2008, the share of foreign currency loans within total consumer loans was 4.9 per cent, while the share of foreign currency housing credit within total housing loans was 9 per cent. In June 2008 a regulatory measure was issued that prevented households from borrowing in foreign currency or by indexation to foreign currency (CBRT 2009: 30). This brought the share of foreign currency credit as a share of total credit down to 3.9 per cent in 2009, while reducing the share of foreign currency loans within total housing loans to 7.4 per cent. Two years later in 2010, the Central Bank, as part of its new policy approach, sought to restrict the impact of capital volatility on exchange rates and credit. It thus developed further tools to prevent exchange rate instability (i.e. excessive appreciation or depreciation). One of these measures was an 'asymmetric interest rate corridor', which allowed interest rates to fluctuate within a predetermined range in reaction to capital flows, thus setting a maximum cap in the short term on the impacts of capital flows on interest and exchange rates (Alper et al. 2013: 342). Another measure, namely the Reserve Options Mechanism, allowed banks to hold some of their Turkish lira reserves in foreign exchange or gold. It thus provided the banks with flexibility to respond to changes in external financing conditions (i.e. acceleration or deceleration of capital flows) thus alleviating the impact of capital flows on exchange rates and credit volumes (Alper et al. 2013: 347; Marois and Muñoz Martínez 2016).

Provision of Personal Loans to Lower-Income Borrowers

Both consumer credit growth and rising household debt have not been class-neutral processes. Rather, their effects have been disproportionately concentrated among particular social groups, such as wage earners and low-income groups. The Turkish Banks Association's data on occupational distribution of consumer credit users (see Table 11.4) show that the wage earners form the largest group (50 per cent) among the users of consumer loans (CBRT 2013: 64). Reliance by wage earners on consumer credit has also increased over the years. The level of credit used by this group increased from 42 per cent of all credit used in 2006 to 52 per cent of all credit in 2014 (see Table 11.3). However, the Turkish Banks Association's data on wage earner categories do not differentiate between multiple occupations with diverse incomes (from managers to unqualified workers) that can be included in this category. It is therefore meaningful to complement the analysis of occupational distribution data with the income-based distribution of consumer loans.

In 2013 the distribution of consumer loan use on the basis of income groups reveals that the lowest two income groups (with a monthly income of up to TL1,000 and TL1,001–2000, respectively) use 44 per cent of all consumer loans, and constitute close to 60 per cent of all consumer loan users (CBRT 2013). The share of the lowest two income quintiles within consumer loan users consistently increased: from 49 per cent in 2006 to 62 per cent in

Table 11.2 Household Disposable Income and Debt Ratio, TL billion

	2003	*2004*	*2005*	*2006*	*2007*	*2008*	*2009*	*2010*	*2011*	*2012*	*2013*
Household Obligations	13.4	28.3	48.8	73.4	99.5	128.9	147.1	191.1	251.9	299.9	372.1
Household Disposable Income	180.3	218.8	233.4	404.7	466.0	352.8	408.9	463.9	531.2	613.9	673.6
Obligations/Disposable Income, %	7.5	12.9	20.9	18.1	21.4	36.5	36.0	41.2	47.4	48.9	55.0
Interest	3.8	6.9	9.4	12	15.5	19.7	21.1	20.4	23.1	30.0	36.5
Interest/Disposable Income, %	2.1	3.2	4.2	3.0	3.3	5.6	5.2	4.4	4.4	4.9	5.4

Source: The values for household obligations and disposable income are taken from CBRT 2006: 11,CBRT 2008: 22, CBRT 2011b: 19 and CBRT 2013: 54. Starting with 2010, the Central Bank uses the results of 2008 Income and Living Standards surveys to identify household disposable income; hence there are different values for 2008 and 2009 values in reports before 2010. The household disposable income and obligations values for 2008, 2009 and 2010 are taken from CBRT 2011b: 19. 2011, 2012 and 2013 values are taken from CBRT 2013: 54.

2012 (see Table 11.6). Likewise, the level of credit used by the two lowest incomes quintiles increased from 37 per cent of all credit in 2006 to 44 per cent in 2012 (see Table 11.5). Both the amounts of credit and credit users in the lowest two quintiles have recorded a declining trend since then.

There is also evidence that rising demand for housing credit, especially after the global financial crisis in 2007, originated from lower-middle and middle-income groups, whose share within total housing credit increased by over 100 per cent during 2009–13 (Altunok et al. cited in CBRT 2014a: 47). Over the same period, the share of highest income groups within total housing credits contracted by around 40 per cent (ibid). In 2014 the share of housing loans within personal loans stood at 35 per cent.

Reliance on consumer loans declines as income levels rise (ibid). When the age distribution of individuals who use consumer loans is analyzed, the dominance of middle-aged individuals can be seen. Half of consumer loans are used by individuals who are between the ages of 36 and 55, while 28 per cent of consumer loans are used by individuals, who are between 26 and 35 years of age (CBRT 2011a). As the provision of student loans is not widespread in Turkey, the access to finance of individuals between the ages of 18 and 25 is limited, with only 6 per cent of total consumer loans being used by individuals in that age group (ibid).

The Political-Economic Context of Rising Household Debt

Growing reliance on consumer credit, and rising household debt in Turkey have been underpinned by wage suppression, and low rates of employment and labour force participation, high levels of unemployment, and rising inequalities in income distribution. As Karaçimen (2014) argues, in this context consumer loans perform a wage substitution function, yet at the expense of further transfers from wage earners to financial institutions.

An extensive body of critical research on the Turkish economy associate the short-term capital-led nature of the growth models, which became prominent in Turkey during the era of financialization, with wage suppression, and the declining wage share in national income (Mütevellioğlu and Işık 2009; Yeldan 2010; Onaran 2009). Given the low value-added and import-dependent nature of local production (Taymaz 2015; Becker 2016), the export surge during 1990–2006, (1990=100) was sustained by significant declines in unit labour costs in US dollars (on average 22 percent) and rises in labour productivity (2.6-fold) (Mütevellioğlu and Işık 2009: 175). Frequent crises that characterized this short-term capital-led model of growth further cemented the downward pressure on wages and aggravated distributional outcomes. The Turkish economy experienced two such crises, one in 1994, and the other in 2001, both of which materialized following sudden outflows of funds and resulted in prolonged wage declines (Boratav, Yeldan and Köse 2000: 7; Onaran (2009: 251). Inflation-targeting policies implemented during the second phase of financialization in the Turkish economy during the 2000s also generated significant effects that suppressed wages. Yeldan (2007:17) shows that the surplus sustaining the high interest rates offered to the financial sector during this period was generated through a significant suppression of real wages (Yeldan 2007: 17). Mütevellioğlu and Işık (2009:191) report that during 2000–06 (when the year 2000 is taken as the base year), real wages declined by 25 per cent, despite economic growth. When 1997 is taken as the base year, during the 1997–2006 period, the real wage index declined from 100 to 83 (Mütevellioğlu and Işık 2009: 192). Wage suppression has also been prominent in the aftermath of the 2007 global financial crisis. Başak and Taymaz (2015: 103) point out that the worst effects of the crisis were shouldered by unregistered labour (that is, workers not covered by any social security scheme), whose hourly average real wage declined continuously during 2007–10. Taymaz (2015 cited in Yalman 2016) also noted that "the 2008 crisis has intensified pressures on manufacturing wages because cost competitiveness achieved on the basis of depressed wages is still the most viable strategy for Turkish manufacturing".

The 1994 and 2001 crises also resulted in extended declines in wage shares (Onaran 2009: 249). The falls in wage share continued into the 2000s. Mütevellioğlu and Işık (2009: 195) note that the share of labour income as a proportion of total national income declined from 29.2 per cent to 26.2 per cent during 2000–06, and the share of capital income stabilized at around 50 per cent over the same period. Using a GDP estimated income approach, which includes the firms' undistributed profits, Bahce et al. (2014: 28) also show that during 2002–2012 wage share declined from 44 per cent to 32 per cent. Focusing on wage share (within the labour share), Boratav (2014), likewise estimates that the wage share declined from 29 per cent in 2002 to 24.4 per cent in 2012.[1] Boratav (2014) further indicates that the declining trend in the wage share was steeper during 2002–07, while during 2007–13 it stabilized at around 25 per cent. Further declines in wage share over the same period were prevented through increases made to the minimum wage (Sönmez 2014; ILO 2015). However, this minimum wage growth was not enough to raise the proportion of wages in total national income, in the absence of improvements at the higher end of wage distribution (Bakış and Polat 2013).

Table 11.3 Occupational Distribution of Consumer Credit Used, %

	2006	*2007*	*2008*	*2009*	*2010*	*2011*	*2012*	*2013*	*2014*
Waged	42	43	48	56	58	52	55	48	52
Free Occupations	16	15	12	13	11	12	12	12	12
Other	16	20	32	26	26	30	12	34	31
Uncategorized	27	22	8	5	5	6	6	6	5

Source: The Banks Association of Turkey, Consolidated Reports on Consumption and Housing Credits. https://www.tbb.org.tr/tr/bankacilik/banka-ve-sektor-bilgileri/istatistiki-raporlar/59.

Table 11.4 Occupational Distribution of the Number of Credit Users, %

	2006	*2007*	*2008*	*2009*	*2010*	*2011*	*2012*	*2013*	*2014*
Waged	51	49	48	55	57	51	52	47	50
Free Occupations	7	7	6	8	7	8	8	8	8
Other	11	16	39	32	31	33	34	38	35
Uncategorised	32	28	7	5	6	8	6	7	7

Source: The Banks Association of Turkey, Consolidated Reports on Consumption and Housing Credits. https://www.tbb.org.tr/tr/bankacilik/banka-ve-sektor-bilgileri/istatistiki-raporlar/59.

Table 11.5 Distribution of Total Amount of Consumption Credit Used, by Income Group, %

	2006	*2007*	*2008*	*2009*	*2010*	*2011*	*2012*	*2013*	*2014*
Up to TL 1,000	21	19	27	21	22	27	22	21	17
TL1,001−2,000	16	19	23	25	25	22	21	23	20
TL2,001−3,000	8	10	11	14	17	15	19	18	15
TL3,001−5,000	10	9	10	13	13	11	13	12	12
TL5,001 +	18	17	18	19	16	16	15	17	22
Uncategorized	28	25	10	8	6	9	10	10	13

Source: The Banks Association of Turkey, Consolidated Reports on Consumption and Housing Credits. https://www.tbb.org.tr/tr/bankacilik/banka-ve-sektor-bilgileri/istatistiki-raporlar/59.

Table 11.6 Distribution of Consumer Credit Users, by Income Group, %

	2006	*2007*	*2008*	*2009*	*2010*	*2011*	*2012*	*2013*	*2014*
Up to TL1,000	30	30	45	41	41	42	35	31	26
TL1,001–2,000	19	22	25	29	28	25	27	28	27
TL2,001–3,000	7	7	8	11	13	12	15	14	13
TL3,001–5,000	7	6	5	6	6	6	7	7	7
TL5,001+	6	7	6	7	6	6	7	10	15
Uncategorized	31	30	11	6	6	9	9	9	11

Source: The Banks Association of Turkey, Consolidated Reports on Consumption and Housing Credits. https://www.tbb.org.tr/tr/bankacilik/banka-ve-sektor-bilgileri/istatistiki-raporlar/59.

Wage suppression, the declining wage share, and deteriorating income distribution generate deficits in household income, which hit the lowest-income quintiles hardest. As the analysis of Bahçe et al. (2014: 38) of household income and consumption for the period 2002–11 reveals, the lowest-income quintiles were persistently in deficit throughout the whole period. Their distribution of income, and household consumption data on the basis of social classes, also reveal that subsistence farmers and rural labourers had the largest share within deficit households while at the end of 2011, and nearly 40 per cent of urban labourer households were also in deficit (Bahçe et al. 2014: 40). This is compatible with the finding in the previous section, which stated that the lowest-income quintiles and wage earners are the largest customers of consumer credit. In this respect Karaçimen's work (2014, 2015) further reveals that wage suppression, deteriorating income distribution, rising labour flexibility, the insecurity of labour markets, and changing consumption habits are trigger factors for wage earners' greater reliance on consumer loans.

A financialized growth model, based on inflows of short-term capital, also proved incapable of generating employment. This inability came to be recognized as the phenomenon of 'jobless growth' and was defined as the weakening of the relationship between economic growth and employment creation (Yeldan 2007). Tight monetary and fiscal policies implemented in the post-2001 crisis period, as well as high interest rates and overvalued Turkish lira components of these policies significantly undermined the production structure of the real sector by shifting investment away from this sector towards the financial sector (Yeldan 2010). This resulted in significant contraction in production and employment creation in the manufacturing sector. During 2002–06 average economic growth in Turkey reached 7.2 per cent, while employment growth was only 0.8 per cent (Mütevellioğlu and Işık 2009: 174). During 2008–12, in the aftermath of the global financial crisis, employment growth in the industrial sector was again stagnant (Aydın etal. 2015: 68).

While the short-term capital-led growth model failed at employment generation, the dissolution of small-scale commodity production in agriculture in the 2000s further depressed labour force participation, employment, and income distribution. Agricultural reforms, which have been implemented with increasing vigour since the early 2000s under the auspices of the World Bank and the International Monetary Fund, reduced support payments for agricultural inputs, such as fertilizers, seed and fuel, and halted the government's purchases of a number of key crops (Kendir 2007; Pamuk 2014: 265). Meanwhile, the World Bank initiated a direct income support system, which provided support based on landownership rather than cultivation, reduced the incentives for production, and urged subsistence farmers to migrate to urban centres. The policies concerned thus generated record reductions in agricultural production, and a concomitant reduction in the agricultural labour force (Aydın 2009). They also resulted in large waves of migration to urban centres and expanded the urban labour force. Employment in agriculture shrank from 40 per cent of total employment in Turkey in 1999 to 26.4 per cent in 2007 (Mütevellioğlu and Işık 2009: 171–172). While these reforms reduced agricultural employment, non-agricultural sectors were trapped in a model of economic growth dependent on inflows of short-term capital and high interest rates, which undermined industrialization policies, reduced public investment and sustained jobless growth patterns (Mütevellioğlu and Işık 2009). Manufacturing sector employment, which stood at 17 per cent of total employment in 1999, rose to 19.8 per cent by 2007, while employment in the services sector increased from 42.7 per cent in 1999 to 48 per cent in 2007, of which construction services comprised 5.8 per cent (Mütevellioğlu and Işık 2009: 171–172). Employment in agriculture rose from 23.6 per cent of total employment in 2008 to 24.5 per cent in 2012. (Aydın et. al. 2015). A further change in the support system, coupled with reverse migration triggered by the global financial crisis, could have contributed towards the reverse of the declining employment trend in the agricultural sector during 2008–13 (Aydın et al. 2015: 61). Despite this increase, the share of agriculture within total employment in 2012 was still lower than its 2007 value of 26 per cent. The recent reforms on the use and inheritance of agricultural lands (cf. Ministry of Agriculture 2016) are likely to further influence employment patterns in the agricultural sector.

The demise of small-scale production in agriculture also affected unregistered employment—a long-lasting attribute of the labour market in Turkey. During 2004–11 the average share of unregistered employment—i.e. employment not covered by any form of social security—within total employment reached 44 per cent (Başak and Taymaz 2015: 97). The overall trend in unregistered employment is a declining one: from 50 per cent in 2004 to 39 per cent in 2012, and this can be attributed to the declining employment rate in agriculture (ibid). Mütevellioğlu and Işık (2009: 180), however, note that while the rapid reduction in agricultural employment contributes to reductions in total unregistered labour, this decline is partly offset by increases of unregistered labour in non-rural sectors. Unregistered waged labour in non-rural sectors continues to form the most insecure section of the labour force in Turkey. As Başak and Taymaz (2015: 102) noted, hourly average wages received by this group of workers in urban areas during 2004–11 were always around half of the hourly average real wages received by registered labour.

The demise of small-scale production in the agricultural sector also reduced the income of agricultural labour. As Bahce et al. (2014: 25) in their analysis of functional income distribution show, during 2002–11 the share of agricultural income halved: from 16 per cent to 8 per cent of total household factor income. Poverty associated with the demise of small-scale commodity production in agriculture thus emerges as an important source of social exclusion in the Turkish context (Yükseker 2009).

During the 2000s, the demise of small-scale production in agriculture and the jobless growth pattern emerge as the main causes underlying further declines in already low levels of labour force participation and employment. During 1990–2007 the working-age population increased by 48 per cent, the labour force increased by 25 per cent, while the employment rate increased by 22 per cent (Mütevellioğlu and Işık 2009: 168). Hence, during the 1990s and 2000s there was a constant decline in both labour force participation rates and employment rates. The labour force participation rate, which was 57.6 per cent in 1990, declined to 50.5 per cent in 2014, which effectively means that half of the labour force is out of the labour market. Low levels of female labour force participation, which declined rapidly as a result of migration from rural to urban centres, is the most important source of low levels of labour force participation. As such, female labour force participation, which was 35 per cent in 1990, declined consistently until 2007, when it reached 23.6 per cent. It improved thereafter to 28.8 per cent in 2011 and reached 30.3 per cent by 2014 (SIT 2016). While the current male labour force participation rates are closer to EU15 rates, a consistent declining trend is also observable in the male labour force participation rate, which declined from 80 per cent in 1990 to 71.5 per cent in 2013 (SIT 2015).

A downward trend is also observable in the employment rate, which fell from 53 per cent in 1990 to 45.5 per cent in 2014. During 2002–06, when the Turkish economy recorded significant growth in terms of gross national product, the employment rate declined from 44.4 per cent to 41.5 per cent. This downward trend in the employment rate continued until 2011, when it rose to 43 per cent and eventually reached 45 per cent in 2014 (SIT 2015). Unemployment started to increase, especially after 2002. During the strong growth period of 2002–06, unemployment was stable at around 10 or 11 per cent. Non-agricultural unemployment rates are higher than total unemployment rates and during 2002–06 there was a volatile and negligible decline from 14.5 per cent to 12.7 per cent. The values for 2014 for unemployment and non-agricultural unemployment were 11 per cent and 12 per cent, respectively.

As a result, wage suppression, declining wage share, low levels of employment and labour force participation are important factors that led low-income households to rely on bank credits to meet basic needs. Perpetuation of such factors in the Turkish economy is also closely related with the financialized growth model based on inflows of short-term capital.

Inequalities in, Access to, and Use of Financial Services

Despite the rapid growth in retail banking activities and household debt, there are significant inequalities in access to and use of financial services across Turkey. The Macro Access Index, developed by the World Bank, calculates the index value for access to financial services in Turkey as 49 points, which means that half of the Turkish population is excluded from access to financial services (CBRT 2011a: 19). A more recent financial index, developed by Boğaziçi University and Turkish Economy Bank, calculates the financial access value as 39 out of 100. (TEB-Boğaziçi University 2014). The low access value in this index indicates that ordinary consumers do not use most financial services other than the most basic, such as bank accounts and credit cards (TEB-Boğaziçi University 2014: 7) A similar index that was developed to measure financial literacy, where this is defined as financial knowledge, attitudes and behaviour on a scale of 1 to 100, generated a value of 59 (ibid). TEB-Boğaziçi indices also reveal that demographic groups that lack both financial literacy and access to financial services overlap. Those who lack both financial literacy and access to financial services are predominantly women, belong to lower socioeconomic groups, live in rural areas, and tend to be unemployed, housewives or students. Those with greater financial literacy and access to financial services predominantly tend to be male, live in urban areas, belong to higher socioeconomic groups with higher levels of education, and are usually employers, entrepreneurs, managers and/or professionals (TEB-Boğaziçi University 2014).

Spatial inequalities in access to and use of financial services across Turkey are also abundant. Access and use of financial services are highly concentrated in regions and provinces that ranked among the most developed in the 2011 socioeconomic development index (cf. Ministry of Development, 2013). These regions are İstanbul, East Marmara (including provinces such as Kocaeli, Bursa and Eskişehir), Western Anatolia (including the capital city Ankara), the Aegean (including provinces such as İzmir and Muğla) and the Mediterranean (including Antalya). Meanwhile, socioeconomically the least developed regions of Mid-East Anatolia (including provinces such as Van, Muş, Bitlis and Hakkari), North-East Anatolia (including provinces such as Ağrı, Kars, Iğdır and Ardahan), and South-East Anatolia (including provinces such as Mardin, Şırnak, Siirt, Şanlıurfa and Diyarbakır) lag significantly behind. Although there appears to be a significant catch-up development process, the distribution of that catch-up is also unequal.

A total of 41 per cent of all bank branches are concentrated within İstanbul, East Marmara and West Marmara (including the provinces of Balıkesir, Tekirdağ, Kırklareli and Edirne) while the respective shares of the least developed regions such as South-East Anatolia and North-East Anatolia have only 4 per cent of total bank branches (BRSA 2011a: 16). Provincial distribution of bank branches is also highly concentrated. The share of the most developed five provinces within the total number of bank branches across the country is 51 per cent (BRSA 2011a: 16). İstanbul alone has 30 per cent of all bank branches, followed by Ankara (10 per cent), İzmir (7 per cent), Antalya (4 per cent) and Bursa (4 per cent) (ibid).

There are also extensive variations in population per bank branch. The lowest populations per bank branch, indicating potentially greater access to financial services, are found in İstanbul (4,368 people per bank branch), Muğla (4,720 people per bank branch) and Ankara (4,755 people per bank branch), which are significantly lower than the national average population per bank branch figure, which is 7,352. This stands in sharp contrast to provinces in the Mid-East Region, such as Muş (33,707 people per bank branch), Şanlıurfa (28,817 people per bank branch) and Van (28,398 people per bank branch), which has up to eight times more population per bank branch than the most developed provinces, and four times more population per bank branch than the national average. On a regional basis, a smaller population per bank branch is seen in West Anatolia (5,706 people per bank branch), the Aegean region (6,600 people per bank branch) and West Marmara (7,615 people per bank branch). The largest population per bank branch is seen in Mid-East Anatolia where an average bank branch serves 19,561 people, and in South-East Anatolia, where the relevant figure is 17,601 (CBRT 2011a: 55).

Regional and provincial distribution of bank loans and deposits is another important indicator of access to financial services. Like bank branches, loans and deposits are also concentrated in more developed regions. Istanbul alone accounts for 46 per cent of all deposits within the banking sector, containing close to 18 per cent of the total population. Regions such as West Anatolia, Aegean, and Mediterranean (all including most developed provinces, such as Ankara, İzmir, Antalya) account for larger shares within deposits, respectively 15 per cent, 9 per cent and 6 per cent. Meanwhile, regions such as East Black Sea, North East Anatolia or Mid East Anatolia attain 1 per cent or less of total deposits (TBB: 2015).

Likewise, bank loans are also concentrated in İstanbul, West Anatolia and Aegean regions. In 2014, 41 per cent of all bank loans were used in İstanbul. This was followed by West Anatolia and Aegean regions, each of which used 13 per cent and 10 per cent of total bank loans, respectively (TBB 2015). The leading positions of these regions are mainly due to their inclusion of the most developed provinces of İstanbul, Ankara and İzmir. Meanwhile the combined share of some other regions, such as the East Black Sea (2 per cent), the North-East Anatolia (1 per cent), the Mid-East Anatolia (1 per cent), is merely 4 per cent of the total loans. The South East Anatolia region's share within total bank loans is 4 per cent (TBB 2015). A similar outlook emerges when the regional distribution of loans per person is observed. İstanbul leads with highest amount of loans used per person followed by West Anatolia and East Marmara Region. The lowest loans per person are seen in the Mid-East Anatolia and North-East Anatolia (CBRT 2011a: 40).

Distribution of bank loans on the basis of different bank groups, such as private commercial banks, public banks, foreign banks, and investment and development banks, also reveal important insights. Private commercial banks provide a larger share of loans than public banks in both developed and least developed regions. In 2014 private commercial banks provided 51 per cent of loans in the banking sector, while public banks' share remained at 29 per cent. Public banks' share in regional loan markets surpassed those of private banks only in the two least developed regions, namely Mid-East Anatolia (including provinces such as Van, Muş, Bitlis and Hakkari) and North-East Anatolia, (including provinces such as Ağri, Kars, Igdir and Ardahan) (TBB 2015). In 2014 public banks provided more than half of all loans in Mid-East and North-East Anatolia. Meanwhile, in other less developed regions, the share of private commercial banks in total loans are either larger than public banks; such is the case in South-East Anatolia and the East Black Sea region, and their share in total loans is almost equal to those of public banks in the West Black Sea region and Mid-Anatolia (TBB 2015). This being said, however, Önder and Özyıldırım (2013) find that the share of public banks in loan markets in crisis years is significantly higher than their share in non-crisis years in all provinces and in less developed provinces (see also Marois and Güngen 2016). Önder and Özyıldırım (2013) further indicate that credit provided by public banks have a significant positive effect on local growth during crisis years in all provinces, and especially in developed regions.

Despite the high concentration of deposits and loans in more developed regions, loan-to-deposit ratios across different regions also reveal that there is an increasing flow of funds from resource-rich to resource-poor regions. Certain regions such as South-East Anatolia, North-East Anatolia, and the Mid-East and East Black Sea regions appear as net receivers of funds, while İstanbul and Western Anatolia are net exporters of funds. During 2010–14, for example, the loan-to-deposit ratio showed the highest increase in South-East Anatolia, rising from 158 per cent to 285 per cent. Although more modest over the same period, loan-to-deposit ratios also increased in the East Black Sea region, rising from 104 per cent to 148 per cent, while the relevant figure for the Mid-East region was a rise from 94 per cent to 159 per cent.

Inequalities within the financial sector, especially income and wage disparities driven by large bonus payments to reward employee behaviour, have been frequently emphasized by financialization literature (Stockhammer 2010). For the Turkish case, no reliable data is available to comment on this trend of wage and income inequality within the financial sector. However, an analysis of wage differentials within the broader economy reveals that compared with all the other sectors, the finance and insurance sectors provide the highest annual average pre-tax earnings. The wage differential between the finance and insurance sectors and the administrative and support services sector, which provide the lowest pre-tax annual earnings, is 68.7 per cent (TÜİK 2010). Standing at 3 per cent, the gender pay gap is also the narrowest in the finance and insurance sector (ibid).

Conclusion

Financialization of the household sector in Turkey over the course of 2000s took the form of rising credit use by households from the commercial banking sector. Thus, the last 15 years have seen significant growth in retail banking activities of commercial banks, together with greater reliance by households on consumer loans, and rising household debt. This process has been of paramount significance, especially for lower-income and wage earning households. As discussed in this chapter, growing credit reliance by households cannot be considered independently of the political economic context. The effects on the labour market of the short-term capital-led growth model prominent in Turkey throughout the 2000s, led low income households to rely on bank credit to meet basic needs. Wage suppression, low rates of employment and labour force participation, high levels of unemployment, and growing inequalities in income distribution, were among the prominent effects of the short-term capital-led growth model, which fuelled credit reliance among low-income households. The greater share of general purpose loans within consumer loans, as opposed to housing loans, which take the lion's share within bank loan distribution in most other economies, indicates the indispensability of credit for meeting basic consumption needs in the household sector. Against this background, the rising retail banking activities of commercial banks has encouraged large parts of the working population to enter into a relationship with the financial sector.

Throughout the 2000s, borrowing and indebtedness by households formed an essential dimension of the consumption-based and short-term capital-led growth model in Turkey. Foreign capital inflows facilitated credit expansion by commercial banks and financed the loans used by the household sector. The consumption power of households became an important engine of economic activity throughout the 2000s (Orhangazi and Özgür 2015; Becker 2016). As has been discussed throughout the chapter, the significance of household borrowing for the growth model can also be observed in various regulatory measures introduced by the state to mediate, contain or encourage credit use by the household sector. Hence, during the early 2000s, and well into the 2010s, regulatory measures that encouraged household borrowing were prominent. During 2010–13 a more cautious approach emphasizing financial stability was adopted and measures were introduced to contain credit expansion. Most recently, in 2016, amid increasing unemployment and stagnant growth, earlier policies were reversed in order to encourage consumption and economic activity.

Credit reliance and growing indebtedness by low-and middle- income households in Turkey has several implications. As discussed in this chapter, and as widely emphasized in financialization literature, the most obvious implication is that growing debt service obligations result in income transfers from wage earners and workers towards the financial sector. Second, greater integration into credit relations increases the market exposure of low-income households, magnifying the risks from financial market instabilities. Thirdly, as noted by some financialization theorists, greater dependence on credit for meeting basic needs expands the disciplinary power of capital on labour and spreads market logic into the everyday lives of wage earners (Bryan, Martin and Rafferty 2009; Karaçimen 2014).

To conclude, household borrowing from the commercial banking sector and the ensuing household debt were the principal means in financialization of the household sector in Turkey. This process has been significant, due to its rapid growth, its extensive breadth across different social groups, with greater prominence among the low- and middle-income households, as well as its indispensability both for meeting the needs of households and sustaining the consumption-based economic growth model in Turkey. However, financialization of households has also been restricted, as use of financial services is often limited to basic bank services, such as credit cards and consumer loans, and even such limited use is marked by extensive inequalities.

Note

1 *ILO Global Wage Report 2015* (p. 77) defines income accruing from employment to include both wage income and self-employment income. While calculating labour share, Boratav notes that earners of self-employment income in Turkey constitute a heterogeneous group, ranging from rural labourers to professional groups. Boratav therefore distinguishes and calculates wage income separately (Boratav 2014).

REFERENCES

Akçay, Ü. (2015) "Türkiye Ekonomisinin Finansallaşması: Merkez Bankasının Bağımsızlığıve 'Borcun Özelleştirilmesi'", *Paper Presented at the 13th National Conference on Social Science, organized by the Turkish Association of Social Sciences, 23–25 December 2015.*

Alper, K., H. Kara and M. Yörükoğlu (2013) "Alternative Tools to Manage Capital Flow Volatility", *BIS Papers*, 73: 335–352.

Altunok, F. Çağacıoğlu, T. and Y. Hacıhasanoğlu (Forthcoming) "Türkiye'de Konut Kredisinin Mikro Dinamikleri", *CBRT Research Notes in Economics.*

Aydın, Z. (2009) "Deagrarianization and Depeasentization: Dilemmas of Neoliberal Restructuring in Turkish Agriculture" in Z. Öniş and F. Şenses (eds.) *Turkey and the Global Economy: Neoliberal Restructuring and Integration in the post crisis era*, London and New York: Routledge, 223–242.

Aydın, Z., M.K. Bayırbağ, P. Bedirhanoğlu, A. Benlialper, H. Cömert, Ö. Çelik, A. Göksel, Ö. Orhangazi, G. Özgür, E. Taymaz, G. Yalman, E. Yeldan (2015) "Financialisation, Uneven Development and Faltering Governance: The case of Turkey", *FESSUD Working Papers*, 143.

Bahçe, S., H. Cömert, S. Çolak, N. Erdem, E. Karaçimen, A.H. Köse, Ö. Orhangazi, G. Özgur, G. Yalman (2014) *Financialisation and Financial and Economic Crises: The Case of Turkey*, FESSUD Studies in Financial Systems, No. 21.

Bagimsiz Sosyal Bilimciler - BSB (2015) *AKP'li Yillarda Emegin Durumu*, Ankara: Yordam.

Bakır, C. and Z. Öniş (2010) "Regulatory State and Turkish Banking Reforms in the Age of Post Washington Consensus", *Development and Change*, 41(1): 77–106.

Bakış, O. and S. Polat (2013) "Wage Inequality in Turkey" *GIAM Working Paper Series*, 13–9, July.http://giam.gsu.edu.tr/wp-content/uploads/2014/07/WP-13-09.pdf.

Banking Regulation and Supervision Agency – BRSA (2015) *Turkish Banking Sector, Basic Indicators*, Ankara: BRSA.

Banking Regulation and Supervision Agency – BRSA (2004a) *Banking Sector Evaluation Report*, October, Ankara: BRSA.

Banking Regulation and Supervision Agency – BRSA (2004b) *Banking Sector Evaluation Report*, February, Ankara: BRSA.

Banking Regulation and Supervision Agency – BRSA (2006) *Financial Markets Report*, December, Ankara: BRSA.

Banking Regulation and Supervision Agency – BRSA (2007) *Financial Markets Report*, December, Ankara: BRSA.

Banking Regulation and Supervision Agency – BRSA (2009) *Turkish Banking Sector Overview*, Ankara: BRSA.

Banking Regulation and Supervision Agency – BRSA (2010) *Turkish Banking Sector Overview*, March, Ankara: BRSA.

Banking Regulation and Supervision Agency – BRSA (2011a) *Structural Developments in the Banking Sector*, Issue 6, December, Ankara: BRSA.

Banking Regulation and Supervision Agency – BRSA (2011b) *Turkish Banking Sector Overview*, December, Ankara: BRSA.

Banking Regulation and Supervision Agency – BRSA (2011c) *Turkish Banking Sector Overview*, June, Ankara: BRSA.

Banking Regulation and Supervision Agency – BRSA (2012) *Turkish Banking Sector Overview*, June, Ankara: BRSA.

Banking Regulation and Supervision Agency – BRSA (2014) *Turkish Banking Sector Overview*, May, Ankara: BRSA

Banks Association of Turkey (TBB) (2008) *50. Yılında Türkiye Bankalar Birliği ve Türkiye'de Bankacılık Sistemi 1958–2007*, Publication No. 262, November 2008, Ankara: TBB.

Banks Association of Turkey (TBB) (2015) *Turkiye'de Bankacılık Sistemi Seçilmiş Göstergelerinin İllere ve Bölgelere Göre Dağılımı 2014*, Report YT06, June 2015, Ankara: TBB.

Barba, A. and M. Pivetti (2009) "Rising household debt: Its causes and macroeconomic implications–a long-period analysis", *Cambridge Journal of Economics*, 33: 113–137.

Başak, Z and E. Taymaz (2015) "Bölüşüm Göstergeleri ile 2008–2009 Krizi: Türkiye Örneği", in E. Özçelik and E. Taymaz. (eds.) *Turkiye Ekonomisinin Dünü, Bugünü, Yarını, Yakup Kepenekve Oktar Türel'e Armağan*, Ankara: İmge Yayinevi, 91–120.

Becker, J. (2016) "Financialisation, Industry and Dependency in Turkey" *Journal für Entwicklungspolitik*, 32(1–2): 84–113.

Bedirhanoğlu, P., H. Cömert, İ. Eren, I. Erol, D. Demiröz, N. Erdem, A.R. Güngen, T. Marois, A. Topal, O.Türel, G. Yalman, E. Yeldan, and E. Voyvoda (2013) *Comparative Perspective on Financial System in the EU: Country Report on Turkey*, FESSUD Studies in Financial Systems No. 11.

Boratav, K., A.E. Yeldan and A.H. Köse (2000) "Globalisation, Distribution and Social Policy: Turkey, 1980–1998", *CEPA Working Paper Series I*, Working Paper No. 20.

Boratav, K. (2014) "ILO'dan Emek Dünyası'na Bakışlar", *sendika.org website*, Accessed 17 June 2017.

Bryan, D., R. Martin, M. Rafferty (2009) "Financialisation and Marx: Giving Labour and Capital a Financial Makeover", *Review of Radical Political Economics*, 41(4), 458–472.

Bryan, D. and M. Rafferty (2014) "Financial Derivatives as Social Policy Beyond the Crisis" *Sociology*, 48(5): 887–905.

Catte, P., N. Girouard, R. Priceand C. André (2004) "Housing markets, wealth and the business cycle", *OECD Economics Working Paper*, No. 394.

Central Bank of the Republic of Turkey (CBRT) (2005) *Financial Stability Report*, Ankara: CBRT.

Central Bank of the Republic of Turkey (CBRT) (2006) *Financial Stability Report (December 2006)*, Ankara: CBRT.

Central Bank of the Republic of Turkey (CBRT) (2008) *Financial Stability Report (November 2008)*, Ankara: CBRT.

Central Bank of the Republic of Turkey (CBRT) (2009) *Financial Stability Report (November 2009)*, Ankara: CBRT.

Central Bank of the Republic of Turkey (CBRT) (2010) *Financial Stability Report (December 2010)*, Ankara: CBRT.

Central Bank of the Republic of Turkey (CBRT) (2011a) *Dunyadave Turkiye'de Finansal Hizmetlere Erisimve Finansa lEgitim*, March 2011, CBRT website, Accessed 19 November 2012.

Central Bank of the Republic of Turkey (CBRT) (2011b) *Financial Stability Report (May 2011)*, Ankara: CBRT.

Central Bank of the Republic of Turkey (CBRT) (2011c) *Financial Stability Report (November 2011)*, Ankara: CBRT.

Central Bank of the Republic of Turkey (CBRT) (2012) *Financial Stability Report (May 2012)*, Ankara: CBRT.

Central Bank of the Republic of Turkey (CBRT) (2013) *Financial Stability Report (November 2013)*, Ankara: CBRT.

Central Bank of the Republic of Turkey (CBRT) (2014a) *Financial Stability Report (May 2014)*, Ankara: CBRT.

Central Bank of the Republic of Turkey (CBRT) (2014b) *Financial Stability Report (November 2014)*, Ankara: CBRT.

Central Bank of the Republic of Turkey (CBRT) (2015). *Financial Stability Report (May 2015)*, Ankara: CBRT.

Central Bank of the Republic of Turkey (CBRT) (2016) *Financial Stability Report (November 2016)*, Ankara: CBRT.

Ergüneş, N. (2009) "Global Integration of the Turkish Economy in the era of Financialisation", *Research on Money and Finance, Discussion Papers*, No. 8, February 2009.

Ertürk, I. (2003) "Governance or Financialisation: The Turkish Case", *Competition and Change*, 7(3): 185–204.

Fine, B. (2012) "Financialisation on the Rebound", *Actuel Marx*, 51(1): 73–85.

Inter Bank Card Center (2015) "Domestic and International Transactions with Domestic Credit Cards", https://bkm.com.tr/en/yerli-kredi-kartlarinin-yurt-ici-ve-yurtdisi-kullanimi/

International Labour Organization (2015) *2014/15 Global Wage Report: Wages and Income Inequality*. Geneva: ILO.

Karaçimen, E. (2014) "Interlinkages between credit debt and labour market: evidence from Turkey", *Cambridge Journal of Economics*, advance online publication. 14 May 2014.

Karaçimen, E. (2015) "Consumer Credit as an Aspect of Everyday Life of Workers in Developing Countries: Evidence from Turkey", *Review of Radical Political Economics*, advance online publication, 10 July 2015.

Kendir, H. (2007) "Küreselleşen Tarımve Türkiye'de Tarım Reformu", in F. Ercan et al. (eds.) *Türkiye'de Kapitalizmin Güncel Sorunları*, Ankara: Dipnot, 143–177.

Lapavitsas, C. (2009) "Financialised Capitalism: Crisis and Financial Expropriation", *Historical Materialism*, 17: 114–148.

Marois, T. and A.R. Güngen (2016) "Credibility and Class in the Evolution of Public Banks: The Case of Turkey", *The Journal of Peasant Studies*, 43(6): 1285–1309.

Marois, T. and Muñoz-Martínez, H. (2016) "Navigating the Aftermath of Crisis and Risk in Mexico and Turkey", *Research in Political Economy*, 31: 165–194.

Ministry of Agriculture, Food and Livestock (2016) *Structural Changes and Reforms in Turkish Agriculture 2003–2015*, Ankara: MAFL.

Ministry of Development (2013) *Research on Socieconomic Development Ranking of Regions and Provinces (SEGEM 2011)*, General Directorate on Regional Development and Structural Harmonisation, Ankara: Ministry of Development.

Mütevellioğlu, N. and S. Işık (2009) "Türkiye Emek Piyasasında Neoliberal Dönüşüm", N. Mütevellioğlu and S. Sönmez (eds.) *Küreselleşme, Krizve Turkiye'de Neoliberal Dönüşüm*, Istanbul: Bilgi Universitesi Yayinlari, 159–204.

Onaran, Ö. (2009) "Crises and Post Crisis Adjustment in Turkey: Implications for Labour" in Z. Öniş and F. Şenses (eds.) *Turkey and the Global Economy*, London and New York: Routledge, 243–261.

Önder, Z and S. Özyıldırım (2013) "Role of Bank Credit on Local Growth: Do politics and Crisis Matter?",*Journal of Financial Stability*, 9: 13–25.

Orhangazi, Ö. and G. Özgur (2015) "Capital Flows, Finance led Growth and Fragility in the age of Global Liquidity and Quantitative Easing: The case of Turkey", *Political Economy Research Institute, University of Massachusetts, Amherst, Working paper Series*, No. 397, September.

Pamuk, Ş. (2014) *Türkiye'nin 200 Yıllık İktisadi Tarihi*, İstanbul: İş Bankası Kültür Yayınları.

Şahbaz, N. and A. İnkaya (2014) "Non performing Loans in Turkish Banking Sector and Macroeconomic Effects", *Optimum Ekonomive Yönetim Bilimleri Dergisi*, 1(1): 69–82.

Selimler, H. (2015) "Sorunlu Kredilerin Analizi, Banka Finansal Tablo ve Oranlarına Etkisinin Değerlendirilmesi", *Finansal Araştırmalarve Çalışmalar Dergisi*, 12: 131–172.

Sonmez, M. (2014) "İşçinin İliğini Sömürdüler", *Sözcü, Turkish Daily*, 19 May 2014.

Statistical Institute of Turkey–SIT (2010) "Türkiye Kazanç Yapısı Araştırması", *Turkstat News Bulletin*, Accessed 8 October 2012.

Statistical Institute of Turkey – SIT (2015) "Women in Statistics", *News Bulletin* No. 18619 5 March 2015.

Statistical Institute of Turkey – SIT (2016) "Women in Statistics", *News Bulletin* No. 2151 9 7 March 2016.

Stockhammer, E. (2010) "Financialisation and the Global Economy", *Political Economy Research Institute, University of Massachusetts, Amherst, Working Paper Series*, No. 240, November.

Taymaz, E. (2015) "Transformation of trade and industrialization", *Unpublishedbackground paper to FESSUD Work Package 6.*

TEB and Boğaziçi University (2014) "Türkiye'de Finansal Erişim ve Okuryazarlık", *TEB website*, Accessed 17 June 2017.

Yalman, L.G. (2016) "Crises as Driving Forces of Neoliberal 'Trasformismo': The Contours of the Turkish Political Economy since the 2000s" in A. Cafruny, L.S. Talani and G. Pozo Martin (eds.) *The Palgrave Handbook of Critical International Political Economy*, London: Palgrave Macmillan, 239–266.

Yeldan, E. (2007) "Patterns of Adjustment under the Age of Finance: The Case of Turkey as a Peripheral Agent of Neoliberal Globalisation", *Political Economy Research Institute, Working Paper Series*, No. 126, February 2007.

Yeldan, E. (2010) "Global Crisis and Turkey: A Macroeconomic Assessment of the Effects of Fiscal Stimulus Measures on Employment and Labour Markets" in H. Ercan, E. Taymaz and E. Yeldan (eds.) *Crisis and Turkey: Impact Analysis of Crisis Response Measures*, Ankara: ILO, 9–40.

Yükseker, D. (2009) "Neoliberal Restructuring and Social Exclusion in Turkey" in Z. Öniş and F. Şenses (eds.) *Turkey and the Global Economy: Neoliberal Restructuring and Integration in the post crisis era*, London and New York: Routledge, 262–280.

Index

Note: Page numbers in *italics* and **bold** denote references to Figures and Tables, respectively.

For Product Safety Concerns and Information please contact our EU representative GPSR@taylorandfrancis.com
Taylor & Francis Verlag GmbH, Kaufingerstraße 24, 80331 München, Germany

www.ingramcontent.com/pod-product-compliance
Ingram Content Group UK Ltd.
Pitfield, Milton Keynes, MK11 3LW, UK
UKHW021017180425
457613UK00020B/959
* 9 7 8 0 3 6 7 5 8 4 9 6 2 *